HITLER THE SCIENTIST

HITLER THE SCIENTIST

HOW PSEUDO-SCIENCE AND ANTI-SEMITISM SHAPED HITLER'S DESTINY

ANDREW PIKE

Pen & Sword
MILITARY
AN IMPRINT OF PEN & SWORD BOOKS LTD.
YORKSHIRE – PHILADELPHIA

First published in Great Britain in 2024 by
PEN AND SWORD MILITARY
An imprint of
Pen & Sword Books Limited
Yorkshire – Philadelphia

ISBN 978 1 39907 974 7

Typeset in Times New Roman 10/13 by
SJmagic DESIGN SERVICES, India.
Printed and bound in the UK by CPI Group (UK) Ltd.

Pen & Sword Books Limited incorporates the imprints of Atlas, Archaeology, Aviation, Discovery, Family History, Fiction, History, Maritime, Military, Military Classics, Politics, Select, Transport, True Crime, Air World, Frontline Publishing, Leo Cooper, Remember When, Seaforth Publishing, The Praetorian Press, Wharncliffe Local History, Wharncliffe Transport, Wharncliffe True Crime and White Owl.

For a complete list of Pen & Sword titles please contact
PEN & SWORD BOOKS LIMITED
George House, Units 12 & 13, Beevor Street, Off Pontefract Road,
Barnsley, South Yorkshire, S71 1HN, England
E-mail: enquiries@pen-and-sword.co.uk
Website: www.pen-and-sword.co.uk

or

PEN AND SWORD BOOKS
1950 Lawrence Rd, Havertown, PA 19083, USA
E-mail: uspen-and-sword@casematepublishers.com
Website: www.penandswordbooks.com

MIX
Paper | Supporting responsible forestry
FSC® C013604
www.fsc.org

Contents

Introduction

When Hitler came to power in 1933, he promised the German people a technocratic state where science, education and intelligence would grow and flourish. However, many of his promises failed, due largely to his own education and understanding of science.

Hitler's schooling was a troubled time, where he struggled with many areas of education, especially so with science and its place in the world. For example, he found difficulties accepting competing views from science and religion, such as evolution and creationism, which, in his words, caused him to 'run his head against the wall'. He was also heavily educated in alternatives to science and religion such as myths, magic and the pseudo-sciences. Unfortunately, these educational problems followed him into adulthood where, as Fuhrer, his mentality and mindset towards science was highlighted when he described his ideology by saying: 'A new age of magic interpretation of the world is coming, of interpretation in terms of the Will and not the Intelligence.'

Hitler's ideology and rise to power also came at an interesting time for physics. The early decades of the twentieth century saw a revolution occurring in two key areas known as quantum mechanics and relativity. Whereas today, physicists realize these two theories must combine, at the time of Hitler, they were seen as competing theories by the Nazis. Quantum mechanics was the brainchild of non-Jewish German physicist Max Planck, while relativity was the brainchild of Jewish physicist Albert Einstein. It was quantum mechanics that the Nazis believed was important to their physics research and development of new weapons for their war machine, while relativity was seen as a justification for anti-Semitism and rejection of Jewish science. Yet Hitler's intellectual strains from childhood and his inability to grasp these theories and the many other scientific advances of the early twentieth century remained steadfast.

Both quantum mechanics and relativity had important connections to the decade preceding Hitler's rise to power, leading to the Aryan physics under his dictatorship. Both were replacing the ideas of classical physics developed by the likes of Galileo Galilei and Isaac Newton, providing better theories that would have a dramatic influence on the physics community to this day. Gone was the idea of a determined or clockwork universe, replaced instead by a universe governed by probabilities and a new way to interpret reality. It is no surprise these two theories would also influence the physics of the Third Reich and the approaching world war. Furthermore, Einstein had experienced significant anti-Semitic attacks during the decade as he quickly became the first science celebrity following proof of his theory—proof that was difficult for the Nazis to accept. To add to this situation, many of his anti-Semitic enemies of the time later found posts in Hitler's government.

On the one hand, quantum mechanics suggested a strange underlying world governing physics and a new way of understanding reality, where the observer determined that reality. As war approached, it became clear that just by observing an experiment, the scientist could change reality and the outcome of that experiment. This was particularly exciting to the Nazis, who sought new and hidden sciences; in its early stages, quantum mechanics looked like a gateway into the magical beliefs of Hitler and willpower. On the other hand, Einstein had been attacking quantum mechanics during the 1920s with his view that 'God does not play dice with the Universe', referring to its probabilistic properties breaking with a determined or clockwork universe of classical physics. Einstein also dismissed certain elements crucial to Nazi pseudo-science, like the belief in an ether.

As a result, this played perfectly into the hands of Nazi Germany by providing justification for anti-Semitism and rejection of relativity as they turned instead to quantum mechanics. In short, these two theories inevitably allowed the Third Reich to both support its pseudo-scientific beliefs and anti-Semitism in one package, a situation that was set to drag on and drag down Hitler's ambitions, only amplifying his problems as the war progressed. By using the so-called 'magical properties' of quantum mechanics in the hope it would provide new wonder weapons against the Allies, the Nazis believed they could win the war. As such, these two theories aptly demonstrated how Nazi Germany chose to go down a route of experimental applied physics rather than the Jewish theoretical physics that had dominated the years leading up to war, and introduced their pseudo-scientific beliefs into their research too. With this rejection of Jewish theoretical physics, Hitler actually put yet another obstacle in his way to victory.

As Hitler prepared to tear up the Versailles Treaty in stages to release Germany from the restrictions it proposed to his technocratic state, the Third Reich called for a spirit of *gleichschaltung* (marching in step) so that all were in co-ordination, an effort that was essentially designed to shape public opinion in his own revolution of a National Socialist state. This spirit was to apply to all areas of life, including science, education, technology, medicine, research and even psychology and the media. To this end, efforts were made by Propaganda Minister Joseph Goebbels to brainwash and manipulate the people, while equally determined efforts were made by other high-ranking Nazis like Heinrich Himmler, who would play a major role in science and technology side-by-side with pseudo-science.

Importantly, Hitler's belief of 'Will, not Intelligence' appears to have been emphasized in his mind following his first attempt to overthrow the government in 1923. It has been suggested that, with this, he was reaching back into the German culture of Arthur Schopenhauer's *The World as Will and Representation* and it is significant that the mastermind behind this and Nazi occultism, General Karl Haushofer, not only was an avid scholar of Schopenhauer but also was one of the individuals who visited Hitler in his prison cell during 1924. Furthermore, as well as being an avid scholar of Schopenhauer,

Haushofer was also the architect of Nazi geopolitics, with its own interpretation of *lebensraum* (living space), which played a major part in Hitler's invasion of other countries and the necessary science and technology that required. It was quantum mechanics and the will of the observing scientist during experiments that fitted well with Schopenhauer's ideas and Hitler's education.

This set in motion a battle between science, education and Hitler's 'Will not Intelligence', leading to events such as the famous book burnings encouraged and orchestrated by Goebbels, who said: "There was no point in seeking to convert the intellectuals. For intellectuals would never be converted and would anyway always yield to the stronger, and this will always be the man in the street. Arguments must therefore be crude, clear, and forcible, and appeal to the emotions and instincts, not the intellect. Truth was unimportant and entirely subordinate to tactics and psychology."

Unsurprisingly, many of the reforms initiated throughout the Third Reich involving science and education were based on Hitler's troubled school years: reforms that saw a bias towards the unconventional and a continued lack of understanding of true science, which was replaced by Nazi pseudo-science, magic and even the occult. In order to achieve this, Hitler and Himmler worked together as theorist and facilitator, respectively, while twisting the position so as to regard pseudo-sciences as the true Aryan sciences, while actual true sciences became the pseudo-sciences (especially relativity). This inevitably led to the politicizing of science in all branches, which quickly became 'Aryan sciences' with Aryan physics, Aryan chemistry, Aryan biology, Aryan mathematics and so on. From there, science experienced an era of division and decline, with the loss of freedom and diversity, misapplication of innovation, and the inevitable decline in some areas of the natural sciences, especially physics, as all disciplines strived to be acceptable to National Socialism.

Within days of coming to power, Hitler set his destiny in motion as his brownshirts invaded scientific research and educational institutes across the country. Having little or no choice, German scientists readily turned over their civilian science institutions, the Kaiser Wilhelm Institutes. Immediately upon this invasion, the first wave of Jewish scientists were dismissed, with non-Jews, often with inferior qualifications and experience, replacing them. Following their dismissals, the lucky ones managed to escape the country one way or another, while the unlucky ones ended up in concentration camps or were simply murdered, again in the name of pseudo-science. The justification for this and further waves of dismissals was the pseudo-scientific view of National Socialist Germany and a radically hygienic body, where the body politic expelled unwanted pathogens. Put in its simplest terms, the Jewish scientists were seen as being rejected by the body's immune system, like germs; a further expansion eliminated any lives that were considered not worthy of living.

After the brownshirts had succeeded in their task, a split occurred: some scientists were only too willing to jump into some form of Nazi uniform, while others fought to maintain a distance from politics, arguing that science was apolitical. In the case of medical doctors and anthropologists, this desire to conform was particularly strong, leading to the horrific medical experimentations on concentration camp inmates. Some scientists, preferring to support an apolitical viewpoint, introduced an element of sabotage, where they tried their best to exercise selective ignorance to deprive Hitler of certain advances; a particular example is the enigma surrounding one German quantum physicist, Werner Heisenberg, who appeared to have mental blocks involving the physics necessary to develop an atomic bomb. This led to the good scientist/bad scientist scenario still debated today when scientists and politicians co-operate.

However, the desire to pursue pseudo-science was equally strong, and under the Third Reich, there was an intense quest to investigate the scientific basis of esoteric and occult notions, no matter how bizarre or flawed they appeared to be, in order to discover new science and its possible application to wonder weapons. Interestingly, the occultist element was kept from the German people and largely pursued within Himmler's SS *Ahnenerbe* (Ancestral Heritage), an organization prepared to explore all areas of research, including the occult, and in particular the origins of the Aryan bloodline and proof of its superiority. Amongst the many efforts of the *Ahnenerbe* was the task of finding new and hidden sciences within ancient manuscripts, which became a key area of global research for the Nazis. However, despite the rejection of Jewish science, by the desperate last years of war, the Nazis did include elements of Jewish research in an attempt to win the war.

All this clearly affected Hitler's war machine and the many technologies it relied upon, especially with the development of the atomic bomb, which was largely Jewish science. However, those who saw worth in conventional areas, like rocketry, managed to push ahead, even if Hitler was initially sceptical and cold towards such research. The justification for such research was not only its necessity as part of the war machine, but it was Aryan in the sense that it was largely experimental or applied physics, and not Jewish theoretical physics. However, it was not without its share of problems, with waste, duplication, delayed deadlines and infighting. There were also problems causing a serious split between science and pseudo-science, resulting in even further duplication, wastage, loss and infighting between competing power cartels. Indeed, the infighting was even encouraged by Hitler and regarded as a positive. As Himmler's *Ahnenerbe* took more control over scientific research, the problems increased, as did the ineptitude.

By the war's end, Himmler's SS had taken control of much of Nazi scientific research; with the unthinkable dawning on the Nazis (that they might lose the war), Hitler placed SS General Hans Kammler in charge of producing new wonder weapons, even super weapons, through his own think tank along the lines of the *Ahnenerbe*. Kammler was only one rank below Himmler, working with him in an intense effort to turn the war around. To the very end, Hitler continued to declare that these weapons from Kammler would save Nazi Germany, putting strain on his generals by ordering troops to make a last ditch attempt to protect certain areas that his generals did not fully understand; areas that made no tactical sense as the D-Day invasion progressed. Once again, Hitler had failed to understand the true situation. Meanwhile, Kammler and Himmler had other plans.

It is clear the foundations Hitler set in place after coming to power, based on his upbringing and schooling, shaped his destiny as Fuhrer and the ability of the Nazis to win the war. Consequently, over time the promised veneer of scientific and educational modernization under his technocratic state suffered seriously; although this did not initially cause his government to collapse, it neither allowed it to thrive anywhere close to the many promises he made to the German people.

All this was a far cry from Germany's scientific research of the nineteenth century, which saw staggering achievements spanning almost a century up to Hitler's rise to power. These golden years built an unrivalled global reputation from the foundations of chemistry in all areas organic, inorganic and industrial. Furthermore, this was an era that also created advances in the associated area of medicine and ran parallel to major discoveries in other disciplines like astronomy and physics. In doing so, the subject of chemistry had greatly expanded Germany's economy; by the early twentieth century, with the creation of the Nobel Prize, German and German-speaking scientists, including Einstein, had won over half of its prizes in chemistry, physics and medicine. However, it was not just the sciences that saw advances during the golden years: there were also advances in subjects like history, literature and philosophy.

Whereas such an unequalled series of national advances and discoveries should have placed Germany in a good position to win a world war, the Nazis failed to take full advantage of the opportunities, despite Hitler's claims that he planned to build on the golden years. Again, it was his inability to understand science and how science worked, in particular, that stood in his way. It is clear the golden years had provided great advances in science for both sides, especially during the Weimer period, but it was the Allies who really fully appreciated its opportunities and took advantage of fleeing Jewish scientists, while Germany failed to do so under a dictator focused on pseudo-science and seething anti-Semitism, aided by his like-minded, high-ranking Nazis.

Chapter One

Missed Opportunities and the Mind of Hitler

Before Hitler came to power in 1933, Germany had gone through a scientific rollercoaster lasting over a century, with the country developing from an agricultural society to one of scientific envy throughout the world. Then, with the First World War, the country's scientific reputation collapsed, only to recover during the 1920s and then further during the Second World War, but for many of the wrong reasons.

This rollercoaster started in the early 1800s with what is regarded as the golden years of chemistry, with successes spreading to other areas of science as industry and academia benefited from one new discovery after another. However, because of developments in harmful chemicals, this golden period eventually led to the horrors of chemical warfare during the First World War; the gassing of enemy troops in their trenches clearly led to Germany losing in scientific reputation. Following the war, the scientific communities of the world turned their backs on Germany, adding to the restrictions and sanctions generally imposed as part of their unconditional surrender; Germany was defeated in science as it was in war.

Matters did improve during the years between the two world wars, but only to end up in a further decline of scientific reputation as a result of the next war under Hitler. Scientifically speaking, we found a chemists' war turning into a physicists' war as the world built on the golden years of Germany's science.

The chemical revolution within Germany started back in 1824, and although Hitler would talk of this period, and promise the people great advances as a result, we will see that scientifically he was technologically lacking, mentally strained, and clearly did not fully appreciate the significance of how that revolution played out and the essential connections it forged. In short, the lessons learned by both German scientists and the state from 1824 to the First World War did not appear as important to Hitler and were demolished in part thanks to his mindset. Consequently, this deprived the Nazi war machine of many advantages they might otherwise have taken onboard. As we will see later, this mindset was a result of his schooling, and both science and education itself would feature highly in his reforms after he came to power; often these reforms were far from positive.

During the nineteenth century, the golden years revolutionized the German economy as it brought together many scientific discipline like physics, chemistry, mathematics, pharmaceuticals, dyes, electrical power, iron and steel production, and the liquification of gases, to name but a few. The result of all this was to set the scene for the scientific connections that would become part of the war machine in both world wars. For example, whereas the liquification of gases served to weaponize the gassing of troops in the trenches during the First World War, it went on to develop liquid propellants for rockets such as the V-2, increasing their power ever further as new fuels and engineering developed. There was also the discovery of the electromagnetic spectrum, a band of radiation stretching from radio and microwaves to infra-red, visible light, ultraviolet radiation, X-rays, and gamma rays. This one area of electromagnetism allowed both conventional and unconventional technology, including the development of radar and radio communications on the conventional side of science, as well as less conventional attempts involving exotic new weapons that the Nazis particularly considered as a result of their love of pseudo-science. Those weapons included electromagnetic disruption, death rays, long-range X-ray guns, and even flying discs, or what we might today call 'flying saucers'. Many of these exotic ideas were based on unsound science like endless free energy from mysterious sources.

There were also serious consequences for race and anti-Semitic propaganda with the dismissal of Jewish sciences and the rise of Aryan sciences, including the search for Aryan purity through genetics; this had serious consequences with medical experimentation in the death camps. In short, under Hitler there would no longer be physics, chemistry, biology and mathematics, but Aryan physics, Aryan chemistry, Aryan biology and Aryan mathematics. To fully understand how all this came together and its consequences, we need to look deeper into those golden years of discovery.

The foundations in chemistry leading to the First World War had been laid early by the likes of Justus von Liebig who, in 1824, founded a laboratory at Giessen where he would train large numbers of chemists. Liebig is probably best known for his discovery of the nitrogen cycles, finding a law now named after him. This law states that plant growth is limited by the element's presence in soil in the least adequate quantity; this helped Germany both to improve its agriculture amongst a young growing population and develop its science, which freed it from dependency on other nations. However, in later years under Hitler, the subject of chemistry became a toxic mix, as it provided a means of both giving life and taking it away, something that Hitler had become aware of during the gassing of troops during the First World War. Ironically, although Hitler saw gassing as distasteful, he would later use its advances in the gas chambers of concentration camps to rid the Third Reich of Jews and others he found undesirable or not worthy of living. Much of the efficiency of such camps was delegated by Hitler in later years to Hans Kammler, a doctor of engineering who was a ruthless, evil and cold-minded SS general. In addition to his skills in building, he improved the efficiency of the concentration camp gas chambers and ovens. Yet, on the other hand, as part of Hitler's health policies for a hygienic and healthy Aryan race the scientific advances in medicines and foods coming from chemistry would play a very different role.

The discovery of the nitrogen cycle was followed in 1828 by important biological developments when Friedrich Wohler converted ammonium cyanate into urea, an important molecule that until then could only be synthesized by living organisms; now it was possible to artificially produce it in the laboratory. With this discovery chemists realized they were on the brink of something big: a whole new world of manufacturing a host of substances that do not occur in nature. Then, in 1841, a student at Liebig's laboratory, August Wilhelm von Hofmann, received his doctorate for a thesis on the derivations of coal tar, a waste product from burning coal. One of these substances was aniline, which would prove an important substance in the new world of chemistry for its use in chemical transformations. In the past aniline had been distilled from indigo, but this new method would prove more productive. As a result of this discovery, Hofmann wondered whether artificial dyes could be obtained from coal tar, a thought that would eventually develop into reality following a royal visit four years later.

It was then that Queen Victoria and Prince Albert visited Bonn to celebrate the seventy-fifth anniversary of Beethoven's birth, and while visiting Hofmann in his laboratory, a set of rooms Prince Albert once lodged in while a student, the prince invited him to head the Prince's new Royal College of Chemistry in Oxford Street, London, an invitation Hofmann readily accepted. It was there that he was able to bring together a group of chemists, both British and German, and in doing so selected and directed various research projects for them, allowing an entire new industry to be born in his new laboratory.

One of Hofmann's chemists was a 17-year-old student by the name of William Perkin who, in 1856, found himself working on a way to make quinine from coal tar. It was then he stumbled upon a process for making a rich artificial dye yielding the colour of mauve. He immediately realized the commercial possibilities of this popular colour and left Hofmann's laboratory behind to set up a rapidly successful, but modest, business with his father. Following the setting up of the business, the colour mauve quickly became the rage of Europe with the French Empress declaring the colour matched her eyes, while Queen Victoria decided to promote the discovery by wearing a vivid mauve dress to a wedding. Hofmann continued in his quest for other artificial dyes, eventually producing colours such as violets, reds, greens and blues.

However, despite the discoveries being made in Britain, it was to be Germany that reaped the industrial and commercial benefits of these new products. Germany, unlike Britain, was looking for more than a short-term investment, so they invested heavily in new technology aimed at exploiting the new chemical techniques. They also actively pursued patents and market strategies to ensure a monopoly for Germany. Following this, many chemistry graduates migrated to England to gain experience in industry but then returned to Germany to take part in the Fatherland's expanding industries. Perkins himself did not like this situation and complained bitterly that Britain was losing out with its short-sighted approach to the opportunities possible from this new industry, especially those he had helped to develop.

Back in the 1800s, such co-operation between academia and industry was seen as more important with an expansion in the number of universities and general educational institutions; there were new education investments in schools of chemistry set up in Giessen, Heidelberg, Berlin and Bonn. It was at Bonn that August Kekule, a Bohemian-born chemist, discovered the benzene ring with the famous story of the chemical links coming to him in a dream when he saw atoms linked like a serpent grabbing its own tail in its mouth. This discovery eventually proved essential for the future chemical formulae of many carbon-based molecules. However, this is a significant point that Hitler would miss in many ways because of his extremely warped ideas about both science and education. This missed opportunity would make a significant difference to how science played out under his dictatorship; whereas he expanded industry as part of his war effort, co-operation suffered, with many self-inflicted wounds. Instead, Hitler introduced significant damage to education, as well as a corrupt regime. Moreover, where there was co-operation, it was usually only when it suited the Nazi physicists.

In contrast, German industry and academia of the past sported a host of chemical achievements, many coming as a result of dye technologies. These included Bayer's organic chemistry laboratory in Munich, and F.W. Beneke's successful staining of plant and animal cells with aniline dyes in the 1860s. This then led to the realization by Paul Ehrlich in Frankfurt that it was possible to develop techniques for staining biological cells, highlighting particular parts of the cell's structure. For example, the important nucleus of a cell was highlighted green using methyl green, while cytoplasm highlighted other parts in red and in doing so gave colour-coded visualization. Following on from this, Ehrlich's cousin, Carl Weigert, showed that methyl violet highlighted bacteria, which in turn helped Robert Koch's research in Berlin on bovine anthrax bacillus and tuberculosis. All these achievements revolutionized biology, giving birth to the new science of biochemistry.

From this starting point in dyes, German chemistry went on to other areas, including the new global pharmaceutical industry. This is highlighted by the development of aspirin in the 1890s at the Bayer plant, which transformed pain and fever control. Meanwhile at Hoechst am Main, Albert Einhorn's invention of novocaine had its own revolutionary influence in local anaesthetics, especially in dentistry. With such German achievements mounting, Ehrlich went on to win the Nobel Prize for Salvarsan, a synthetic pharmaceutical product for the treatment of syphilis. Indeed, by the start of the First World War, German chemistry had reduced the costs of products dramatically while also flooding the world with its new products, including medicines, soaps, paints, inks, dyes, explosives, fertilizers, improvements in iron and steel production and much more.

Physics also saw developments which further aided biological achievements when Carl Zeiss set up his famous optical instrument workshop in Jena. Not only did this help subjects like biology, pathology, histology and embryology through the development of the microscope, it also helped advance areas of physics such as astronomy with better optics from which telescopes could advance further. By the end of the nineteenth century, the German optical industry was also flourishing, resulting in Carl Zeiss and Ernst

Leitz's companies becoming world leaders in optics, while also providing industrial and production improvements, reducing costs and making the German optical instruments far cheaper and of better quality compared to their rivals.

At this stage, industry and universities were closely associated, enjoying ever-greater personal ties, contracts, formalized research and the production and flow of trained chemists from universities to industry. Consequently, well-funded research establishments flourished with new ones being developed, bringing everything into a mutual, professional framework. This also led to a reductionist approach to science, especially biology, narrowing the scope of scientific enquiry and abandoning the associations with philosophy. In the case of biology, scientists would seek to understand its workings and mechanics on the smallest scales of atoms and molecules, with the foundation of these approaches being credited to Liebig. In fact, through his training of future chemists, Liebig also proved to be instrumental in the rejection of vitalism and speculation about the meaning of living things, concentrating instead on the physico-chemical components of biology and its processes.

Ironically, these were just the areas needed by the Nazis, but the route, methods and co-operation necessary to achieve this were not completely appreciated by Hitler; although he encouraged a form of 'togetherness', it was in his unique form thanks to his unconventional schooling in science, with his own ideas about education and academic co-operation with industry. Nevertheless, some areas did strike a chord with him. For example, it was Liebig's training of chemists and his instrumental rejection of vitalism and speculation and the meaning of living things through physico-chemical components that had a profound influence on Hitler. This was particularly significant with his search for the perfect Aryan race and its origins, driven by genetics and racism, but the medical and pharmaceutical advances of the past would lead to the horrors of medical experimentation on concentration camp detainees as a result. Hitler also believed in a strong race connection with unconventional areas of physics, especially in astronomy, with a universe he and Himmler believed was made of ice; another pseudo-scientific idea that linked the origins of the Aryan race with shoots from ice.

In short, what escaped Hitler was the essential co-operation between industry and academia and the organization of the many parts involved in such achievements, as well as a clear understanding of how science really works.

Another key German scientist from the golden years was Hermann Helmholtz, who brought together physics and physiology, being qualified in both disciplines. Helmholtz made many contributions to science in these areas; so much so that he became known as the 'Reich Chancellor of Physics'. Helmholtz was also a key contributor to the understanding of electromagnetism and, in particular, its connection with the so-called ether and Einstein's theory of relativity, something we will come to in detail later because the ether was a key pseudo-scientific belief of the Nazis that connected with their ideas about electromagnetism, gravity and exotic weaponry.

Helmholtz was born in 1821 in Potsdam. His father taught philosophy and literature, and his mother was a descendent of William Penn, the founder of the US state of

Pennsylvania. Helmholtz thrived on scholarship; his father taught him Latin, Greek, Hebrew, French, Italian and Arabic and he showed a talent for physics in the early years of his schooling. His unusual dual skill as a physicist and physician was due to his father being unable to afford his tuition in physics at university; however, to study medicine, there was financial assistance. So, in 1838 he entered the Friedrich Wilhelm Institute in Berlin to study medicine and physiological studies.

Dominating the subjects of physics and physiology during the latter half of the nineteenth century, Helmholtz developed a list of achievements in both these scientific disciplines that is quite amazing. Throughout his life, Helmholtz's phenomenal intellectual capacity and grounding in philosophy were at the basis of his work and this was encouraged through his supervisor, Johannes Muller, who was also interested in various ideas promoted by philosophers. However, during his working life, Helmholtz rejected many ideas of the philosopher Immanuel Kant which his supervisor subscribed to, in particular the assumption that the organism as a whole is greater than the sum of its parts. As a result, Helmholtz's work was guided by an effort to disprove these fundamentals, convinced instead that living things did not possess an innate vital force and that their life forces are driven by the same forces, and obey the same principles, as non-living systems. It was a further sign of science narrowing and breaking from philosophy.

Helmholtz's doctoral submission in 1842 concerned the relationship between the nerve fibres and nerve cells of invertebrates which led to an investigation into the nature and origin of animal heat, after which he went on to investigate muscle action. Following his training as a doctor, Helmholtz became a surgeon in the military, but it soon became clear he had a stronger ability in science than medicine and he was released from his military duties in 1848. As a result of his work, by 1848 he had discovered that animal heat and muscle action are generated by chemical changes in the muscles, leading to his appointment as associate professor of physiology at Konigsberg the following year. This appointment placed him on a more suitable career path which allowed him in 1850 to measure the velocity of nerve impulses, after being stimulated by a statement from Muller that vitalism caused the impulses to be instantaneous. Helmholtz measured the impulse velocity of a frog by experimentation and found it to be about a tenth of the speed of sound. In 1855, he moved to Bonn to become professor of anatomy and physiology, and then in 1858 he was appointed professor of physiology at the University of Heidelberg. He finally took up a scientific post in 1871 as the chair of physics at the University of Berlin, and in 1887 became director of the new Physico-Technical Institute (later called PTR) of Berlin.

To give some examples of his dual physics and physiology work, he developed the first precise formulation of the principle of the conservation of energy, which is one of the most important principles in physics; he was the first to measure the speed of nerve impulses; he invented the ophthalmoscope; and he revealed the mechanism by which the ear senses tone and pitch. He also worked with thermodynamics, observed that the energy of life processes is derived entirely from oxidation of food, and derived a general equation that expressed the kinetic energy of a moving body as being equal to the product of the force and distance through which the force moves to bring about the energy change—that could then be used in many fields to show that energy is always conserved, which is another basic principle of physics. Helmholtz also went on to develop thermodynamics in physical chemistry, advancing the German efforts further in the chemical research that would be so important to the country. He also worked with acoustics, producing a comprehensive explanation for how the upper partials in sound combine to give them a particular tone or timbre, and how resonance may cause this to happen, for example, in the mouth cavity to produce vowel sounds. He also produced an important paper in 1858 in hydrodynamics in which he established the mathematical principles that define motion in a vortex. Again, this will link to the vorticular motion that would become another important element of Nazi physics while supporting their ideas about the ether through which electromagnetic waves were thought to move. Vortex ideas would also come into James Clerk Maxwell's work in understanding electromagnetism. In biological research, Helmholtz's work on nerve impulses would lead him to important discoveries in the physiology of vision and hearing, and also revived the three-colour theory of vision first proposed in 1801 by Thomas Young who, like Helmholtz, was both a physicist and physician. Helmholtz also took the physics of classical mechanics to its limits, paving the way for other German scientists who developed a radical departure from tradition with the modern physics of quantum mechanics and relativity in the early twentieth century. As we will see, these two theories were destined to become further key elements of Nazi physics, but for different reasons: one positive (quantum mechanics) and one negative (Jewish relativity).

These are just a sample of the many achievements Helmholtz made to German science during the latter half of the nineteenth century, an era he dominated with his wide range of work, and in doing so brought the achievements of German science to the forefront of world attention as well as serving as a great inspiration to others, not least his many students.

Helmholtz died in 1894 without seeing how his work would develop in important associated areas and new discoveries during the early decades of the next century, although he was spared the future visions of his advances when the Nazis attempted to build on his discoveries with medical experimentations performed on concentration camp inmates.

Advances in Germany led to others throughout the world. One key area was the understanding of electromagnetism, which eventually led to those two new theories of quantum mechanics and relativity, significant areas in our understanding of Nazi physics, and both great German discoveries. We start our story at the time of Helmholtz, when a Scottish physicist by the name of James Clerk Maxwell was developing his own theories involving electromagnetism, one of the four fundamental forces of nature (the others being strong nuclear force, weak force and gravity). It was Maxwell's work that led to Max Planck developing quantum mechanics in 1900, and then an unknown physicist called Albert Einstein developing his theories of special and general relativity in 1905 and 1915, respectively. However, the immediate problem here was one considered by the Nazis as a true Aryan science (i.e., quantum mechanics), while the other was considered Jewish pseudo-science. This would prove to be a fatal flaw for Nazi physicists.

We now understand that electromagnetic radiation is a spectrum of frequencies running from the shortest frequencies (longest wavelengths) of radio waves and microwaves through to infra-red radiation, with light at the middle of the spectrum range (the only part our eyes detect), increasing further in frequency (shorter wavelength) to ultraviolet radiation, X-rays and, finally, the highest frequency (shortest wavelength)—gamma radiation. Many of these would play an important part on both sides during the Second World War, as would Maxwell in his understanding of the physics involved. Maxwell would also introduce the idea of an ether as a medium or means of transmitting the waves, like water for ripples on a pond or sound through air. Again, this would be crucial to areas of Nazi physics.

Maxwell's development of the electromagnetic theory of light, which took many years, started with his paper *On Faraday's Lines of Force* in 1855 and 1856 and eventually resulted in his famous equations of electromagnetism. In that paper, Maxwell built on the views of Michael Faraday that suggested electric and magnetic effects resulted from fields or lines of force that surround conductors and magnets. In particular, this involved drawing on the analogy between the behaviour of the lines of force and the flow of an incompressible liquid, thereby deriving equations that represented known electric and magnetic effects.

The next step was the publication of Maxwell's paper *On Physical Lines of Force* in 1861 and 1862. Here Maxwell developed a model for the medium in which electric and magnetic effects could occur that was thought likely to throw some light on the nature of these lines of force. He then devized a hypothetical medium consisting of an incompressible fluid containing rotating vortices that responded to magnetic intensity and was separated by cells responding to electric current, effectively introducing the ether. These ideas of electromagnetism and vortices were particularly eye-catching to the Nazis, who produced similar theories, often of the pseudo-scientific variety.

By considering how the motion of these vortices and cells could produce magnetic and electric effects, Maxwell was successful in explaining all known effects of electromagnetism, which in turn showed that the lines of force must behave in a similar way. From there, Maxwell went further by considering what effects would be caused if the medium was elastic rather than an incompressible fluid. It transpired that by making the medium elastic, the movement of a charge would set up a disturbance within that medium which would take the form of transverse waves, the type of wave that appears as an up-and-down motion with peaks and troughs, also known as sinusoidal waves. These waves would then be propagated through the medium with a velocity equal to the ratio of the value for a current when measured in electrostatic units and electromagnetic units. In fact, this part of the physics had already been established by Rudolf Kohlrausch and Wilhelm Weber, and it was found to be equal to the speed of light. The importance of the speed of light would also show up later in Einstein's theory of relativity with dramatic consequences for mainstream physics and the rise of Aryan physics. As we will see later, it is not surprising that the Nazis placed much importance on all these areas of physics—except for the Jewish interpretations, of course.

From all this, Maxwell inferred that light was therefore a transverse wave in the same medium that causes electric and magnetic phenomena; the so-called medium of the ether was born. Because of its association with the transmission of light, it is often known as luminiferous ether. It is important to also realize that this does not only apply to visible light; it applies to all those other frequencies in the electromagnetic spectrum mentioned above. It is also important to realize that whereas this idea of ether would be a major element in Nazi physics, as was a distinction between an incompressible and elastic version, it also plays a memorable role in the anti-Semitic activities of the Nazis.

Maxwell's conclusions were further strengthened by work carried out to define the basic definitions of electric and magnetic quantities in terms of mass, length and time. In a further paper, *On the Elementary Regulations of Electric Quantities,* in 1863, Maxwell found that the ratio of the two definitions of any quantity based on electric and magnetic forces is always equal to the velocity of light. As a result, he considered that light must therefore consist of electromagnetic waves, but he first needed to prove this idea by abandoning the vortex analogy and arriving at an explanation based purely on dynamic principles. This he achieved in the paper *A Dynamical Theory of the Electromagnetic Field,* published in 1864, in which he developed the fundamental equations that describe the electromagnetic field. That paper showed that light is propagated in two waves, one electric and the other magnetic, which vibrate perpendicular to each other and in the direction of propagation. This was then confirmed in Maxwell's *Note on the Electromagnetic Theory of Light* in 1868, which used an electrical derivation of the theory instead of the dynamical formulation. The whole work on the subject was then summed up in *Treatise on Electricity and Magnetism* in 1873, in which it was also established that light has a radiation pressure and further suggested that a whole family of electromagnetic radiations must exist.

Eventually this resulted in the formation of the electromagnetic spectrum consisting of radio waves, microwaves, infra-red radiation, visible light, ultraviolet radiation, X-rays and gamma rays. This belief was then confirmed in 1888 with the discovery of radio waves by the German physicist Heinrich Hertz (the unit of frequency now bears his name: Hertz). Eventually all the different frequencies were discovered to complete the picture. This electromagnetic spectrum would then play important roles in wartime developments, for example, detection methods using infra-red, radio and microwave frequencies such as radar and communications, and even weapons involving deadly X-rays.

Sadly, Maxwell died in 1879 without seeing the full vindication of his work, but the legacy he left to physics would dramatically affect the subject to this day. By the start of the twentieth century, there was to be a bumpy ride to come with quantum mechanics and relativity as a result of the ether legacy he left.

With the belief in a luminiferous ether, physicists set about detecting its existence shortly after Maxwell's death from 1880 to 1881. The attempt was yet another first for

Germany, being performed by A.A. Michelson at Helmholtz's laboratory, where a light beam was split in two and recombined as an attempt to detect the velocity of the Earth with respect to the hypothetical ether; if the ether existed, then the recombining beams should show an interference pattern on a screen due to a phase shift. It was during a leave of absence from his teaching duties at the US Naval Academy in Annapolis, Maryland, that Michelson made his attempts, attracting great excitement from the scientific press. However, this excitement did not extend to the military academy, where it met with disapproval. Nevertheless, after much effort, the experiment failed to detect the ether, with no interference pattern obtained.

Later, in 1887, the experiment was refined by Michelson and Edward Williams Morley in the United States, this time at what is now Case Western Reserve University in Cleveland, Ohio, becoming known as the Michelson-Morley interferometer experiment. The procedure was much the same as the first attempt using the Michelson interferometer, but with greater sensitivity, comparing the optical paths of a split light beam, each beam moving in a mutually perpendicular direction. When the two beams were later made to interfere, the difference due to their travels through the ether in different directions would be the order of a fraction of a wavelength and should produce an interference pattern on the screen. Michelson's reasoning was that, for the speed of light to be constant with respect to the proposed stationary luminiferous ether ('the ether wind', as it was now being called) through which Earth was moving, that motion could be detected by comparing the speed of light in the direction of Earth's motion and the speed of light at right angles to the Earth's motion. Put simply, there should be a difference between the speed of light in the direction of movement through the presumed luminiferous ether and the speed at right angles due to the Earth's drag through the ether and that would reveal itself as an interference pattern. The results were published that November, but again showed no trace of the elusive ether.

Meanwhile, physics was also grappling with another problem involving electromagnetic radiation known as the ultraviolet catastrophe, which would lead directly to the discovery of quantum mechanics in 1900. In 1862, the German physicist Gustav Kirchhoff introduced the idea of what is called a 'perfect black body' that absorbs and emits radiation at all frequencies, reaching an equilibrium that depends on temperature and not the nature of the surface of the body. A series of investigations then took place into the nature of the thermal radiation emitted by such a body, which included measurements of the frequency distribution of black body radiation by another German physicist, Wilhelm Wien, in 1893. These measurements suggested the distribution is a function of the frequency and temperature, and when a graph was plotted of the radiation against the frequency, it resulted in a series of curves at different temperatures with the peak value of energy occurring at a higher frequency with greater temperature. An everyday example is found in the observed varying colours produced by a heated, glowing object, such as a metal rod in a blacksmith's furnace; at low temperatures, it glows red, but as the temperature rises, the peak energy is emitted at a greater frequency and the colour becomes yellow and then white.

However, following this research, the graphs that were plotted showed an obvious problem. Using classical physics, the distribution of energy (or 'partition function', as physicists call it) calculated using the principles of thermodynamics gave a result that only agreed with actual experimental measurements of the spectrum at long wavelengths. Indeed, the displacement between experimental results and theory became more pronounced as the wavelength decreased (or frequency increased). At short wavelengths (high frequency) corresponding to the ultraviolet part of the electromagnetic spectrum, the displacement between experiment and theory was so great it became catastrophic, producing a curve wildly out of alignment with experimental results. This became known as the ultraviolet catastrophe. What physicists found was a set of curves that peaked at various temperatures and dropped back again, but with the ultraviolet wavelengths it shot up dramatically instead of reducing downwards again. Clearly, experimental results were not holding with classical theory. As if this was not bad enough, a further catastrophic element became apparent; the theoretical results also contradicted the principle of the conservation of energy. Yet as we saw with Helmholtz, the conservation of energy had become a cornerstone of physics, and therefore of the theory of the very thermodynamics being used; effectively physicists ended up with a theory that even contradicted itself!

By 1896, the position improved somewhat when Wien discovered a radiation law that was valid at high frequencies only, while Lord Rayleigh later found a similar equation that held for radiation emitted at low frequencies. This at least gave some clarity, but was far from perfect. The final step came from yet another German physicist, Max Planck, who was able to combine the two radiation laws to arrive at a formula that represented the observed energy of the radiation at any given frequency and temperature, solving the ultraviolet catastrophe. However, this achievement was to come with a surprise that would shape the whole of physics to come, starting at the sub-atomic level. What Planck had effectively done was to discover quantum mechanics, and it was the point where physics followed the work of Liebig and biology inasmuch as it dealt with the smallest parts, atoms and sub-atomic particles.

It transpired that the only way Planck could achieve his goal of uniting the two radiation theories of Wien and Rayleigh was to assume energy came in discrete packets and not as a continuous flow as in classical physics. This simple assumption would result in some of the weirdest discoveries of the fundamental workings at the smallest scales of our universe. These packets, or quanta, also followed a simple mathematical equation where the energy (E) of each quantum is given by multiplying the frequency (f) with a constant that is extremely small and now called the 'Planck constant' (h), giving the simple equation $E = h \times f$. To put it technically, by directly relating the energy of a radiation to its frequency, an explanation was then found for the observation that radiation of greater energy has a higher frequency distribution. The ultraviolet catastrophe was solved, and with it the curve of the graph shooting off at ultraviolet frequencies for which classical physics had been unable to account. Planck's idea that energy must consist of indivisible packets was revolutionary, completely overturning the accepted belief that radiation consisted of continuous waves. This era was to become known as modern physics, replacing the classical physics that was now understood as an approximation of the new physics.

The reason the effects of quantum mechanics had not been noticed earlier was simply because the Planck constant (h) is incredibly small and the reality we inhabit is extremely large in comparison; if the Planck constant was to be much larger, we too would experience its weird effects in everyday life. However, as the subject developed over the following century, its weirdness would become even more obvious with amazing consequences even on the large scale too. For example, we now understand that particles can be in several places at the same time, they can quantum-tunnel through barriers, and if the Planck constant was much larger, the theory says we could see things pass through walls like a ghost. It also led to ideas of parallel universes or what is called the 'many-world theory', or 'Multiverse', where every decision we take splits into the possible alternatives in different universes. For example, if we choose between having coffee or tea, then the two universes split: one in which we have coffee and one in which we have tea. However, the complexities of the Multiverse were unknown at the time of the Second World War and would be a whole book in itself, so we need not worry about that here. Nevertheless, what was understood about the weirdness of quantum mechanics at the time of Hitler certainly had a profound influence on him and the Nazi physicists charged with carrying out his will, because to them, it was magical and fitted their ideology all too well. During the 1920s and 1930s, it would have serious consequences for the rapidly approaching Second World War, physics, and for Nazi Germany's pseudo-science, anti-Semitism and the anti-relativists.

By the turn of the century, physics was starting to go through a revolution, with the discovery of quantum mechanics in 1900 closely followed by Einstein's theory of special relativity in 1905 and then his general theory of relativity in 1915 shortly after the First World War broke out. It was general relativity that brought gravity into Einstein's theory, superseding Newton's theory of gravity which was now understood to be an approximation of Einstein's theory. Although gravity, along with anti-gravity, would be another favourite research area of unconventional Nazi physics, its Jewish origins meant they turned to quantum mechanics as an alternative, a decision that caused them many problems. Ironically, today we realize these two great discoveries must unite to form quantum gravity, which is something Einstein battled with for the last thirty years of his life with his Unified Field Theory; today we pin our hopes for unification on string theory, or M-theory. All this was a shock for physics because it was assumed at that time that all of physics was known and all that was needed was to fine-tune a clockwork, classical, Newtonian universe.

Like biology, the physics of quantum mechanics was also starting to understand science through its smallest parts and was moving forwards by breaking free from the old ways of vitalism, philosophy and speculation. In particular, this new area of physics was starting to rebuild ideas about the smallest building blocks of nature with a better, stronger and stranger view of atoms and sub-atomic particles together with energy. Again, this would become particularly significant to the war machine of the Second World War, especially with the development of the atomic bomb, yet another lost opportunity for Hitler given that the nuclear physics on which the bomb depended was dominated by Jewish physicists in Germany. Consequently, Hitler got rid of its Jewish physicists by dismissals from universities and research institutes, detention in concentration camps or even death. The lucky ones fled to the Allies, who took full advantage of their skills and knowledge.

Whereas the problems of energy and its connection to electromagnetism had effectively been solved by Planck, there was still the problem of the elusive ether as a medium for the transfer of electromagnetic waves, and it is here that an important connection with Nazi physics persisted. Einstein's theory of relativity had by now shown that the ether was unnecessary, causing more anti-Semitic problems, but attempts to detect it still persisted and there was much resistance to the idea that it should be abandoned altogether. For example, there were further attempts to detect the ether from 1902 to 1905, just as Einstein's theory of special relativity was about to appear on the scene. A further attempt was made in 1913, eight years after the publication of the concept of special relativity, by the French physicist Georges Sagnac using his rotational version of the Michelson-Morley interferometer experiment. In Sagnac's version, the beam of light is split into two and sent in two opposite directions around a closed path on a revolving platform with mirrors on its perimeter; the beams are then recombined to see if they form that elusive interference pattern. Sagnac carried out his experiment with the hope it would show that the rotation of the Earth experienced an ether drag by measuring what is called the 'Sagnac effect', originally predicted by Max von Laue in 1911. The result apparently showed there was indeed an interference pattern, and for that reason, some took it as a more significant outcome than the Michelson-Morley attempt. The result is now disputed, but it is significant that Sagnac was an anti-relativist, strongly opposed to Einstein's theory of relativity, and wanted to prove the theory wrong, as indeed were several other physicists, especially those who were right-wing and anti-Semitic in nature. Sagnac had hoped to show that the speed of light is not a fixed universal speed limit as relativity suggested. With his rotational version, he thought he had done that, because it showed the expected interference pattern; however, this was not due to the ether, but the fact that one of the two split beams of light had travelled further due to the rotation of the device.

A further intriguing point is the timing of Sagnac's experiment. This came just before another attempt in the early 1920s by an assistant to the original Michelson-Morley experiment to use a more sensitive version of the experiment; that, too, appeared to detect the ether. However, it was also found to be in error. In fact, all attempts since then have shown no evidence of an ether, including attempts in the 1960s, and as recently as 2009 using optical resonator experiments. The point we need to take away from the 1913 and 1920 results is they showed positive results at just the time Aryan physics was on the rise during the 1920s along with anti-Semitism, anti-relativists and personal attacks on Einstein.

Interestingly, in 1921 there was an incident that occurred when Einstein was on a tour of the United States and was asked to give a series of lectures that were often followed by cocktail parties. During one of these parties at Princeton University, somebody excitedly informed him about the more sensitive rework of the Michelson-Morley experiment that had recently taken place and its 'confirmation' that the ether exists. Moreover, he was informed that the results showed the speed of light does indeed vary after all, something that was a cornerstone of his theory. Einstein refused to accept the news, knowing quite well that his theory was sound. He simply uttered one of his now famous quotes: 'Raffiniert ist der Herr Gott, aber boshaft ist er nicht', usually translated as: 'Subtle is the Lord, but malicious he is not.' Professor Oswald Veblen of Princeton University who was next to Einstein when he uttered these words later asked him for permission to have them carved into the stonework above the fireplace in the university's common room. Einstein happily agreed.

By the time Hitler came to power in 1933, the physics community was sure the ether did not exist, with the Nazis convinced it did. From that point onwards, Nazi physicists would have strong impetus, and ideological pressure from above, to accept the existence of the ether and in particular to also investigate associated Nazi physics such as rotating media, vortices or vorticular physics, physical fields of the gravitational and electromagnetic kind, and the possibilities obtainable from the ether theory, generally in the search for wonder weapons and new, 'hidden', physics.

However, it must be said that the Nazi form of the ether did have some subtle differences. One difference was the Nazis considered ether to be a 'dynamic ether'; until then, ether was considered to be stationary, which was a contributing factor to its downfall under relativity and the rejection of absolute space, absolute time and a fixed point of reference (something we will deal with later). Another important difference was an attempt to fit it into their mindset by bringing in an area of non-Jewish quantum mechanics known as the 'quantum background foam', or zero-point field. This served as an alternative way of dealing with the ether and also allowed a way to introduce their ideas about gravity, anti-gravity and endless supplies of so-called 'free energy' as a result of sub-atomic particles, energy and fields (like electric and magnetic fields) popping into and out of existence according to the Heisenberg Uncertainty Principle (HUP) of 1926. This was another great German discovery by the German quantum physicist Werner Heisenberg, who won the Nobel Prize. That would later be important because of the energy crisis in Germany during the war. It would also be a means to powering exotic weapons, including flying discs, or 'field propulsion discs', with anti-gravity capabilities. As such, it was another part of the theory that fitted well with Nazi pseudo-science. In chapter five, I will cover in detail how and why the Nazis regarded the ether as different.

The Nazis also considered an ether that would harden using electricity, a form that also fitted with the many exotic ideas and experiments carried out during the latter half of the nineteenth century and early twentieth century by the Croatian physicist Nikola Tesla; the work of Tesla was not surprisingly another favourite research area for Nazi physicists.

Heisenberg had another significant role in Nazi physics because he would also be important to developments in nuclear physics, including atomic reactors and atomic bomb research, which could be pursued without the Jewish science of nuclear physics. However, Heisenberg's part in all this would reveal something of an enigma with the man when it came to his abilities and loyalty towards the war effort, particularly involving the development of an atomic bomb for the Nazis.

Significantly, the theory of relativity had also provided another important principle involving energy and its connection to matter in the form of Einstein's energy/mass equivalence equation now famously known as $E = mc^2$ which would also be key to building the atomic bomb. This also made for more difficulties within Aryan physics and the way Hitler in particular saw nuclear physics, calling it 'the spawn of Jewish pseudo-science'. That undoubtedly influenced the Nazi physicists trying to interpret the will of the Fuhrer when considering their areas of research.

At the end of the day, what all this amounted to in the minds of key Nazi physicists are intriguing connections between many areas of physics such as nuclear physics, the ether, quantum mechanics, vortex physics and even unconventional subjects like anti-gravity, flying discs (or flying saucers), numerology, and even how the human will and consciousness can affect their research leading to new physics. Furthermore, it also links to ideas about reality from 2,500 years ago when Anaxagoras suggested reality is forged from vortices, linking to their faith in ancient hidden sciences.

So far as the long battle to detect the ether is concerned, the ironic part to the whole story is despite whatever form it may be considered to take, we now know that the electromagnetic waves of Maxwell that introduced it do not actually require a medium through which to travel after all. It has become clear that electromagnetic radiation is a flow of energy that is produced when electrically charged bodies, such as electrons, are accelerated. Light is the most familiar form of this radiation. These electromagnetic waves consist of oscillating electric and magnetic fields that travel through a vacuum or through air, carrying their energy, and therefore requiring no ether as a medium. The two fields vibrate in planes at right angles to each other and to the direction of the wave motion. So, with electromagnetic radiation made up of a periodically varying electrical disturbance and a periodically varying magnetic disturbance travelling like a wave in the direction perpendicular to the direction of the disturbance, it becomes self-propagating. That is because of the relationship between electric and magnetic fields; the magnetic field creates an electric field which creates a further magnetic field that creates the next electric field and so on along the direction of travel. This does away with the need for a medium through which to travel like the water of a pond for water waves or the air for sound waves. Einstein was also right in his view the ether is unnecessary (see later) because he had shown that one of the key principles of his theory is we can only know measurements of relative motion with the speed of light in a vacuum being a universal constant; this effectively ruled out the requirement for a stationary ether as a fixed point of reference.

To fully appreciate the theories of quantum mechanics and relativity within the Third Reich we need to look at Einstein's theory of relativity in more detail. This will then place in context the backlash towards Einstein, the anti-Semitic propaganda of the 1920s, and why an ether as a fixed point of reference was such a problem.

The theory of special relativity is concerned with the laws of physics as viewed by observers moving relative to one another at constant velocity (what physicists refer to as observers in inertial frames) and deals with how relative motion affects measurements made by these observers. If the velocities are relatively low, special relativity predicts the same results as the classical Newtonian laws of mechanics, which is why everything appeared to work fine until Einstein came along. In that respect, it was another area of physics, like quantum mechanics, inasmuch as it only becomes obvious at extremes; in quantum mechanics, it is the very small, and with relativity, it is greater velocities as we approach the speed of light (with his general theory we will introduce acceleration and gravitational fields where the extremes kick in).

There are two important elements to special relativity known as the fundamental postulates. The first is essentially the principle of relativity, which asserts that all the fundamental laws of physics, including Maxwell's equations, are the same for all observers moving at constant velocity relative to each other (or as the physicist would say, observations made in inertial frames of reference). More precisely, they are the same for all inertial frames of reference, the same for someone at rest relative to the Earth as for someone travelling at a uniform velocity on a train or spaceship. So, all inertial frames are totally equivalent for the performance of all physical experiments. The second postulate deals with the velocity of light through a vacuum, treating it as always being a constant relative to an observer (in all inertial frames). In other words, it does not matter what the velocity of the observer might be: the consistency in the speed of light holds. As we will see, it is mainly the first of these postulates that answers the dilemma of the ether, although because ideas about the ether also allowed for the variation in the speed of light, both postulates play their part in the story of the ether's downfall. So let us start with the first postulate, which addresses relative motion.

An important basic principle of special relativity is that the speed of light remains the same in any direction in free space, and it is the same for all observers and is independent of the motion of the body emitting the light or other regions of the electromagnetic spectrum (such as radio waves, microwaves, infra-red radiation, visible light, ultraviolet light, X-rays and gamma rays). This violates the classical concepts of relative motion but has been conclusively verified experimentally. The other main principle is that all physical laws are the same for every inertial frame. So, any laws deduced in one inertial frame will also be true in every other inertial frame. The values of the numerical constants appearing in these laws are also independent of the inertial frame in which they are measured; however, this is not true for certain variable quantities measured by different inertial frames, which we will come to later.

To illustrate this, let us take a simple example of relative motion. Imagine you are on a train looking out of the window as you travel through a station without stopping.

If you concentrate on the station as you pass through, it is easy to imagine that it is the station moving past you in the opposite direction rather than the station being fixed with you being the one in motion aboard the train. It will not be long before your imagination returns to your train being in motion and the station being fixed, because you know that is the case. This led to a famous claim that Einstein once asked a fellow train passenger: 'What time does Oxford station arrive at this train?' It is an easy experiment to perform and is also possible in other walks of life. For example, when watching a passing truck from your car on a road where the truck appears to be moving but you are not because of the relative velocities, or when standing on a bridge, watching the water run underneath, where if you stare at the water you get the feeling it is stationary, with you and the bridge moving along the river. Again, these visions will pass because you know the true situation.

Now let us look at a situation where it will not be easy to determine which of the two motions are possible. Take an astronaut, Fred, speeding away from Earth in a rocket at, say, 5,000km/hr. As he looks out of his window, he sees another rocket approaching, ready to overtake him, which must be moving faster, let us say 1,000km/hr faster. It might seem logical to assume the other rocket is therefore moving at 6,000km/hr if Fred 'knows' he is moving away from the Earth at 5,000km/hr. But what relativity shows is it all depends on the observers, because to the other rocket, piloted by Jane, she could argue she sees Fred's rocket as stationary, with her rocket passing by Fred's rocket at only 1,000km/hr. So, Fred looks at his radar, which tells him Jane's rocket is moving at 1,000km/hr with respect to him, and that is the key. Relativity tells us that the relative motion is, in fact, all that Fred and Jane can determine. So, the question becomes: Is Fred's rocket moving at 1,000km/hr and is Jane's stationary, or is it the other way around? The answer is: It depends on the observers themselves; all that can be said is with no fixed object as a reference point, out there in the depths of space, well away from Earth, you can only say there is a relative motion of 1,000km/hr. This situation could also easily be determined another way by saying Fred's rocket is moving at 2,000km/hr, having lost speed, and Jane's is moving not at 6,000km/hr but now only 3,000km/hr, but it still gives a relative motion of 1,000km/hr confirmed by the radar. Even stranger: it could be that Fred's rocket is now travelling backwards towards the Earth at 1,000km/hr!

To resolve the problem, the astronauts need a motionless, fixed, or stationary object as a reference point, something akin to the idea of the ether we have just explored. Moreover, it is impossible to develop an instrument to determine what is happening other than that you are moving with respect to something else. It was this fact that Einstein recognized: all motion is relative, hence the name 'relativity'. It is true that Einstein did not like the word relativity—he preferred 'invariance theory'—but we need not confuse the issue here with that point.

As a result, we cannot speak of absolute motion as such, but only of motion relative to something else. So, we are not able to say an object has a velocity of such-and-such but only that an object has a velocity of such-and-such *relative* to so-and-so. The reason why we snap out of our illusions on Earth with the train, truck and river is because we know these velocities are relative to the Earth. Likewise, a speed limit along the highway of, say, 50km/hr is understood to mean 50km/hr relative to the Earth; in the depths of space with no Earth or other body as a fixed reference, a velocity in itself has no meaning.

An obvious answer might appear to be the use of a planet, star, asteroid or other heavenly body as a reference point, for example, the Earth in our rocket scenario. However, this will not do because the Earth rotates on its axis, is also in orbital motion around the sun, the sun in turn orbits around the Milky Way Galaxy, and our Milky Way Galaxy is in relative motion with respect to all the other galaxies in the universe. The whole universe is filled with motion such that nobody can say what is moving and what is stationary; we can only say all the heavenly bodies are moving relative to one another with no one of these moving bodies different in this respect; none have a privileged position about which all others move, so there is no fixed reference point.

At the end of the day relativity did away with the Newtonian ideas of absolute motion, absolute time and absolute space that were the same for all observers. There was no universal clock for all observers, and no stationary reference point. In particular, as a direct result of the invariance of the speed of light (hence Einstein's name preference), the concepts of space and time could no longer be considered as separate, but instead are a composite entity called 'space-time'. As a result, any event in an inertial frame must be described by four space-time co-ordinates, three spatial (length, width and height) co-ordinates and one time co-ordinate. This means the space-time co-ordinates of the same event measured in two different inertial frames will differ. To interconvert these, we need to use the Lorentz transformations.

This fundamental starting point of relativity was difficult to accept, and with many other similar features of the theory adding to the 'strangeness' of everyday common sense, it led to many being unable to accept the theory following its publication and instead dismissing it as nonsense. In turn this view was adopted by the Nazis and was combined with their anti-Semitic views in general, and to Einstein in particular, as well as an excuse to hold on to the idea of a stationary ether, which was a fixed reference point, although, as we saw, they did adjust the idea to a dynamic ether as part of their ongoing research. It became the perfect reason to reject the whole theory of relativity as 'Jewish pseudo-science'.

So, how does this rather long explanation fit with the ether? The answer is a stationary ether would allow absolute motion by being the one thing that is motionless. However, because of special relativity, we now know that we can only measure relative motion. From this, it follows that we cannot detect the absolute motion of the Earth through space, and it is therefore meaningless to talk about absolute space or the ether providing some fundamental frame of reference for the measurement of velocity (see the Michelson Morley experiment). This, oddly enough, does not technically mean special relativity proves the ether does not exist; it shows we cannot detect it. Moreover, special relativity does not require an ether in any form. So, whereas relativity does not technically dismiss the ether idea, it shows it is unnecessary (as we will see later Einstein did resurrect an ether of sorts to explain the space-time fabric as a medium for gravitational waves, but that was different). There was also that further blow when self-propagating electromagnetic waves also did away with Maxwell's ether as a medium for its transmission through space, the idea of an ether he left to physics in the last year of his life. We must also remember that it was Maxwell's work that played a major role in the development of Einstein's work.

Nevertheless, despite the troubles this might cause, the understanding of electromagnetism was important to developments in weaponry during the Second World War, both conventional and unconventional, allowing for the development of areas like communications and radar.

By the time Hitler came to power in 1933, modern physics was a well-founded scientific discipline providing the backbone to a world war that would see physics and engineering develop even further in leaps and bounds as an essential part of the war machine on both sides. The timing of these advances in physics has an almost spooky element, coming as they did at maybe just the wrong time for world peace and the Jewish community. That said, an equally spooky element is the uniquely Nazi way these advances were interpreted and implemented. Here we had conventional physics invaded by politics and pseudo-science, and because of the anti-Semitism developing in the 1920s, this toxic mix was wrapped up with the foundations of prejudice and hatred that would eventually develop just in time for Hitler's Germany, and in doing so helped shape the fate of both Hitler and the Nazis generally.

As the world entered the twentieth century, German science was really on a high that continued for another fourteen years until the outbreak of the First World War. It therefore came as a surprise in 1900 that Germany failed in its bid to host the great International Exhibition, the honour going to Paris instead. Exhibits stretched over fifteen locations, with millions of Germans attending to glow in their country's achievements, the general theme being to show how science and technology was useful across nations. The achievements on display were from so many fields of science and technology it was quite overwhelming, showing how co-operation could be a reality. Furthermore, following the creation of the Nobel Prize at the beginning of the twentieth century, Germans or German speakers would find themselves winning half of the awards by 1921, with Einstein continuing the trend in 1922. There was no doubt that German science and technology was advanced, active and healthy, and as we saw, there was more to come as the new century dawned.

However, all this glory turned sour at just about the time quantum mechanics and relativity were taking off when, in 1914, the First World War broke out. Whereas the Second World War could be regarded as the physicists' war, the First World War was the chemists' war, having been built on the golden years driven by chemistry. The horrors of a chemical war with the gassing of soldiers in the trenches and the relentless drive for better gases and chemicals to fight that war led to the downfall of German science in the eyes of the world's scientific community. There was also, of course, the political problems for Germany as a result of losing the war.

The use of chemicals was hardly surprising given the level of expertise the Germans had developed throughout their golden years, but it would see Germany defeated in science as it was in war, and it did not take much to achieve that scientific defeat—the first attack was enough. That attack came at 5.00 pm on the afternoon of 22 April 1915 when the chemist Fritz Haber and his troop, known as Pioneer Regiment 36, were dug in along a 6.5km front on the German lines at Ypres facing the French Territorials and an Algerian division of the French Army. Haber's troop possessed 5,730 cylinders, each 91kg in weight, of liquid chlorine gas made possible as a result of another German advancement in the liquification of gases. The order came to attack. With the wind blowing in the right direction, the troop, wearing protective clothing and masks, opened the valves to release the entire contents of the cylinders across no man's land. It took only 10 minutes for the cloud of dense, heavier-than-air, yellow-green gas to sweep westwards into the Allied trenches. Some troops were almost instantly suffocated while others fled in panic, abandoning their guns. The Germans crossed no man's land and took the trenches.

The attack was widely condemned on both sides and broke the Hague Conventions of 1899 and 1907; it was a major act of inhumanity. In later years, as we will see, Hitler would regard such devastating and surprise attacks as acceptable in general, making his philosophy clear at one of his so-called 'table talk dinners' in 1942. He said: 'What's important is to have technical superiority in every case at a decision point. I know that; I'm mad on technology. We must meet the enemy with novelties that take them by surprise, so as continually to keep the initiative.' No doubt this kind of action pleased him to a point; however, there is evidence he found gas attacks in particular distasteful. Indeed, when Hitler came to power in 1933, his reaction to Haber as instigator of such actions was negative, but that was essentially due to Haber being Jewish; as far as Hitler was concerned, Haber had no worth in his war.

One of the more enthusiastic colleagues of Haber, Otto Hahn, would say in the 1960s: 'At first the English were very surprised by our disregarding the Hague Convention, but from 1916 onwards they used at least as much poison as we did.' Haber's attack was indeed later emulated by the other side, in particular by British physicist J.B.S. Haldane. He, like others, saw the new technology in weapons as having the power to actually save lives by bringing about a swift victory. It is said that both Haber and Haldane considered the act of gassing 'a higher form of killing': being killed or injured by gas was better than being blown up.

Further gas attacks would be carried out by Haber, including one at the eastern front involving the Russians on 12 June 1915. In Galicia, the Germans used gas—this time a mixture of chlorine and phosgene, the latter being even more deadly (its inventor died after only a brief sniff).

In the end, these attacks did not bring the hoped-for swift victory but, instead, retaliation in kind and more inhumanity and violation of treaties of war. In fact, things only escalated, and by the war's end some twenty-two different agents were used on both sides, including blood-poisoning chemicals delivered by shells, mortars, and aerial attacks. The consequences of these attacks were dug-outs full of casualties as the chlorine attacked the mucous membranes of the nose, mouth and throat, causing asphyxiation and blindness. Faces also turned blue as soldiers choked and gasped for breath, and lungs were scorched. Eventually the whole head turned blue with black lips, resulting in victims choking to death through suffocation and haemorrhages. Those lucky to have gas masks often underestimated the length of time the gasses lingered, removing them too soon; the heavier-than-air chlorine gathered in trenches and lingered in some areas. Those lucky enough to be far enough away still suffered horrific pains to the eyes, and violent vomiting which passed relatively quickly. Other agents had differing effects, but all were deadly. Developing better gas masks did not help either because Haber and his team carried out a series of experiments to deliver ever more deadly gas combinations and ways to bypass the gas mask. One of these was known as *Buntkreuz*, involving a mixture of a form of phosgene gas and an irritant which was capable of penetrating gas masks. The result was simple but deadly: the irritant would force soldiers to rip off their masks, exposing them to the ever-more-deadly gases Haber had perfected.

Hahn's justification for this was expressed after the war when he said: 'As a result of continuous work with these highly toxic substances, our minds were so numbed that we no longer had any scruples about the whole thing. Anyway our enemies had by now adopted our methods.' He added: 'As they became increasingly successful in this mode of warfare we were no longer exclusively the aggressors but found ourselves more and more at the receiving end.' Maybe most significant was the comment: 'Another factor was we front-line observers rarely saw the direct effects of our weapons.'

For years Haber continued his work through several projects of chemical warfare, even after the war and against restrictions by the Treaty of Versailles, often using the go-between Dr Hugo Stoltzenberg. These projects included the use of poison gas by the Spanish army to put down Abd el-Krim's Morocco revolt, secret deals with the Soviets and the establishment of a gas factory near Wittenberg. One of the developments Haber encouraged was that of hydrocyanic acid, which had the more innocent use as a pesticide. Later, it would double as another gas for killing humans under its alternative name, Zyklon B; it was used under that name by Hitler as the principal means for killing Jews in the death camps. Even when Haber ceased to be a leader in gas warfare, the Kaiser continued to consult him as part of a possible future revenge against the Allies. In 1927, living in exile in Holland, the Kaiser had expressed a special interest in Haber helping with the possibility of 'the total gassing of large cities'.

After Germany lost the First World War, the Allies tried to bring Haber to trial as a war criminal; however, according to Hahn, to escape the authorities he began wearing a beard. He then disappeared to Switzerland. Eventually he was allowed to return to Germany. Then, in 1918, to the disgust of the Western scientific community, Haber won the Nobel Prize, awarded for his discovery of ammonia. He then remained an honoured member of German science for more than a decade.

Haber did make attempts to revive Germany's scientific reputation during the immediate aftermath of the First World War as the country was plunged into crisis, but the golden years that saw great advances in the country's chemical industries had led to inhuman consequences unacceptable to both the scientific community and world at large. As a result, there was an almost-immediate cessation of international scientific collaboration with Germany. There was now little money for the experimental research that had allowed the country to grow in wealth as well as science; all that was really left was a concentration on the areas requiring less in the way of financial support and more on brainpower, like the theoretical and mathematical sciences. That situation was well-suited to quantum mechanics and relativity in particular, both of which flourished during the 1920s. Even so, the theoretical physicists found themselves continuing their work against a backdrop of economic collapse, alliances in shreds, a defeated military and a country left vulnerable to revolution and civil war. Furthermore, the Treaty of Versailles had delivered a harsh underfunding problem to the country, which inevitably had its fallout in science and technology. By 1919, Allied powers had funded the International Research Council, but Germany and Austria found they were barred (as were countries that were neutral during the hostilities). This situation would span a period of time at least as long as the war itself, until 1925, when the Locarno Treaties provided a more relaxed approach, resulting in Germany being invited into the council. However, not all went as well as expected when both German and Austrian scientists turned down the invitation.

In no small part the problem for German scientists was augmented by their being boycotted by many foreign peer groups, with visiting professorships and access to conferences and symposia denied. In total, German scientists had been barred from 165 of the 275 international meetings between 1919 and 1925, which included the famous Solvay Conferences. Nonetheless, there were some positive elements to come from this situation. One such attempt was to encourage understanding in science during the 1920s with the construction of a planetarium by the Zeiss Lens Corporation in Jena. This interest in astronomy had been sparked by new discoveries in the sciences following Einstein's achievements in relativity and the work of the American astronomer Edwin Hubble in showing that the universe was expanding and there were many galaxies external to our own; until then, our Milky Way Galaxy was thought to be the entire universe. Hubble's discovery would also see Einstein solve one of the key problems with relativity, which he later regarded as the biggest mistake of his life—a static universe neither expanding nor contracting. Yet this was not all good news. For example, Hitler, and indeed Himmler, would take a different view towards astronomy, providing a warped interpretation tailor-made to the Nazi ideology, particularly the purity of the Aryan race.

This desire to understand the workings of the universe appeared to shine through the isolation Germany faced after the war, much to the disgust of extreme right-wing physicists and anti-relativists because it was heavily aided by Einstein and his theory of relativity. By now, Einstein had become the world's first true celebrity scientist and he was much in demand, popularizing astronomy and physics through the media during the rest of his life. Anti-relativists not only based their backlash on anti-Semitism but also on his theory being complicated and incomprehensible. That backlash would then develop alongside Einstein's celebrity status during the 1920s and into the Second World War. To add further to the anti-relativists' disgust, as the world was now getting back on its feet, attention returned to proving his theory correct, thus escalating the troubles.

With the First World War over in 1918, a fortunate opportunity arose to test relativity in 1919 with a total solar eclipse in May of that year. The idea was to measure the displacement of stars near the sun caused by their light being bent by the curved space-time created by the sun's mass. That opportunity did indeed prove Einstein right, as we will see later. The discovery was made by an English astronomer by the name of Arthur Eddington. Given the strained relationship between Britain and Germany at the time, an English astronomer proving a Jew right was not appreciated by the extreme right-wing physicists of Germany.

The general theory of relativity presented in 1915 describes how the relationship between space and time already developed in the special theory is affected by the gravitational effects of energy and matter. The basic idea is that gravitational fields change the geometry of space-time, causing it to become curved, and in doing so dictates the natural motions of bodies. The famous expression to sum up this principle is: Matter tells space-time how to curve and space-time tells matter how to move. In a similar fashion to comparing special relativity with Newtonian motion, the two theories of Newtonian gravity and Einsteinian gravity (general relativity) only diverge when conditions like gravitational fields become extreme and therefore warp space-time, so Newtonian gravity is an approximation of general relativity. For most cases, such as sending space probes to the planets, Newtonian gravity is used because its mathematics are far simpler, but for an object orbiting a massive black hole, for example, Newtonian laws break down and general relativity is then required. In fact, even for our own sun, the gravitation can become a problem at close range. This became evident when astronomers before Einstein's day found they could not predict the orbital behaviour of Mercury, the closest planet to the sun. As a result, many decades were wasted trying to find a planet closer to the sun than Mercury, which was thought to be pulling Mercury from its predicted path. Such was the confidence it existed that this planet was even given a name: Vulcan. When general relativity appeared on the scene, the orbital behaviour of Mercury was solved by Einstein and the agreement between theory and observation became the first successful test of relativity. This was known as the perihelion problem, where the closest point to the sun in Mercury's orbit, perihelion, was slipping around its orbit unexpectedly.

The basic postulate from which general relativity was developed is the principle of equivalence between gravitational and inertial forces. Essentially, gravitation and acceleration are equivalent; the same laws of nature apply, and thus the same phenomena will be observed. This is usually illustrated by a person standing on a planet, such as Earth, compared to one in a rocket accelerating at 1 G and with no windows out of which to look. The person in the rocket would not observe anything different versus the person on the planet's surface. A G is a unit of measurement of the force resulting from gravitation, where 1 G is equivalent to the force of the Earth's gravitational pull. In other words, 1 G is the force of gravity we experience on Earth, but it does vary elsewhere. It would be less on the moon (1/6 G) because the moon is less massive than the Earth and greater on planets more massive than the Earth, the value depending on the planet's mass. So, the person in the rocket would be unable to determine if he was accelerating into space at 1 G or sitting on the launch pad; for the person in the rocket, the feel of the floor pushing against his feet due to acceleration would be the same as the feel of gravity for the person standing on Earth. That is why, when sitting in a car or train, cruising at a constant velocity, you feel no push on your back, but if the vehicle then accelerates, you feel as if you are being pushed back in your seat. You are then in an accelerating frame rather than an inertial frame, as described above with special relativity.

Einstein was also able to show that the natural motion of a body was in a straight line along the shortest path between two points (called a geodesic) in the geometry required to describe the physical world (compared to Newton's first law). However, the usual three-dimensional Euclidean geometry could not be used for this purpose; the geometry needed to be more flexible, and this became the geometry of space-time. The curvature of space-time can be calculated from Einstein's field equations which he produced as part of his general theory, and which he struggled to develop right up to a couple of weeks before November 1915, when it all fell into place.

The three main tests of general relativity are the bending of light around gravitational masses, proved at the 1919 total eclipse of the sun (see below); the predicted gravitational redshift in spectral lines of radiation emitted from a massive body, also proved; and the effects of curved space-time on the motion of orbiting bodies, again proved with Mercury. Other predictions are gravitational waves, or ripples in the space-time fabric akin to throwing a pebble in a pond, recently discovered; the existence of singularities in the structure of space-time leading to black holes; and the constancy of the gravitational constant. In short, the evidence for general relativity was mounting all the time as it passed test after test with flying colours. It was no surprise the Nazis rejected Einsteinian gravitation following confirmation at the 1919 eclipse using instead some uncertainty about the results to fuel their 1920s backlash (see below). That said, they did consider certain elements of Einsteinian gravitation when researching their pseudo-scientific ideas involving mass, inertia, superluminal speed and exotic aviation ideas, but with a quantum mechanical twist. One such connection was the uniting of electromagnetism and gravity, something Einstein went on to investigate with his Unified Field Theory during the last 30 years of his life without success. This unification was essential for their theories of electrogravitation (or electrogravitics) involving anti-gravity devices like their 'field propulsion discs' or flying saucers. In fact, the uniting of electromagnetism and gravity is still a goal today with string theory, or M-theory, and has even been investigated by NASA and several aviation companies.

It was this idea of putting physical meaning to the space-time geometry, or fabric of space-time, that caused Einstein to resurrect the idea of an ether during the 1920s. However, he was clear to distinguish this ether from that proposed by Maxwell during the last year of his life. This act might appear to be a way to address the backlash he experienced, but that is unlikely. From a scientific viewpoint, he did make his views clear as part of a scaling back on some of his bolder, earlier ideas, possibly because he was now world-famous: 'To punish me for my contempt of authority, fate has made me an authority myself.' This scaling back included the description of the ether as 'superfluous' in his 1905 paper on relativity. After finishing his theory of general relativity in 1915, he concluded that it contained something that characterized the physical qualities of empty space that served as a medium to transmit disturbances such as gravitational waves—the gravitational potentials—which he started referring to as a new way to conceive of an ether. In 1916, he wrote to Hendrik Lorentz, saying: 'I agree with you that general relativity theory admits of an ether hypothesis.' Then, in a lecture in Leiden in May 1920, Einstein publicly proposed a reincarnation, though not a rebirth, of the ether. He said: 'More careful reflection teaches us, however, that the special theory of relativity does not compel us to deny an ether. We may assume the existence of an ether, only we must give up ascribing a definite state of motion to it.' He believed this was justified by the results of his 1915 general theory of relativity in particular and reintroduced it in order to explain struggles he and other physicists had been having since Newton's time with rotation and inertia. Nevertheless, the idea of gravitational waves, proved correct today, would undoubtedly have been significant to the exotic gravity and anti-gravity research of the Nazi physicists together with their ideas on inertia. For those interested in the struggles from Newton's time involving rotation and inertia, these were associated with Ernst Mach and Newton's bucket, which can be followed up by the reader if they wish. Essentially this part of Einstein's work does not come into our story here, except to say Einstein was a great fan of Mach and his work, which played an important role in Einstein's initial interest in physics, but it would also bog him down at times while trying to develop general relativity and again with his United Field Theory; he found it difficult to accept certain new ideas because of this faith in Mach. The true nature of the fabric of space-time remains unresolved to this day.

When it came to the hatred of Einstein and his theory amongst the right-wing anti-relativists, a further problem was evident; Einstein did not like quantum mechanics, especially its probabilistic nature. 'God does not play dice with the Universe,' he said. With that in mind, he approached the problem of uniting electromagnetism and gravity by actually doing away with quantum mechanics in a paper from 1929. Initially the idea looked promising, but unfortunately it had no physical meaning and was universally rejected by physicists, although it did generate considerable media attention.

Advanced physics, like quantum mechanics and relativity, and later nuclear physics, certainly caused more confusion and misunderstanding in Hitler's mind, although it did allow him to cherry-pick what suited him best as he grappled with the scientific revolution taking place around him and its Jewish connections. That said, Hitler did have a documented comment that appears to be connected with the two great theories of quantum mechanics and relativity: 'Science has taught us that we are hemmed in not only by the infinitely great, but the infinitely small in the macrocosm and microcosm.' Maybe, from the psychological viewpoint, Hitler himself felt hemmed in.

Despite Hitler's strained understanding, he did talk of the golden years of German science, although it appears he saw that period of German history in his own unique way and from a military perspective; Germany had been a prosperous country, a world leader, and had a rich history, and leisure pastime, in aviation and rocketry that could now turn the defeat of the First World War into a victory in the Second World War. The blame for defeat and Germany's current global position, which he placed on Jews, was, of course, to be a further driving factor. Hitler certainly rejected a fair amount of theoretical science developed during that time because of its Jewish connections, turning instead to experimental science and, in particular, applied physics. Those times saw experimentation and applied physics flourish with national hobbies like gliding, aviation and even rocketry, especially during the 1920s and 1930s. Interestingly, some of the extreme right-wing physicists who went all out to attack theoretical science were experimental physicists who found the concepts of its advanced mathematics hard to understand; many of these individuals would continue their attacks under Hitler's regime in one way or another.

The emphasis placed on applied physics was arguably one of the good decisions of the Nazis, because applied physics, together with engineering, allowed them to build on these past developments with aviation and rocketry. Indeed, they had already been experimenting with new designs and airfoils well in advance of the war. Of course, their preference for quantum mechanics over relativity and other Jewish science was more of a disadvantage and a fatal one; it left them searching for alternatives that simply did not exist through pseudo-science, myths and legends. That said, the Nazis saw some worth in theoretical science so long as it was not Jewish in nature and they could incorporate it into applied science and applied physics; there was also an element of twisting Jewish science and crowbarring it into their projects too when it suited them.

One particular area that stood out amongst their research was the atomic bomb. Whereas their applied physics fitted well with many projects like the aviation and rocket programmes, it did place them at a disadvantage when it came to the development of an atomic bomb. So, instead, the nuclear project followed a somewhat haphazard and unconventional path; there is still debate to this day as to how far they really got with its development, spawning many a conspiracy theory along the way.

However, generally speaking this preference for applied physics was a double-edged sword when combined with Hitler's mindset. Whereas it would lead to major technological advances in conventional weaponry, it also opened a Pandora's box of pseudo-science leading to much delay as Himmler's SS pursued all manner of controversial science projects with all kinds of trial-and-error experimentation on a wide variety of devices. This pursuit was largely tied up with the belief that ancient manuscripts and texts held those secrets that would win the war for the Nazis. It was a misplaced justification that created a toxic mix and disastrous consequences, and set in motion unconventional and chaotic pursuits that sent research into a downward spiral. Much of this was through Himmler and his pet society, the *Ahnenerbe*.

As we will see, many of Hitler's beliefs were also shared by Himmler. Himmler was convinced he was the reincarnation of Henry the Wildfowler, Emperor of Germany; backed up by Hitler, Himmler demonstrated some of the best examples of pseudo-science in history. These two worked well together, Hitler as the theorist and Himmler as the facilitator, resulting in a lethal mix based on an amateurish approach as well as lack of judgment and scientific know-how. Other issues included reasoning by analogy, classifying phenomena according to superficial observation rather than empirical evidence, trial, error, 'lost science' and combining science with religion into a single discipline.

Running parallel to these problems was conventional science that helped built the hardware of war like tanks, cannons, aircraft and rockets. It is also particularly significant how much of the unconventional fitted into the thinking of other areas, with overlaps and twisted facts involving all manner of ideas and theories.

Chapter Two

The Rise of Aryan Physics

The troubled times of the post-war 1920s saw the German science community fragmented both intellectually and politically; many found themselves restricted by being civil servants. However, there was an eventual uniting of physicists as a result of an intense dislike of the Weimar Republic. Politically, as we have seen, there were also far-right scientists who not only had a problem with theoretical physics but also the heavy influence Jewish scientists had with many of those theoretical subjects developing at the time. Inevitably this fanned the flames of what would become a decade of anti-Semitism leading up to Hitler's rise to power; it would also see many of the extreme right-wing physicists finding roles within Hitler's regime. Two such names in particular who played key roles in the troubles of that decade were the German Nobel Laureates Philipp Lenard and Johannes Stark; it is, therefore, no surprise these right-wing aggressors found a welcoming home within the Nazi Party, which they eagerly joined at the earliest opportunity.

A more immediate problem following the First World War and the defeat of Germany was funding for German and Austrian science, which became hard to come by until about 1923; it was a far cry from the golden years, with scientists now facing a shortage of resources and funding that had to be shared out sparingly. For that reason, as we have seen, theoretical physics flourished more than applied or experimental physics; it needed little, if any, equipment, as it was largely a matter of researching the work of others and applying brainpower to build on those past achievements. This would further agitate the likes of Lenard, who was an experimental physicist. There was also further resentment towards the Weimar government; under them, scientists had forced cuts in wages as a result of being civil servants. Nevertheless, there was some extra money to be had from industry and certain foreign sources.

A new agency was eventually established in Weimar Germany called the *Notgemeinschaft der Deutschen Wissenschaft* (Emergency Society for German Science). This agency represented the Kaiser Wilhelm Society and its institutions, together with the universities, technical institutions and other academic and scholarly areas of science. Its purpose was to provide money, institutions and research programmes as well as providing individual scientists with funding from the Reich government in Berlin, General Electric, and the Rockefeller Foundation in the USA. There was also a rival Helmholtz Society, which German industry tended to support. It was at this point that German industry enters our story as a key element of things to come.

Yet another problem, and one which would escalate out of all proportions after Hitler came to power, was anti-Semitism, especially in science. Of course, German science was not alone in this. Other countries also actively practicing this form of discrimination included France, Britain and the United States, for example. Later, more global anti-Semitism would be particularly evident through what became known as the Academy of Nations, which supported anti-Semitism aimed at theoretical physicists in general because of the often lack of experimental verification to their theories. By the 1920s, anti-Semitism reigned supreme in many of the German universities and research institutes, and by the 1930s, it had become a fact of life in just about all such areas.

As we have seen, the focal point for much of this anti-Semitism was none other than Einstein himself. Einstein's fame had already taken off by the 1920s following the first experimental confirmation of the theory of general relativity with the long-awaited explanation for Mercury's orbit, a verification that anti-relativists did not see as proof at all. It was also a case that the theory of relativity was gaining ever-more interest in the press, something that would follow Einstein for the rest of his life in all his endeavours. Matters were not helped either by the fact Einstein also loved the publicity and was only too happy to embrace it. As the first true international celebrity scientist, the situation of public fascination and prejudice became an extremely toxic mix.

Despite the many boycotts and financial problems, areas like experimental science also had their moments, as the number of German Nobel Laureates of the time shows. For example, Wilhelm Konrad Rontgen was awarded his prize for the discovery of X-rays, Emil Adolf Von Behring for serum therapy, Adolf von Baeyer for organic dyes, Wilhelm Ostwald for chemical equilibria and reaction rates, Philipp Lenard for cathode rays, Max Planck for quanta of energy, Fritz Haber for synthesizing ammonia, Walther Nernst for thermodynamics and, of course, Albert Einstein for the photoelectric effect and his contributions to theoretical physics. Therefore, scientific achievements were still recognized following the First World War and these would advance despite the scientific community's reluctance towards German scientists. In short, Germany continued as best it could with efforts to build on the golden years. That said, when it came to theoretical physics, a key problem was the concentration of Jewish scientists researching the subjects, a situation that made itself evident with those two keystones of modern physics, quantum mechanics and relativity; Einstein was certainly Jewish but Max Planck was considered to be non-Jewish, resulting in a scientific dichotomy that sent the Nazis down a unique and fatal path as a result of anti-Semitism building up.

Mathematics under the Nazis did not seem to have such a clear Jewish and non-Jewish split in quite the same way and appear to have been treated somewhat differently, although some right-wing individuals like Lenard did rebel, mainly because they themselves did not keep up with the mathematics so essential to theoretical physics as a result of being experimental physicists. Nevertheless, many Jewish mathematicians would be persecuted. Interestingly, things could have been very different because of this mathematical element had history played out an alternative reality regarding the final formulation of general relativity.

The story centres on a 2-week period in November 1915 which could have seen a split in credit between special and general relativity, with the special theory being credited to Einstein and the general theory going to the German mathematician David Hilbert. Both physicists found themselves in a race to complete the final details surrounding the geometry of general relativity, with Einstein almost pipped at the post. Einstein had essentially created this situation for himself due to him stubbornly holding onto old ideas; had he not seen sense at the last moment, it might have become Hilbert's theory of general relativity, but Hilbert came up with the solution just a bit too late. Hilbert, being considered non-Jewish, may have also changed the Nazis' view of relativity; the general anti-Semitism from the anti-relativists may have been less severe. Hilbert essentially solved the problem just after Einstein went public with his solution; he presented at a series of lectures.

Of course, under this alternative history, special relativity would still be Einstein's achievement and therefore Jewish, but no doubt the mindset of the Nazis would have circumnavigated that detail somehow—after all the general theory essentially incorporated the special theory. As a result, they may have simply suggested a Jewish scientist had failed to find the whole answer but a non-Jew had. Moreover, Hilbert's reputation would have no doubt played a role; he was already regarded as a great German mathematician and invited to many functions to speak on mathematics, setting the world's mathematicians a series of unsolved problems. Hilbert explained that these problems 'Show how rich, how manifold and how extensive mathematical science is today.' Hilbert went on to say: 'Mathematics is the foundation of all exact knowledge of natural phenomena. . . .may the new century bring it gifted prophets and many zealous and enthusiastic disciples.' Hilbert was no doubt held in high esteem and might have taken the Nazis down a different scientific route and possibly an alternative outcome to the Second World War.

The 1920s also saw a significant advance in the understanding of quantum mechanics with the subject seeing a growth from around 1923 to 1930, when the theory gained experimental verifications. After that, it started to take off in leaps and bounds, and today we have all manner of exotic discoveries and even more exotic theoretical possibilities, from parallel universes and time travel to warp drive engines capable of taking us to the stars like something out of a sci-fi movie. There are also advances in super-quantum computers more powerful than anybody ever imagined.

As we saw earlier, quantum mechanics is a fundamental theory of physics that describes physical properties of nature at very small scales, on the order of atoms and sub-atomic particles. As such, it is the foundation of quantum physics, including quantum chemistry, quantum biology and quantum information science. So, let us summarize and pull together this area of physics as it developed during the 1920s.

With this branch of physics, physicists can explain how everything works and it is the best description we have of the nature of the particles that make up matter and the forces with which they interact. This means quantum physics underlies how atoms work and so why chemistry and biology work as they do. In this small-scale world, objects exist in a bizarre haze of probability; they have a certain chance of being at point A, another of being at point B and so on; essentially, they can be in more than one place at the same time. As we have also seen, properties like position, velocity and energy can only occur in specific set elements called quanta and not as a smooth continuous spectrum of all values as with classical physics; physicists say these properties are quantized. Another startling property of this theory is that particles can also behave as waves, giving them a wave/particle duality; some experiments highlight their wave nature, and others their particle nature. Furthermore, as we have seen, the reason why these bizarre quantum rules only apply to the very small domain of atoms and subatomic particles is because they are governed by the Planck constant, h, which is an extremely small number.

It was the Danish physicist Niels Bohr, the youngest of the early quantum physicists of the pre-First World War era, who was responsible for taking quantum theory forwards into the 1920s. He summed up the nature of the subject in his now-famous quote: 'If you are not profoundly shocked by quantum theory, you have not understood it.' His relationship with another German quantum physicist, Werner Heisenberg, resulted in a historic meeting during the depths of the Second World War in occupied Denmark during 1941, a meeting that was key to trying to determine whether Heisenberg, the future head of the Nazi atomic bomb project, really appreciated this area of physics and in particular the building of an atomic bomb. To this day, the enigma surrounding Heisenberg's behaviour makes it unclear whether he was deliberately depriving Hitler of that weapon of mass destruction by stalling its development or whether his knowledge surrounding its true implications was lacking. That said, Heisenberg did develop his Uncertainty Principle in quantum mechanics that led to many other Nazi projects.

It was while considering problems with atomic physics that Heisenberg came up with answers involving observations on the quantum level as he joined, accompanied by Arnold Sommerfeld, the world-famous team of quantum physicists at a Gottingen 'Bohr Festival' in 1922. Here, Bohr was giving a series of lectures on quantum mechanics that led to the Heisenberg Uncertainty Principle, which we will cover shortly.

Bohr, however, was not part of the Nazi Party, despite Heisenberg's attempts in Denmark to recruit him, although he did favour scientific collaboration and wanted an international community of physicists operating as an ideal society. Unfortunately, such a goal was in conflict with the more hostile extreme right-wing physicists of the Nazi regime, particularly the likes of Philipp Lenard and Johannes Stark.

There was also tension between Einstein and the Bohr-Heisenberg group throughout the 1920s and into the 1930s because of Einstein's mistrust of quantum mechanics. Initially Einstein did not believe the theory was correct because of its nature being based on probability and uncertainty. However, after much experimental confirmation in the 1920s, including his own quantum law of photoelectricity for which he won the Nobel Prize, he concluded it was 'incomplete'. Even so, to his dying day Einstein did not believe that 'God plays dice with the Universe' and described quantum entanglement, another confirmed phenomenon, as 'Spooky action at a distance'. This is when two or more particles appear to be connected no matter how far apart, even if on opposite sides of the universe.

At his Manchester, England laboratory during the first decade of the twentieth century, Bohr worked on the model of the atom originally suggested by Ernest Rutherford. Rutherford had shown that the bulk of an atom's mass (99.9 per cent) resided in its nucleus with particles of much less mass, electrons, orbiting the nucleus like a mini solar system (the nucleus representing a sun and the electrons representing planets). The problem with this particular arrangement was it did not account for the stability of the atom. So, what Bohr did was to apply Planck's quantum theory to the problem by first using the simplest atom, hydrogen, which had only one particle as a nucleus, a proton, and one orbiting electron. The problem was eventually solved when it was found that the angular momentum of electrons also come in discrete packets, or quanta, which meant that they too are quantized, like many other quantities in physics. Bohr won the Nobel Prize for his work in 1922, a story we will cover later.

However, although this was a better, quantized, model it was not without problems and it was then up to the German quantum physicist Otto Frisch to resolve matters. It was he who would fully realize the nature of these problems and start asking awkward questions. He questioned why the electrons should 'orbit' in confined circular paths around the nucleus like planets in a solar system. He also asked how exactly electrons jumped from a higher orbital energy to a lower one, throwing out the loss of energy as photons of light. He further questioned the exact structure of atoms with more than one electron and how those electrons orbited without collisions. Answers to some of these questions were provided in the early 1920s by the physicists Arnold Sommerfeld from Munich and Wolfgang Pauli from Vienna. Sommerfeld classified possible orbits, including elliptical orbits, while Pauli came up with the exclusion principle, whereby more than one electron cannot exist in the same quantum state within one atom. Pauli won his Nobel Prize for this work in 1945. Many of these characters and their work would later play major roles in the race to develop the atomic bomb, but they also showed how quantum mechanics was becoming a major subject during the 1920s and therefore influenced Nazi physics above relativity.

It was also significant that Heisenberg was a German quantum physicist who featured centre stage in Nazi physics. Heisenberg was a stereotypical German youth with blond hair, blue eyes and a fondness for dressing in lederhosen, as well as being a member of The Pathfinders, which emerged in 1919 from the German Youth Movement (*Jugendbewegung*). Heisenberg also subscribed to what would be a central theme in National Socialist Germany: a radically hygienic 'body' of clean living and the vision of the body politic expelling unwanted pathogens. This 'body' would not only refer to the human body, but also the body of the German state itself; he therefore was well-suited to the Nazi ideology.

In his early life, Heisenberg had been taught at Gottingen, one of the great mathematical centres of the world, by Max Born, who had coined the name *quantum mechanics* (*quantenmechanik*) in 1924. In 1921, Born became the director of the Institute for Theoretical Physics at Gottingen and after a visit by Bohr the following year, called for a new rigour in the discipline. It was Heisenberg who was then taken on as his assistant a year later. This set in motion the three physicists of Born, Bohr and Heisenberg, who formed one of the most prominent trios in physics.

It was in 1925 while on the island of Heligoland recovering from an asthma attack that Heisenberg produced what is called *matrix mechanics*, providing a formula relating different quantum states of electrons, and in doing so solved some more of the outstanding problems with the Bohr atomic model. The following year while working with Bohr in Copenhagen, he came up with his famous Heisenberg Uncertainty Principle, which he published in a paper titled *On the Intuitive Content of Quantum Kinematics and Mechanics* in 1927. This showed that properties like position and velocity of fundamental particles cannot both be determined with precision simultaneously. In other words, the more accurately you know the value of one, the less accurately you know the other; any attempt to measure one will unavoidably disturb the other. This, by the way, is not a problem with experimental measurement but an immutable property of our universe. This means that we can never predict where a particle will be at any given moment—we can only list its probability of being somewhere. Another way of looking at this is to say it can be considered that it does not exist until it is observed; in other words, until we observe the particle, we must regard it as being at once everywhere and nowhere. This is the part that had a profound influence on Nazi doctrine, especially involving their views on 'Will, Not Intelligence' and consciousness, which we will look at later because it made the observer part of the experiment.

There is also another version of the HUP involving energy and time, and it was this version that would later lead to the idea that energy can be borrowed from a quantum vacuum, or bubbling quantum foam, resulting in ideas of endless free energy, another favourite area of Nazi physics. However, with this energy/time principle, the more energy taken from the vacuum, the shorter the time before it must be paid back. Despite this limitation, free energy would find its way into the more pseudo-scientific ventures of the Nazis under Himmler's direction; moreover, this was augmented by the fact Heisenberg was one of the prized non-Jewish physicists within the Nazi regime.

The HUP effectively meant that particles, fields (like electric and magnetic) and even time itself could be created from nothing so long as they popped back out of existence in accordance with Heisenberg's formula. Not surprisingly, the formula contained the Planck constant, h. This had further profound implications for exotic ideas within Nazi physics and also for the backlash to Einstein's ideas on the ether. It also gelled with free energy, anti-gravity, and flying disc technology. The bubbling quantum background of the HUP, or foam, became known as the zero-point field from which zero-point energy is obtained as part of the Nazi's interpretation of the ether, and more importantly avoided problems with Einstein's Jewish theory of relativity. This zero-point field and zero-point energy concept persists to this day in many of the fringe areas of science but has been seriously investigated particularly in aviation involving the likes of NASA and several big aerospace companies.

Interestingly, there is some uncertainty about the use of the word 'uncertainty' in regard to the HUP! In various translations, the German words *unsicherheit, unscharf, ungenauigkeit* and *unbestimmtheit* have been used; however, none of these quite equates to the English word 'uncertainty'. It has therefore been suggested that a better word may be 'indeterminability'. As maybe a way of settling the matter, it is known that Heisenberg himself used *unbestimmtheit,* which is generally regarded as the closest to 'uncertainty' or 'indeterminability'.

The next quantum physicist in our story was another key influencer in Nazi doctrine, Erwin Schrodinger. Schrodinger was an Austrian mathematician and physicist famous for his equation of wave mechanics, which related to the idea that particles also have a wave nature, or a wave/particle duality. This is probably one of the weirdest parts of quantum theory. A particle can sometimes act like a wave and sometimes act like a particle, but in essence, the Schrodinger equation is simply an equation that equates the total energy over time as the sum of the kinetic energy and potential energy. Each part contains what is called the wavefunction and to solve the equation we need to find that wavefunction that fits all three parts. However, it is a particular thought experiment proposed by Schrodinger, known as Schrodinger's cat, that makes him particularly world famous. Perhaps the most significant feature of this part of quantum physics is it has intriguing consequences for consciousness. Indeed, it is a further part of quantum physics that highlights the Nazi views concerning their 'Will, Not Intelligence' interpretations, which was a favourite of Hitler's. As such it is yet another important part of quantum physics that fitted well with Nazi doctrine.

So, what is Schrodinger's cat? This is a thought experiment originally introduced to show how ridiculous this consciousness position is, but has now become known as a way of accepting the consequences. The cat is shut in a box which contains a radioactive substance with a 50-50 chance of decaying within an hour. If the decay takes place, the radiation triggers a poisonous gas and the cat dies. Assuming the principles of this area of quantum theory to the box and its contents leads to the implication that at the end of the hour, before a conscious observer lifts the lid to determine the fate of the cat, the cat is in an even-handed superposition of being both alive and dead. Only after the lid of the box is opened and the observer looks inside will the reality fall into place, or as physicists say, the wavefunction collapses.

Now, as many would say, surely the cat is a conscious observer and will determine if it is poisoned or not and therefore dead or alive. Here is one of those difficulties because how far do we go? What about a mouse instead of the cat, or a butterfly, a worm or an ant, or even bacterium? Do any of these have enough consciousness to collapse the wavefunction? Difficulties like this have prevented many physicists from believing that hypothesising a unique role for consciousness is the way to solve the measurement problem. Is there a limit to how conscious a being needs to be? Is it like quantum physics itself when we need to know how big something becomes before it shows none of the weirdness of the small quantum world, the value of the Planck constant, h, in other words? Where is that boundary line? Is there a 'consciousness value' equivalent to h? Yet out of this quantum weirdness came the fact the observer is part of the experiment and consciousness does appear to play a role, and as such it is hardly surprising this would become yet another key element of Nazi physics developing just as war approached.

Another possibility which has been put forwards and is perhaps even more unusual is that everything has consciousness to varying degrees, even inanimate objects. So what if we were to consider Schrodinger's *ornamental* cat by placing a porcelain ornament of a cat in the box with a hammer triggered by the radioactive decay. After the hour would the ornamental cat be in a state of smashed and unsmashed until a conscious observer like a human (or real cat?) looked inside, or would the ornament's consciousness decide before the lid is opened? This may appear weird, but it is something that is seriously debated even today and was not out of place in Nazi thinking, as we will see later. The measurement problem is somewhat simpler when we know that the act of observing something changes it and the observer becomes part of the system, and that much was enough for the Nazis to expand upon accordingly.

To summarize, the essential point for this part of the story centres on the idea consciousness is the ill-understood but undeniable experience of the interface between matter and the mind or the mental. We know that the effects of drugs, or indeed brain damage, make it clear that the material can act upon the mental, but the interesting idea here is why we should not expect a reciprocal situation whereby the mind can affect the material. In fact, it seems that through quantum physics something along these lines does indeed happen and that is why it caught the eye of the Nazis. It is now clear that the observer is actually part of the system that he or she is observing, and the very act of observing can influence and change the outcome of experiments. In short there seems to be a link between consciousness and experimentation, yet another of the weird consequences of the quantum world. A further consequence of this is the idea that things do not exist until we actually observe them. So, this link between the mind, consciousness, and the material universe certainly appeared exciting to the Nazis, especially as it was a non-Jewish science and might contain hidden science they could use in warfare.

Einstein, on the other hand, had his own view. Because this situation is essentially based on observation, Einstein, with his difficulty in accepting whether God plays dice with the universe, was reluctant to accept that the moon, for example, does not exist simply because nobody on Earth was observing it at a particular moment.

We can expand this further. At most times, and in most places, the universe has been devoid of any consciousness. So, are we to believe that throughout the vastness of space and time, across the billions of light years, no quantum process resulted in a determinate consequence? Furthermore, what if we were to set up a system by which a random phrase or series of numbers are generated by a computer which then prints out the result with them placed in an envelope for years to come unseen. Then years later an observer opens the envelope and looks at what the computer printed out. The point is, would only then a printout appear on the paper because some consciousness observed it? If quantum physics is to be believed, that might well be the case. However, today physicists are starting to move away from this interpretation in its different forms, and although this conclusion is not impossible, many physicists do not think it plausible.

Back in the 1920s this new physics of quantum mechanics saw the classical Newtonian mechanics with its accurate clockwork nature to the workings of the universe give way to the modern physics of quantum weirdness, uncertainty and the need for probability functions. In those early days, the ideas we have explored may well have looked like magic; they are not, but magic was a part of the Nazi world of science. To the Nazis and their views, it was akin to magic, and as we will see, such ideas were associated with the esoteric, occult and consciousness to play a major part in their research on many levels. Quantum mechanics augmented these areas of their doctrine. With Hitler and Himmler supporting such weirdness as part of 'Will, Not Intelligence', this and other quantum effects would be a welcomed alternative to the Jewish science they hated. As such, quantum theory would become a cornerstone of Aryan physics as it did with conventional physics, but for very different reasons. It also fitted particularly well with Hitler's early education as we will see later.

For the conventional world of physics, developments took a different route. Visualizing this strange fuzzy quantum world and its uncertainties is not easy and measuring properties was beyond perception. As the end of the 1920s approached and quantum mechanics developed further, Otto Frisch tried to sum up the view of an atom by saying the electrons were pulsating clouds and not orbiting 'planets' like a mini solar system. It was then up to Paul Dirac at Cambridge to bring together Schrodinger and Heisenberg's matrix mechanics to create a quantum mechanical theory in line with Einstein's special relativity and describe the behaviour of the electron, which he achieved in 1927. Dirac also developed solutions to explain problems with fast-moving electrons; the original ideas worked well for slow-moving electrons but not when moving close to the speed of light. The obvious answer was to use special relativity to solve this problem, which Dirac did. He also used the same theory to explain the problems with light bouncing off an object. Dirac went further still in explaining how electrons move in what became known as *Dirac's Equation*. Max Born then put forwards the idea that the waves in quantum mechanics are probability amplitude waves, suggesting the electron did not have a specific location but when orbiting the hydrogen nucleus it had a certain probability. It was physicist John Polkinghorne who summed it up by saying: 'It had a probability of being found here and a certain probability of being found there.' However, whereas ideas from Heisenberg and others involving the physics of atoms would play a major role in the later development of nuclear power for the Nazis, the ideas Dirac developed did not, being as they were based on special relativity. Nonetheless, this work was an important step in marrying together the two great theories of quantum mechanics and relativity into what will one day be a theory of quantum gravity and maybe a theory of everything.

By the late 1920s, German physics was taking pride of place once again in the eyes of the world, although in Germany there was ever-growing general dissatisfaction with the Weimar Republic. That said, there was some optimism, but this was mixed with unease as the country approached Nazism and the uncertainty of what that might bring. Whereas there had been great scientific advances during the decade, there was also another important element that would play a far more negative role in physics and science generally: the subject of anti-Semitism to which we now turn.

This unease in the scientific community was eventually realized when many of the scientists responsible for past achievements gave their support to the Nazi party. This created a system where some would gain further honours and achievements under the Nazis, while others would find themselves fleeing the country by whatever means they could, scattered around the world as they desperately escaped the horrors of Nazism. However, these horrors would start developing before Hitler gained power in 1933; they were advancing in readiness during much of the 1920s along with developments like quantum mechanics and relativity.

Amongst the most prolific agitators were Philipp Lenard and Johannes Stark, who centred their dislike on Einstein as much through anti-Semitism as anti-relativity. In the case of Lenard, even his description was sinister. Physically he had sunken eyes, very bushy eyebrows and wild hair accompanied by an equally wild and bushy beard. He also had a lymph node disease which had resulted in one of his ears dropping to shoulder level, requiring intensive surgery to correct. Mentally he possessed a seething envy and was vitriolic and fanatical, with grudges against many individuals. This anger would manifest itself in particular ways, especially with his xenophobic and racist rages that developed through the early years of the Third Reich and further under Hitler.

One such early grudge was against the German physicist Wilhelm Rontgen, who discovered X-rays. Lenard had always considered the discovery as belonging to him, and his seething anger towards Rontgen for being credited with this discovery was obvious, to say the least. Lenard had certainly helped Rontgen obtain highly sensitive tubes necessary to generate X-rays, but Rontgen had 'failed', as Lenard put it, because he did not give him the appropriate credit. Nevertheless, Lenard himself, in 1905 at the age of 43, had won the Nobel Prize for his own work involving cathode ray tubes, but that was not enough for him. This award meant he was certainly credited with the Lenard Window, involving methods whereby the beam can pass through atoms, demonstrating how much of an atom was empty space; but, to him, the main point was Rontgen had stolen his associated discovery of X-rays.

Lenard also hated English scientists, in particular. By the end of the First World War, he had come to the conclusion that England was an island of self-seeking, duplicitous tradesmen, whereas Germany was a nation of heroes. Another of his beliefs was Europe should impose an intellectual blockade on England. He further believed that England had suffered an intellectual fall from grace; to him this was confirmed by reading the racist works of Englishman Houston Stewart Chamberlain, who had adopted Germany as his homeland.

It is here that we see a link with his hatred of Einstein and theoretical physics. He particularly hated the English physicist J.J. Thomson, who discovered the electron: the particle associated with the beams in cathode ray tubes. He accused Thomson of exploiting his own research on the photoelectric effect without acknowledgment. It is significant that the physicist who actually won the Nobel Prize in 1922 for the discovery of the photoelectric law was none other than Einstein. This law governs the emission of electrons from a metal when illuminated by electromagnetic radiation. It is also significant that the prize also credited Einstein for his work in theoretical physics. Lenard was an experimental physicist and fell short when it came to mathematics and theoretical physics; as a result, his hatred extended to theoretical physics too. This situation was partly due to the fact mathematical skills were becoming increasingly necessary to do modern physics; much of the 1800s saw its discoveries through experimentation, but with the start of the new century and discoveries like quantum mechanics and relativity, mathematical skills were now essential, and indeed they were becoming more so with every discovery. Furthermore, the photoelectric effect is an effect of quantum theory, and its understanding required a theoretical and mathematical approach as much as an experimental one. In short, to Lenard, experimentation was more important than theory. In his acceptance speech for his Nobel Prize, Lenard denounced Thomson, explaining that his dislike of him was due to Thomson's love of mathematics and a further link to theoretical physics.

In later years, this mentality would focus on Einstein, with great efforts from Lenard to deprive him of his Nobel Prize. Of course, Lenard's speech was at about the time Einstein's work was published on special relativity and long before general relativity appeared, so it would have been interesting to know what Lenard would have said about Einstein then. He certainly made up for it during the 1920s and beyond.

Oddly enough, all this hatred was actually set against an earlier respect for Einstein which was held by Lenard as late as 1913 and long after the 1905 publication of special relativity. In that year he had considered inviting Einstein to a chair in theoretical physics at the University of Heidelberg, but with the outbreak of the First World War, he seems to have revised his opinion of Einstein; Einstein began to associate Lenard with an anti-relativity campaign that was gaining pace in Germany. By the 1920s, Lenard had completely changed his view about Einstein—he hated him and everything he stood for in physics and life. However, to really put all this into proper context we need to look at what happened during and after the solar eclipse of 29 May 1919 that proved Einstein's theory of general relativity.

In his 1916 popular book, *Relativity: The Special and General Theory*, Einstein issued yet another call for scientists to test his conclusions gained from general relativity. Before the completion of general relativity in 1915, it was obvious space-time curvature would bend light around massive objects like the sun, so the earliest solar eclipse of 1914 might help prove Einstein right. However, that eclipse occurred just as the First World War broke out; the attempt failed when the astronomers were taken as prisoners by the Russians because their telescopes and cameras were considered to be spying devices. In his book,

Einstein said: 'Stars ought to appear to be displaced outwards from the Sun by 1.7 seconds of arc, as compared with their apparent position in the sky when the Sun is situated at another part of the heavens.' He added: 'The examination of the correctness or otherwise of this deduction is a problem of greatest importance, the early solution of which is to be expected of astronomers.' The event to determine this displacement then fell to the next available eclipse of 1919.

At this point, it is necessary to explain what is meant by a shift of 1.7 seconds of arc. This is an angular measurement whereby there are 60 seconds of arc in 1 minute of arc, and 60 minutes of arc in 1 degree, there obviously being 360 degrees in a full circle. Because the sky extends 360 degrees around us it is the angular measurement used by astronomers against the sky. So, we are dealing with an extremely small angular shift in a star's position by looking for, and measuring, just 1.7 seconds of arc. This small value would only add to the controversy of the exercise and consequently the attack by anti-relativists and their associated anti-Semitic views.

The Dutch astrophysicist Willem de Sitter had managed to send a copy of Einstein's general relativity paper across the English Channel in 1916 during the midst of war and got it to Arthur Eddington, director of the Cambridge Observatory. At the time, Einstein was not well-known in England, moreover, those scientists who were familiar with relativity tended to take pride in the ether theory more often than not, even ignoring or denigrating the counter claims from Germany for its existence through relativity. This unfortunate position of favouring the ether may have also been due to the war between the two countries; science is not immune to politics and war. It is well worth remembering the saying in science: 'When science becomes political, stick with the science.' However, Eddington was a pacifist, like Einstein, and was one of the few to have embraced relativity enthusiastically, even writing an account of the theory to popularize it throughout the scientific community and the public.

Eddington consulted the Astronomer Royal, Sir Frank Dyson, who decided a team of astronomers should take up Einstein's challenge and prove the deflection of starlight as genuine even though the two nations were at war. This had an added bonus for Eddington because, being a pacifist and Quaker, he feared the danger of being called up for the war effort. As a young man of only 35 with no genuine reason to resist military service and the demands of the government, he would face imprisonment if he refused to serve. Dyson therefore convinced the British Admiralty that Eddington would be better served as a leader of an expedition to test the theory. To add weight to the idea, Dyson also pointed out what a unique opportunity this would be for all concerned. There was also a genuine scientific reason for this eclipse being particularly appropriate; at the 1919 eclipse, there would be many stars appearing close to the sun's limb. For example, the sun would appear close to a particular cluster of stars in the constellation of Taurus known as the Hyades. As a result, plans for the expedition were set in motion.

One of the earliest concerns centred on the track of totality, which stretched across the Atlantic near the equator from the coast of Brazil to equatorial Africa; this was known to be an area where U-boats were active, and therefore placed the astronomers in danger. Fortunately, because these types of expeditions need to be planned well in advance by the time of the eclipse, the war had ended. This was both a relief to the astronomers in general and Eddington in particular, who now faced no danger of being called up for military service. With the expedition starting in March 1919, Eddington sailed from Liverpool with two teams: one to set up telescopes and cameras at the isolated town of Sobral in the Amazon jungle of northern Brazil; the other, which included Eddington, headed for the tiny island of Principe, a Portuguese colony only a degree north of the equator, just off the Atlantic coast of Africa.

The eclipse started at 3.13 pm local time on Principe, lasting for the relatively long time of about 5 minutes; the maximum possible for this type of solar eclipse is a little over 7 minutes. As is typical of such astronomical events, the morning of the eclipse saw heavy rain and cloud cover; however, this fortunately cleared slowly as the eclipse time approached, with the clouds teasing Eddington's team until the last minute; it was a typical cat-and-mouse game, with the clouds cloaking then revealing the sun periodically. As the eclipse began, Eddington concentrated on taking his series of photographs, busily changing the plates to maximize the possibility of getting the data he needed to prove Einstein right. Such was his concentration with this task he saw little of the eclipse himself, but was able to take a total of sixteen photographs, later writing in his diary: 'They are good of the Sun, showing a very remarkable prominence; but the cloud has interfered with the star images.' His telegram back home read: 'Through cloud, hopeful. Eddington.' Meanwhile in Brazil, there was better weather, but a problem of another sort; the heat of the jungle had affected the telescope mirror which, like all telescopes, had a carefully crafted curve to bring images to as sharp a focus as possible. Nevertheless, they too managed to capture the eclipse.

There then followed a delay in announcing results partly due to the fact that all the photographic plates from both observing sites had to be returned to Britain for analysis. After arrival, the plates had to be developed, measured and compared, which caused further delay until September. Once all this was done, the key part of the story became evident; there was no clear-cut answer. One set of particularly good pictures from the Brazil site showed a deflection of 1.98 seconds of arc, close to the 1.7 predicted by Einstein. Another from Brazil, a blurred image due to the temperature affecting the focal length of the mirror, showed an uncertain deflection of 0.86 seconds of arc, closer to the 0.85 predicted by Newton's theory of gravity. This confusion did not help, especially amongst those who had seen this as a contest between England's theory put forwards by Newton several centuries earlier and the new German theory. Amongst the two arguing sides was the undeniable fact that the value of 0.86 did carry a high degree of error because of the blurred images. With Eddington's plates, there was less of an error, but they contained fewer visible stars because of cloud and therefore required some complex calculations to extract the data. After much work, Eddington's plates suggested a deflection value of 1.6 seconds of arc, closer to Einstein's theory.

Then came the controversial part. Eddington had such faith in Einstein's theory he decided to reject the values from Brazil because of the faulty equipment. Possibly that decision had some justification, but there were cries of bias when Eddington decided to take an average value from his own sixteen plates to arrive at 1.7 seconds of arc: exactly what Einstein had predicted. It was not an elegant result, but with hindsight we now know Einstein's theory is correct and 1.7 is the correct answer. Universal acceptance did not come until the 1970s. However, at the time, this was good enough for Eddington, who described the result as 'the greatest moment of my life'.

Through all this delay and uncertainty, back in Germany, Einstein awaited the results. He wrote to his ailing mother on 5 September, saying: 'There is still no news about the eclipse.' On 12 September, he then wrote to his friend Paul Ehrenfest in Holland, ending the letter with the casual question: 'Have you by any chance heard anything over there about the English solar eclipse observation?' Although Einstein was trying to hide his eagerness, it was certain he would have heard from one of his many friends if there was any news. Finally, on 22 September, Hendrik Lorentz sent him a cable that said he had just heard from a fellow astronomer who had spoken with Eddington at a meeting: 'Eddington found stellar shift at the solar limb, tentative values between nine-tenths of a second and twice that.' It was a carefully worded piece of news because it only amounted to the values found at the two sites, a Brazilian value about 0.9 (nine-tenths) and Eddington's value of about 1.7 (twice that).

Nevertheless, Eddington and the scientific community had little doubt in the value of 1.7 and that was also true of Einstein himself, who had great faith in his theory; he simply knew his theory was correct. A student present shortly after Einstein received the telegram, Ilse Schneider, later told how Einstein handed her the telegram from his window sill, saying: 'Perhaps this will interest you.' Calmly, he added: 'I knew the theory was correct.' She said to Einstein: 'What if the experiments had shown the theory to be wrong?' Einstein replied: 'Then I would have been sorry for the dear Lord; the theory is correct.'

As more precise details started to circulate about the eclipse results, Max Planck was amongst those who gave a word or two of caution to Einstein. Writing to him on 4 October 1919, he said: 'You have already said many times that you never personally doubted what the results would be but it is beneficial, nonetheless, if now this fact is indubitably established for others as well.' Einstein replied on 23 October, saying: 'The intimate union between the beautiful, the true and the real has again been proved. ...It is a gift from gracious destiny that I have been allowed to experience this.' Planck's letter was clearly a warning that any doubt would later play into the hands of the anti-relativists and add fuel to anti-Semitic attacks, which indeed it did.

The first unofficial announcement of the result came at a closed meeting of the Dutch Royal Academy. Einstein was present, sitting proudly on the stage as Lorentz gave details of Eddington's findings to an audience of almost 1,000 cheering students and scientists. No press officials were allowed into the meeting because the official announcement was set for 2 weeks later, on 6 November in London at the Royal Society.

The Royal Society meeting was held at Burlington House, Piccadilly, where the findings were presented by the Astronomer Royal, Sir Frank Dyson, who announced:

'After a careful study of the plates, I am prepared to say that there can be no doubt that they confirm Einstein's prediction.' He added: 'The results of the expeditions to Sobral and Principe leave little doubt that a deflection of light takes place in the neighbourhood of the Sun and that it is of the amount demanded by Einstein's generalised theory of relativity.' However, this careful wording by the Astronomer Royal did not satisfy everybody in the audience; there were those present who expressed scepticism and they were not alone. It was not long before claims appeared that the data had not been proved to the requirements demanded by science and this was enough for some to cast further doubt on the whole theory within anti-relativistic and anti-Semitic circles. Einstein missed the excitement at the Royal Society, being back in Berlin, but he did treat himself to a new violin.

Whatever the views circulating within the physics community, the findings from the 1919 eclipse saw Einstein's fame increase exponentially as he became a household name. As a result, his theory of relativity burst into the consciousness of the world that had become weary of war and was yearning for a positive triumph of human achievement; it has remained a public fascination to this day. Indeed, it was almost a year to the day after the end of fighting that the achievement was announced and the world officially learned that a German Jew had been proved correct by an English Quaker. 'Scientists belonging to two warring nations had collaborated again,' an excited physicist by the name of Leopold Infeld announced. He went on to say: 'It seems the beginning of a new era.' This all seemed perfect except that behind the scenes the confirmation was still unclear and that provided Philipp Lenard and his fellow anti-Semitic associates a golden opportunity to attack Jews, the Jewish science of relativity and, in particular, Einstein himself.

By November 1919, news was fast spreading around the world, but it was mixed. *The Times* of London carried stories on 7 November about the defeated Germans being summoned to Paris to face treaty demands from Britain and France, together with the eclipse news and Einstein's theory of relativity. The triple headlines read: 'REVOLUTION IN SCIENCE, *NEW THEORY OF THE UNIVERSE*, NEWTONIAN IDEAS OVERTHROWN.' It went on to report: 'The scientific concept of the fabric of the Universe must be changed.' The paper then boldly claimed that Einstein's newly confirmed theory will 'require a new philosophy of the Universe, a philosophy that will sweep away nearly all that has been accepted'.

Two days later, the *New York Times* caught up with the news, but not having a science correspondent in London, the paper assigned the story to its golf expert, Henry Crouch. The first mistake by Crouch was his initial decision to skip the official news conference at the Royal Society. On reflection he realized this may have been a mistake, so he changed his mind, only to find his late arrival meant he was not allowed entry. So, he decided to telephone the astronomer responsible for the confirmation of the theory, Eddington, to get a summary. Crouch was somewhat blinded by the science and asked Eddington to repeat the details in simpler words. The result was one of overexcitement from Crouch, and maybe feeling a bit out of his depth, he produced the headlines: 'ECLIPSE SHOWED GRAVITY VARIATION, DIVISION OF LIGHT RAYS ACCEPTED AS AFFECTING NEWTON'S

PRINCIPLES, HAILED AS EPOCHMAKING, BRITISH SCIENTIST CALLS THE DISCOVERY ONE OF THE GREATEST OF HUMAN ACHIEVEMENTS.' This was both a sign of things to come as well as the greatest of irritations for the anti-relativists and only served to heighten their anti-Semitism.

The reporting of the *New York Times* over the next few days played up the complexity of the theory with ever more elaborate headlines such as: 'LIGHTS ALL ASKEW IN THE HEAVENS, MEN OF SCIENCE MORE OR LESS AGOG OVER RESULTS OF ECLIPSE OBSERVATIONS, EINSTEIN THEORY TRIUMPHS, STARS NOT WHERE THEY SHOULD OR WERE CALCULATED TO BE, BUT NOBODY NEED WORRY.' As for Einstein's 1916 book, *Relativity: The Special and General Theory*, the paper's headlines read: 'A BOOK FOR 12 WISE MEN', claiming: 'No more in all the world could comprehend it, said Einstein when his daring publishers accepted it.' This book was originally published in German but was now re-released in English. As the paper got more and more carried away, Einstein said: 'The newspaper drivel about me is pathetic.' This was also true of the claim only twelve men in all the world could understand relativity, a claim physicists still hear to this day. I do not hear the claim as often today as I did, but recall my father being convinced of the so-called fact up to the 1980s. The theory is difficult mathematically, but can be understood, in principle, by anybody prepared to stick with it.

Fortunately, Einstein had the opportunity to explain the theory, and misconceptions, in his own words when *The Times* of London commissioned him to write an article called, 'What is the Theory of Relativity?' The article appeared on 28 November 1919, with Einstein hinting about the issues that could arise by saying: 'By the application of the theory of relativity, today in Germany I am called a German man of science, and in England I am represented as a Swiss Jew. If I come to be regarded as a bete noire, the descriptions will be reversed, and I shall become a Swiss Jew for the Germans and a German man of science for the English.' Months later, following his newfound fame, that prediction came true.

In the normal course of things, fame can cause resentment, and this is also true in science and academia, especially with self-promotion. Here, we had resentment from the likes of Lenard and his followers, but in the case of Einstein it went beyond self-promotion, which he was famous for, because we also had the fact it was Jewish science, and the likes of Lenard were building that hatred up during the 1920s long before Hitler came to power in 1933. In a letter to his friend Paul Ehrenfest during the initial weeks of frenzied headlines, Einstein wrote: 'Anti-Semitism is very strong here.' He also wondered: 'Where is all this supposed to lead?'

The rise of anti-Semitism after the First World War produced a counter-reaction in Einstein; he started to identify more strongly with his Jewish heritage and community. He was also all too aware that anti-Semitism was not the result of national causes, writing in early 1920: 'In Germany today hatred of the Jews has taken on horrible expressions.' The problems were heightened partly due to inflation, which was now out of control; the

German mark was worth twelve cents at the beginning of 1919, half its value before the war. By the beginning of 1920, it was worth only two cents and collapsing further by the month. Furthermore, Germany had lost six million men in the war, been humiliated and forced to surrender land containing half its national resources, as well as all its overseas colonies, and many thought this was due to betrayal. The Weimar Republic that emerged after the war supported by liberals, pacifists and Jews was disdained by much of the old order and even the middle classes. As a result, people sought out a scapegoat and made the Jews responsible. 'They are a target of instinctive resentment because they are of a different tribe,' wrote Einstein.

The dramatic announcement in November 1919 that the eclipse observations had confirmed parts of Einstein's theory should have made 1920 his year. Indeed, in Germany relativity promoted lively and informed debates, as it did worldwide; however, a sign of things to come appeared when Einstein experienced his first public collision with this rising anti-Semitism in the summer of 1920. That collision took the form of anti-relativists, including extreme right-wing physicists involved in politics but also extended to mainstream scientists who had particularly conservative views within the scientific community. Indeed, there was direct antagonism towards theoretical physics, such as relativity and even quantum theory, through anti-Semitism and the phenomenon of Aryan physics, which Hitler would develop further during the 1930s.

This collision involved a somewhat-shady German nationalist named Paul Weyland who had turned himself into an active member of a right-wing nationalistic political party that pledged in its 1920 programme to 'diminish the dominant Jewish influence showing up increasingly in government and in public'. Weyland realized Einstein was a highly publicized Jew and had engendered resentment and jealousy. He further saw the potential of turning Einstein's theory into a target because of the way it had unnerved many members of the public, including scientists. The key to this was relativity's undermining of absolutes; remember the theory had shown there was no absolute motion, absolute space and absolute time as Newton had proposed in his classical theories. It was also seen as being built on abstract hypotheses rather than grounded in solid experiment. This latter point is where the somewhat carefully worded conclusions from the 1919 solar eclipse experiment could be crowbarred into the general plan. So, Weyland went to work writing an article that denounced relativity as 'a big hoax', allowing him to form a mysteriously well-funded organization of dubious misfits called the Study Group of German Scientists for the Preservation of a Pure Science. The group started by making a few personal attacks on Einstein and the 'Jewish nature' of relativity theory, after which they arranged a series of meetings around Germany which included a large rally at Berlin's Philharmonic Hall on 24 August 1920. As well as Weyland, other members of the group included Ernst Gehrcke and Philipp Lenard.

At the meeting both Weyland and Gehrcke were speakers, with Weyland being the first as he took on an imposing and pompous manner as if a leader of the populace. He accused Einstein of engaging in a 'business-like booming of his theory and his name'. Weyland also declared 'relativity was a hoax' and was 'plagiarized' too. These, and other, claims were then backed up by Gehrcke but with a more technical and scientific gloss to them while reading from a prepared text. It was also claimed that the *New York Times* 'had a decidedly anti-Semitic complexion'.

In the middle of the talk, a quiet murmur circulated amongst the audience—'Einstein, Einstein'—as none other had arrived to see what was being said. Einstein took a seat in the audience with his friend, the chemist Walther Nernst. As somebody who was averse to neither publicity nor controversy, Einstein repeatedly laughed and cackled loudly, and at the end, declared the meeting 'most amusing'. As his friend Philipp Frank noted: 'He always liked to regard events in the world around him as if he were a spectator in a theatre.'

Although Einstein gave every indication he was not angered by the proceedings, he obviously was, because he then made what is generally regarded as a tactical mistake. On 27 August, 3 days later, he responded with a highly charged article titled, 'My Response' which was published in the *Berliner Tageblatt*, a liberal daily owned by Jewish friends. He said: 'A motley group has joined together to form a company under the pretentious "syndicate of German scientists" currently with the single purpose of denigrating the theory of relativity and me as its author in the eyes of non-physicists.' He went on to say: 'I am well aware that the two speakers are unworthy of reply by my pen.'

Unfortunately, Einstein did not take his own advice and proceeded with a detailed reply. As for one of the principal speakers, Weyland, Einstein said: '[He] does not seem to be a specialist at all (is he a doctor? engineer? politician? I could not find out), he presented nothing of pertinence. He broke out in coarse abuse and base accusations.' Indeed, Einstein spent most of the piece refuting both Weyland and Gehrcke. It should be noted that neither of these speakers had been explicitly anti-Semitic at this stage, neither did they overly criticize Jews in their presentations, but Einstein alleged that they would not have attacked his theory 'if I were a German nationalist, with or without a swastika, instead of a Jew'. To clarify this point, Einstein was quick to point out that the anti-relativist campaign was in fact about anti-Semitism.

Although he was not present at the meeting, Einstein chose to attack the more reputable physicist, Philipp Lenard, because he had given support to the anti-relativity course and allowed his name to be used in connection with the meeting, particularly in the brochures that were distributed at the time. As we have seen, Lenard was also a Nobel Laureate, and this was believed to have added to his authority. As for Lenard, Einstein said his objections to relativity 'are already invalidated on the basis of my general proof that on first approximations the statements of the general theory of relativity conform with those of classical mechanics'. It is certainly true that what Einstein had shown was in its simplest form of approximation the theory reduced to Newtonian mechanics. It is hardly a surprise to find that this attack from Einstein sent Lenard into one of his famous rages.

Another popular rant from Lenard which Einstein objected to was the claim his famous mass-energy equivalence equation of relativity, $E = mc^2$, was stolen by Einstein from a little-known Austrian physicist of pure Aryan descent, Friedrich Hasenohrl.

In fact, Lenard even wrote a paper to that effect in 1921. His argument on this point centred on electromagnetic mass, a concept of classical mechanics denoting how much the electromagnetic field (or self-energy) contributes to the mass of charged particles; first devised by J.J. Thomson in 1881, it was for some time considered as a dynamical explanation of inertial mass. Certainly, it is true that the formulae for electromagnetic mass like those of Hasenohrl were similar to Einstein's equation, but it was not quite that simple. Lenard also gave credit to Johann Georg von Soldner and Paul Gerber in relation to some effects in general relativity. However, it was Max von Laue who quickly rebutted Lenard's claims by pointing out that the inertia of electromagnetic energy was known about long before Hasenohrl; in particular by Henri Poincare in 1900 and Max Abraham in 1902. Furthermore, Hasenohrl only used their results for his calculation involving cavity radiation, an alternative name sometimes given to the black body radiation we explored earlier with the ultraviolet catastrophe and discovery of quantum mechanics. Max von Laue continued by saying that credit for establishing the inertia of *all* forms of energy, in other words, the real mass-energy equivalence, goes to Einstein, who was also the first to understand the deep implications of the equivalence in relation to relativity. Today, the relation of mass, momentum, velocity and all forms of energy (including electromagnetic energy) is analyzed on the basis of Einstein's special theory of relativity and mass-energy equivalence.

Because Lenard had not actually turned up to the meeting at the Philharmonic Hall, and because his published critiques of relativity had been academic in tone, Einstein did not really need to attack him in his newspaper response, but unfortunately, he did. As an introduction to that attack, Einstein wrote: 'I admire Lenard as a master of experimental physics, but he has not yet produced anything outstanding in theoretical physics, and his objections to the general theory of relativity are of such superficiality that, up until now, I did not think it necessary to answer them, I intend to make up for this.'

As we saw earlier, Lenard originally had great admiration for Einstein, certainly as recent as 1913; however, that would change, especially following the publication of general relativity in 1916. A major catalyst in this would be due to him being an ardent German nationalist, which saw him becoming ever more bitter towards the British as well as the Jews, so having a British astronomer, Eddington, working to prove Jewish science was no help in this matter. A further problem was the publicity Einstein was gaining day-by-day around the world as a result of his theory and Eddington's confirmation. Lenard considered the various conclusions drawn from relativity as 'absurd' and by this stage was becoming more vocal himself regarding his beliefs. Not surprisingly, Lenard became outraged by Einstein's newspaper response and demanded an apology, especially as he had not even attended the meeting. Mediation in this argument was attempted by the chairman of the German Physical Society, Arnold Sommerfeld, who urged Einstein 'to write some conciliatory words to Lenard'. However, Einstein refused to back down. This incident appears to have edged Lenard even further towards his outright anti-Semitic views.

Of course, this newspaper response had mixed reactions within the scientific community, but generally Einstein's friends supported him in public if not in private. A group which included Max von Laue and Walther Nernst published a letter claiming somewhat inaccurately: 'Whoever is fortunate enough to be close to Einstein knows that he will never be surpassed in his...dislike of all publicity.' In private, matters were quite different, as shown through a series of private letters to Einstein. Generally, his friends were appalled and felt he had been provoked into this public display of anger. They felt those who had organized the rally were unworthy of a reply.

On 8 September 1920, Max Born's wife, Hedwig, wrote to Einstein to say '[you should] not have allowed yourself to be goaded into that rather unfortunate reply'. She felt he should have shown more respect for 'the secluded temple of science'. In a reply to the Borns on 9 September, Einstein said: 'Don't be too severe with me.' He added in his defence: 'Everyone must, from time to time, make a sacrifice on the altar of stupidity, to please the deity and mankind. And I did so thoroughly with my article.' As such, he made no apologies. Einstein's good friend Paul Ehrenfest went even further in a letter dated 2 September 1920. He said: 'My wife and I absolutely cannot believe that you yourself wrote some of the phrases in the article.' He also added: 'If you really did write them down with your own hand, it proves that these damn pigs have finally succeeded in touching your soul. I urge you as strongly as I can not to throw one more word on this subject to that voracious beast, the public.' Einstein replied to Ehrenfest's letter on 9 September, saying: 'I had to do this if I wanted to stay in Berlin where every child recognizes me from photographs.' He went on to say: 'If one believes in democracy, then one must grant the public this much right as well.'

The next key stage in the anti-relativity saga came with the upcoming annual meeting of German Scientists scheduled for late September. This was due to be held in the spa town of Bad Nauheim and was due to be attended by both Lenard and Einstein, who had never actually met face to face. Furthermore, Einstein had ended his newspaper piece by issuing the challenge that, at his suggestion, a public discussion of relativity would occur at the meeting: 'Anyone who can dare face a scientific forum can present his objections there.' This was clearly directed at Lenard.

During the week-long gathering, Einstein chose to stay with Max Born in Frankfurt, 32km from the venue; the two would commute there and back daily. It was not until later in the week that both Einstein and Lenard were due to face each other, on the afternoon of 23 September. Lenard was due to speak before Einstein, who would listen to his presentation and take notes, except Einstein had forgotten to bring anything to write with and had to borrow a pencil from the person seated next to him. Max Planck was chairing the meeting with his commanding, yet soothing presentation, in an attempt to avoid any personal attacks from either side. Lenard's presentation was typical of a non-theorist, suggesting the theory was abstract, rejected absolutes and certainties, was built on mathematics, was theoretical rather than experimental and was not supported by observational data. He summed up his views by saying: 'It offends against the simple commonsense of a scientist.' Clearly Lenard was choosing not to accept the proof from Mercury's orbit or Eddington's eclipse results, the latter still being somewhat controversial. Einstein's response to Lenard was that what seems obvious changes over time and that was true of even Galileo's mechanics. Although Einstein and Lenard refused to shake hands and clearly were never going to progress beyond their individual positions following the Philharmonic Hall episode, both managed to remain relatively calm thanks to Planck's chairing skills. The two were never to agree and future dealings would take a turn for the worse. Planck was able to bring the meeting to a conclusion before hostilities escalated by making a joke. He said: 'Since the theory of relativity unfortunately has not so far been able to extend the absolute time available for this meeting it must now be adjourned.' Although it does not appear in the minutes of the meeting, Born later recalls: 'Einstein was provoked into making a caustic reply.' A few weeks later, he wrote to Born to assure him that he would 'not allow himself to get excited again as in Nauheim'.

For a short while, things did look as if they might improve; Lenard decided to distance himself from The Study Group of German Scientists for the Preservation of a Pure Science, but this decision was really to do more with Weyland in particular rather than the group's views. Lenard later said: 'Unfortunately, Weyland turned out to be a crook.' His antipathy towards Einstein survived intact and if anything, following the Bad Nauheim episode, he became ever more anti-Semitic regarding his views about Jewish science and Einstein in particular. He also became viler in nature, generally. He later decided to create a Deutsche Physik that would purge German physics of any Jewish involvement or influence, of which he saw Einstein and his theory of relativity as prime examples. From then, matters would only get worse.

Indeed, a sign of future things to come appeared a few months later on 3 January 1921 from an obscure Munich party functionary. 'Science, once our greatest pride, is today being taught by Hebrews,' wrote Adolf Hitler in the controversial newspaper *Volkischer Beobachter*. But before that episode unfolded during the 1930s, Einstein faced another problem.

Following the fallout from the results of the 1919 eclipse and the subsequent problems of 1920, Einstein was to experience a further backlash when it was considered by members of the physics community that he should be nominated for the Nobel Prize. By this stage, Lorentz was no longer such a sceptic, so he, along with Planck, Bohr and six others wrote in support of Einstein's nomination by mostly focusing on his theory of relativity. Unfortunately, Planck's letter arrived after the deadline. Lorentz pointed out in his letter that Einstein 'has placed himself in the first rank of physicists of all time', while Bohr wrote 'one faces here an advance of decisive significance'. However, politics would intervene. With a similar running theme, the primary justification for denying Einstein a Nobel Prize was that the theory is purely theoretical in nature; there was no experimental evidence to satisfy the committee, despite the results from the 1919 eclipse. Furthermore, the theory's correct interpretation of Mercury's wandering orbit suggested from Newtonian gravity was not considered as proof; at the time there were alternative explanations, including a periodic variation in the sun's size, and the existence of Vulcan had not yet been disproved. Indeed, the troubles that had arisen from the likes of Lenard, Weyland, Gehrcke and their anti-relativity followers had only served to complicate matters with the experimental interpretations. In a nutshell, these results were now tainted with political, cultural and personal bias. Also highlighted by his critics was Einstein's superstar status, which was used against him as being unworthy of a Nobel Laureate.

In a seven-page report, the committee chairman, Svante Arrhenius, outlined why Einstein should not be awarded the prize in 1920. This report included the criticized eclipse results and their ambiguous interpretation; other scientists had not yet confirmed the theory. There were also problems with confirming that light coming from the sun would be red-shifted in the spectrum as a result of it climbing out of the sun's gravitational well. Also in the report was the argument from the 1920 rally where Gehrcke had pointed out that the problems with Mercury's orbit could also be explained by other theories. Interestingly, these objections still simmer away quietly in the background of fringe science to this day amongst die-hard anti-relativists.

Worst of all was the fact that, behind the scenes, Lenard was busy at work preventing Einstein from winning the prize by whatever means was open to him; indeed, the following year Lenard would propose Gehrcke for the prize. It was Sven Hedin, a Swedish explorer and prominent member of the Academy, who later recalled just how determined Lenard was to convince those concerned that Einstein was unworthy of the prize. Hedin remembers Lenard working hard to persuade him, and others, that 'relativity was really not a discovery' and that 'it had not been proven'. In Arrhenius's report, he cited Lenard's 'strong critique of the oddities in Einstein's generalized theory of relativity'. Lenard's views were that the theory was not grounded in experimentation and concrete discoveries. There was also a strong element in the report concerning Lenard's animosity to the type of 'philosophical conjecturing' that he often dismissed as being a feature of 'Jewish science'. This behaviour by Arrhenius was not entirely surprising; with his position of power over the Nobel committee, he became well-known for manipulating nominations so that they went to his friends but not his enemies.

What occurred as a result of all this appears odd, but the oddity went further. The Nobel Prize for 1920 eventually went to another Zurich Polytechnic graduate by the name of Charles-Edouard Guillaume, the director of the International Bureau of Weights and Measures. Guillaume had not exactly made any shattering discovery in the world of science; instead, he made his modest mark by assuring that standard measures were more precise and discovering metal alloys had practical uses, particularly in making good measuring rods. Indeed, it was considered that his work could not be described as the typical beacon of achievement usually recognized by the committee. In the words of Robert Friedman: 'Even those who opposed relativity found Guillaume a bizarre choice.'

The best explanation might lay in the idea of standard measurements and in particular the good measuring rods of his work. One of the consequences of special relativity shows that objects travelling close to the speed of light appear to shorten to an outside observer. For example, if a rocket sets off travelling faster and faster towards the speed of light, somebody observing its departure will see it shorten in length along its direction of travel; however, to those on board, no shortening is observed. This would be the same for a measuring rod and is known as Lorentz contraction. A clock, and therefore time, will also be observed to run slower as it approaches the speed of light, but not to those onboard. Furthermore, it will also appear to an observer that the object gains mass as it approaches the speed of light. In short, measurements depend on velocity and with the absolutes and fixed points being dismissed by relativity, the whole idea of measurements, especially standard measurements, is seen differently, being based on particular observers. Could this have been a subtle nod to the possibility that the likes of Lenard were considered right by the Nobel committee following Arrhenius's report? It is hard to believe, but the decision becomes less bizarre if true. This point seems to be clarified with the next stage in the story.

Meanwhile, Einstein was gaining in fame with support coming from both theoreticians and experimentalists and, of course, the public worldwide. With his fame came pressure on the Nobel committee to award the prize to Einstein. That pressure came as much from public fame as it did from the scientific community, with Einstein now gaining fourteen official nominations, far more than any other contender. Planck was still supporting the nominations, as was Eddington, a member of the Royal Society. Eddington wrote: 'Einstein stands above his contemporaries even as Newton did.' As a result, the prize committee was forced to consider the matter again and this time assigned the task of providing a report to Allvar Gullstrand, a professor of ophthalmology at the University of Uppsala. Gullstrand himself was a Nobel Laureate, having won the prize in 1911, but once again this was a bizarre choice because Gullstrand had little experience in physics or mathematics; he won his prize in medicine. Nevertheless, he produced a report consisting of fifty pages. Perhaps not surprisingly, Gullstrand's report criticized Einstein's theory in a clearly determined knowing tone designed to undermine Einstein at all costs. He concluded that the bending of light was not a true test of Einstein's theory and that the results were not experimentally valid. Furthermore, even if the results were valid, other theories may explain the phenomenon from classical physics, such as Newtonian mechanics. Once again Mercury's orbit played a negative role, with Gullstrand saying: 'It remains unknown until further notice whether the Einstein theory can at all be brought into agreement with the perihelion experiment.' As far as the effects of special relativity are concerned, he decided they 'lay below the limits of experimental error'. To bring things back full circle to Guillaume, there was a comment about rigid rods. Here Gullstrand was particularly 'appalled' by the fact that Einstein's theory could suggest measurements of such things vary relative to moving observers. Highlighting this point again was not surprising because Gullstrand's reputation was built on devising precision optical measuring equipment. Choosing another scientist involved in precision measurements, and a non-physicist at that, did not look good for the Academy.

However, a point being missed here regarding measuring devices and rigid rods, is relativity has a negligible effect in everyday life, at speeds far less than the speed of light. We now know such devices are indeed affected by relativity, but the results are unnoticeable. What appeared to be dismissal of relativity based on personal reputations and lifelong work on standards of precision was unfounded due to a lack of understanding about relativity, which also did not sit well with either Guillaume or Gullstrand's reports. Nevertheless, a pattern was emerging. That said, there were those on the committee that considered Gullstrand's report as unsophisticated and were opposed to the conclusions; yet, on the other hand, the prize could not be given to a speculative theory. As a result, the vote was taken to choose nobody for the 1921 prize and roll it over a year.

Of course, at the end of the day, this was all becoming very embarrassing for the Nobel Prize committee and had the potential to be even more so if it dragged on; after all, the two failed attempts were heavily backed by the physics community, who would only try again. That third attempt came when French physicist Marcel Brillouin sent in a 1922 nominating letter. In it he said: 'Imagine for a moment what the general opinion will be fifty years from now if the name of Einstein does not appear on the list of Nobel Laureates.' Brillouin had a point, especially as Einstein was not only famous for his theory of relativity but had made other great achievements in physics too, in particular his explanation of the photoelectric effect; to have the stigma of refusing the prize because of the anti-relativity lobby would be wrong. It is exactly that point that shone a light on a way out of the mess, but it would be more bad news for Lenard.

The solution came from Carl Wilhelm Oseen, a new committee member who took up his position in 1922. Oseen was a theoretical physicist from the University of Uppsala who was a colleague and friend of Gullstrand. What Oseen did was to gently show Gullstrand's errors in his ophthalmologist's ill-conceived and stubborn conclusions presented in his report the year before. The other key breakthrough from Oseen was he could see that relativity had become such an issue that matters needed a different course of action. With that in mind, Oseen pushed for the prize to be awarded to Einstein not for his theory of relativity but for the experimentally proven law of the photoelectric effect. The photoelectric effect had already been considered along with relativity, but it was the latter that appeared to drag down the whole process with the committee. Oseen then made a carefully worded proposal which included the all-important word *law* so that the prize was not for any theory. Moreover, he also circumnavigated the theory of relativity by ignoring it and therefore throwing out the *theory* part of any proposal. Oseen made his report using the title *Einstein's Law of the Photoelectric Effect* so that the previous year's discussion of *Einstein's Theory of the Photoelectric Effect* would not be an issue (along with the theory of relativity); it omitted the word 'theory' and introduced the word 'law'. In his report, Oseen emphasized that it was a fundamental natural law and, moreover, it had been fully proved by experimentation; it had a mathematical description and it was possible to show experimentally that this relationship of discrete light quanta absorbed and emitted relate to the frequency of the light. A final touch came with Oseen suggesting that Einstein be given the prize for 1921, leaving 1922 available for someone else and effectively solving the roll-over issue from the previous year. This was proposed so that the 1922 prize would then go to Niels Bohr as a coupled-award because Bohr's model of the atom was based on the laws that explained Einstein's photoelectric effect. That seemed to cover all issues and Gullstrand agreed to go along with the plan, with Arrhenius accepting the inevitable. The committee voted in favour of the proposal on 6 September 1922, with Einstein and Bohr receiving the prize for 1921 and 1922 respectively.

However, the story does not end there because when Einstein was notified of his win, the citation and letter from the committee secretary was most intriguing. Although the citation read 'for his discovery of the law of the photoelectric effect', it came with an interesting caveat too. Both documents specified that the award was given 'without taking into account the value that will be accorded your relativity theory and gravitation theories after these are confirmed in the future'. A further interesting addition was the inclusion that the award was also for his theoretical contributions to the subject of physics, which in an indirect way, could be considered to include relativity anyway. So, it is open to debate as to what this really amounted to, but it looked like all bases had been covered. As it was to be, Einstein never did win a further Nobel Prize for relativity although, indirectly, he could have been considered to.

For Lenard, the outcome of this battle was not good news. Not only had Einstein won a Nobel Prize, but it was for the photoelectric effect, the very area of physics that was based primarily on observations made as a result of Lenard's experimentations. Indeed, in Einstein's 1905 paper on the subject, he credited Lenard and his 'pioneering work'. Lenard was doubly outraged at this dark irony and wrote an angry letter to the secretary, the only official protest received. In his letter he stated: 'Einstein misunderstood the true nature of light' and was a 'publicity seeking Jew whose approach was alien to the true spirit of German physics.' With Lenard being an experimental physicist, the inclusion that the award was also for Einstein's theoretical work, which could be an indirect reference to relativity, only angered him further.

After Gehrcke died, it was found he had left behind boxes of papers which for many decades were not properly examined. In more recent years, these have now been looked at and have provided a unique view of what was happening at the time. Amongst the papers was a box containing documents from a mysterious organization setup in 1921 called 'The Academy of Nations', an alliance of laymen and qualified scientists who, at best, can be described as misguided misfits and at worse dangerous right-wing political troublemakers. As soon as Arvid Reuterdahl founded the academy, he set about contacting Einstein opponents across the world. After successfully achieving this task, he made the Academy of Nations an international organization involving ten countries, including Britain and the United States, in its first year of operation. It was clear from the organization's letterhead that it was meant to have the aura of a scholarly academy. The main purpose was to build a home for an international network of Einstein opponents, with its members exercising their worries about the way science was heading as a result of such theories as relativity. Reuterdahl was then dean of the faculty of engineering and architecture at the University of St Thomas in St Paul, Minnesota. He was also a devoted theist who attempted to reconcile religion and science into a 'new science', as he put it. One of his concerns was that science was becoming ever more specialized and so his academy would reconnect different branches of knowledge by integrating scientific findings into a unified, religious account of nature. This idea of a new science and religious associations would later be a favourite of the likes of Hitler and Himmler under the Nazi regime, spawned from Hitler's struggles with science and religion from his school days—something we will explore later.

The boxes of papers left behind by Gehrcke are revealing and still have not been fully incorporated into the history books. Einstein himself had, to a certain extent, played down the anti-Semitism towards him at the time; however, the Gehrcke papers show that matters were far worse than previously appreciated and had far-reaching effects. To understand what was really happening, its significance to the rise of Aryan physics and its baggage, we need to examine those papers further, especially the driving force behind the creation of the Academy of Nations and its connections to Nazi history.

Members of the Academy of Nations found themselves marginalized; they considered themselves outsiders and their arguments were dismissed as old crop by mainstream physicists. As a result, scholarly journals and scientific organizations closed their doors to them, so they exercised their voice through self-governed publications which they hoped would allow them to break from their marginalized position. They also feared for the future of physics, and science in general, and this went beyond simply attacking relativity because they opposed the new, modern physics altogether. With modern physics taking over from classical physics, the subject was becoming ever more mathematical, theoretical and abstract. This they did not like because it collided with their experimental approach and widely held view that science is essentially simple mechanics and comprehensible to every layperson; consequently they saw the likes of Newton and Galileo as having all the answers science needed. As we saw, that was certainly the general view within physics up until 1900, but with the discovery of quantum mechanics and relativity, that view changed amongst most physicists. Besides, it was clear classical physics was really only an approximation of the new modern physics anyway, but members of the Academy of Nations thought otherwise.

Clearly the beliefs of this organization were set in the nineteenth century, the golden years of German science, much of which was experimental. Moreover, it was an era when ordinary citizens devoted leisure time in the pursuit of scientific understanding, building things such as gliders and simple rockets. There were also popular articles in many magazines explaining science in simple terms, including the theories of electricity and gravitation, where open debate by all was encouraged, including personal theories. Furthermore, all this could be explored without fear of becoming lost in an ocean of equations and theoretical terminology. Nevertheless, there were attempts to extend this type of debate to modern physics; there was lively open debate in *The Times* of London during December 1921 about the nature of space-time and whether its fabric had physical meaning in the old-fashioned way. Interestingly, it was at about this time that Einstein started to consider a resurrected form of the ether to address this problem. Inevitably things got very technical very quickly, with opinion divided as the theory spread around the globe; indeed the layperson felt they were drowning in scientific jargon and equations. Before long the theory became a different way of understanding the world.

Gehrcke, co-founder of the academy, was clear in his views. 'Mathematics is the science of the imaginable, but natural science is the science of the real,' he said in 1921. Another member, Eyvind Heidenreich, an engineer who found relativity incomprehensible, said: 'This is not a science. On the contrary, it is a new brand of metaphysics.' The academy therefore saw itself as a salvation of real science, with Gehrcke saying the academy 'must become an alliance of truth'. Of course, to the founder, Reuterdahl, nothing demonstrated how science was becoming too specialized better than Einstein's theory of relativity, which is why in 1921 he contacted Gehrcke with the view of making him head of the German branch of the academy, a post Gehrcke eagerly accepted. Other members of the academy included Philipp Lenard and Johannes Stark, both openly right-wing political troublemakers.

The bitterness of Lenard would only increase throughout the 1920s, beyond just Einstein and relativity. In February 1922, his only son, Werner, died, which was put down to years of malnutrition during the war. In fact, Einstein also suffered as a result of food shortages during war time, resulting in a lot of stomach pains during his life—pains which never really went away, although he did have some luck from medical suggestions with diet. That year would also see Lenard pushing his rants about the 'alien spirit' that he claimed relativity incorporated. However, it was in June 1922 that Lenard managed to also anger his students and became the target of demonstrations at Heidelberg when he failed to fly the flag of his institute at half-mast to honour the death of Walther Rathenau. Lenard did this because he felt that Rathenau, as a Jewish politician and industrialist, had done irreversible harm to Germany. There then followed a student revolt and, probably on Lenard's orders, the students were hosed with water. They then broke into the building and frog-marched Lenard to an auditorium where he was subjected to a verbal torrent of political abuse. Lenard was then disciplined by the university over the episode. It appears that this set him on course to join the National Socialists, augmenting further his anti-Semitic views on science and Jewish physics and a return to Aryan experimental science. The awarding of the Nobel Prize to Einstein that same year did nothing to help matters, as we have seen. From there, Lenard was of the opinion that Jews were well-known for twisting objective arguments into personal conflicts and he charged colleagues with betraying their race.

The attacks on Einstein, relativity, modern physics and the theoretical and mathematical approach to science over experimentation continued for much of the 1920s through the likes of the Academy of Nations, although it did lose steam towards the final years of that decade. As the academy became ever more aware of their developing marginalized position, many of the anti-relativists turned more towards anti-Semitic conspiracy theories to boost their cause. One of many such theories from Lenard was the considerable amount of money he lost by investing gold for bonds. These become worthless in the inflationary Weimar years; he concluded that he had been swindled out of his fortune by Jewish politicians. However, it was not just politics that anti-relativists believed was dominated, even run, by Jews. The press was also a key target because of journals and scholarly publications ignoring their views. In 1923, for example, Reuterdahl wrote: 'Our trouble in America is that all scientific journals are closed to the anti-relativists through Jewish influence. The daily press is almost entirely under the control of the Jews.' It was easy for Einstein's opponents to see themselves as victims rather than aggressors; in their reality the mere existence of relativity and non-acceptance of arguments against it qualified as a personal attack on them.

Lenard's partner in crime for the support of Aryan physics was Johannes Stark, a native of Bavaria and son of a landowner. Stark made a number of discoveries during his scientific career and won the Nobel Prize in 1919 for the Stark Effect, involving the influence of electric fields on spectral lines. He also discovered the Doppler Effect in canal rays, a form of radiation emitted from holes in positive electrodes. Like Lenard, he started off respecting Einstein and his work and even invited him to write a review in a science journal he founded and edited. For 2 years they had a cordial relationship, writing to one another on subjects like quantum physics, where Stark was one of the first to employ the idea of quanta in light in his own research. That research even resulted in papers that verified Einstein's own work in the same area. Stark had many good and original ideas, including the appreciation that photo-chemistry was a quantum effect; almost as good as Einstein's ideas on the subject. Indeed, Stark was a prolific writer of scientific papers which included ideas of modern physics. It is therefore strange he took the views he did against these subjects. That said, there are clues to account for this behaviour.

Stark did have an irritating side to his nature; he was described by one physicist, James Franck, as 'a pain in the neck'. Things were fine in his early career, but later he became more active in trying to control the physics community. With this he became ever more intemperate and particularly vitriolic, like Lenard had become. He also tried to influence funding in the subject, and when his efforts failed, he set up an opposition society called the German Professional Community of University Physicists to further his aims; he considered the existing setup, the German Physical Society, as being too liberal. However, he was constantly frustrated that his efforts led to nothing.

Matters really took a turn for the worse when he was particularly mocked by the physics community for a thesis by one of his proteges, Ludwig Glaser, on optical properties of porcelain. As a result, Stark resigned his chair at the university in the early 1920s and made efforts to become the president of the *Physikalisch-Technische Reichsanstalt* (Reichs Physical-Technical Institute, PTR); however, his ever-increasing hostility was fuelled further when he was rejected. At this point, he concluded that he was surrounded by 'Einstein lovers'. Like Lenard, he had been embittered further when Einstein won the Nobel Prize, because for a few years he was a Nobel Laureate whereas Einstein was not, something he particularly liked amongst all his hatred. From that point, he repeatedly failed to get another academic post until Hitler came to power in 1933.

All this resulted in a torrent of abuse and venom towards both Einstein and relativity. That abuse took pride of place in his book *The Contemporary Crisis in German Physics*. His attacks did, however, stop short of all-out anti-Semitism, preferring to use the term 'anti-German' instead. A further blow for Stark came with reviews for his book; some in the physics community were not exactly impressed. One of the most distinguished physicists of the time and Nobel Prize winner in 1914, Max von Laue, who had already rebutted Lenard over claims that Einstein's mass/energy equivalence equation was plagiarized, dismissively reviewed the work with a conclusion that read: 'All in all, we would have wished that this book had remained unwritten, in the interest of science in general, of German science in particular, and not least of all in the interest of the author himself.'

Like so many others, Stark was not impressed that Einstein had gained world fame and publicity at such a rapid pace. He denounced Einstein's method of 'self-publicity' and called it 'a betrayal of Germany and German science'. He also accused Einstein and his followers of promoting the 'revolutionary nature' of the theory around the world, suggesting it was a social and political revolution of the type currently taking place in Germany at the time. Stark went on to condemn Einstein's theory as laughable, degenerate and, above all, unproven. With such views it is not surprising Lenard and Stark would form a very unpleasant double act under Hitler.

Both Lenard and Stark also declared that a four-dimensional space-time, with space and time curved by mass and energy, lacked physical meaning. As for the twin paradox—they said that was ridiculous. This paradox involves one twin speeding off in a spaceship while the other remains on Earth. The twin in the spaceship travels close to the speed of light; as a consequence of time dilation, when he returns to Earth, his twin has aged considerably compared to him. It is certainly true the twin paradox did have problems under the 1905 special theory, but by the time Lenard and Stark were in full swing 10 years later, the general theory resolved the problems by bringing in gravity and acceleration and, with it, the equivalence principle between the two. This did not matter to Lenard and Stark either. They insisted relativity had nothing to do with science: the theory was ideological and linked with internal politics of power in German science. This was quite some claim, considering that their very own efforts could essentially be summed up using the same words.

Another key feature of the rise in National Socialism during the 1920s was to provide a convincing link between German racial purity and Jewish fake science. An early sign of things to come is found with an article published in the *Grossdeutsche Zeitung* on 8 May 1924 jointly penned by Lenard and Stark and titled 'The Hitler Spirit and Science'. This article appeared 2 years after Stark's book and only 6 months after Hitler had led the march from a beer hall in Munich in an attempt to topple the city government. In the article, Lenard and Stark compared Hitler with the giants of science and celebrated Aryan genius while condemning the corrupting influences of Judaism throughout the ages. It also promoted a 'spirit of total clarity and honesty' towards the world while linking these virtues with past great scientists like Newton, Galileo, Faraday and Kepler. The article also glorified Hitler with various great qualities and declared how privileged people should be to have such a great genius living among them in the flesh. From the racial purity viewpoint, the article told of how the Aryan-Germanic bloodline and its carriers of this unique spirit are in rapid decline, while an 'alien spirit' flourished in its place, the same that 'brought Christ to the cross and Jordanus Brunus to the stake'. This was followed by the rallying cry: 'We now place the highest emphasis on protecting that which is inherited in our blood because we have learned to recognize it as the blessing of all mankind. But we will not simply protect our own intellectual identity, we will first start digging it out again from under the alien-spirited rubble within ourselves - primarily in order to find ourselves again we need lucid minds not only as scientists - no, people should not be segregated according to their occupation (a frequently used Semitic deception!).' This article highlighted much that was wrong with the Hitler years ahead and the way science would be interpreted and pursued during the Second World War; in hindsight, it served as a warning. As we will see later, this fitted perfectly with Hitler's schooling on many levels.

Many of the scientists mentioned in this article, in particular Newton and Galileo, give a clue to the early stages of the phenomenon of Aryan physics. These two scientists are associated with a mechanical or clockwork universe and experimentation, which were the keystones of classical physics. Physicists like Einstein were therefore further despised because the anti-relativists like Lenard and Stark were convinced he actually headed a disruptive Jewish conspiracy within physics. Furthermore, the stand that Einstein had taken during the First World War was despised by the same Conservative Nationalists; he was a pacifist and supported a democratic spirit in the Weimar Republic. All these qualities and more were the very things Lenard, Stark and their followers hated, and in doing so helped to start the ball rolling for Hitler and his National Socialists 10 years later.

However, the extreme right-wing conservative scientists did not have it all their own way and did not always have an easy ride. By the mid-1920s, the tide was starting to turn, with anti-relativists facing more resistance which became overwhelming over time. Such was the backlash that most refrained from taking part in public rallies, especially against relativity, while others simply gave up. The Academy of Nations eventually ceased to serve as the central organization campaigning against Einstein and for 'real' science, although die-hard anti-relativists survived by revising their opinions. Despite these difficult times during the final years of the 1920s, they survived long enough to take their views into the 1930s, where they found a boost under Hitler. After the war, decline set in again, although some members of the academy managed to hang on in one form or another until as late as 1951, only 4 years before Einstein's death. At that time Gehrcke in particular was still campaigning against relativity, writing: 'The day will come where everything, but everything about this theory will be abandoned by the world at large, but when will this be?' Well, the theory went from strength to strength between the 1920s and 1951 and even more so during the 1960s and 1970s when research in astronomy started to develop in leaps and bounds. Relativity was not only put to the test time and again; it passed each and every test with flying colours. Moreover, new discoveries were made about the universe that fitted perfectly with the theory. Indeed, even today relativity survives and there is no doubt Einstein's theory is correct, although not complete. Even so, the marginalized, die-hard critics and opponents still exist to this day and no doubt always will. They are akin to those who stubbornly believe we did not go to the moon, regardless of the evidence to prove we did, and the Flat-Earthers, who still have supporters around the globe.

Shortly before Hitler came to power, Lenard wrote what was probably his greatest influential piece, *Grosse Naturforscher* (*Great Natural Scientists*), which was published in 1929. It amounted to a pseudo-anthropological and biographical encyclopaedia of sixty-five scientific heroes from history. All were of Aryan-Germanic heredity, from the time of the first century with Hipparchus of Nicea to Heinrich Hertz, who was Lenard's mentor. Interestingly, Hertz was half Jewish on his father's side; however, that was no problem for Lenard because it allowed Hertz's work in theoretical physics to be put down to his Jewish father while his achievements in experimental physics was due to his Aryan mother. Indeed, a popular rant of Lenard would be the idea of this Aryan bloodline in a person's make-up, something shared by Hitler. All in all, he was destined for pride of place in the horrors to come under the Fuhrer.

In December 1932, Einstein left Germany for a lecture tour of the United States. With the growing troubles in his home country, he was not sure whether he would be able to return. In tow was a tell-tale sign of thirty pieces of luggage, far more than would be required for the 3-month trip. It turned out he would not return following Hitler's rise to power on 30 January 1933.

Einstein's destination was California, where one of his public duties was to deliver a speech in Pasadena to celebrate German-American friendship, a somewhat painfully ironic booking. His stay at Caltech was funded to the tune of $7,000 by the Oberlaender Trust, a foundation that sought to promote cultural exchanges with Germany and was arranged by its president and physicist, Robert Millikan. Upon his arrival, Millikan made the announcement that Einstein was 'coming to the United States on a mission of molding public opinion to better German-American relations'. The idea was that Einstein would make one helpful broadcast to achieve this aim. The broadcast was due to be made on NBC radio, with big donors attending a black-tie dinner preceding it at the Pasadena Civil Athenaeum. Not surprisingly, this was a big draw with a long list for tickets.

Einstein's speech was not quite as intended, which is not really a surprise. He chose to attack people who used words 'laden with emotion' to intimidate free expression, such as 'Heretic' during the Inquisition. He also cited examples that had similar hateful connotations for people in a variety of cultures, such as 'the word "communist" in America today, or the word "bourgeoisie" in Russia, or the word "Jew" for the reactionary group in Germany'. This was typical of Einstein and probably went as far as possible given the nature and funding requirements of the grant. He also attacked capitalists regarding the current world crisis, giving as an example the economic depression in America. However, he did make a couple of attempts to express sympathy to earn the grant funding. He suggested America would be wise not to press for payment of debt and reparations from the

First World War and even justified Germany's demand for military equality. He hastened to add it did not mean they should re-introduce mandatory military service; 'universal military service means the training of youth in a war-like spirit,' he concluded. Ironically, this had all come about because Millikan had tried to prevent any such controversy by forcing Einstein to cancel a scheduled speech at UCLA's War Resister's League some days earlier. Einstein managed to get away with it because Millikan was happy enough that he spoke pro-German views and not pacifist sentiments, and allowed some talk of politics.

Following Hitler's rise to power in January 1933, Einstein appeared initially unsure what all this meant for him. During the first week of February, he wrote letters back to Berlin about his planned return in April, which included details about his salary. It seemed at this stage a return was not out of the question. Interestingly, there are some clues to be gained from his travel journal about the way his mind was working. During that week there are only entries about serious scientific discussions, an example being cosmic ray experiments. There were also details of social contacts and events such as spending the evening playing Mozart quartets and talking of a fat lady whose occupation was making friends with all celebrities. However, by the end of February, the Reichstag was in flames and Hitler's brownshirts were running amok, ransacking Jewish homes and businesses, events that made matters clearer in Einstein's mind. On 27 February, he wrote a letter to a female friend, Margarete Lebach, in which he said: 'Because of Hitler, I don't dare step on German soil.'

On 10 March, the day before Einstein was due to depart Pasadena, he took a stroll through the gardens of the Athenaeum with Evelyn Seeley of the *New York World Telegram*. The two talked for 45 minutes, during which he made a declaration that would become headline news, saying: 'As long as I have any choice in the matter, I shall live only in a country where civil liberty, tolerance, and equality of all citizens before the law prevail.' What Einstein did not realize at the time was that the same afternoon, his apartment in Berlin was raided twice by the Nazis. Cowering inside was Margot, the daughter of his second wife, Elsa. Her husband, Dimitri Marianoff, was out doing errands at the time and was almost trapped by one of the roving gangs of thugs. He sent word to Margot to get Einstein's papers to the French embassy for safety and then meet him in Paris. Unfortunately, she was unable to do both, but the papers were saved. More fortunate were Ilse, one of Elsa's daughters, and her husband, Rudolph Kayser, who successfully escaped to Holland. During the next 2 days, Einstein's apartment was raided a further three times. There seemed little chance of Einstein returning to Germany, although he did tell friends and family the only place in the country he really wanted to see again was his cottage in Capula. However, his cottage did not escape the Nazi's attention either; Einstein received word that they had raided the cottage too under the pretence of looking for a cache of communist weaponry. They returned a second time and confiscated his beloved boat since it might be used for smuggling. This sealed the decision that Einstein would never return to Germany.

His problem now was he remained unclear about where he would live, a worry that remained right up to the moment of sailing from the United States. Paul Schwartz, the German consul in New York who had been Einstein's friend in Berlin, met with him privately to make sure he would not return to Germany. 'They'll drag you through the streets by your hair,' he warned him. The ship Einstein planned to sail on was due to stop next at Belgium; he suggested to friends that after getting off there his final destination might be Switzerland. Another possibility in his mind was to make the United States a final home. The following year saw the opening of the Institute of Advanced Studies, where he decided to spend 4 or 5 months each year, perhaps more. On the day before he sailed, he and Elsa slipped away to Princeton to look at houses they might buy.

As soon as the ship docked in Antwerp on 28 March 1933, Einstein had a car drive him to the German consulate in Brussels, where he turned in his passport and renounced his German citizenship. His arrival also took a further worrying turn. Having found a house to rent on the dunes of Le Coq sur Mer, a resort near Ostend, word got to him that there was a rumour going around that his name was now on an assassination list with a price on his head of $5,000. In typical Einstein style, he pointed to his head and said: 'I didn't know it was worth that much!' Despite this display, Einstein's lack of worry did not extend to the Belgian authorities, who supplied him with two burly policemen to guard him. They proved alert when they pounced on one of Einstein's friends who had turned up to visit him unannounced.

While in Belgium, Einstein gave a lot of thought to his future home. He was certainly not short of opportunities; he had received many offers of appointments at universities including Madrid, Paris, Brussels and even Oxford. He had expressed a particular liking for the latter, corresponding about the possibility with his friend, Professor Frederick Lindemann, later scientific advisor to Winston Churchill. Einstein decided to visit Oxford in May 1933, but problems with his son, Eduard, meant he had to delay the trip so he could go to Zurich to be with him. He wrote to Lindemann to say: 'I could not wait six weeks before going to see him. You are not a father, but I know you will understand.'

Einstein had already mailed a letter during his Atlantic crossing to resign his membership to the Prussian Academy. 'Dependence on the Prussian government is something that, under the present circumstances, I feel to be intolerable,' he wrote. Max Planck, who had recruited him to the Academy some 19 years earlier, was relieved at the news, considering it the only way for an honourable separation that could be made by Einstein. He later wrote to Einstein saying: 'Despite the deep gulf that divides our political opinions, our personal amicable relations will never undergo any change.' Unfortunately, there was still the possibility of disciplinary action against Einstein, which government ministers had been calling for; this particularly came from the troublemakers Lenard and Stark. This action, feared Planck, would cause the academy historic embarrassment and himself personal agony. As a result, Planck wrote to the academy's secretary, saying: 'Even though on political matters a deep gulf divides me from him, I am, on the other hand, absolutely certain that in the history of centuries to come, Einstein's name will be celebrated as one of the greatest stars that ever shone in the academy.' However, the academy was not prepared to leave the matter there;

moreover, the Nazis were furious that Einstein had pre-empted them by announcing his resignation publicly using the newspapers before they could kick him out.

A further problem was that the Prussian Academy's secretary was a Nazi sympathizer and had issued a statement in the American press denouncing the comments of Einstein. That announcement accused Einstein of 'participation in atrocity mongering' and accused him of 'activities as an agitator in foreign countries'. In a concluding remark, the secretary said the academy 'has, therefore, no reason to regret Einstein's withdrawal.' It was Max von Laue who tried to get other members to join his protest as a lifelong colleague and friend and to disavow the secretary's comments. However, nobody agreed, not even Fritz Haber, one of Einstein's supporters and closest friends. Unsurprisingly, Einstein responded to this situation by saying: 'I hereby declare that I have never taken any part in atrocity mongering. …I described the present state of affairs in Germany as a state of psychic distemper in the masses.' From there, the exchanges descended into predictable irritation.

By early April 1933, the German government effectively settled the matter when it passed a law declaring that Jews, defined as anyone with a Jewish grandparent, could not hold an official position, which included the Prussian Academy and universities. As for Lenard, he had already made an announcement in the Nazi propaganda newspapers earlier that week: 'The most important example of the dangerous influence of Jewish circles on the study of nature has been provided by Herr Einstein.'

By 10 May, Germans were gathering in front of Berlin's Opera House as a parade of swastika-wearing students and beer hall thugs carrying torches threw books into a huge bonfire. They were joined by ordinary citizens carrying books from looted libraries and private homes to add to the blaze. Yells accompanied the event from Propaganda Minister Joseph Goebbels, standing at his podium to declare such things as 'Jewish intellectualism is dead' and 'The German soul can again express itself.'

Einstein eventually made it to Oxford after visiting his son, hoping to spend half of each ensuing year in Europe. He gave lectures at Oxford and Glasgow, and enjoyed his visit so much he planned to return in July following an invitation from British Commander Oliver Locker-Lampson, who was a Member of Parliament and had studied in Germany. He was also an early supporter of fighting the Nazis. During his visit, Locker-Lampson took Einstein to visit Winston Churchill; they talked at Churchill's home, Chartwell, about Germany's rearmament. Later Einstein described Churchill as 'an eminently wise man'. He also said: 'It became clear to me that these people have made preparations and are determined to act resolutely and soon.' During his visit, Einstein also met with Austen Chamberlain and former Prime Minster Lloyd George. On arrival at Lloyd George's home, Einstein was asked to sign the guest book. He gave some thought over the entry for home address, finally writing 'Ohne': 'without any'.

Following his visit, Einstein planned a return to Oxford the following spring to spend another term at Christ Church, but it was not to be. Eventually, he set sail for his new home in the United States on 7 October 1933, arriving in New York on 17 October; he would never visit Europe again.

Chapter Three

Educating Hitler

Hitler's first attempt to overthrow the government (i.e., putsch) came in 1923, but it was a failure and he found himself imprisoned. Nursing his grievances with greater fury than ever, he was visited by what might be called a dark angel of death, General Karl Haushofer. Haushofer was a Prussian officer as well as a remarkable scholar of Eastern mysticism, and by coming into Hitler's life, he 'unleashed the demon', to quote the general's son, Albrecht Haushofer. Indeed, those words were written on the walls of the cell in which the young man later awaited death for his part in the generals' plot against Hitler's life. General Karl Haushofer was professor of oriental studies at the University of Munich and came to lend his support to the imprisoned ex-corporal and to instruct him in *geopolitik*, Haushofer's original political theory. The Prussian professor had been brought to see Hitler by Rudolf Hess, a wartime pilot friend of Hermann Goering, and a fellow student of oriental ritual magic. As a consequence, fate had made Haushofer the instrument that would bring Hitler out of the darkness of failure and defeat into the light of a Germany reborn by giving him a coherent political creed.

The rigid class structure of the German military caste meant it was quite extraordinary for generals like Haushofer and Field Marshal Hindenburg or other officers to concern themselves with Hitler, a mere corporal; the gulf between officers and non-commissioned ranks was so great that it was virtually feudal. Yet General Ludendorff, Haushofer, Goering, Hess and, above all, Field Marshal Hindenburg, second president of the Weimar Republic from 1925 to 1934, surmounted this abyss of German class distinction to find a saviour for the Fatherland. In the case of Hindenburg, he actually despised Hitler, yet would eventually accept him as chancellor. It appears the generals had seen unique qualities in Hitler amongst which was a hypnotic effect on his followers.

Haushofer had devised a master political plan for a Third Reich, the *Drang nach Osten* ('the Drive towards the East'), for a reborn Germany to win new territories with plenty of *lebensraum* ('living space'): a basic principle of Nazi foreign policy, for the German master race to develop its plan of world conquest. As we will see in due course, the occult and black arts would feature heavily in the Nazi regime, and Hitler's hypnotic effect on his followers would fit into this plan perfectly. It is believed by some scholars that these men used the principles of ritual magic to bring about the almost total enslavement of the German people. What emerged was the focus of a new putsch to seize power from a weakly governed Weimar Republic.

General Karl Haushofer was a great supporter of geopolitics with his *geopolitik* theory, which was just one of the many twisted contributions to National Socialist ideology: this one being in geography and its influence on mankind and race. He was also an avid scholar of Arthur Schopenhauer's 'Will to Power', which was another twisted contribution (we will address him later). One way *geopolitik* theory achieved its goal was through the justification for an expansion of *lebensraum* ('living space'), therefore endowing Hitler's aims for conquest with scientific legitimacy.

To call geopolitics a science is strictly wrong, certainly from the Nazi perspective, but it has been sold as such and really originated with the ideology of the Swedish politician Rudolf Kjellen, who coined the term in 1905. Indeed, today we are also graced with the subject of political science—another subject that cannot really be regarded as a science under the strict definition. However, like then, today it gives extra legitimacy to the politicians. If anything, these subjects are arts, and as we will see later, that provides a nice Freudian slip involving Haushofer. Nevertheless, it is easy to see how this was also seized upon by the Nazis as a scientific justification and legitimacy for many of their plans, something that is not uniquely Nazi, as today's politics clearly show. Putting aside the debate about geopolitics being a science or not, we will see that one thing we can say about the subject is it was certainly an idiosyncratic version of cultural and political history and nothing to do with geography either.

Kjellen, in turn, was influenced by the British geographer Sir Halford Mackinder, who became director of the London School of Economics in the first decade of the twentieth century, at about the time Germany was enjoying great scientific recognition following the many discoveries from the golden years of German science and, of course, the world discovering quantum mechanics and relativity. It was Mackinder who devised and promoted the idea of a people's heartland with the concept of a nation–state as organic in nature, or as a living organism. This links with the Nazi idea we saw earlier of a body politic expelling unwanted pathogens, and the horrors of the Holocaust. This particularly appealed to Hitler and Himmler in the same way as many other thinkers of the time because Mackinder was convinced of the need for a country to expand beyond its boundaries, when necessary; something that even today is not uniquely Nazi.

However, things become more significant when we discover how this linked with true sciences like physics and biology. In particular, it links with quantum mechanics, the human will and consciousness, going on to link further with racial types and Darwin. In fact, Mackinder held with the belief that different racial types adapted through Darwinian natural selection to their geographical environment. For example, the climate and temperature of Britain created the 'John Bull' type with the aptitude of freedom and civilized values. Russians were more adapted and acquiescent to despotic rule, attributed to them being raised on the open, level, grassy plains (steppe) common to the country that were devoid of forests, especially in cold and harsh climates like Siberia. Mackinder concluded that until complete adaptation to geography and, particularly, climate had been achieved, people should submit to the guidance of the Anglo-Saxon type. Furthermore, in the event they failed to recognize this wisdom, Pax Britannica should be imposed for the benefit of the world.

All this had obvious consequences for the Nazis. It was the German geographer Friedrich Ratzel who coined the term *lebensraum* in an essay titled *Der Lebensraum* in 1901 where he described the term as 'a geographical region within which living organisms developed'. However, the main scope of this work was the study of plants and zoogeography, but somewhat unfortunately he also applied his sociobiological treatment of *lebensraum* to warfare between nations. Consequently, Haushofer took on Ratzel's ideas, then exploited and applied them to the process of expelling disruptive minorities in the interest of an expanding nation–state; in other words, ethnic cleansing.

Kjellen and Ratzel also believed a thorough knowledge of a country's geography was an essential element when shaping its national policy, especially on a grand scale. Because Haushofer was one of Hitler's prison visitors at Landsberg in 1924, we can see how many of these subjects like geography, geopolitics, physics, quantum mechanics, racial purity and expansion of a nation–state came together in Hitler's mind and in the 'Will to Power' of the Third Reich in general. Moreover, those dark visitors were already aware of how the mind of Hitler had been shaped in his schooldays in these subjects, as we will see later. Following these visits, the notion of *lebensraum* linked with fear for the survival of *volk* ('the people') and entered Hitler's thinking. Hitler wrote in *Mein Kampf*: 'Our German nation must find the courage to gather our people and their strengths for an advance along the road that will lead this people from its present restricted living space to new land and soil, and hence also free it from the danger of vanishing from earth or of serving others as a slave nation.' Furthermore, Haushofer declared that Germany's predicament following its defeat in the First World War demanded geopolitical expertise for that crisis of defeat which included the economy as much as the loss of territory.

It is interesting to compare this situation with a true science, in this case, physics and the discovery of quantum mechanics, for much of this keeps coming back to that element of the subject as well as its discoverer, physicist Max Planck. Indeed, Planck was no stranger to meeting Hitler face-on and experiencing the Fuhrer's rage; it was Planck who had urged the importance of science as the Fatherland's best asset in its post-war situation, and that included Jewish science and its scientists. However, others cited as the country's salvation the 'science' of geopolitics and did so in today's familiar political fashion of 'alternative science', 'alternative facts' and 'fake news'.

As a means of protecting this so-called 'alternative science', Haushofer founded and edited the journal *Zeitschrift fur Geopolitik* in the same year that he visited Hitler in prison: 1924. It will come as no surprise that it followed the general trend, especially that of 'alternatives', being crammed from cover to cover with inflated claims, and a lack of objectivity and rationality as well as any empirical method; as such, it was at odds with true science journals in just about every way possible. This dichotomy is evident when we look at how Haushofer described his subject, saying it was 'the science of the earth relationships of political processes'. He went on to add it was 'based on broad foundations of geography, especially on political organisms in space and their structure'. He summed it all up: 'Geopolitics sets out to furnish the tools for political action and the directives for political life as a whole. Thus, geopolitics becomes an art, namely, the art of guiding practical politics. Geopolitics is the geographical conscience of the state.' The change from science to art is telling and maybe was something of a Freudian slip.

Given the rise of Aryan physics and the anti-Semitism of the 1920s that we have explored in detail, this new publication became another of the many Nazi propaganda publications. With this, Haushofer was able to hammer home key points, one of which was Germany's defeat in the First World War and how it had resulted from 'ignorance of the geographical realities on the part of Germany's leaders'. As for science, he said that geopolitics emerged from an 'elementary craving for better scientific protection of the political unit'. What this amounted to, according to his publication, was that the West was in decline and argued that it was the destiny of Germany to lead Europe back to primacy as the defender of civilized values in the world. This, as we can see, still has its parallels in the current problems of the political world, particularly with dictator states.

This was all fitting together nicely for the Nazis and their ideology and had been set in place along with other elements during the 1920s, ready for Hitler's eventual rise to power and the plans to make Germany the heart of Europe. However, initially, in a similar way with physics, mathematics and just about any discipline, it was critical that geography fitted with National Socialism, which was particularly difficult for mathematics, as we have seen. Now we had a similar situation with geography needing to show its worth as a true Aryan subject, which produced obvious tensions. Therefore, Haushofer urged geographers to become politicized in a similar fashion as other disciplines and in a way that had become necessary with science and mathematics. However, as in other disciplines, there was resistance and bewilderment. Again, like other disciplines, there was a counter-urge to be seen as apolitical and remain as such.

Nevertheless, Hitler adopted Haushofer's geopolitics and incorporated it into Nazi ideology. Shortly after he gained power in 1933, it became a key element of Hitler's education and science reforms along with other warped elements in his mind. Under the Nazis, from 1933 onwards geopolitics became a compulsory subject in schools and universities. Indeed, textbooks were even drafted promoting the works of Haushofer and Ratzel and how they supported Hitler's *lebensraum* rhetoric. Part of this educational reform was to encourage school children to look forwards to the new German Empire and its influence on the world, or *Germanisches Weltreich* (Germanic world empire), which was seen as a necessary result of the country's quest for *lebensraum*. This was also promoted through 'Will', in this case, 'Iron Will', with the words 'the meaning and the Iron Will of National Socialist Statesmanship are the securing of our Lebensraum and a sensible organization of space…To create a spatial organisation suitable to Germany means to undo the damage caused by an unavailing population'.

Of course, in a similar fashion to other disciplines, there were always those only too ready to adopt the state view and jump into a Nazi uniform of one type or another. Some promoted German imperialism, *Drang nach Osten* ('Push to the East') and *Volks-und Kulturboden* ('Soil of the People and Culture'), and with this we have those interpretations of territory and belonging; the Reich, or 'State'; ethnic communities outside these borders; and wider cultural links with Germanhood.

The state of geopolitics continued to rise under Hitler's rapid conquest of territories to the east with the invasions of Poland and Russia. In the wake of this expansion and the establishment of German settlements in Poland, coupled with the treatment of Jews and their subsequent transportation as slave labourers westwards, the 'science' of geopolitics was set to work establishing demographics and assessing the Germanic populations and optimal population densities in Russia and Ukraine.

Naturally, as the father of German geopolitics, Haushofer assumed a central role under Hitler's regime. Furthermore, during the 1930s he was happy to praise National Socialist foreign policy as a manifestation of his own views and theories. However, oddly, this was done even though his form of geopolitics did not actually imply a racist ideology. Because of this sticking point, in later years, he would come to deplore Hitler's invasion of Russia as the reverse of his beliefs that Germany, Japan and Russia should make common cause.

Undoubtedly another key influence in Hitler's early years was a close companion and hard-drinking, ranting Prussian poet, journalist, publicist and political activist, Dietrich Eckart, who was also a participant in the Beer Hall Putsch of 1923. He was a strange and violently anti-Semitic man running a broadsheet publication, *Auf Gut Deutsch* (*'In Good German'*), which was an anti-Semitic weekly first appearing in 1918 and ceasing publication in 1921. In August of that year, Eckart then became editor-in-chief and original publisher of *Volkischer Beobachter* (*'Volkisch Observer'*), the newspaper of the German Workers' Party, the predecessor to the Nazi Party. Eckart was also a founding member of the party and lyricist of the first party anthem, *Sturmlied* (*'Storming Song'*). He died in December 1923 from excessive drinking. Hitler greatly admired Eckart; his name appeared in *Mein Kampf* along with a eulogy of praise. According to Albert Speer, Hitler's architect, Eckart was one of the few people whom Hitler addressed as 'du', indicating a close relationship.

With these essential starting points, we now need to look at how Hitler himself arrived at this stage of his life as a result of his education. First, Hitler received little real schooling, not even getting beyond elementary level, although he was considered to be relatively intelligent. However, he was also considered to be indecisive and lethargic, qualities that appear to have dogged him both from a scientific perspective and a military one. By the time he came to power, he seemed to have acquired only a sketchy knowledge of the natural sciences, especially physics, engineering and mathematics. In *Mein Kampf,* he claimed he had sabotaged certain aspects of the curriculum he considered unimportant and unattractive. He also claimed that his best subjects were geography and history, fitting nicely with geopolitics. The reality was these turned out to be amongst his worse subjects, and things were even more disastrous when it came to mathematics. Nevertheless, it does appear he was taught a history of sorts, but that focussed on its specific relationship to

German myths, legends and pseudo-science taught by Leopold Poetsch, for whom he later expressed a high regard.

There were also claims that he provoked his teachers by highlighting contradictions between science and religion. This would also show through in his later life when religion also became wrapped up with the myths, legends and pseudo-science taught by Poetsch. It explains his determination to combine science and religion into a 'new science' in the same way as Arvid Reuterdahl and the Academy of Nations. A particular problem seems to originate with requirements to attend Bible classes immediately followed by natural science classes, never a happy mix; his natural science classes taught him evolution, whereas the Bible classes taught creationism. In Hitler's words, this forced him to 'run his head against the wall'.

Hitler's vision included putting 'Will' over education, especially as the driving force of the state. He believed that science in German schools had resulted in fragmentation and, above all, the chaos of the Weimar Republic. This point was emphasized in *Mein Kampf* when he cited science and technology in education, describing it as 'The plague of our present day cowardly lack of will'. Indeed, his idea of 'Will, Not Intelligence' would be an obvious key element to much of his understanding; it also links with ideas appearing in quantum mechanics, as we have seen. All this undoubtedly accounts for his desire to change the curriculum once he came to power and the political appointments of less-than-sympathetic characters to head a ministry which combined both science and education. He declared that all state educational work would be taken over by the *Volkisch* state who he said 'will have to put general scientific instruction into an abbreviated form, embracing the essentials'. This further showed a lack of understanding of science, holding the belief that Germany's scientific education was turning ever more towards practical subjects like physics, chemistry, biology and mathematics, subjects he clearly failed to grasp and saw as too complex. These, as we have seen, would become Aryan physics, Aryan chemistry, Aryan biology and so on. This situation, he warned, was creating preoccupations which were dangerous, neglecting an ideal education and preservation of the nation. In short, he placed this above technical or other similar abilities. However, some of his views expressed at this time would change during the course of the war, but there was a clear and worrying mentality that no doubt contributed to many of Hitler's scientific woes and the eventual outcome of the war.

A further worry, according to Speer, was that Hitler had the habit of seeking scientific and technological opinion and expertise from unreliable sources usually having no scientific training and with a preference towards the unconventional and pseudo-scientific way of thinking. This practice was seen by him as more productive than to consult responsible experts and may explain his behaviour when attending official scientific gatherings. It is clear this showed through when he would 'tune out' at times as new ideas and technology was demonstrated then suddenly 'tune in' again when some form of fanatical destructive element entered the conversation. Speer records an episode from the autumn of 1939, barely weeks before Britain went to war with Germany, when Hitler saw a newsreel where, in the final scene, a plane dives towards the British Isles. The outcome was a blinding flash of light, and Britain is blown into smithereens by an atomic device. Hitler sprang to life on seeing this, his enthusiasm unbound. Although still in its early development, nuclear power and the potential for bombs of mass destruction was becoming well developed in physics, so the concept was a real possibility. However, despite his preference for more conventional hand-to-hand combat, this really showed not so much his desire for science but his fanatical mass-destruction dreams, which was also an awkward mix in his mind.

This desire for mass destruction was also demonstrated by another incident, reported by Speer. When the head of the Nazi rocket development programme, Walter Dornberger, spoke to Hitler in the summer of 1943 about the potential for ballistic missiles, he said: 'A strange fanatical light came into the Fuhrer's eyes.' Hitler then responded with: 'What I want is annihilation, annihilating effect!' There was a clear pattern in these gatherings, where Hitler would be less enthusiastic with the science until somebody spoke of the mass destruction the technology could deliver; at that point a switch was thrown in the Fuhrer's brain and he was suddenly 'tuned in', often excitedly pacing around with great enthusiasm.

On 23 April 1942, Speer had a meeting with Hitler about the atomic bomb and advances taking place in that area of nuclear physics, a meeting which also showed how his desire for annihilation was more important than understanding the science behind it, and which was also a throwback to that 1939 newsreel. In his memoirs, he recalls that the Fuhrer's intellectual capacity was quite obviously strained by the idea and he was 'unable to grasp the revolutionary nature of nuclear physics'. This, according to Speer, was again largely due to the Fuhrer seeking garbled knowledge about such subjects from his pseudo-scientific contacts. In the case of the atomic bomb, he sought advice from his photographer, Heinrich Hoffmann. In turn, Hoffmann had obtained his understanding from Wilhelm Ohnesorge, Reich Minister of the Reich Postal Ministry, because the German postal service was sponsoring an atomic bomb project. Although Ohnesorge was a member of Hitler's cabinet and had an interest in the atomic bomb, much of his time was taken up running the postal service; he supported the research interests of nuclear physicists Manfred von Ardenne and Fritz Houtermans. In his memoirs, Speer stated the advice Hitler had obtained through that chain of contacts had led him to think that the bomb would turn the Earth into a 'glowing star' as a result of a nuclear chain reaction. It is true that there were many secret projects underway and hidden within the post office, including super-computer development (as was also true in Britain), but the advice Hitler was to eventually get from his photographer was far from accurate and out of scientific context.

Interestingly, further details to muddle the issue came from the quantum physicist Werner Heisenberg, and his contradictory claim that absolute certainty showed that a sustained chain reaction could not be maintained. However, when it came to nuclear physics and the atomic bomb, Heisenberg was an enigma; he really should have been in a position to understand and develop this line of research from other physicists, and it is a debate to this day whether it was all to deprive Hitler of the atomic bomb. Speer also wrote that other scientists went off in the opposite direction to Heisenberg and did, in some cases, support the view of a controlled reaction, while some even feared an uncontrolled one. However, at the end of the day, it was early for this branch of physics and even physicists were still piecing together the science. It is true there was talk of an uncontrolled reaction eventually destroying the whole planet and possibly beyond, but most physicists appreciated this was highly unlikely; indeed some were uncertain such a reaction could be achieved at all.

Speer also reported that Hitler liked to turn it into a joke by saying that scientists 'in their unworldly urge to lay bare all the secrets under heaven might someday set the globe on fire'. Summing up Hitler's understanding, Speer wrote in his memoirs that much of these scientific and technological problems were because 'of his love for amateurishness and his lack of understanding of fundamental scientific research. Instead Hitler pontificated on science and technology as if he understood by process of intuitive genius.'

In contrast, Winston Churchill, President Roosevelt and later President Truman respected and sought scientific expertise. Although none were particularly educated in science and technology, they did not take decisions in such areas without consulting the best experts at their disposal. They listened, took advice and learned from formal groups of experts and committees as well as from migrant experts thrown out by Hitler, like Albert Einstein, Leo Szilard and others. What they were told was not always what they wanted to hear, learning some painful lessons along the way; something in stark contrast to Hitler. As for Stalin, he fell somewhat in the middle of this spectrum; he subscribed to certain areas of pseudo-science but not to the same extent as Hitler. He also held with certain characteristics of inheritance. However, eventually he moved away from such views somewhat more towards Churchill and Roosevelt, no doubt as a result of the many meetings with them. He also came more into line with seeing sense in scientific and technological advances from true science, which, after the war, allowed him to keep up with Anglo-American advances, especially with the hydrogen bomb and other key developments. This difference was a key factor in winning the war, one that Hitler did not appreciate or even understand.

Hitler eventually came to power and was sworn in as Chancellor on 30 January 1933; however, one of his immediate problems was power sharing because he had failed to gain an overall majority. As a result, he immediately called for new elections on 5 March. As chancellor, he was now in a good position to influence the outcome of the election by control of the media, oppression of opposition democratic parties and the launching of attacks on Jews as well as Socialists. However, the outcome of the March election still saw Hitler with no absolute majority for the National Socialists. Nevertheless, he did have a temporary majority with the help of Hugenberg's right-wing nationalists, securing 340 of the 647 seats and giving him a 52 per cent majority.

The opening of the newly constituted Reichstag was celebrated on 21 March in the Old Garrison Church in Potsdam. As Hitler spoke to the nation on the radio, his brownshirts were already at work rounding up anybody Hitler regarded as an enemy of the regime. Within 2 short days, parliamentary democracy ended following an arson attack on the Reichstag, which lay in ruins; Hitler secured a majority in the Kroll Opera House in favour of the Enabling Act. This act gave him dictatorial powers under spurious legality. The result of all this allowed Hitler's brownshirts more power to carry out their attacks, which included turning their attention towards the scientific community as well as a carefully organized series of appointments and ministerial shuffling within the areas of science and education.

When Hitler came to power, science, technology and medicine were pressed into the service of the new regime. The Third Reich called for a spirit of *Gleichschaltung*, or 'Marching in Step', where all the resources of the regime were to work in co-ordination. Education, psychology, communications and the media were also important areas for this goal and were adopted to serve the Nazi ideology, shaping public opinion as part of the National Socialist revolution. Many in these key disciplines were surprisingly quick to accept the challenge, some willingly while others required varying degrees of pressure. However, behind this modernization there were sinister elements of dismissals of key Jewish scientists, the book burning of 12 May 1934 and oppression from within institutions and universities as well as from outside. Unfortunately, this did not provide a suitable environment for the survival of many key academic disciplines Hitler would need to fulfil his plans. What was once a thriving part of Germany's achievements throughout the world thanks to the golden years was now heading in the general direction of further collapse augmented by little rebuilding after the First World War. If Hitler's knowledge and understanding of science, education and technology is to be summed up, it would be something along the lines of 'profoundly warped and racist'.

Hitler's understanding, reaction and views on how science should be reformed were put into practice early after seizing power; only months afterwards, in the spring of 1933, he started dismissing Jewish scientists from their posts. These jobs would be immediately taken by non-Jewish junior colleagues, many of whom were less qualified and less experienced. In effect, these dismissals constituted one of the first exercises by the state in racial hygiene. Indeed, Hitler was particularly keen on cleansing science and technology; it is a sad fact that German science allowed this to happen, but, in many ways, they really had little choice, although there was some protest. Hitler had quickly established those willing to make sure his plans were carried out from the start, for example, Hermann Goering, Minister of Aviation and Prussian Minister of the Interior, now controlled the police with wide-ranging powers against opponents.

There were also early indications suggesting how Hitler was to reshape the academic and intellectual life of the scientific community with the closure of publishing houses, or alternatively converting them through Nazification, and the establishment of the Reich Chamber of Culture in pursuit of *Gleichschaltung*. Wrapped up in these plans was a key character by the name of Bernhard Rust, a 50 year-old who, in February 1933, was appointed Prussian Minister for Culture with responsibility for science and education;

Rust was to bring particular despair to the world of many scientists. He started as he meant to go on with the following statement: 'Everybody must recognize that what we are experiencing is not a change of direction but the fundamental fact that the German people is waking up to itself. This movement is progressing relentlessly until one day the whole German people will have been won over to the new cause and will have created for itself its own organisations for politics, the economy, and culture.' Most significantly, perhaps, was the added comment that: 'Our Gleichschaltung means that the new German ideology, as the only valid one, will assume the supreme position over all the others.'

It was after Rust's February 1933 appointment, on 10 March, that Einstein realized he could never return to Germany. Einstein's parting words were that 'civil liberty, tolerance, and equality of all citizens before the law had vanished in Germany, and that justice was now in the power of a raw and rabid mob of Nazi militia.' Following his resignation from the Prussian Academy of Sciences on 28 March, pre-empting the decision of Rust to expel him, Einstein said: 'The conduct of German intellectuals as a group was no better than rabble.' After Einstein's departure, Rust quickly rose up the ranks to cause even more trouble for science and education.

This ideology was a major driving force in Nazi science generally, including physics, with more than a little help along the way from Heinrich Himmler himself. In the case of Himmler, who, by the closing years of the war, had complete control over science through his SS, far too much of this ideology was based on just about no scientific fact, extremely unconventional ideas and what can only be described as pure pseudo-science.

The following month, the new regime passed a law for the Restoration of the Career Civil Service (*Gesetz zur Wiederherstellung des Berufbearmtentums*), throwing Socialists and non-Aryans out of their civil service jobs. Under this law, a non-Aryan was defined as somebody with one parent or grandparent non-Aryan, so as to include even those with one-quarter Jewish blood. As most scientists, academics and members of the Kaiser Wilhelm Institutes were technically civil servants, along with about 1,000 university teachers, this would have consequences for them in the form of instant dismissals. Overseeing this was Hitler, who refused to acknowledge the obvious damage this would bring not only to science but to his war efforts. As a result, the spring of 1933 saw hundreds of scientists dismissed from their jobs throughout German universities and scientific institutions.

Also overseeing all this was Rust, who himself was once dismissed as a schoolteacher for suspected mental instability and for being accused of abusing a schoolgirl. It has even been suggested this may have been due to a head wound he received in the First World War, for which he was awarded the Iron Cross. Subsequently, he had been unemployed since 1930. Whatever the reason, Rust was now doing well under the Nazis, and by 1934 he had been elected to the Reichstag, rapidly rising to the rank of four-star general (Obergruppenfuhrer) and by the following year had been appointed Reich Minister for Science, Education, and Popular Culture. With perhaps a sense of revenge for his dismissal as a schoolteacher, he would gloat that overnight he had 'liquidated the school as an institution of intellectual acrobatics'.

Two of the top nuclear physicists working on atomic power and the bomb were Otto Hahn and Lise Meitner, colleagues at the Kaiser Wilhelm Institute of Chemistry. Hahn was away in the United States lecturing at Cornell University, leaving Meitner as acting director of the institute in his absence, which included overseeing twenty-five scientists and experiencing Hitler's brownshirts, who promptly invaded the buildings. Within days of the 5 March election, Meitner wrote to Hahn to inform him about what was happening back home at the Kaiser Wilhelm Gesellschaft/Kaiser Wilhelm Society (KWG). In her letter, she said: 'Today the accounting office ordered us to estimate the cost of our national flag because it is to be replaced with a black/white/red one which the KWG will pay for.' In a further letter 2 weeks later, she informed Hahn that: 'Everything and everyone is influenced by the political upheavals. Already last week we were notified by the KWG that along with the black/white/red flag, we must also display the swastika.' She also added: 'It must have been very difficult for Haber to raise the swastika.'

One young colleague of Meitner's who had left Germany of his own accord, like Einstein, was Leo Szilard. He was of Hungarian-Jewish descent and, although there was no immediate threat to him, he was wise to follow in Einstein's footsteps. Cancelling his lecture series with Meitner, Szilard first headed to Austria, then Britain, eventually arriving in the United States complete with his life savings hidden in his shoes. He later told of how he was fortunate to leave on the day he did, just a few days after the Reichstag arson attack that was believed to have been ordered by Hitler. He said: 'I took the train from Berlin to Vienna on a certain date, close to 1 April. The train was empty. The same train on the next day was overcrowded and was stopped at the frontier. People had to get out and everybody was interrogated by the Nazis.' He summed up events nicely by adding: 'This just goes to show that if you want to succeed in this world you don't have to be much cleverer than other people, you just have to be one day earlier than most people.' Things could have been quite different for Szilard, who later joined Einstein in convincing the president of the United States, Franklin D. Roosevelt, that the Nazis could develop the atomic bomb, and do so before the Allies. He would go on to be one of the main physicists involved in the Manhattan Project to develop the bomb for the Allies.

Meanwhile, others loyal to Hitler were taking their own control of the situation, including the two right-wing physicists Philipp Lenard and Johannes Stark. Having shown their true colours throughout the 1920s, they now showed their allegiance to Hitler, the 'celebrated Aryan genius', as they had put it. Now in a position to continue their efforts under the Fuhrer, they took a new pride of place, and with it matters worsened for German physicists. Lenard had a meeting with Hitler to tell of the deplorable state of German science in the universities and that it needed to be reformed. Not surprisingly, he was quick to offer his services to secure appropriate posts for suitable Germanic physicists. Hitler's reaction to this meeting is not on record but it would be easy to imagine his response; we can certainly gain many clues from events that unfolded following that meeting. Lenard's partner in crime, Stark, sought control of the Emergency Foundation with its authority over funding and choice of research programmes, as well as the presidency of the

Physikalisch-Technische Reichsanstalt (PTR), which he got in May 1933. At last, Stark's many failed attempts to control scientific funding and failed attempts to become head of various scientific establishments during the 1920s was turning in his favour, but he would not have it all his own way.

Following this move, it is no great surprise that Lenard then welcomed the appointment of Stark, writing in the Nazi newspaper *Volkischer Beobachter*: 'It signifies a definite renunciation of the apparently already inescapable predominance of what might briefly be called Einsteinian thinking in physics; and it is a move towards reaffirming the scientist's old prerogatives to think independently, guided only by nature.' He added: 'Einstein's theories were already falling to pieces, which is the due fate of unnatural products.' Of course, in reality, Einstein's theories were gaining proof throughout science at this time. What we actually had here was a predictable cherry-picking of details, anti-Semitism and a twisted ideology fuelled by the Nazi regime because of Einstein's world fame, all of which allowed the Nazi propaganda to gain ground.

Having secured the appointment of president to the PTR, Stark also become president of the German Research Foundation by 1934; together with Lenard, he now controlled the universities. Moreover, this allowed them to also develop their own research programmes along the lines of Aryan science in general and Aryan physics in particular. Not surprisingly, what this amounted to was a general preference for applied or experimental physics over that of pure theoretical research. There was, however, a fly in the ointment for Stark and his attempts to manipulate the situation, which appeared in the form of Rust. Rust had wangled his appointment of a supreme ministerial post controlling education, science and culture, securing the position by methods similar to those used by Lenard and Stark. As a result, Stark would find himself in conflict with large power-brokering members of the Nazi cartels. Of course, this was really no surprise, given that most of these appointments to positions of power had Hitler's involvement somewhere along the line; he felt it advantageous to have this type of rivalry and infighting within his regime. With so many individuals jostling for positions of power or simply grabbing power, and many with overlapping responsibilities driven by personal agenda, Stark found his plans suffering. For example, his dream of a super version of the PTR with as many as fifty large institutes and 300 laboratories manned with thousands of personnel came to nothing. Instead, he had to settle for securing an assortment of research programmes with military applications involving the Luftwaffe (Air Force) and Wehrmacht (German Army).

In August 1934, Hitler combined the offices of president and chancellor following President Hindenburg's death, and with that effectively became unchallenged dictator. With this, he was able to extend his plans for science, particularly applied physics over Jewish theoretical physics. This also allowed Stark the opportunity to further impose propaganda that was going around at the time to secure further support from the physicists that remained in Germany. Once again, Stark met with failure when many of the big names in physics refused to give their support on the grounds that science and politics had nothing to do with each other. This distancing of science and politics further angered Stark, but it did allow him the opportunity to drag Einstein into the argument, and his plans, again. Stark's abrupt and abrasive response was that praising Einstein while at the same time refusing to support the Fuhrer was indeed a political act. However, physicists were not so easily intimidated and remained determined that politics would not rule science, regarding both as separate entities.

By the following month, allegiance to the Fuhrer was effectively imposed upon the civil servants; they were now required to take an oath of loyalty to the Fuhrer and because physicists in universities were technically civil servants, they were also required to take the oath. However, some refused to do so for as long as possible, with Heisenberg leaving it as long as the following year. This action by Heisenberg may be telling given what we know about the man, his enigma and his involvement in the Nazi atomic bomb project. Intriguingly, Heisenberg also took part in a conference at Hanover during September 1934 where theoretical physics was the theme and Einstein's theories were wholeheartedly endorsed and further promoted. As a result of these actions, Lenard and Stark were now also firmly opposed to Heisenberg, as they continued to seek out those who supported Jewish science; Heisenberg was in for years of further vitriolic offerings from both.

Despite the opposition to the way things were going, in particular towards Lenard and Stark, not all physicists or, indeed, scientists of other disciplines felt the same about the apolitical position. In fact, just about as soon as the brownshirts entered the universities, a surprisingly large number of scientists started wearing some form or other of Nazi uniform.

It was not only scientists who were subjected to dismissals; mathematicians were also subject to the same treatment. Indeed, Nazi Germany lost many of its distinguished mathematicians in a manner identical to the scientists, and again many of these ended up in Britain or the United States. In 1934, Rust asked the mathematician David Hilbert, who had almost beaten Einstein to the final formulation of general relativity, how Gottingen, one of the world's great institutions for mathematics and theoretical physics, had fared following the dismissal of Jewish scientists and mathematicians. Presumably expecting a positive response along the lines that things had greatly improved now that Jews and Jewish staff had been banished, Hilbert abruptly replied: 'Suffered? It hasn't suffered, minister. It doesn't exist anymore!'

Like physics, mathematics did not lend itself to the parallels of other disciplines such as medicine, genetics and anthropology in being easily shaped to Nazification and the ideology of National Socialism. Nonetheless, like in physics, there were some mathematicians only too eager to give it their best try, at the very least to crowbar it into shape by associations with other disciplines and, of course, to attack Jewish science. German mathematics had a driving desire to see the subject taking its place alongside National Socialist sciences, so there was also a desire to be connected with racial hygiene. That meant if such associations were not seen to be part of the subject of mathematics, it was in danger of being left behind and suffering damage to its reputation as a result of being international and value-neutral. There was also another urgency; Nazi ideology insisted that only those disciplines which directly served the national policy had a right to exist. The problem here was, so far as

Lenard was concerned, mathematics had already been dismissed by him as simply 'the science of counting' and belonged in the humanities. So, in an attempt to save mathematics and prove its place in National Socialism, mathematicians proceeded to write a flood of papers and essays to justify connections between the two.

Ludwig Bieberbach was one such mathematician of repute who set about making the necessary links. Bieberbach appears to have quickly converted to Nazi ideology and anti-Semitism following Hitler's rise to power for, it seemed, no real apparent reason; the only answer seemed to be personal advancement and to stand out, or 'to shine', as the physicist Max Born put it. However, to others the answer was somewhat different. Bieberbach struggled against almost impossible odds to crowbar mathematics into Nazism; many felt it was more likely he was under some kind of pressure to do so. A clue may come from April 1933 when Bieberbach joined the SA (Storm Troopers); it was then that he was promoted to dean of philosophy at Berlin University, which conveniently included mathematics and natural sciences. Consequently, that may be where his pressure to conform came from; it may have simply been payback time.

Certainly, Bieberbach showed how it was possible to adapt himself, and others, through what could be regarded as independent thought, and being a philosopher as well, he was ideally placed to illustrate his art. Many of his ideas were also based on the anthropology of Erich Rudolf Jaensch of Marburg University, which suggested vague connections between psychology and racial types. The German Society of Psychology had also suffered from Jewish dismissals, having had its Jewish board members expelled in April 1933, with the remaining members left infighting to establish their own research programmes and theories. Hitler, not surprisingly, was declared 'a great psychologist' and, in a 1933 keynote speech, a 'bold and emotionally deep Chancellor'. Future meetings of the society focused on racial matters combined with the inevitable twisting of facts to fit Nazi ideology. Bieberbach himself believed that Jewish and French mathematicians had a tendency towards abstraction rather than the truth of hard empirical reality and, importantly, the Nordic intuition which was important to the Nazis bloodline. Nazi mathematics called for a tangible dimension that could be clearly visualized even when it referred to pure mathematics. At the end of the day trying to link mathematics to this racial element of Nazi ideology seemed ad hoc and incapable of proper description or meaning.

There were many other such attempts to bring mathematics into line with Nazi ideology. In January 1936 an essay was written by a colleague of Bieberbach and Nazi supporter, Professor Erhard Tornier, titled *The Reality of German Mathematics,* in which we find the following statement: 'Every theory in pure mathematics is justified which is truly capable of answering concrete questions about real objects.... If not, such theories are... a document of Jewish-liberalistic obfuscation, born of the intellect of rootless artistes who juggle with intangible definitions to simulate mathematical creativity to their unthinking captive audience, which is glad if it can slowly learn a few tricks that it can itself use to show off.' This seems to be aimed at the Jewish science of Einstein again with the views that relativity and its mathematics of geometry have no real substance or reality.

There was another essay which looked at the links between Nordic man and mathematics penned by Claus Heinrich Tietjen. This essay dealt with education and was aimed at schools. He wrote: 'Science teaching therefore brings the school pupil into close contact with two decisive realities of natural life; large-scale war and the question of work. These are just the realities which have begotten the National Socialist movement and for which that movement must fight. All the same, little account has been taken of the fundamental issues in arithmetic books for the Volksschule, and they are also insufficiently brought out in the books for the higher schools. These books are brimful of economic problems and questions about the global economy which breathe much less national spirit. It is both possible and necessary, therefore, to throw out a good deal of ballast which is soon forgotten anyway and is in some cases irrelevant to what is being learnt.' This rejection of ballast was broadly along the lines of Hitler's thinking.

Of course, none of this helped Jewish mathematicians who suffered dismissals too, and in some cases worse. For example, Robert Remak was arrested and detained in 1938 and sent to Sachsenhausen concentration camp. That was only temporary, but he was arrested again in 1942 in Holland and sent to Auschwitz, where he died. Paul Epstein committed suicide in 1939 shortly before war broke out and before the Gestapo caught up with him, and Felix Hausdorff committed suicide in 1942 to avoid being sent to a concentration camp. The Gestapo deported Ludwig Berwald to Lodz, where he died in 1942, as did Walter Froehlich. Stanislaw Saks was murdered by the Gestapo in 1942, as was Juliusz Pawel Schauder in 1943. As for Otto Blumenthal, he ended up in the detention camp Theresienstadt, where he died in 1944. The list goes on and on with many either sent to concentration camps, murdered, deported, or committing suicide before the inevitable consequences caught up with them.

Fortunately, some were lucky enough to escape the country, in similar fashion to key physicists. One such mathematician was John von Neumann, who settled at Princeton University, while Richard Courant and Max Born experienced long journeys to eventually arrive in the United States and Britain, respectively. All of these became a great loss to the German mathematics community, leading to David Hilbert's comment to Rust. Lost also was arguably Germany's greatest pure mathematician, Emmy Noether. She had left Germany in 1933 for a post in the United States at Bryn Mawr. Two years later, she died as a result of an operation, with her departure only marked by a brief mention in the American press. This prompted Einstein to write a letter to the *New York Times,* saying: 'In the judgment of most competent living mathematicians, Fraulein Noether was the most significant creative mathematical genius thus far produced.' The dismissals and general treatment of German mathematicians was as much of a loss to Hitler's war machine as were physicists; it left yet another serious hole in the expertise he would later need to draw upon. It was amongst one of Hitler's early mistakes.

Amongst the physicists departing Germany was Lise Meitner's nephew, Otto Frisch, who had lost his job at the University of Hamburg. His original plan before Hitler's intervention was to first go to Copenhagen to work in Niels Bohr's Physics Institute, then to move onto Britain to work at the University of Birmingham. As for Lise Meitner herself, she decided to stay in Germany following Szilard and others' departures; after all, she was an Austrian citizen and was under no pressure to leave her post or Germany. Of course, like many others, she could have protested the dismissals by resigning, but she decided not to do so. It was later, after the war, that she explained how she regretted her decision not to resign in protest: 'I knew that it was not only stupid but very wrong that I did not leave at once,' she said in 1946. However, in 1938 she did flee Germany. On 12 March 1938, the Wehrmacht entered Austria and, in doing so, enforced its annexation (Auschluss), thus making all Austrian citizens part of the Third Reich. That meant she was now subject to the Nazi race laws in Germany and was now no longer able to depend on her Austrian citizenship to protect her.

Meitner had received many invitations from colleagues to work abroad; however, her dedication to her work had led to a delay in making any decisions amongst the increasing dangers developing around her. Eventually that delay became too long, and she found her Austrian passport was worthless. Moreover, due to her Jewish origins, she was unable to secure a German one. A further problem she faced came from a new law passed by the Nazis which prevented technical specialists from leaving the Reich. Meitner also discovered many of her colleagues at the institute found it difficult to help her, or simply refused to do so because they felt it was safer to side with the Nazi anti-Semitism as a precaution. It was Hans Krebs who summed up the situation while he was working at the laboratories of a hospital in Freiburg at the time. He said: 'Within a few days of Hitler's assumption of power, Nazi uniforms appeared everywhere. Colleagues in the hospital who had admitted at most only mild sympathies with Hitler were suddenly to be seen in the uniforms of Nazi organisations.' This was true of just about all scientific establishments.

Krebs, too, had been on the receiving end of Nazi intimidation. Four months earlier, the dean of the faculty, Professor E. Rehn, had signed a letter in which he had recommended Krebs be appointed as a teacher in the medical faculty. However, on 12 April 1938, Krebs received a second letter from Rehn, this time stating that on the orders of the Ministry of Education he was now on immediate leave of absence. The difference in tone between the two letters was obvious, with Krebs saying: '[It] demonstrated the breakdown of social tenets under ruthless political pressure - threats of being deprived of one's livelihood, of being discredited by public defamation, of being thrown into jail or a concentration camp, or of being murdered.'

Meanwhile, for Meitner, things were still not going well. Kurt Hess, an institute member responsible for the hospitality of visiting scholars, was one of the first to threaten those who spoke out in defence of Meitner. Even her loyal colleague, Hahn, was cautious about defending her; indeed, he told her she should no longer be a member of the institute. He did suggest that she might be able to continue her research there unofficially. Meitner would never forgive him.

Meitner's fortunes did change for the better when one of her colleagues, Carl Bosch, came to her rescue. He applied for a permit allowing foreign travel based on the many outstanding invitations she had to visit colleagues abroad. Amongst these many invites was one from Holland as well as one from Bohr's institute in Copenhagen and others from Cambridge, England. It was thought one of these might give her an escape route from Nazi Germany. Bosch made his application to the authorities on 22 May, stating: 'Miss Meitner is non-Aryan, nevertheless, with the concurrence of all the official departments she has been allowed to retain her position as she is engaged in important scientific discoveries.' Interestingly, these important scientific discoveries included nuclear physics that was vital to the development of the atomic bomb, research that was eventually completed with the help of her nephew, Otto Frisch, but for the Allies after her escape from Germany. Unfortunately, the application was somewhat forcefully rejected with the statement: 'There are political objections to the issuing of a passport to Professor Meitner. It is considered undesirable that renowned Jews should leave Germany for abroad to act there against the interests of Germany according to their inner persuasion as representatives of German science or even with their reputation and experience.'

It was then left to Dutch physicist Dirk Coster to come to her rescue. He offered her a post for at least one year at Groningen University. The problem now was getting her out of Germany by less-official blessing. On the eve of her departure, she continued her routine as usual so as not to attract attention that she was about to do a bunk for Holland. Packing two small cases and spending a sleepless night at the home of Hahn, she prepared to leave Germany. Hahn, now more sympathetic to her plight, gave her his mother's diamond ring as a source of finance; those leaving Germany for abroad could not take more than ten marks with them.

Meanwhile Coster waited at Berlin's railway station but was careful not to draw attention to the situation by making contact with Meitner on account of ever-watchful Gestapo agents. A 7-hour train journey ended at the border with Holland, with both arriving safely. Days earlier, Coster had visited the border immigration officers with Meitner's official entrance permit and asked that they allow her to pass using what was described as 'friendly persuasion'. She passed the border guards with no problem. When the train arrived at Groningen, Coster made contact with Meitner and they went to his waiting car. Coster later sent a telegram to Hahn saying: 'The baby has arrived.'

However, not all went as planned. Coster's hope of securing a post for Meitner fell through, so she moved on to Stockholm to take up an offer of work at Manne Siegbahn's new laboratory, not far from Niels Bohr's institute in neighbouring Denmark. A few years later, in 1942, Jews in Holland were being sent to concentration death camps, so her failure to secure a position of work in Holland might have been a blessing in disguise. Meitner went on to play a key role for the Allies with the fission (splitting) of the uranium atom and the subsequent development of the atom bomb.

Interestingly, in amongst all this trouble, there was actually a form of exemption for Jewish scientists; initially they were allowed to apply for this exemption if they had been employed before the First World War, had fought in the war, or lost a father or son in the war. However, the idea was not attractive to many scientists because they did not like the idea of having to ask for permission to continue to serve their country after so many years of loyal service in the first war. Unfortunately, many later discovered this exemption would hamper both their chances of survival in the academic world and as a scientist. At the end of the day, this exemption did not amount to much anyway because Jews would still be persecuted whether they were scientists or anyone else. Indeed, that is exactly what they experienced if they applied for exemption and remained in Germany; they found themselves on the receiving end of intense intimidation, relentless heckling and general treachery from colleagues and students. The added incentive for such intimidation was if a Jewish academic was forced out of their job, those who had been the perpetrators of such acts would easily take up the now-vacant post for their own good.

That said, there were rare examples of refusals to take over a post from a dismissed or sacked Jewish scientist. One such example occurred at the University of Dusseldorf, when the biologist Otto Krayer rejected the offer of a chair that had fallen vacant as a result of a Jewish colleague being sacked. Indeed, Krayer even complained to the government. Not surprisingly, he, too, was sacked and had to depart for the United States. Another example was the geneticist Kurt Kosswig who refused to apply the racist doctrines of the Nazi regime and denounced the treatment of Jews. He managed to escape the country shortly before attempts to arrest him.

There were also objectors amongst the big names of science, like Max Born, director of the Institute of Theoretical Physics in Gottingen, and Nobel Prize–winner James Franck, a war veteran and one of Fritz Haber's poison gas colleagues. Another to object to the way Jews and Jewish scientists were treated was Max Planck. Indeed, it is something that Hahn claims Planck said that sums up the situation: 'If today 30 professors get up and protest against the government, by tomorrow there will be also one hundred and fifty individuals declaring their solidarity with Hitler simply because they're after the jobs.' In short, complaints made to the government would simply be dismissed, or the complainant would suffer the consequences.

Given details from a later meeting with Hitler, it is quite likely Planck did openly express such views. In his 1947 transcript of his meeting with Hitler, Planck said he told the Fuhrer 'that there were different sorts of Jews, some valuable and some valueless for mankind among the former old families of exemplary German culture and that one had to make distinctions in such matters'. Hitler replied: 'That's not right! A Jew is a Jew, all Jews cling together like burrs. Whatever one Jew is, other Jews of all types immediately gather.' As Hitler's thunderous temper started to appear he said: 'Our national policies will not be revoked or modified, even for scientists.' He continued his rant with: 'If the dismissal of Jewish scientists means the annihilation of contemporary German science, then we shall do without science for a few years.' Planck also commented that the work of Jewish scientists carried an importance for Germany and it would be no less than an act of self-mutilation to force valuable Jews to emigrate, and that foreign countries would be the first to reap the benefits. Planck wrote that Hitler did not respond to this observation, instead he went into one of his angry rants, speaking faster and faster. As he continued to rant, he started slapping his knee with a powerful blow, while saying things like: 'People say that I sometimes suffer from weak nerves. That's slander, I have nerves of steel.' Hitler was working himself up into such a rage that Planck felt he had no alternative but to gracefully retreat from the conversation and take his leave.

From that point on, all Planck could do was try to convince his Jewish colleagues not to leave Germany but to wait for better times. Of course, better times did not come under Hitler's regime; quite the opposite. Planck appears to have tried to act as diplomatically as possible in this matter for both sides, but he was also putting himself in danger by trying to resolve this matter, especially when confronting Hitler to his face. He was aware he could not go too far or protest too much.

Planck's objections had appeared at an early stage. The year following Hitler's rise to power Planck opened the new Kaiser Wilhelm Institute of Metals where he gave a speech. As he approached the rostrum the audience waited for him to begin with the Nazi salute and the words 'Heil Hitler'. It was clear that Planck was in two minds about doing so. He started by half raising his arm, twice. It was only on the third attempt that he managed to raise his arm to a full salute and say before the audience 'Heil Hitler'. Many commented later that there was really no choice; he had no option but to obey. From that point on Planck would give the salute with observers saying he managed to do so with greater comfort and confidence as time passed. He also took to the habit of signing official documents with the words Heil Hitler. Following these episodes Planck would always encourage people to remain on good terms with the Hitler regime.

Einstein could not bring himself to be angry with Planck. In the usual formal and respectful style he used whenever writing to him he said: 'In spite of everything, I am happy that you greet me in old friendship and that even the greatest stresses have failed to cloud our mutual relations.' He added: 'These continue in their ancient beauty and purity, regardless of what, in a manner of speaking, is happening further below.'

There was one story that showed how being a Jew was really all there was in Hitler's mind when it came to rejection, even if the individual had shown loyalty to Germany stretching back to the First World War as required with the so-called exemption. The episode involves the poison gas scientist Fritz Haber. In Haber's case, he had started by encouraging his colleagues to help Hitler and the war effort. He had also attempted to turn his back on his Jewish past by converting to Christianity. However, none of this impressed Hitler. So far as the case of conversion to Christianity is concerned, Hitler had trouble with that faith and how he saw its connections to science. In short, it was not going to do Haber any good at all. We know Hitler's view was 'a Jew is a Jew' and as far as he and his regime were concerned, Haber was still a Jew. At this time Planck was president of the Kaiser Wilhelm Society, where Haber was forced to resign as president of the Kaiser Wilhelm Institute of Physical Chemistry. At his meeting with Hitler about Jewish scientists, Planck also asked that Hitler himself put in a good word for Haber, but given the way that meeting went, Haber's fate was sealed on many levels. As a result, his work for Germany during the First World War obviously counted for nothing.

Haber always regarded himself as German and had always put Germany first while serving the country as a scientist. In the end, Haber was lucky that he escaped with just a dismissal but he nevertheless felt that he had no way to continue his loyalty and concluded his only option was to leave the country. Haber wrote a letter to Richard Willstatter, in which he said at his time of life he felt he could not start a new career abroad. In summing it up he wrote: 'I am bitter as never before.' Even Einstein wrote to him from the United States, saying: 'I can conceive of your inner conflicts. It is somewhat like having to give up a theory on which one has worked one's whole life. It is not the same for me because I never believed in it in the least.' Another problem for Haber was Hitler did not particularly favour gas attacks; he favoured hand-to-hand combat, finding gas attacks particularly distasteful.

Haber did have some comfort in the only thing left for him which was to help his fellow Jewish scientists find alternative work abroad. He departed for Cambridge, England, where he met up again with a fellow poison gas scientist William Pope, professor of chemistry. On the whole, Haber was not welcomed in England, which was no surprise given his record during the First World War. He therefore accepted a post in Palestine at the Daniel Sieff Institute (now the Weizmann Institute). Einstein then wrote again to him to warn against working with the Hebrew University; however, he never made it to his new life; he died in Switzerland from heart disease at the age of sixty-five while he was visiting family in January 1934. The Haber Institute for Physical Chemistry in Berlin still bears his name and controversy to this day.

The end result of this mass dismissal and mass exodus of scientists from Hitler's regime is best summed up by Planck. He pointed out that the exodus of Jewish scientists had devastating consequences for Germany. A quarter of the pre-1933 physics community was now lost. Einstein had gone, as had Born, Frank, Gabor, Hess, Stein, Hevesy, Hertz, Debye, Bloch, Schrodinger, Herzberg, Wignar, Bethe, and Gustov, all of whom were Nobel Laureates. Amongst the mathematicians were Richard Courant, Emmy Noether, and Hermann Weyl. All of these were original thinkers, highly experienced, highly qualified and irreplaceable. In the end, half of the country's theoretical physicists had gone including top experts in quantum mechanics and nuclear physics. The huge loss to Hitler's regime was an even greater gain for Britain and the United States.

As war loomed, there was a further problem for Hitler: the German scientific community was becoming ever more isolated, foreign powers were no longer sending scientists to the country and collaboration was no longer possible. There were also cancellations of memberships to scientific societies and subscriptions to scientific journals. Within the regime itself there was restrictions on scientists who wanted to travel out of Germany, as we saw with Meitner. These problems would only worsen with time. The Nazi regime retaliated by introducing measures to block any co-operation with scientific establishments considered inappropriate to National Socialism.

With many of the theoretical physicists now gone from Germany, Hitler was able to move away from Jewish science and concentrate on applied physics, experimentation and trial and error in developing his war machine. Despite the dismissals, the actual numbers working in universities did not drop dramatically overall, but what did decline was the quality of work, expertise and experience, with a shift to applied physics and a decline in basic research. Numbers would increase further as Hitler's ambitions grew throughout the 1930s and into the war years, but it was always to suffer from the mass exodus of all those big names. The university that lost out the most was the world centre of mathematical physics, Gottingen, the university famous for much of the theoretical physics developed in Germany up to Hitler taking power. They, together with all other universities and institutions, declined, except for Berlin.

In Britain, however, full advantage was being taken of these dismissals and fleeing scientists. For example, an Academic Assistance Council was being set up by William Beveridge, A.V. Hill, and Nobel Laureate in biology Frederick Gowland Hopkins to help provide jobs for the displaced German scientists. Beveridge would later head the London School of Economics. One of Beveridge's closest associates in this project would be Leo Szilard, who helped to secure positions for the dismissed German scientists before moving on to the United States in 1938 to convince President Roosevelt, together with Einstein, to start work on the atomic bomb before the Nazis. Szilard later worked on the Manhattan Project.

As Hitler turned his thoughts to the conquest of Europe, a key scientific area occupied his mind, the power and scope of applied science and its role in the war effort which was based somewhat on the values of the golden years of German science. Indeed, there was an obvious attempt by Hitler to build on those years and their achievements to some extent. However, what he did not appreciate was how that had been achieved through structure, organization and co-operation. Nevertheless, Hitler was keenly interested in weapons and at times was surprisingly quick to grasp details of new ideas and developments presented to him, but it was often selective and difficult to interpret. Many of those closest to Hitler claimed he would listen to some extremely long and complicated technical explanation and summarize it in a short, concise and understandable way, but much of our understanding about him, scientifically speaking, makes this hard to accept. However, despite this claim there was also that interesting observation that at times he appeared to 'tune out' from his surroundings during demonstrations.

Underlying this was a deeply worrying appreciation of science. For example, there were serious blockages which in later years would also manifest in his tactical and military judgment. One such blockage took the form of a stubborn refusal to see the full advantages put before him, let alone take them onboard, and this also applied to science. This blockage was something he never lost from the days of his schooling. In some ways, this science and pseudo-science mix may explain many of his reactions to technological advances during demonstrations and discussions; there appeared to be a battle going on between the two in his mind.

Hitler's grasp of science and exactly what scientists do as well as how results are arrived at was extremely worrying; it was narrow and, above all, it was ill-informed. A particular mental blockage was in propositions and metaphysics, where Hitler had the inability to distinguish between the two, regarding them as essentially the same thing. Moreover, he regarded them as tools for immediate temporary solutions rather than seeing the long-term bigger picture. Furthermore, experimentation and empirical techniques were areas of understanding in which he found himself severely lacking. As if this weren't bad enough, there was a further problem whereby educational training was seen by him as nothing more than just accumulating facts, a view that puts Bernhard Rust and his efforts into perspective. That said, arguably the most serious part of his scientific thinking hinged on a complete lack of understanding when it came to the freedom scientists needed to do their jobs, a feature which would run throughout his dictatorship, culminating in his devastating decision to allow Himmler's SS to take absolute control over scientific research. Eventually experimentation would be important to Nazi physics and its development, for example, in aviation and rocketry, but not without considerable problems involving how that was achieved thanks to the cartel.

A further clue hinting at things to come is found in comments by Speer who said Hitler was 'anti-modern in decisions on armament'. For example, Hitler opposed the machine gun. In later years this thinking by Hitler was explained by Speer: 'It made soldiers cowardly and made close combat impossible.' Hitler was also said to be opposed to jet propulsion because he thought its extreme speed was an obstacle to aerial combat. Nevertheless, jet propulsion did see advances by German physicists and engineers, as did the development of atomic power and attempts to produce an atomic bomb, although the latter was far less advanced than jet power by the end of the war. That was caused by it being heavily dependent on theoretical physics: partly due to the loss of Jewish physicists, and partly due to the way Heisenberg went about things. As we saw, according to Speer, it was summed up by Hitler as 'a spawn of Jewish pseudo-science'. However, despite this situation, there was actually much conventional science that became important to his ideal and was pursued in the form of mostly applied science; even here, there were familiar problems.

The course of the Second World War saw remarkable advances in new technologies, many of which were war-winners; although due to experimentation there was some failure, especially on the side of Germany. There were advances in aviation, rocketry, radar, computers and radio communication between land forces, ground-to-air and air-to-air. There were also developments with weapons from the First World War including tanks, submarines, guns and cannons. In fact, to a veteran of the previous world war, many of the weapons used in the Second World War would look familiar. There were also weapons still in development as the war drew to an end. For example, despite phenomenal advances in rocketry, there were still problems with guidance and power required for the ever-increasing weight of payloads; such advances were left to the future Cold War. The same was true of radar; starting in the 1930s, the development made great advances, particularly on the British side, but proved to still be relatively primitive compared to post-war developments. There were also advances in automatic weapons and their efficiency, including new designs of clips and magazines allowing rapid fire. Despite advances, much of the fighting in all theatres of war was performed with conventional technology developed during the 1930s and rapidly brought up to optimum efficiency as the war progressed. That said, lingering in the background was that impressive list of new ideas both scientifically sound, as well as some more unsound and even harebrained.

Germany's tactical efforts had developed in the pre-war years, focussing on tanks, aircraft, artillery and the mobilization of troops and their carriers, or Blitzkrieg, with concentrated efforts in punching holes in the enemy's defences and rapid outflanking movements. There was also the idea of gigantism, when conventional machines of war were built bigger and bigger as a fear factor, supported by Hitler. As expected, Hitler missed the point because of his misunderstanding of science and engineering. For example, in Germany there was an 80cm gun, called Dora, requiring 4,400 personnel to operate it while mounted on a railway track; it ended its days rusting away after firing only 48 shells at the siege of Sevastopol in June 1942. There was also a gun more than 90m long known as the V3 which worked on the principle of several explosions along the barrel to propel the shell; it was overengineered and not the success the Nazis had hoped. The V3 was erected on the Channel coast to fire at London but, like Dora it failed in its expectations, only being used against Luxemburg.

Another example of gigantism came with the tank; it was a huge beast but slow moving and amounted to a pile box on wheels. It was another failure. However, the redevelopment of conventional-sized tanks was more successful. Both sides of the war had been improving their tanks during the 1930s, developing them beyond the ponderous models seen in the First World War. The Germans concentrated production on their Mark II and Mark IV versions, finding efficiency by deploying them as massed Panzer divisions, particularly in Poland, France and early in the invasion of Russia; this weapon was particularly effective with the open, flat spaces of Northern Europe and grasslands of Russia. Such advances, together with superior German tactics, enabled the Wehrmacht to bring the Red Army to the brink of defeat in the early stages of the invasion with 3,500 German tanks rolling back about 15,000 Russian vehicles. At least this was something of an achievement for Hitler, because he had a relatively small, mechanized army supported by a much larger one, amounting to nineteenth century means of transport involving 700,000 horses and railways.

This virtual destruction of the Russian armoured divisions forced them to design a new generation of tanks mimicking the German tactics used against them, in some cases becoming superior: the T34 was built for speed, whereas the KV-I and the later Stalin were designed for firepower. By 1943, the Russians would carry two-way radios, augmenting the battle tactics. These designs were reliable and robust, as well as being highly standardized and speedily mass-produced, something gigantism had failed to deliver.

A further advantage over the Germans was the way the Russians maintained their forces; their tank armies were accompanied by skilled and well-equipped motorized maintenance teams. The Germans retaliated with their Panzer divisions like the Panther, which was the equal of the T34, followed by the Tiger, which was supposedly superior.

However, during the second half of 1942, the German tanks were rushed into service, which made them cumbersome and technically complex. Moreover, they were plagued by another Nazi problem as they proved to be difficult to mass-produce and repair.

Interestingly, this turnaround by the Russians appears to explain Hitler's racist views towards them. Some of the most extraordinary ideas Hitler held regarding science and technology were connected with Russia; views that probably swung the war away from him and into the hands of the Allies. One belief was that the Russians were incapable of fighting a technological war. Blinded by racial prejudice, he believed the Russians were incapable of making things; indeed, he would often declare, 'Russians never invented anything'. Nonetheless, he did accept they were quite capable of copying things—a conclusion probably reached by the fact the Russians had designed their new generation of tanks by mimicking the German tactics. But when it came to actually inventing things in the first place, Hitler believed they were incapable. There was a further belief that they were incapable of systematic thought and organization. Moreover, should any qualities to the opposite emerge, it was due to the little Aryan blood that coursed through their veins. This belief did not stop with the Russians; Hitler declared regarding the Chinese and Japanese: 'These people are inferior to us. In the sphere of chemistry, for example, it's been proved that everything comes to them from us.' It is almost certain these beliefs came from the golden years of German chemistry and the horrors of chemical warfare during the First World War, it also showed again his inability to grasp science and his ability to twist the facts where necessary towards an Aryan answer.

At the time Russia was showing its superiority over Germany with its tank designs, production and maintenance skills, Hitler was commandeering a prodigious collection of vehicles from all over occupied Europe. It is believed over 2,000 vehicle models were then used against the Russians, requiring over a million spare parts in tow. One battle had 96 types of personnel carriers and 111 types of truck, together with 37 different types of motorcycles. All these were vulnerable to breakdown because of the terrain, mud produced in battle, rain, and the harsh Russian winter; this was a far cry from the organized efforts of the Russians. Moreover, Russian training and tactics proved the T34 a good match for German armour in battles like Kursk and Stalingrad, greatly improving matters by the autumn of 1944. Given the production skills of the Russians they achieved a numerical advantage over the Germans of three to one by 1943, spelling disaster for Hitler's armies, his racist views and scientific abilities. This was followed in 1944 with a numerical advantage for the Allies with the Sherman tank.

Aircraft research, development and production were also expanded. For example, one scientific advance of note was with jet propulsion, developed by Germany as well as Britain. However, for Germany, these new technologies needed time to evolve; time that the war did not fully allow. Matters were also bogged down by bureaucracy, infighting, corruption and lack of raw materials and energy.

In the early days, there were certainly technological challenges with aircraft, particularly to produce single-engine, single-wing fighters that could fly faster and further, carry heavier armour and provide greater firepower than the enemy. A further challenge was to produce bombers with greater range and the ability to carry ever-greater bomb loads. At this same time, developments were required for synchronization with radar and communications to allow for air-to-air detection, accurate targeting and organization; for communications, this was also required between bases and other aircraft.

German aviation was motivated by speed, with Britain catching up thanks to the Rolls-Royce Merlin engine developed in 1938. By 1940, Merlin had proved extremely reliable, first being cooled by evaporation systems working off condensers in the wings, then ethylene glycol, which was more effective than water. This situation was also aided by better fuels produced in the United States, giving speed a further boost, further augmented by sophisticated superchargers. Germany had its own advantages but never really equalled many developments by the Allies while struggling with its own bureaucracy and internal problems. Nevertheless, there was plenty of money ploughed into aircraft manufacturing, allowing scientists and engineers to indulge their wildest dreams in aircraft design. However, many exotic designs like the Horten 229 (reportedly) stealth aircraft came too late, despite being based on uncontroversial ideas from early in the war. This showed how experimentation in exotic ideas did not fully take off until around 1943 and 1944, when the SS had just about full power over scientific projects.

Although Germany's general problem involving lack of co-operation between industry and academia was obviously a result of Hitler's mindset in that area, there was some collaboration between the army and academia, including aircraft design and the rocket programme. In the mid-1930s, the rocket programme involved contributions from Dr Rudolf Hermann, who was an assistant at the *Technische Hochschale* at Aachen. Here, he worked on sub-scale rocket models at the university's wind tunnel. Hermann was most definitely a Nazi and it is here that a departure from academia was apparent. He was presented with irresistible prospects if he went over to working at Peenemunde, which had been designed for rocket research even before the outbreak of war. Other members of the *Technische Hochschale*, especially from Dresden and Darmstadt, joined Hermann, where they worked on guidance system technology.

When at Peenemunde, Hermann was required to construct larger and more powerful wind tunnels. These were completed in the autumn of 1939, just as war between Britain and Germany was declared. These wind tunnels would prove beneficial for both the aerodynamic designs of rockets and aircraft, building on the pre-war love of gliding and rocketry within Germany. Rocketry and aviation were now combined with the forming of an alliance with Goering. From the unconventional side of things, it is also said that Peenemunde helped in the design of disc-shaped aircraft, or flying saucers. However, Goering's alliance would eventually break down, partly due to him losing the Battle of Britain and partly due to priority going over to the development of the A-4 rocket (later known as the V-2). It was only at this point that Hitler saw the potential of rocket development, and as such the rocket had replaced the aircraft as a weapon of mass destruction. That said, in Britain the aircraft, together with advances in onboard radar, would serve as a better weapon of mass destruction towards Germany with better-targeted carpet bombing from about the same time of 1943 onwards.

Eventually, three supersonic wind tunnels were built, beginning with 60 staff, rising to 200 by 1943, then rising further to 9,000. With these developments, the Peenemunde directors tried to bring together all aspects of rocketry and aviation under one roof; the idea was to design, develop and mass-produce these weapons from raw materials coming in at one end to the firing of the finished product at the other end. This was a goal set for an SS general, Hans Kammler, who was in charge of many such all-in-one fortresses, designing many with Hitler's blessing (we will expand on this later).

Wind tunnels were also used in submarine development, providing better designs for U-boats. The German navy enjoyed enormous advantages over Britain's merchant shipping in the Atlantic, pushing their submarine technology to its limits before the build-up to British radar and code-breaking developments from around 1943; these would eventually help defeat the U-boats. However, before these advances, the Atlantic lanes were still perilous for the U-boats, partly due to enemy attack and partly due to their submarine technology not always being successful. Again, the latter was sometimes due to new experimental devices and a mix of pseudo-science. However, one area where they did have significant success was with new aerodynamic designs, thanks to the rocket wind tunnels. Added to this were additional approaches to increase speed by other methods, but again this sometimes employed a mix of conventional ideas and pseudo-scientific beliefs, and difficulties with equipment were often made more problematic due to rushed deployment.

Experiments with wind tunnels were carried out by marine engineer Helmut Walter using applied mathematics to discover new streamlined hulls. Eventually, Walter's work resulted in a type of submarine known as electro boats, and with the approval of Hitler, 7,000 vessels were ordered by Admiral Doenitz. Unfortunately, with time against them, these ocean-going U-boats were another example of war machines that never saw the light of day.

Nevertheless, Walter did have other ideas to improve U-boats. One such idea considered before the war involved a system to release oxygen from hydrogen peroxide. This 1930s invention was supposed to allow diesel engines to work while submerged by decomposing pure hydrogen peroxide with a catalyst of permanganate. The diesel fuel was injected into a reaction chamber to combust with the oxygen, where it produced steam and other gases at high temperature, powering the turbines. Following this reaction, the steam and gases would be ejected from the submarine. Again, this was aimed at increasing speed rather than submersion time, which was one of Walter's early goals; in fact, early prototypes achieved speeds of 28 knots compared with the top conventional speed of 10 knots, but it was not without its problems.

Possibly with his usual lack of scientific understanding, Hitler authorized construction of two Walter prototypes early in the war; the project was plagued with long-term problems, along with a lack of urgency as a result of the huge success of alternatives like the U-boat

VII and XI series. There was also a further problem with the hydrogen peroxide, which was not a renewable source of power in the same way as rechargeable batteries. It was also a somewhat exotic source of power that had more priority in the rocket programme's development of the A-4; this produced a shortage for use in submarine research. Walter also had a problem with the limited space available in submarines; there was not enough room for both tanks of hydrogen peroxide and rechargeable batteries. That problem meant a further development was needed to find a way to replenish hydrogen peroxide tanks at sea, which left the U-boats open to further attacks. On top of the low priority given to the project, there was a further blow when the building of production plants required for developing the prototypes was also given low priority. A final setback came in March 1942 when Walter's development of the ocean-going test bed, the U-791, was destroyed in a bombing raid on Kiel.

As a result of all these setbacks, Walter's engineering skills were instead applied to upgrading classes of submarines with an improved snorkel (*schnorchel*) known, and hated, by crews as the 'snort'. This was composed of two tubes that could be raised like a periscope when submerged; one tube sucked in air to assist the diesel engines while the other expelled exhaust. This was not a new idea and had been experimented with since the beginning of the century during the golden years of German science. The German version was now based on a Dutch design from the 1930s, but it was far from perfect.

Amongst the many problems with the design was one that occurred when submerged by waves. It was then the snort sucked air from the submarine interior and released its exhaust inside the submarine. It was also the case that early versions used double the fuel and made a lot of noise, making them vulnerable to sonar detection. Walter made changes using valves, but it was far from satisfactory and was only a temporary fix; it then caused a vacuum within the U-boat when it jammed. Attempts to unjam the valves proved difficult, causing men to gasp for air with bulging eyes. Attempts would then be made to detach the snorkel's float, which was often unsuccessful, making breathing even more difficult and suffocation imminent. The best the captains could do was to order the crew to lie low on the floor. If the crew was lucky enough to detach the float, it would do so with a snap, causing air to be sucked back into the U-boat with a long sigh; the sudden pressure change resulted in burst eardrums and extreme pain. At the end of the day, these improvements were rushed and far from successful.

Interestingly, there does seem to be evidence for submarine improvements, including the hydrogen peroxide research, seeing the light of day. There is a declassified document with the title 'Production and Further Investigation of Wesch Anti-Radar Material, CIOS Black List Item 1 Radar BIOS Target No. 1/549', which contains several areas of interest: invisible aircraft (early stealth research), radar, U-boats, computing and torpedo technology. The British Intelligence Objectives Sub-Committee (BIOS) reporting system and its successor, the US/UK–administered Combined Intelligence Objectives Sub-Committee (CIOS), were sources of such research and investigations. These were published in the immediate aftermath of the war and were systems employed by the British and Americans for assessing German high technology. In the report, there is mention of a small flotilla of new type XXI U-boats with the revolutionary hydrogen peroxide underwater turbine propulsion, allowing extraordinary underwater cruising speeds. This May 1945 document also reports the annihilation of a flotilla of British destroyers. The report goes on to mention the inclusion of new types of German wire-guided and magnetic torpedoes and details of the encounter: 'Vierling has heard of electrical homing devices for torpedoes and their firing by proximity effect. Torpedoes were built by AEG in Berlin. Some work was done also at Gdynia. These torpedoes were reported to have sunk 12 Destroyers in one engagement in Atlantic waters.'

Above the waves, there were also problems with battleships. One of the most expensive and greatest war machines in the military hardware is the battleship; yet these became one of the most dramatic demises of the Second World War, together with the battle cruiser. The vulnerability of these ships became apparent in the early weeks of the war with the sinking of Britain's *Royal Oak* by a lone U-boat on the night of 13 October 1939. She lay at anchor in Scapa Flow, which was considered a safe harbour for the British home fleet. Her sinking saw 800 hands lost along with the ship.

The Royal Navy took its revenge two months later when the German *Graf Spee* was trapped in the harbour of Montevideo by the cruisers *Ajax* and *Achilles*. The German pocket battleship was then scuttled by its commander on 17 December 1939. However, it would be Germany's proudest vessel at the time that became vulnerable to attack. At the outbreak of war, the German battleships *Bismarck* and *Tirpitz* were considered the most advanced vessels of their type in the world. Powered by three massive diesel turbines, these would operate three propellers and were capable of top speeds of 29 knots. They also carried state-of-the-art, radar-assisted gunfire controls and eight 38cm guns with 36cm armour plating around the turrets. To add to this, the deck housed a hangar of four Arado 196 sea planes with 2 more stowed on the open deck. These planes were launched by compressed air, operating catapults together with cranes and derricks for their retrieval from the sea.

The *Bismarck* was launched by Hitler in person on 14 February 1939 while lecturing the assembled audience on the spiritual world view of National Socialism together with its technological and organizational abilities of 'defeating the enemies of the Reich now and forever'. Hitler also planned a series of battleships under the gigantism programme involving a fleet of vessels over 100,000 tons, making them twice as heavy as the most massive fighting vessels already afloat.

On 19 May 1941, the *Bismarck* was heading for the Atlantic via Iceland, escorted by the cruiser *Prinz Eugen*, determined to destroy the British merchant convoys vital to supplying the country, especially food. On 24 May, the HMS *Hood* came upon the two German vessels. The *Hood* was somewhat elderly, having been launched in 1920, but it was the pride of the Royal Navy and was their largest cruiser. It took only 8 minutes of exchanges before *Hood* was hit, exploding its magazines. After a further 3 minutes, *Hood* had sunk below the waves. The cruiser had been accompanied by another, *Prince of Wales*, which was also hit before retiring from the battle.

The shock from the loss resulted in Winston Churchill giving the order: 'Get the *Bismarck* at any cost.' The search for the battleship took just 2 days, a search that included two aircraft carriers and tracking by HMS *Suffolk* using gunnery-controlled radar. It was eventually located heading for Brest by an aircraft using radar. On the evening of 26 May, a Swordfish aircraft deployed a torpedo that jammed both of the *Bismarck*'s rudders, fatally crippling the ship; it was unable to steer, only able to sail in wide circles. To add to this, the aircraft on the *Bismarck* could not be launched due to a malfunction with the catapult mechanism. The end came the following day when four Royal Navy ships closed in to finish her off; out of a crew of 2,200, only 115 survived. The defeat of the *Bismarck* resulted in Hitler recalling his capital ships to base, keeping them there.

This was just the beginning of the end for the battleship; later that year, the Japanese attacked Pearl Harbor, resulting in the United States entering the war. Following this, two Royal Navy ships, *Prince of Wales* and *Repulse*, were dispatched to Malaya because of Japanese troop movements and were lost when attacked by bombs and torpedoes from a large Japanese formation of bombers. These losses, and others like them, saw the days of the battleships numbered as air power on the high seas took over. U-boats too would be defeated in the Atlantic when Britain developed superior onboard centimetre wavelength H2S radar for the Royal Air Force.

The use of the electromagnetic spectrum was somewhat different with the Nazis. Amongst the many ideas for powering the war machines were various unconventional or pseudo-scientific attempts, one of which was the Schappeller device, also known as the Schappeller coil, said to have been used in submarines. This alternative to Walter's hydrogen peroxide method seems to have been invented by Karl Schappeller. It was a most odd device and considered to border on perpetual motion, something shunned by physics. However, it did seem to set the scene for various adventures involving electric and magnetic fields and, therefore, electromagnetism and its connections with ideas of so-called 'free energy'; indeed, there was a considerable amount of electromagnetic research of various types carried out by the Nazis.

Some researchers have claimed this device was associated with the new advanced XXI class U-boats coming into service as the war ended; as such, it was another example of Nazi technology that came too late. Again, this seems to be a device that obtained free energy from somewhere, possibly the quantum background foam.

The main device consisted of two separate parts: a rotor and a starter. The starter was a ball-shaped device made of two hemispherical shells of steel which was airtight and contained the internal structure. Attached to each half-shell's pole was an iron bar magnet, most of which was internal to the sphere, with one being opposite the other. Between these magnets was a gap corresponding to the centre of the sphere. A ceramic material insulated the inside of the steel sphere, leaving a hollow central area. Within this hollow and around the sphere between the magnets, internal coils—Coler coils—were wound. These coils were composed of a hollow copper tube filled with a secret substance called 'electret', which is a permanent magnet within the sphere. After leaving the sphere, the electret-filled copper wires were replaced by conventional copper wire. An electrical connection was then made from the outside surface of one pole to one pole of a special type of battery which is grounded at the other pole. Unfortunately, as with many such Nazi devices of the unconventional type, there is a secret component; in this case, the unknown nature of the electret. However, it has been said an alternative type of electret was discovered by Mototaro Eguchi. This substance consisted of carnauba wax and resin and may also have contained beeswax; it was kept in a strong electric field while baked slowly until it solidified. The Schappeller device was said to be a 'no power in, but power out' perpetual-motion machine, but if that is true, it clearly violates physical laws. Nevertheless, to the Nazis and their pseudo-science, that does not appear to matter because it was considered under the 'lost physics' category.

So, how was it supposed to work? It seems this is the point at which pseudo-science really appears. The gap between the magnets internal to the device is called a Bloch Wall and is said to be neutral, being neither north nor south in polarity. However, when grounded and in use, Schappeller claimed it produced a 'new kind' of magnetism, a glowing magnetism, interpreted as stationary with radiating magnetism. It was further interpreted that energy enters here and is radiated as gravity. To the Nazi physicists, this suggested gravity is a quadrupole (four poles) rather than two poles, with a 360-degree push. That push gave them anti-gravity, as opposed to the conventional gravity that is attractive only. Hence the Schappeller device seems to serve two areas of Nazi physics: a power source for a rotor and an anti-gravity source. However, conventional physics suggests it was neither; apart from the nature of the secret electret, it was also claimed to overturn conventional laws of thermodynamics.

Schappeller called this version of thermodynamics 'reverse thermodynamics'. This comes about because of entropy, which is a measure of the disorder of a system. Normally this remains the same or increases as the disorder of a system increases; it is effectively linked to the decay of the universe. However, with this device, the entropy can decrease, in apparent violation of the second law of thermodynamics. This was believed by Schappeller to be possible and the only real reason why he invented his device was to prove his point. Interestingly, in 1977 the Nobel Prize winner, Ilya Prigogine, showed this process is indeed possible with certain chemical reactions. Was this yet another possible area where the Third Reich was way ahead of its time? Physics says no; it is still getting something for nothing. Nevertheless, it illustrates many of the ideas we have encountered so far and their overlapping use in conventional weapons, possibly including submarines. One such overlap is its claim to produce anti-gravity which we will examine in detail later with the extremes of flying disc technology. At the end of the day, we may never know exactly what this device really did, if anything.

However, it appears the Coler coil associated with Schappeller's device was said to have come to the notice of the German Navy (Kriegsmarine) and the Third Reich as far back as the year Hitler came to power, maybe even some 6 years earlier. Yet it is to be believed it did not go into service until the war's end. Given the problems of a power-starved Third Reich, this appears strange, but if it was considered as an anti-gravity device, that research did not really start until 1944. As for the Coler coil, we will revisit this device with a British Intelligence report declassified in 1978, the year after Prigogine showed entropy can be reversed in certain chemical reactions.

There is also another device worthy of mention that is often overlooked and is more scientifically sound. This device is the digital computer, which then was really associated more with code-breaking rather than scientific research, but it was scientifically crucial in many areas during the war. Often considered to be a modern invention, it did advance considerably during the Second World War on both sides. Digital computers are probably best associated with Bletchley Park and the code-breaking of German Enigma machines, but it also played a big part in the development of the atomic bomb during the Manhattan Project when physicists had difficult calculations. However, it is a misconception that the Nazis did not have anything like these machines, as declassified records now show they did, and this has even led to suggestions digital computers were associated with an atomic bomb project in Nazi Germany.

In the above-mentioned BIOS report (1/549) we find this about computers: 'A computing machine was used at Gottingen for researching into aircraft stability and ballistics. Machine could solve equations mentioned in two or three minutes with errors of less than 3 per cent. Only one such machine has been made. It uses ordinary vacuum tubes, a multiplying principle and two cathode ray tubes, one of which has a spiral scan. One tube draws the curve which is the solution and the other indicates the complex roots of the solution.' However, although it appears only one of these machines was built, there is evidence that other computers existed within the Third Reich. Indeed, details and photographs have surfaced since the reunification of Germany to that effect. These photographs are of the enormous 'Eniac'-sized computer built by the postal service. There has been some doubt as to why they needed such an enormous and powerful computer; as we saw, the Reich Postal Minister, Wilhelm Ohnesorge, was not only a member of Hitler's cabinet but also interested in atomic bomb research, supporting nuclear physicist Baron Manfred von Ardenne, for whom Dr Fritz Houtermans was working. Therefore, if such a device was needed by the Manhattan Project, it might also be used for atomic bomb research by the Nazis. For example, it would be able to calculate the neutron free path and cross-sections necessary for the bomb's development. However, does this really mean the Nazis worked on an atomic bomb against official history and Hitler's views on it being the 'spawn of Jewish pseudo-science'?

Returning to his pseudo-scientific endeavours, Hitler had a wide range of beliefs that he was convinced fitted with his war efforts—even to the point that it was his destiny. One area of pseudo-science that Hitler is particularly remembered for is his love of astrology, and it is here that he turned to the astrologer Nostradamus to justify his rise to power. As we will see later, he also turned to astrology at the end to convince himself and his generals that all was not lost, even though Berlin crumbled around him as they huddled in the *Fuhrerbunker*. According to Hitler, Nostradamus predicted a world-conqueror coming from Europe by the name of Hister. However, although the spelling is close, the reality is different; modern interpretation now suggests the name Hister was not a person, but the Latin name for the river Danube. Nevertheless, Hitler used such things to his advantage and it certainly fits with his education. Beliefs along these lines would also be justified by the search for the truth, as he saw it, about the Aryan race, helped along by Heinrich Himmler. Himmler not only shared many of Hitler's views concerning pseudo-science but, with the help of his SS, took matters to a whole new fanatical level, from the science of physics to the horrific medical experimentations in the name of Aryan purity. These interests would also extend to the search for the Holy Grail bloodline and even the search for the lost island of Atlantis.

However, Hitler's love of looking to the heavens was not confined to the pseudo-science of astrology; he also looked to the science of astronomy, but unfortunately even that had a Hitler twist to its interpretation, supported by Himmler. In astronomy, the two chose to believe the unconventional fringe elements developing their own interpretations of the subject, such as crowbarring in beliefs of a universe made of ice (glacial cosmology); a hollow Earth theory, wherein we all live on the Earth's inner, not outer, surface; an original sun 30 million times the size of our current one; our moon being only one of many cycled through history; and, of course, connections with Aryan purity and the lost island of Atlantis, to name but a few.

The Nazis also held many pseudo-scientific ideas regarding health, food and diets but Hitler himself never stuck rigidly to these, although he remained a vegetarian from 1931 until his death. Many of the health fads also had connections with racial purity, following further dubious science advice from all the wrong sources, in this case Hitler's composer, Richard Wagner, who declared eating meat had contaminated humans, along with racial mixing. In fact, Wagner believed we had only become meat eaters because of the last ice age; with that, we were back to the unconventional ideas of glacial cosmology, on which many a dubious idea hung. To reverse the process, fresh fruit and vegetables were required. Of course, there was an element of truth to this because fresh fruit and vegetables are healthy, but the idea that meat eating was connected with ice ages had no scientific basis.

Hitler also had a fear he might develop cancer, which undoubtedly led to many other health fads. This fear seems to have originated from the belief that the condition could be brought about by what he called *Erdstrahlen* or 'Earth rays'. His solution was to get his physician, Gustav Freiherr von Pohl, to test for these rays using dowsing rods. This again illustrated something of a mix between science and pseudo-science, because certain radioactive elements in the ground can cause health problems, even cancer, but there was still the element that dowsing might be effective to detect such radiation.

Consequently, Nazi propaganda gave an impression of technocratic modernism matched with bracing naturalism of exercise, outdoor pursuits and general healthy living with campaigns on anti-smoking and anti-drinking; issues that also influenced Heisenberg's life, as we have seen. When Germany hosted the 1936 Olympics, it gave the country the opportunity to promote this propaganda worldwide. As well as the games themselves, the Berlin stadium would be designed along clean lines, with its neo-classical Nazi pavilion designed by Speer. This healthy living would not only apply to the individual but to the state, expelling the unwanted pathogens in a vision of National Socialist Germany, which was to become a radically hygienic 'body'. To that effect, Karl Haushofer's original political theory of *geopolitik* ('geopolitics') shone the way.

Some groups, notably doctors and anthropologists, not only readily accepted but took a lead in promoting this ideal, which would come to include racist polices and, in some cases, extended to other areas of the scientific community, generating opposition and coercion. The expanding community of doctors, anthropologists and eugenicists aided the advance of both a healthy body in the individual and the healthy 'body' of the state. This would result in the expelling of Jewish elements under anti-Semitism measures as being germs fought by the state's immune system and backed up with legislation. It is therefore no surprise that this eventually led to sterilization and euthanasia to rid the state 'body' of lives not worth living. Biologists and anthropologists had also claimed that population, society and history could be explained by a somewhat spurious, and worrying, historico-biological theory of race. This in turn produced a warped explanation of works such as those of Darwin, appropriated by the likes of Ernst Haeckel and H.F.K. Gunther, which provided ideas that were used to justify Hitler's anti-Semitism and so-called 'racial hygiene'.

As we have seen, Hitler failed to understand the fundamentals of science as a result of his schooling, which had an unfortunate effect on the distinction between science and religion. As far as science was concerned in dealing with ultimate questions, he said: 'As for the way of these laws, we shall never know anything about it.' This was also a mental blockage when it came to ultimate questions in religion, which he believed could not give answers either. Interestingly, what it does appear to show is he still attempted to merge science and religion almost as a new discipline, a new science, because of his love of the magical, mythical and occultist subjects which we will explore later.

Indeed, there was also some contradiction in his mind, because he told Himmler that religion is the enemy of science, and that religion was doomed as a consequence of science, while also believing that Christianity should be left to die a natural death. At one of his so-called 'table talk dinners', it is said that he expressed an opinion that 'the dogma of Christianity gets worn away before the advances of science and that more and more concessions will have to be made by religion. Gradually the myths crumble, all that is left is to prove that in nature there is no frontier between the organic and the inorganic.' There were clearly problems and contradictions here too, and it does not make a lot of sense. That said, although Christianity may have been rejected by him, other religious beliefs played their parts, with twists and pseudo-science to add to the mix.

His views on the science of astronomy and the workings of the universe also appeared to be a part of these table talk dinners involving his views on Christianity. At one, he declared: 'When we understand the Universe, and this has become widespread, when the majority of men know that the stars are not sources of light but worlds, perhaps inhabited worlds like our own, then the Christian doctrine will be convicted of absurdity.' This astronomical view was clearly driven by the unconventional ideas of glacial cosmology, as we will see, and was clearly associated with his racist views; in particular the idea the Aryan race had its roots in ice. As for stars, they were certainly known to be sources of light and different from planets (worlds); indeed they were known to be stars like our sun. Hitler thought science could not answer metaphysical questions, and he also missed significant scientific achievements of the time, including those developing in astronomy, which was entering an exciting new era of discovery.

As we saw, during the anti-Semitic, anti-relativist, and anti-Einstein years of the 1920s, astronomers like Edwin Hubble discovered that many of the faint nebulous patches of light in the night sky, such as the Andromeda nebula, are not within our own Milky Way Galaxy, but are external galaxies in their own right, leading to an expanding universe, or Big Bang. If Hitler ever did realize such discoveries during the 1920s and 1930s, he may well have had reason to dismiss them; in effect, they proved much of his astronomy-based pseudo-science wrong. Moreover, during this exciting time of discoveries and the work of Hubble, Einstein visited the Mount Wilson Observatory where he met with Hubble and looked through the 2.5m Hooker telescope that had allowed the true nature of the universe to be determined. He was also able to meet up with an ailing A.A. Michelson of ether fame at the same time. It was then that Einstein corrected his field equations of general relativity for an expanding universe by adjusting the cosmological constant. These types of discoveries and their support for Einstein would certainly not have been liked by Hitler, or Himmler. Indeed, combined with the discoveries and workings of the very small (the sub-atomic world of quantum theory), as well as the very big (the universe), any advances Hitler did acknowledge only caused more confusion and misunderstanding in his mind. As we saw, this led to another claim that we cannot know of such ideas, with his quote: 'Science has taught us that we are hemmed in not only by the infinitely great, but the infinitely small in the macrocosm and microcosm.' Much of Hitler's views on astronomy will be put into context when we look at the Nazi doctrine involving glacial cosmology, which went beyond a universe of ice inasmuch as it also linked with more extreme views, including the occult. Again, this showed Hitler as the theorist and Himmler as the facilitator.

So, let us now turn to Himmler. There is no doubt that an unfortunate mix of power and fanatical thinking flourished almost unchallenged under Himmler, backed up by Hitler demonstrating some of the best examples of pseudo-science in history. As a recap, Himmler believed in reincarnation and as a result was convinced he was Henry the Wildfowler, Emperor of Germany, in a former life. Much of this lethal mix was based on an amateur approach that Speer had observed as well as lack of judgment. There was also reasoning by analogy and classifying phenomena according to superficial observation rather than empirical evidence, although there was a certain amount of experimentation, often by trial and error. There was also a fixation on seeking out unconventional phenomena and 'lost science' through global expeditions, often with attempts to combine science and religion into a single discipline. These activities would also see any opposition stamped out, especially if serious scientific research and peer review entered the story.

There is no doubt that, running parallel to the drive of conventional science that built the hardware of war, Hitler and Himmler also had a great drive for their version of scientific research. This was not confined to physics, chemistry and mathematics; it was also true of Aryanism, genetics, and medicine, which resulted in murderous medical research and experimentation in the death camps under the SS. It is particularly significant how much of this fitted into the thinking of other areas and how the facts were twisted involving all manner of ideas and theories.

To a certain extent, the subject of mainstream, or conventional, physics was subtly different under the Nazis compared to other disciplines, certainly in the early years. In the case of subjects like medicine, genetics, anthropology and geography, there was plenty of room for National Socialism ideologies and Hitler's racial beliefs. In the case of conventional physics, there were limited opportunities for such matters as there had also been with mathematics. That would eventually change, and it did so in two main ways; firstly, the Nazis found a home for their beliefs in pseudo-science by passing it off as true science under National Socialism, and secondly it allowed Nazis a counter-measure to the threat Jewish science posed when promoting what was really the true sciences.

On the other hand, many have claimed that physics gave just about no opportunity for such parallels and mainly took the form of mass dismissals of Jewish physicists from universities, institutes and various research establishments. However, as we will see, this interpretation is a simplistic one. Certainly, there were mass dismissals, but physics was also used in the effort to seek out the origins and justification for the pure Aryan race. Furthermore, specific branches of physics like astronomy would play a part in some of the crazier theories of Himmler, such as detection techniques using infra-red radiation, a hollow Earth theory, anti-gravity flying discs, and, of course, glacial cosmology.

Himmler's religious origins were rooted in Catholicism, but he eventually rejected it in order to become a devotee of Hitler. Instead, he adopted fanatical religious beliefs which revolved around the superiority of the German people and their bloodline. Within 2 years of Hitler gaining power, Himmler was the major force behind establishing and running his research group, known as the *Ahnenerbe* ('ancestral heritage'), which would become as much to do with attempts to prove this bloodline as it was a service to the Third Reich in many and various ways. Indeed, the *Ahnenerbe* was a research society that encouraged a wide range of pseudo-science and used a heavy mix of physics as a way to achieve its goals. Of course, Himmler appointed himself as both its curator and president.

During the height of the war, the insanity gripping the *Ahnenerbe* and its bizarre theories, beliefs and experimentations became quite surreal. Under complete control of Himmler's SS and following the weird pseudo-science of Hitler's unorthodox education in scientific and religious matters, a huge amount of money and manpower was devoted to the esoteric research projects. In the bureaucratic culture of the *Ahnenerbe* it would be expected that researchers generate and pursue unorthodox ideas and were allowed free rein to brainstorm. It is therefore no surprise there were many failures. However, the culture of all this was supported by the possibility of great success, maybe even the discovery of a new science that would lead to physics that nobody else had even considered, especially the enemy.

There was one experiment which could be considered as an early form of remote viewing. This involved alleged 'adepts' holding a pendulum over pictures of U-boats and then over maps of the ocean in an attempt to detect their current positions. This was right up Hitler and Himmler's street, so the British would allow stories to get out that they were doing the same, as a cover for more conventional scientific methods of detection like radar. It is said that when the higher ranks of the British military were asked if they really believed in such things the answer was: 'No. But Hitler does!' Of course, a somewhat alternative form of remote viewing was considered and experimented with after the war under the Americans and Soviets involving projects like Grill Flame and Star Gate with devastating results to the sanity of many so-called 'psychic spies'. These results took the form of aftereffects that lingered and developed further outside the projects and during their everyday lives. In particular, they manifested as altered states of mind or consciousness. Psychic spies would become detached from their normal daily reality at times and often without warning: a condition their doctors called 'dissociative episodes' where they experienced a co-existence of two or more distinct personalities in the same person. Often these were of an evil or demonic nature, as if possessed by evil spirits, or 'the dark ones', as psychic spies would often describe them. It is open to debate as to whether this was only in their minds, as their doctors believed, or true evil spirits having taken possession after linking to a spirit realm; the procedure undertaken in the projects had a lot of similarities to mediumship and near-death experiences. It is intriguing to consider whether the Nazis experienced similar side effects had they taken remote viewing to the same level, and how this might have added to their already evil mindset. Full details about the post-war projects and their consequences are beyond the scope of this book, but a good starting point can be found in *The Psychic Warrior* (1996) by David Morehouse; he was a CIA remote viewer and whistle-blower who suffered particularly severe apparitions.

Given the years of amazing discoveries like quantum physics, radar, great power from nuclear fission and the preceding golden decades of the great German discoveries, it is easy to see how the Nazis had faith there were even more amazing discoveries to uncover. Moreover, if these discoveries could be weaponized, then maybe the war could be won. This thinking is also present today and not surprisingly also involves some unconventional areas, including unidentified flying objects (UFOs), unidentified aerial phenomena (UAPs) and their sightings, together with Pentagon and political manipulation involving connections to adversaries like Russia and China. Again, that is beyond the scope of this book, but seems to be another form of import from Nazi Germany and connected with the Tic Tac UFOs detected by the USS *Nimitz* in 2004. I will leave that for the reader to follow up on.

Himmler claimed his *Ahnenerbe* society was a serious and proper scientific research establishment; as such, he made many attempts over the years to attract genuine scientists to its rank and file. However, this was yet another of Himmler's delusions, because most serious scientists would not touch his society with a barge pole, and attempts to recruit respectable scientific staff failed time and again. As such, his work went largely unrecognized in the scientific community and was persecuted by official mainstream science. It does, however, survive as an oddity in some modern-day scientific writings. Nevertheless, all this did not stop the *Ahnenerbe* from presenting itself as a serious scientific research establishment that claimed it was breaking down divisions between natural sciences, like physics, and the arts by encouraging a form of 'holism'. The reality of the society was it amounted to a mixture of the good, the bad and the ugly when it came to subjects like history, philology, genetics, archaeology, anthropology, mythology, astrology, astronomy, meteorology, mysticism and, worse of all, the occult. Significantly, it was now possible to control 'occulted science' elements by monitoring, studying and organizing through *Ahnenerbe*'s funding. In doing so, they exploited complete secrecy and encouraged secret society activities. In a letter to one of its scientists, Himmler summed up the *Ahnenerbe* by saying: 'The society is not only to study ancient religion, science and the occult, but also that its principle establishment is an institute for military scientific research.'

To illustrate this type of thinking and activity, there is a story that involved an astrologer by the name of Wilhelm Wulff, who had been made a prisoner of the SS and coerced into working at an SS institute set up during 1939 in Berlin. He described the institute's scientific research centre as being used 'to harness not only natural but also supernatural forces. All intellectual, natural, and supernatural sources of power—from modern technology to mediaeval black magic, and from the teachings of Pythagoras to the Faustian pentagram incantation—were to be exploited in the interest of final victory.' This certainly suggested the darker practices were in place at the beginning of the war and almost certainly earlier. So, it appears clear that there was an odd mix of serious, orthodox science and so-called 'occulted science' within the *Ahnenerbe* as a result of the beliefs of Himmler and, of course, the scientifically warped mind of Hitler himself. That would also be true of other high-ranking SS officers, as we will see later.

So far as the 'orthodox science' is concerned, it really just amounted to the standard physics, chemistry and biology. Of course, in the case of the 'occulted science', there was a wider range of meanings. For example, it could also be taken as meaning 'hidden', which was sometimes deliberate, or 'dark, black, covert and secret'. It could also refer to the mythological, ancient texts, or esoteric and occult traditions of the Orient and the Occident. In fact, this was one of the cornerstones of Nazi doctrine and secret weapons research that was producing mostly spectacular failures and few significant breakthroughs. These esoteric and occult traditions meant not only the standard occult texts, traditions and secret societies, but also legends that are not generally considered as esoteric or occultist in the usual sense; this was because sometimes they were just less known. The ancient mythologies included all legends, texts and scriptures of various cultures: classical Sumerian, Mayan, Chinese, Hindu, Egyptian Olmec, Scandinavian-Teutonic and even Graeco-Roman European culture. In dealing with texts and artifacts, a full range of techniques were employed to understand them. This involved looking for buried, or partially buried, secrets from the mists of pre-history and mythologies, legends, talismans and physical monuments typically associated with them. The Nazis believed that such efforts would provide secrets of science long lost; secrets that they could restore to orthodox science and use in their war effort.

As a result, there was a strong quest associated with the SS to investigate the scientific basis of occult notions, no matter how bizarre or flawed they might appear. It was also Hitler's personal views of 'Will to Power' that suggests his interest as an occultist. He described this ideology himself by saying: 'A new age of magic interpretation of the world is coming, of interpretation in terms of the will and not the intelligence.' It has been suggested that with this he was reaching back into the German culture of Arthur Schopenhauer's *The World as Will and Representation.* It is also significant that the mastermind behind Nazi geopolitics and occultism, General Karl Haushofer, who had meet Hitler when he was imprisoned back in 1924, was an avid scholar of Schopenhauer.

This 'Will, Not Intelligence' leads to the connection in quantum mechanics we explored earlier. As we saw, the world of the quantum is a fuzzy world of inverted cause and effect ruled by probabilities. Another area of quantum theory important here is the Heisenberg Uncertainty Principle, which we looked at earlier. In particular, it involves the uncertainty in measurement whereby we cannot determine the exact position of a particle and its exact velocity at the same time; the more accurately we know its position, the more uncertainly do we know its velocity, and vice versa. This gave rise to the equations of position and velocity together, with one for energy and time breaking with the classical, clockwork views of Newtonian mechanics with its accurate nature. In turn, this gave way to the modern branch of physics, quantum mechanics and its need to introduce probability functions. The point being, all this puts a different slant on reality. It was now clear that this fuzzy and uncertain probabilistic world could be affected by the observer's will; the observer who, in effect, becomes part of the process, or experiment, just by observing.

What this meant, especially to the Nazis, was a way to 'magically' control a realm of new physics which might reveal new laws that they could use in their wonder weapons through their occulted science. In other words, it brought in the 'reality in view', which for them essentially meant that even the probability functions, or wavefunction carrying the information of the quantum state, were themselves predetermined by the attribute the experimenter decided to concentrate upon. So, the Nazis seized upon the idea the experimenter could 'predetermine reality' simply by the way they performed the experiment, bringing in the science of consciousness, or Schopenhauer's will. We have already seen how the conscious observer is part of a measurement in an experiment when we looked at the Schrodinger's cat thought experiment. Most importantly, it meant to the Nazis that they only had to 'scientifically' study the paranormal to grasp hitherto unknown laws of physics, at the scale of the very small. At this level, at least, the ideas of quantum mechanics, gravity and consciousness particularly appealed to certain Nazi physicists; furthermore, it was free from Jewish science. The introduction of gravity would also allow research into anti-gravity and an understanding of the fabric of space and time and its geometry, and in doing so, get away from Einstein's theory of relativity. It would hopefully lead to all manner of possible weapons, as we will see, and bring in favourites like spin, vortex physics, and rotation, which would apply to exotic aircraft designs like flying discs. This, of course, was on the scale of the very small—atomic and sub-atomic levels—but it was hoped that, on the larger scale, the same would be true. By the time the Second World War broke out, all that these dreams needed was somebody to fund them and it fell to the Nazis to do just that, along with the necessary organization and infrastructure.

One of the most important locations for the *Ahnenerbe*'s special occult research was the island of Rugen in the Baltic Sea. This island had many special associations and it is claimed was home to several quirky experiments. Opinion is divided when it comes to some of the stories, one of which was the belief in a hollow Earth theory. This theory is often reported as one of Himmler's pet theories, although it is unclear how far he and Hitler subscribed to such a belief; proof is vague and not particularly supported by any hard evidence. However, there are some details from astronomy regarding a Rugen experiment that is connected to a hollow Earth theory that was something of a blend of conventional warfare and the surreal views of the SS. The report appeared as an article in the June 1946 issue of *Popular Astronomy* titled *German Astronomy During the War*. It involved one of the many unorthodox ideas the SS had about astronomy: that we live inside the planet on the inner surface of its crust rather than on the outer surface. It is said Himmler believed this theory and was convinced the fanatical SS leadership actually lived on the inside surface of our planet. However, this idea leads to a problem with the Earth's curvature. Taking the correct view that we live on the outer surface of a spherical Earth, if you want to locate objects at some distance, the curvature of the Earth makes this difficult at sea level; only a few kilometres away and the object disappears from view as it drops below the curvature of the horizon. For the SS, there was a different view to this problem as a result of living on the inner surface, a view they put to the test with attempts to locate the British fleet. In effect the problem was solved by flipping things upside down such that the curvature of the Earth would not obstruct observation because it would now curve upwards as you looked into the distance. The relevant part of the article reads:

> 'They considered it helpful to locate the British fleet, because the curvature of the earth would not obstruct observation. Visual rays were not suitable because of refraction; but infra-red rays had less refraction. Accordingly a party of about ten men under the scientific leadership of Dr Heinz Fischer, an infra-red expert, was sent out from Berlin to the island of Rugen to photograph the British fleet with infra-red equipment at an upward angle of some forty-five degrees.'

If this experiment did happen, it did not work. Nevertheless, what this story does show is the development of technology that had a variety of uses both in conventional science and bizarre occult beliefs; infra-red detectors would later feature in further strange devices, as well as conventional ones. Therefore, a significant point to take away from this is not so much the irrational beliefs of a hollow Earth theory, but the point that the Nazis possessed the means of detection using infra-red wavelengths at great distances and by using atmospheric refraction. Indeed, this Nazi infra-red technology would be the same type developed for use in heat-seeking anti-aircraft missiles. A further advance in modern times would see another region of the electromagnetic spectrum used—increased wavelength of microwaves—to produce over-the-horizon radar, an area that saw its origins with conventional radar during the war. Of course, this type of radar was developed with the correct view that the surface of the Earth curves down as we look out towards the horizon; in other words, we live on the surface. Another important point to take away from this Nazi experiment is the island of Rugen was chosen for bizarre experiments because of its esoteric history prior to the war, in fact to a time that dates back to at least the First World War.

After the Second World War, Hitler's private library was discovered, hidden in a mine near his idyllic mountain home of Berchtesgaden; not surprisingly, it contained many volumes covering occult literature. Amongst these books was a collection of Lanz von Liebenfels' racist-occult magazine *Ostara,* published in Vienna before the First World War. It is von Liebenfels and his order of the New Templars that forms a connection between the SS and experiments at Rugen. The secret society of von Liebenfels was also dedicated to the purification of the German race from corrupting influences of anyone not Germanic or Aryan. This order not only had its racist ideology but was also interested in astrology, the Cabala, phrenology, homeopathy and nutrition, making it compatible with the ideals of Hitler, Himmler and the *Ahnenerbe*. Of these subjects it is particularly significant that Cabala is present. This was an ancient Jewish tradition of mystical interpretations particularly involving holy texts and first transmitted orally using esoteric doctrine and occult lore methods. With money pouring in from wealthy supporters and the writing of his works, including a secret bible for the initiated, the funding allowed the purchase of several castles, including one on the island of Rugen that was restored as a centre for esoteric research and New Templar activism.

It is unclear whether Hitler ever met von Liebenfels, but it is said he might have done so when the two were in Vienna before the First World War. Some sources suggest Hitler was greatly influenced as a child of twelve by von Liebenfels, who was one of his teachers as well as an ex-Cistercian monk and mystic. Several scholars state that this teacher filled his young pupils' minds with visions of the great pagan past of the Teutonic peoples, an odd pastime for a Cistercian monk. What we do know about the association between the two is that von Liebenfels expressed his views on Hitler in a letter to one of his New Templars, declaring he was 'one of our pupils'. He also said: 'You will one day experience that he, and through him we, will one day be victorious and develop a movement that makes the world tremble.'

Another shared view Himmler had with Hitler was a black and twisted version of King Arthur's Knights of the Holy Grail and Round Table. This also had its connections to the ideal of the Templars and von Liebenfels' New Templars. Here, the Holy Grail (or *sang real*/'blood royal') was the royal bloodline itself with its chalice, or container, being the Germanic Aryan race. This allowed Himmler's *Ahnenerbe* to explore areas of science other than physics, chemistry and biology, the latter resulting in medical experimentation on concentration camp detainees as well as the German people themselves, not only to advance German medicine but to find the basis of genetic and ethnic purity of the Germanic race itself. The headquarters for this cult was situated at the mediaeval castle of Wewelsburg, close to the towns of Paderborn and Detmold in the province of Westphalia. Here, Himmler had a central chamber with a large table; like King Arthur's, it had been designed to seat twelve elite men from the senior generals of the SS. It also came complete with an occult library consisting of 12,000 volumes. Like a stereotypical cult or secret society, these generals would take part in a secret initiation. As a result of his monastic training as a Cistercian monk and in the best traditions and tactics of classical Christian Gnosticism, von Liebenfels also produced a series of texts for the New Templars, including a two-volume *New Templars' Breviary*, the psalms in German, and a secret bible for the initiated, which amounted to ten volumes. There was also a collection of various other works, such as prayer books.

However, following the annexing of Austria, von Liebenfels was forbidden to publish anything further as the Nazis sought to control the occult elements from public knowledge, turning it instead into an internal secret. This control was severe, with strict regulations to the point of non-existence, with any display of public occultism or secret society activity forbidden. In particular, this made things a lot clearer when trying to understand the motivation for Himmler creating the *Ahnenerbe* within the bureaucratic world of the SS; it appears the Nazi regime was fearful of its connections to such activities and societies, especially at its highest levels. That is the point where Himmler and his creation of the *Ahnenerbe* was now able to control occulted science elements by monitoring, studying and organizing through its funding. In doing so they exploited complete secrecy.

It is said there was one particular secret initiation these senior SS generals received that was significant to the anagram SS itself. In the case of the rank and file of the SS, the initials stood for the German word *schutzstaffel*, a term loosely meaning a special staff or military unit; however, to the initiates there was an alternative meaning altogether. That meaning was deeply rooted in the black, occult side to all this pseudo-science and again it has roots in the cosmos, and in particular ancient Sumerian, Babylonian and, to a certain extent, Egyptian beliefs. For these generals, SS referred to *die schwarze sonne*, the black sun.

The doctrine of the black sun goes back to ancient Sumer and Akkadia, and is another area of Nazi doctrine having an astronomical connection. It centres on the idea of their being two suns: the white physical sun at the centre of our solar system, around which the planets orbit, and the black sun, or hidden sun, of spiritual illumination. As for the location of the black sun, it varies somewhat between different mythical themes, but often it is found at the centre of our galaxy, the Milky Way. In some versions, it is associated with the uttermost Hyperborea and Thule, the legendary stellar home and celestial origin of the Aryan race. Others believe it is one of the causes of the immortality and reincarnation of the soul, which would fit with Himmler's view he was the reincarnation of Henry the Wildfowler, Emperor of Germany. As for Babylonian mythology, it is associated with the coming of the King of Kings and the establishment of a New Babylon.

The belief in a black sun located at the centre of our Milky Way Galaxy is maybe amongst one of the most intriguing ideas because we now know that there is a black hole located there, which was not known about at the time of these myths or the Nazis. Furthermore, the way a black hole can form is by the gravitational collapse of a massive enough star at the end of its life; it is then that its gravitational pull becomes so great, not even light can escape. The black hole is then able to pull into it any other stars or matter nearby. What makes this even more intriguing is that the *Ahnenerbe* scientists working on various secret projects held an ideological basis for the more mundane scientific view that the black sun was an extremely powerful gravitational force represented by a large mass rotating around the centre of our galaxy. It is possible that here is the point where unorthodox ideas about gravity control and anti-gravity enter the research for wonder weapons and exotic aviation projects. Moreover, it was believed that these ancient texts may provide the key to the recovery of such lost science. With all this comes an obvious spooky feeling. Was this just coincidence or was it lost science as the Nazis believed?

For the Nazis, that lost science would be different from Jewish science, such as relativity; given the gravitational element, it may act as an alternative to general relativity's interpretation of gravity. This was looking more in line with Aryan physics, which favoured quantum mechanics, vorticular spin, a zero-point field providing infinite free energy, control of gravity for aviation, anti-gravity flying discs and polarization. These areas in particular were amongst those to play a major role in the closing years of the war, when Himmler struggled to bring together everything he believed in to provide Hitler with new and exotic wonder-weapons he promised; promises in which people like Speer had little faith given Himmler's record in such matters. Indeed, the dream centred on all this lost and exotic physics being like nothing conventional science had to offer, and would then turn the war around to the Nazis' advantage. These were the weapons that would leave the enemy no way to retaliate and strike fear into them. Therefore, the black sun symbolism formed a central doctrine to the pre-Nazi secret society, the Thule Society, with the black sun symbol adopted as an emblem for von Liebenfels' New Templars as something akin to the swastika.

The connection between the SS and Egypt comes about through one of the most famous esotericists, R.A. Schwaller de Lubicz, who was well-known to contemporary students of alternative or revisionist Egyptology. Possibly the most famous aspect of de Lubicz is his life-long effort to reinterpret the monuments and writings of ancient Egypt, especially the hieroglyphic system of writing. Of course, contemporary researchers consider his efforts as faulty and sloppy at best and simply wrong at worst. That said, these opinions did not put off the Nazi regime that eagerly took de Lubicz's ideas onboard and elevated them to even greater heights of controversy.

For example, de Lubicz pointed out the weathering of the Sphinx was inconsistent with the Fourth Dynasty origin of the monument, suggesting it was much older. This particular point is actually still active to this day, although a flurry of bestselling books during the 1990s to the early 2000s has been followed by something of a lull today. Interestingly, I encountered this part of Nazi doctrine as an astrophysicist when I was involved with several publications examining the unexplained and paranormal beliefs within fringe sciences. In particular, I wrote for several newsstand magazines of the 1990s and early 2000s during what was considered the 'X-File years', for one of which, the publication *UFO Magazine* (UK), I served as the in-house physics and astronomy correspondent/consultant. In many of these publications I remember how the de Lubicz–style Egyptology played a major role, but rarely did anybody want to bring in the Nazi element. Nevertheless, it became a big subject at conferences with articles and bestselling books appearing on a regular basis. One of the main topics was a somewhat-worrying throwback to the days of Nazis Egyptology and the dating of the Sphinx, which was claimed to date to between 8,000 BC and the Nazi view of 10,000 BC, with some sources even suggesting as far back as 12,500 BC. Again, this was partly based on weathering, but also on astronomy inasmuch as it depended on the positions of stars and constellations at various periods in ancient Egyptian history, particularly their positions relative to monuments. I have to say the latter is based on some dubious astronomy, but nevertheless was presented as being of great significance. In many respects, this too was a somewhat spooky throwback to the past and worrying times.

For de Lubicz, Egyptian hieroglyphics and culture were viewed as the visible signs of a highly developed culture of analogical rather than analytical thought, science and practice. In his mind, analogical thought was synonymous with action at a distance, which he and others have interpreted as compatible with quantum mechanics. This provided further proof within the highest Nazi ranks that Max Planck's ideas were the way to go rather than the Jewish science of physicists like Einstein. Action at a distance was also connected with a particular area of quantum theory known as quantum entanglement, an area that Einstein could not accept and called: 'Spooky action at a distance.' Indeed, this element of quantum mechanics is the same one that links the observer to the experiment and consciousness, the area involving Schrodinger's cat and 'will'.

Quantum entanglement is a physical phenomenon that occurs when a pair (or group) of particles is generated, interact or share spatial proximity in a way such that the quantum state of each particle of the pair (or group) cannot be described independently of the state of the other, including when the particles are separated by large distances. Now that might sound complex, but put simply it means the particles become inextricably linked, and whatever happens to one immediately affects the other, regardless of how far apart they are; the distance can be extremely small or the particles can be at opposite ends of the universe. It is this apparent instantaneous communication that appeared to violate relativity's cosmic speed limit, the speed of light, and worried Einstein. His rebuttal of quantum entanglement came from the EPR paper published in 1935, *Can Quantum-Mechanical Descriptions of Physical Reality be Considered Complete?*, written by Einstein, Boris Podolsky, and Nathan Rosen, and no doubt added to the Nazi beliefs that Jewish science was wrong. We now better understand quantum entanglement and realize the EPR approach and its authors were indeed wrong. However, the phenomenon is correct and does not violate relativity as Einstein feared. That said, the views of the Nazis were equally wrong for different reasons. What we appear to have with this phenomenon is a shared wavefunction and not a communication, as such, over distance. It was not only quantum entanglement that Einstein disliked. As we saw, he also disliked the probabilistic nature, saying: 'God does not play dice with the Universe.' However, he did change his views from this being wrong to being incomplete.

For de Lubicz, this analogical action at a distance, or 'sympathetic magic', brought him to the conclusion that a dualistic world was at play with two sciences: one of genesis or creation, and one of destruction, essentially another 'fire and ice' type view that suited the Nazis' doctrine. Therefore, in this context, any hieroglyphic symbol became a synthesis of polarities of opposition of forces, which are held in balance by the glyph, the information, itself. Again, this has a spooky parallel with quantum entanglement, inasmuch as the wavefunction is associated with information about the quantum states. This dualistic nature also had its parallel with another feature of quantum mechanics: a wave/particle duality, where at times a particle behaves as a particle, and at others as a wave, depending on the experiment. All this was seized upon by the Nazi regime; it fitted perfectly with their ideology and mission statement, particularly within Himmler's *Ahnenerbe*. With further support for anti-Einsteinian views and the dismissal of Jewish science, the Nazis took de Lubicz's views onboard and encouraged them to flourish, but we need to understand that this was a time of discovery for both relativity and quantum mechanics. It was the early days, and coming at the time it did allowed for much uncertainty as well as manipulation within the Nazi regime.

It was not only the so-called 'occulted physics' that was important; central to the early philosophy of the *Ahnenerbe* was a theosophical theory of Nordic connections with the doctrine of 'world ice', which had other important associations in Himmler's mind. In his attempt to prove such connections, he ordered the zoologist Ernst Schafer to lead an expedition to Tibet in 1938. Accompanying Schafer was entomologist Karl Wienert and anthropologist Bruno Beger. The purpose of this expedition was an ideological one, with just about no scientific reasoning to it. Himmler had become convinced that Nazis should 'accomplish far more as SS men and do much more for the lack of understanding for the new Germany by being up front about who they are than by travelling under the disguise of an obscure, if neutral science academy; after all we have a clear conscience.' The aim of this expedition was to collect material about origin, proportion and the significance and development of the Nordic race. This trip to look for traces of a pure Germanic race, which might have been able to keep intact the ancient Nordic mysteries, cost over a million marks and was spent by over fifty departments. On top of this, the *Ahnenerbe* also had archaeologists digging all over Europe for remains of Germanic culture.

The expedition returned, bringing with it the only complete copy of the multi-volume Buddhist *Kang Shur* to reach the West, a collection reputedly containing much lost information from the pre-classical ancient Atlantean world; the legend of Atlantis was of major interest to the *Ahnenerbe*. For his efforts, 2 years later Schafer became chief of the section of the *Ahnenerbe* for Central Asian studies and expeditions, which eventually he helped to develop into the major Institute for the Rebuilding of German Science.

There would be other similar activity, including the armed expedition to South America to recover the well-known crystal skulls to investigate their optical properties—a branch of physics that would feature in other Nazi research, including mysterious devices using crystals. There was also the ransacking of ancient texts and works of Sanskrit for clues to Vedic mathematics. The SS even inducted the Muslim Grand Mufti of Jerusalem into its ranks as an honorary major.

Also important to the origins of the Aryan race was the theory of a universe made of ice, which brought matters back to physics and astronomy, and included subjects like meteorology and geology. This theory was important for the justification of the superior Aryan race originating from living shoots conserved in crusts of ice in outer space, another one of Himmler's pet theories. Also central to Himmler's theories was the belief that leaders of the Third Reich had descended from the Vikings; because of this he arranged another of his expeditions to Iceland to find the proof.

With what he considered as proof, Himmler made yet another attempt to attract respected scientists to his cause, this time with the formation of the Institute of Meteorology; hoping that, unlike his failure to attract respected scientists to his *Ahnenerbe,* this new institute would have better luck. It was also hoped that the institute would attract scientists from associated disciplines, in particular astronomers and geologists, who would validate his theories, especially the one about a universe being made of ice. Again, this did not work, and only attracted more persecution and criticism. Surprisingly, amongst the critics of Himmler's Institute of Meteorology was Philipp Lenard. Despite his extreme right-wing views and support for the Nazis, Lenard took particular exception to a series of articles supporting the belief in a universe made of ice, or *Welteislehre*, published in the *Illustrierter Beobachter* ('*Illustrated Observer*') run by the National Socialists. The editor had announced that this would be a long-running series, but it was abruptly cancelled after Lenard approached him with his views on the matter. The theory was later promoted in a more discreet manner.

The ice theory has gone by several names—cosmic ice theory, glacial cosmogony, glacial cosmology and their German translations, such as *Welteislehre,* being the main ones. Essentially, they were all the same idea except that 'cosmology' refers to the universe, or cosmos, as a whole, while 'cosmogony' really refers to just the solar system (the sun, moon, planets and assorted smaller bodies within it like moons of other planets, comets and asteroids). As such, we need not worry about the interchange of cosmogony with cosmology other than the ideas started with the solar system objects like the moon (cosmogony) and extending to the universe at large (cosmology).

It is not at all surprising to learn that Himmler was not amused by attacks on the theory; he continued to defend the theory and the right for people to know about it. Possibly as a result of Lenard's views on the Nazis, and his support, which grew in leaps and bounds along with his career under Hitler, there was some level of tolerance with Lenard and his attack. However, that was not the case with another critic, Dr Otto Wacker of the Ministry of Science, Training and Popular Education, who had declared the theory as 'nonsense' and forwarded a memorandum to Himmler from Paul Guthnick of the Babelsberg Observatory, west of Neubabelsberg. Himmler replied to the minister, saying: 'I am a defender of free research in all its forms, and this includes free research into glacial cosmogony. Moreover I intend to give this free research my warmest support, and in this I find myself in the best possible company, as the Fuhrer and Chancellor of the German Reich, Adolf Hitler, has for many years been a convinced adherent of this theory, which is disdained by the journeymen of science.' By the following month, Himmler had tracked down the culprit responsible for commissioning the memorandum and relieved him of his job, uniform and party badge. Himmler then wrote to Reinhard Heydrich (his second in command) explaining this action was because 'the man had constantly attacked the theory, and taken a totally unscientific position with regard to the phenomenon.' Himmler's actions are hardly surprising given the fact this theory was one of the main purposes of the *Ahnenerbe*—the historical and ethnographical research to discover the origins and superiority of the Aryan race. Indeed, to Himmler, this was a form of religion. There was also good reason to bring into the mix subjects like meteorology and geology to join with astronomy, all coming together to form fanatical beliefs and the lethal mix and twisting of facts that his society thrived upon.

The Nazis took as their bible on the subject the book written in 1913 by Austrian engineer Hans Horbiger called *Glazial-Kosmogonie,* which, of course, was a complete work of pseudo-science, but advertised as a theory of 'universal ice'. It is not difficult to see why Horbiger's book attracted the attention of high-ranking Nazi officials like Hitler and Himmler when we see what was written on the title page. The book described itself as 'A new developmental history of the Universe and the Solar System, based on the opposition of Cosmic Neptunism to an equally universal Plutonism, following the most up to date results of all exact branches of research, revised and supported by his own experiences and edited by Philipp Fauth: with 212 diagrams.' A key part of Horbiger's book was the 'history of the Universe' because it led not only to the doctrine of world ice, or *Welteislehre*, but echoed the Nordic heroic mythology featuring apocalyptic struggles between fire and ice. Indeed, this fantastical notion had come to Horbiger in a dream, which also appealed to the Nazis. With little effort the book reeled in Himmler hook, line and sinker. All the more attractive was the fact the book supported many of Hitler and Himmler's beliefs in general, especially those of race.

An important element in *Welteislehre* was the moon, which appeared to be a starting point in some respects. Philipp Fauth was Horbiger's chief follower and a famous German lunar astronomer with a worldwide reputation. However, his ideas were somewhat different from a solid ice moon, as proposed by some versions of glacial cosmogony.

Instead, he believed that it had an icy coating over a rocky body. Nonetheless, the ideas of solid and coated ice bodies were largely interchangeable to suit Nazi doctrine and so the distinction was suitably blurred. Despite Fauth's reputation, many other astronomers were not impressed, the general consensus being this idea was all 'quirks' and 'out of character with studies in astronomy', which, of course, was true. However, Fauth's own studies of the lunar surface had led him to believe its mountains were glacial blocks, as were its craters, which were created not by debris impacts from solar system bodies but ice-rain from the depths of the cosmos. Unfortunately, as promising as this sounded, Fauth's personal contribution to Nazi *Welteislehre* was limited; he died during the war, but he did leave his book behind as a legacy from which the Nazis took inspiration and built upon.

However, it must be said that ideas surrounding a moon, or universe, made of ice did not solely originate with the likes of Fauth and Horbiger or, indeed, the Nazis. For example, the main ice-covering theory of the moon actually originated with a Norwegian captain named Ericsson, who published a paper on the subject in 1869. It was then popularized by the British tea-planter S.E. Peal, who also published a book on the theory. At that stage, neither proposed, nor believed, in a universal ice theory, limiting instead the idea to the moon alone.

Under the Nazis, *Welteislehre* did eventually come to incorporate the whole universe; indeed, it was ice, ice everywhere. The moon was ice, as were the planets, and the sun and even the stars. As for the Milky Way Galaxy stretching across the heavens, its stars were simply crystals of ice twinkling away above our heads, which oddly enough did not fit with Hitler's view that they were inhabited worlds or planets. Even the dark spots on the sun's surface (sunspots) were said to be caused by ice blocks dragged into the sun's gravity where they would spiral down and hit the surface; the solar prominences (large ejections of hot plasma) were therefore giant geysers of exploding steam erupting into space, forming ice crystal meteors. The resulting collisions then throw fine-powdered particles of ice out into space, finally arriving on Earth to produce high-altitude cirrus clouds, hence the reason for the Institute of Meteorology. In the case of meteors, or shooting stars, these were said to explode in our atmosphere after being released from hailstones rather than being debris, like rock and dust grains, from space. All this went against astronomical knowledge and was considered by astronomers as nonsense. For example, as we have seen, at that same time astronomers like Edwin Hubble were advancing Einstein's ideas and realizing the true nature of the universe, an expanding explosion of sorts with receding galaxies of hot stars and hot interstellar materials.

Moreover, when the Nazis came to power, the understanding of temperatures in the cosmos was clear and becoming ever clearer. Certainly at the time of the golden years of German science during the late 1880s, the true temperature of the moon's surface was unknown, but by the early 1900s, the value was being accurately determined. In particular, a lot of credit for this work must go to the fourth Earl of Rosse, who set up sensitive equipment at his observatory in Birr, County Offaly, Ireland. The value he determined for the moon was in excess of 200°F on the sunlit side during the middle of the lunar

Affix
stamp
here

Pen and Sword Books
c/o Casemate Publishers
1950 Lawrence Road
Havertown, PA 19083

day; this was clearly too high for ice to survive, which has a freezing point of only 32°F. The values the earl estimated are now known to be correct. However, acceptance was slow, and by the time the Nazis came to power, there was still considerable debate about the values. Nevertheless, temperature values in other areas of astronomy also showed an ice-based universe was wrong. None of this was of interest to the Nazis, who accepted a frozen moon and a similar condition for the rest of the universe, incorporating it into Nazi doctrine.

There were particular reasons why *Welteislehre* and meteorology combined in the minds of Hitler and Himmler, leading to the desire to form an Institute of Meteorology, as well as astronomers and geologists working alongside meteorologists. One reason centred on Himmler's theory involving ice meteors thrown out from the sun and entering Earth's atmosphere to cause cirrus clouds and hailstorms. What Himmler wanted to do is use this theory as an advantage over the enemy by forecasting long-term weather patterns with the help of Horbiger's book that proved Himmler's theory to his total satisfaction. A further bonus was Horbiger also included details in his theory to support a luminiferous ether as well as supporting the biblical flood involving Noah's Ark and effects leading to the fate of Atlantis. In short, Horbiger's book augmented and 'proved' Himmler right with so many of his pet theories. It is therefore no surprise it quickly became close to the 'theory of everything' for the Nazis from the origins of the universe, its apocalypse and everything in between while unifying the fundamentals of science for a true Nordic philosophy of life and world view, or *weltanschauung*. Moreover, it served as a further dismissal of the Jewish science of Einstein and returned the luminiferous ether to its former glory.

Horbiger was convinced he was on solid scientific ground, which is not out of the ordinary with what astronomy politely calls 'independent thinkers'. Of course, the fact remains his theories were pure pseudo-science bound in a tome amounting to some 800 pages of mysticism presented as solid science that was so attractive to the Nazis. To add to the presentation, Horbiger included many diagrams and photographs accompanied by portmanteau words and a Teutonic style, combining heaviness with dogmatism, making it even more attractive to the Nazis.

It is hardly surprising that mainstream science was not impressed and as a result Horbiger, like Himmler, became convinced he was being persecuted by orthodoxy and all official scientists were therefore his personal enemies. Again, this is not at all out of the ordinary for the 'independent thinker'—all the more so today with social media, where ideas and hostility can reign supreme. Furthermore, in a similar fashion as modern-day social media and its backlashes, Horbiger was so convinced he was right that it was said to be absolutely impossible to debate with him, let alone convince him about facts. This would also be true of Himmler, as we have seen with the memorandum he received from Paul Guthnick of the Babelsberg Observatory. Anybody arguing against this theory would be branded as spreaders of 'fake news' and 'fake facts' in yet another familiar modern-day practice where mainstream scientists were not listened to and there was talk of 'alternative facts' and 'alternative science'. For example, the fourth Earl of Rosse's temperature measurements of the moon's surface were dismissed without a second thought, as were the 1930s' photographs from the world's largest telescopes of the Milky Way, stars and other astronomical bodies, all simply branded as deliberately faked. This Nazi dependency on fake news, alternative facts, alternative science, politics and public manipulation is nothing unique; history of this type repeats itself regularly.

What Horbiger wanted from all this at the time of his book was high office to recognize his work, but true recognition was not achieved until after his death, when the Nazis embraced his theories. That said, *Welteislehre* does still survive in specialist astronomy books as a curiosity often referred to by astronomers as 'WEL' (*welt eis lehre*, or cosmic ice theory). Although considered today as a harebrained theory, at its height it is estimated that *Welteislehre*, or WEL, had at least a million supporters, most of whom were in Germany, with others around the world, including Britain.

Let us now look at this theory in more detail. One area where *Welteislehre* was closer to the truth is its view the universe is filled with rarefied hydrogen gas; this gas does dominate the universe, but the theory was certainly wrong in just about everything else. Under the theory, the stars are chunks of ice and the sun is the most important body which was drawing all the planets that orbit it into its surface, dragged in their orbits by this rarefied hydrogen. Smaller bodies would break apart as a result of the hydrogen, allowing them to fall into the larger planets. The key detail of *Welteislehre* was that practically everything is made of ice, or at least is ice coated, except, of course, the Earth, which had just ice at the poles. This was along the lines of Flat Earthers and their view all the planets are spheres except the Earth, which is flat. There were also rather specific details about the ice on the moon, which was given a thickness of 241km with no supporting evidence. For Mars, it extended to a depth of 402km, again with no supporting evidence. As for the famous Martian canals, these were simply cracks in the ice. We now know they are optical illusions and do not actually exist at all. As for our moon's orbit, it was said to be spiralling into the Earth and will eventually be disrupted before the Earth itself falls into the sun, creating a particularly large sunspot.

It also seems that our current moon is not the first; there have been many before, at least six. All of these six moons have spiralled into the Earth, approaching closely before being disrupted. Each time this has happened there have been major upheavals accounting for extinctions like the Dinosaurs sixty-five million years ago. This series of spiralling moons needs to be examined closer as it is one of the keys to the ice theory. Horbiger believed the penultimate moon existed at the height of the near-prehistoric times; it then spiralled in towards the Earth, breaking up as it went because of the drag of hydrogen. This in turn caused the pulling up of our oceans into a girdle around the equator. As a result of the large amount of ice on the moon's surface, the Earth's temperature plummeted, which in turn terrified humanity, causing them to move to warmer climates. At the same time, the moon was swinging closer and was now dominating the sky, which gave rise to folk legends of evil spirits, dragons and the like. With the moon approaching ever closer, it was further broken up by the Earth's gravity, showering ice rain onto the surface of our planet, closely followed by rocks and various items of debris. While all this was happening, the Earth was twisted out of shape and then suddenly returned to a spherical shape so dramatically there were earthquakes and violent eruptions of volcanoes as the girdle of water at the equator rushed back to higher latitudes, accounting for the biblical floods. Fortunately, there was a long period of calm in the moon theory after which our present moon arrived on the scene and was captured by the Earth between 13,000 to 14,000 years ago, causing more earthquakes and volcanic eruptions. It will eventually spiral inwards to repeat the cycle.

Really the only truth in all this is a body coming close to another can break up. In the case of the Earth, if a natural body comes within what is called the 'Roche Limit', named after Edouard Roche, which is 9,173km above the Earth's surface, it will break up due to gravity. Otherwise, the rest is nonsense. In fact, the moon is spiralling outwards by a little over 3cm per year. A similar situation exists with the planets, which are spiralling out from the sun, not into it.

For followers of such ideas, there is a strange familiarity to the theories of Dr Velikovsky and his book *Worlds in Collision* where the planet Venus, as a comet, caused havoc throughout the solar system and in doing so shows that such ideas often repeat themselves throughout history in one form or another. That makes it all the more suitable for the Nazis because they could join all manner of dots throughout history that really only served to develop a warped Nazi history of reality, especially when it came to the origins and evolution of the Aryan race.

Our next character, Hans Bellamy, enters the story with the legend of Atlantis and its demise due to biblical-style floods. Bellamy was a supporter of the penultimate moon theory and was looking for 'proof' that such floods sank Atlantis. It was therefore to Horbiger's book that Bellamy turned because it had much to say about the legend. As a disciple of Horbiger, and with Horbiger no longer alive, Bellamy picked up the cause using the 1913 book and the subject of *Welteislehre*. Furthermore, Bellamy was now in a position to make his mark under the Nazis by publishing all the mystical ideas associated with these areas that were so popular with them. Of course, the Nazis were also happy to twist and add to the details. To help the cause further there were conferences and 'scientific meetings' where orthodox science was reviled as vigorously as Jewish science had been under Philipp Lenard, Johannes Stark and others involved with the Academy of Nations. In place of mainstream astronomy with all its proof, the subjects of glacial cosmogony, glacial cosmology, and the work of Horbiger were applauded as the 'true science' of astronomy.

There was, however, one of the oddest parts to this whole affair, which surrounded opposition to the theory. This opposition resulted in a somewhat unexpected outcome whereby the Nazi government declared that one could still be a good Nazi if one did not believe in a universe of ice. Oddly, this appeared to go against Himmler's views and his actions against opponents, for example, mainstream astronomers like Paul Guthnick of the Babelsberg Observatory .

With the fall of Nazi Germany, the ideas and support associated with the various cosmic ice theories and their popularity started to diminish, although it has never completely gone away to this day. By the 1950s, *Welteislehre* was modified and the Horbiger Institute under the Nazis reappeared. Despite these modifications, the theory remained relatively true to its origins. In 1953, the institute released a pamphlet claiming: 'The final proof of the whole cosmic ice theory will be obtained when the first landings on the ice-coated surface of the moon takes place.' That point was settled on 20 July 1969 thanks to another Nazi engineer, Wernher von Braun, who helped mankind get to the moon. The result was the moon is not solid ice or rocky with an ice coating. However, in recent years astronomers have found some ice on the surface, but it is a far cry from the ice world theory, amounting to just 'puddles' of ice in some craters at the poles. This is believed to have been deposited by comet impacts and exists because the sun does not shine there to melt it. As for the Horbiger Institute today, they have accepted the truth, to a point.

I suspect if they were still with us, Horbiger, Hitler and Himmler would declare the moon landings as faked, with faked photographs and fake news. As for the astronomers, they would be seen as persecuting Horbiger by orthodoxy and all official scientists are his personal enemies. Looking at the modern-day conspiracy theories that NASA faked the moon landings, not a lot has really changed in that direction. Possibly as a result of the ice theories having been largely abandoned, a Horbiger pamphlet published in 1966 by Egerton Sykes, a noted researcher in Atlantis lore, wrote: 'The main emphasis is now on Horbiger's theories of how the moon was captured which he claims are valid.' However, astronomers now believe there is good reason to support the idea the moon was not captured but resulted from a collision of the Earth and another planetary-sized body about the size of Mars, the debris of which formed our current planet and its only orbiting moon. Sykes also revised the dates for the penultimate moon's encounter with Earth as about 25,000 BC, while we acquired our current moon in 10,000 BC. It is interesting to note these revised dates now connect with other revised events, like the building of the Egyptian pyramids and the weathering of the Sphinx. These new pyramid dates are a far more modern unorthodox area of 'independent thinkers', showing that such theories were never the exclusive domain of the Nazis, and will continue, maybe forever, in one form or another. As I mentioned above with the many 1990s presentations, these ideas continue with ever-evolving connections, mixing and matching as we plod along. Furthermore, in between these dates came the height of the Atlantis civilization, a theory which also plods on to this day in the same circles. As for Sykes' views on ice ages, these are still considered to be associated with the previous moons of Earth and their break-ups, remaining true to Horbiger's original theories.

As well as these adjustments over the years, the Institute also speculated that the belt of asteroids orbiting between Mars and Jupiter were once a planet called Phaeton, which was disrupted by a wandering body called Maldek (or Mallona). This body went off course, bounced off the planets Pluto and Neptune, knocked Jupiter so violently that it produced its famous Red Spot, and finally crashed into Phaeton, smashing it into smithereens to produce the asteroid belt. Again, these views by Sykes are much along the lines of Velikovsky. Either way, they are both scientifically wrong.

At the end of the day, these unorthodox theories have a strange and fascinating charm to them and it is sometimes clear modern supporters do not always realize where they originated as history repeats itself. The trick is to see them for what they are and not to get fanatical about them. Unfortunately, Hitler and Himmler had indeed become fanatical, and that may go some way to explain Hitler's habit of swinging from indifference to fanatical excitement at many conventional scientific ideas and advances presented to him by his scientists; he never really settled down one way or the other. Indeed, his love of the pseudo-sciences meant that to the end he would still rant about secret developments in science and technology capable of turning around Germany's fortunes, wild claims from the scientific disciplines which he had trouble understanding, particularly those less conventional ones. In reality, by then many of the conventional scientific projects had become intermixed with his pseudo-scientific beliefs and even occulted science, all helped along by Himmler and his SS.

It has been claimed that Hitler's unconventional beliefs had significantly contributed to a delusional insanity, which included beliefs that certain geographical areas were important when it came to turning around Germany's looming defeat. These areas were likely to be the esoteric locations developed during his dictatorship. Wherever they were, he believed they must be protected at all costs. This is something we will examine later.

In summary, by the time Hitler had established himself as Fuhrer, his own philosophy of science and technology, as well as other areas, had become firmly established in his mind and there it stayed until he died. He had demoted science, religious and political associations, and even the universe as a whole, to suit his own mentality. He had taken a holistic, pseudo-scientific view of life, the universe and everything. He had convinced himself he had grasped all there was to know about science and technology. Moreover, he would declare that his war against the Allies was technological, but would talk as if this technology could be plucked from thin air like magic, and that he was able to conjure up wonder weapons within unrealistic time scales while expecting no questioning or attacking on his planning or logic.

In reality, there is no evidence that Hitler was a true scientist; there is no evidence he had grasped the way science worked or the scientific legacy of German science during its golden years. He also failed to understand the history and philosophy of science and the structure and organization it required to work. As for the benefits science could afford him, he was severely lacking in his understanding. There were great technological advances, but these were largely due to the efforts of others, while Hitler played at being more of a know-it-all mad scientist. The true element of Aryan physics, and Aryan science in general, is found in the continuation of the 1920s anti-relativist and anti-Semitic attacks on Jewish science from the likes of Lenard, Stark, Rust and the Academy of Nations. Of course, he put his own twist on that and took it to ever more evil heights; worst of all, he had also taken the road to the occult, and that added yet another dimension to his 'scientific' legacy. It may even be said he made the fatal mistake of forging a pact with the devil.

Chapter Four

Into the Labyrinth of the Beast

We have seen how the surreal pseudo-scientific mindset of both Hitler and Himmler helped shape the scientific understanding of the Third Reich. However, they were not alone in such views, and with Himmler's control over the SS, other characters would emerge with equally warped minds. As a result of the confidence in what can generally be termed 'occulted science', the SS became a key part of what was to be an extensive building programme to pursue new physics and the black arts.

We have also seen how many of the beliefs in pseudo-science, and even the occult, that developed in leaps and bounds under Hitler started before he came to power and were put in place during the 1920s amongst a decade of anti-Semitism, anti-relativity and rejection of Jewish science. Now, with Himmler as a facilitator, it was possible to follow the wishes of the dark angels who visited Hitler in prison during 1924. With his own version of the Knights of the Round Table, Himmler gathered together those who could aid him in his task and, while doing so, also implement his own plan to make the SS a self-sustained body free of the Third Reich's bureaucracy and funding, something that eventually led Hitler to declare Himmler a traitor as the war ended.

Wrapped up in this strange world was a further essential element that shaped the inner workings of the Third Reich from a scientific perspective, and that was how the will of Hitler was interpreted by those around him and how it filtered down to lower ranks. Because of the confusion, contradictions and mixed messages surrounding the Fuhrer, any attempt at interpretations must have carried problems. Although it might be seen as an advantage for him to appoint those with the same traits as himself, it simply aggravated the situation, as we will see with Hans Kammler. In fact, there was a clear element of control amongst these high-ranking Nazis in the form of personal agenda with power-grabbing and corruption flourishing, oddly encouraged by Hitler. Essentially, there was a striking image depicting the relationship between the power struggles of the Third Reich and the way science and technology played out under Hitler's will.

From the scientific perspective, it becomes obvious that the Third Reich was not a dictatorship under the tight executive rule and control of its dictator, Adolph Hitler. Instead, he chose to support what can be best described as a cartel of power blocs: the behemoth, monstrous beast of polycratic coalitions of the military forces, business, civil service, the Nazi Party and the power-grabbers. Much of the problems caused by the cartel came from their exercising what they believed was their power by virtue of Hitler's favour and not according to the requirements of science and research; as such it was incumbent on each to interpret the mind and will of the Fuhrer. Unfortunately, as we have seen, when it came to science and technology, the mind and will of the Fuhrer was warped and racist in nature, and this only served to spread like a virus throughout the sciences under his regime. What the mind and will of the Fuhrer actually amounted to was due to his most unfortunate schooling and the dark angels who played upon it.

One of the results of Hitler's mindset and subsequent lack of understanding meant, contrary to beliefs of a fascist leadership principle, he only interfered intermittently in the scientific research of the Third Reich. Furthermore, any interference was often too late and often resulted in disastrous effects. Whereas there have often been claims that Hitler did not know what was going on in his name within certain quarters of the Third Reich, rightly or not, it is certainly true that science was one of those areas, and it clearly stemmed from his education. Therefore, much of the true research and its directions were left to the cartel and their own agenda, as well as their interpretation of the Fuhrer's will. Indeed, there were many only too willing to pursue science and research under those conditions, which meant Hitler himself had little control over the direction of research, development and, often, production in the Third Reich. That said, there is evidence he had more control over production than research, especially production of weapons of mass destruction, but that evidence also shows the results of his control were often disastrous.

Essentially what evolved was a collection of power barons fighting amongst themselves, with some areas of science and technology encouraged, even flourishing towards their ultimate conclusions, while others were opposed, even repressed, all amongst a backdrop of corruption and power-grabs. As such the future of the Nazi war machine with its research, development and production was dependent on a regime that lacked a centralized executive capable of prioritizing these many competing elements. Fritz Todt as minister for armaments and munitions did try to resolve matters, but he had a strained relationship with Hitler. Wrapped up in this unfortunate mix were the pseudo-scientific obsessions of high-ranking Nazis like Hitler and Himmler, who saw their pseudo-science as the true science, while regarding the many areas of true science as pseudo-science. This element of the mix flourished alongside Himmler's desire for an economically self-sustained SS separate from the Third Reich, which, in turn, brought in slave labour and the horrors he and Kammler saw necessary to achieve that goal through concentration camp detainees. This situation was further augmented by Hitler when, at the war's end, he delegated all exotic wonder weapons research and development to Kammler. This was a huge mistake; the great faith in Kammler and belief in his promises that were never delivered served the final blow and the suicide of Hitler.

The only way this cartel seemed to work scientifically was when members would co-operate rather than be in opposition to each other. However, when there was clearly a conflict of interest or corruption at play, the infighting and power-grabbing would show through, and co-operation was easily lost. Unfortunately, science does not work that way and as such was in direct contrast to the Allied efforts in scientific research. For the Allies, science was exploited to the full, and scientists were allowed to do their jobs without the equivalent of the SS breathing down their necks. That said, the Allies were not totally immune to such disadvantages. Even so, given Hitler's unfortunate education, he was in many ways doomed to failure.

An example of how these troubles played out comes with Todt. It was on 17 March 1940 that Todt appeared on the scene as the new minister for armaments and munitions, with the authority to exercise influence over the whole array of weapons production, including the rocket and missile programmes. Todt was a qualified engineer coming from a prosperous middle-class family and with an impressive record, which included his service as an officer during the First World War. Amongst his achievements was the famous building of Germany's autobahns during the 1930s. He was also responsible for building the West Wall, also known as the 'Siegfried Line', a 480km-long defensive line opposite France's Maginot Line, running from Basle to Kleve. The so-called 'Organisation Todt' employed about half a million men to complete the work and consumed a third of Germany's annual supply of cement; the workforce eventually rose to millions by the time war broke out.

Hitler had given Todt the task of ending the bottleneck in army weapon production that was becoming more of a problem than he had liked due to the competing polycratic nature, power-grabbing and infighting, ironically a situation largely caused by Hitler himself. Unfortunately, this proved to be impossible, especially as the war progressed. To add to Todt's problems, he had not been given any authority over the German Navy or Goering's Luftwaffe, the latter being a particular obstacle to his efforts. One of his first orders was to cut back funding on any projects that did not have a short-term chance of success. However, the chaos and confusion continued, even causing suicides and muckraking in attempts to destroy reputations. One such example was the suicide of Karl Becker at the rocket programme. Eventually Todt himself would lose his life after a mysterious explosion aboard his departing plane, just after a blazing row with Hitler. Goering then appeared on the scene in the hope of grabbing the late Todt's power, but Hitler had immediately transferred it to Speer.

The problems continued to drag on during 1940 with overlapping projects, lack of organization and failing momentum. This was further amplified by Goering losing the Battle of Britain from July to October, with the losses to the Luftwaffe marking the Nazis' first real defeat. Furthermore, the promotion of Goering to Reich Marshal of the Greater German Reich (Reichsmarschall), effectively out-ranking all other field marshals, did nothing to help matters. To add to the problems, raw materials were in short supply and Goering had put in place an ineffective rationing plan that only added to production problems.

As we have seen, all these problems and the attitudes towards co-operation were in stark contrast to the past, when Germany was the scientific envy of the world, with its industry and academia working closely together. Now, any remnants of that were suffering under Hitler because of education and science reforms, infighting and the general behaviour of the cartel. As a result, the increasing strains of wartime production mounted, and the situation became a severe disadvantage to Hitler's war machine. Whereas the golden years should have served as a solid foundation to make Hitler's Germany a force to be reckoned with, the downturn following the First World War diminished that possibility and was never fully regained. Even though Germany recovered to some extent during the two world wars, Hitler effectively started demolishing any recovery that had been achieved the moment he came to power in 1933. Moreover, it took much of the war to recover that lost advantage, only to find they were often too late to put into practice new technology. In a last desperate attempt, Hitler turned ever more towards his own 'alternative science', having placed its progress in the dubious hands of Kammler of the SS. Ironically, whereas the golden years had freed Germany to rise from an agricultural economy, setting itself up in serious competition to Britain, France and the United States, wartime Germany saw these countries destroying any remaining elements of the past golden years that Hitler had not already destroyed himself.

Nevertheless, technology did develop and flourish during the war. As the losses to the Luftwaffe mounted, there was a new priority in the form of rocket science, which was now brought forwards in the Fuhrer's mind as a result; until then, Hitler was somewhat cold about the project. In a memorandum from the top rocketeer, Walter Dornberger, for the attention of Field Marshal von Brauchitsch, he said the A-4 rocket (later known as the V-2) should be regarded as a 'significant relief for the employment of aircraft against England, and especially London and the port cities.' He also pointed out that the advantages were an inability to defend against rockets and the element of terror it would bring to Britain in undermining the will of the British. There was also the added bonus that rockets were unaffected by weather and, overall, they were a crucial contribution to the 'defeat of England'. Rocketry was certainly one area of the Third Reich that saw advanced technology, extreme effort and organization, but it also saw the efforts of the cartel and shortage of materials, energy and labour, producing considerable setbacks. These problems were added to by Allied bombing raids. Had things been different, V-2 rockets might have rained down on Britain possibly 2 years earlier than 1945; then, Hitler's original dream would have materialized when he said: 'What I want is annihilation, annihilating effect!' The same was true of the V-1 doodlebug, which suffered the same kinds of delay.

Hitler's promise to the people to build an arsenal of offensive missiles resulted in Germany's bold attempt to apply the necessary high technology to fulfil this promise. With a rich German history in rocketry already in place before the outbreak of war, the Nazis had started building its research and production plants as early as 1936, like Peenemunde, designed and constructed by the Luftwaffe in a neo-classical style. This was just the start of a set of fortresses planned under the control of Kammler. Goering then forged an alliance between the rocketeers and his Luftwaffe, a relationship that would eventually turn sour.

There were also similar problems in store for aviation. Although under Hitler the aviation industry was awash with funding, allowing its physicists and engineers to indulge their wildest dreams, the corruption and infighting of the cartel was ever-present. Not only were there the shortages of raw materials affecting production; there were also many delays piled upon delays. Often, just as a design was about to go into production, high-ranking Nazis would decide on a change of design, resulting in a return to the drawing board. There was also a trend of spending considerable amounts of money and time building each aircraft individually with teams of skilled craftsmen rather than on a production-line basis as the Allies did. One individual who caused a lot of problems was Colonel-General (*Generaloberst*) Ernst Udet, who had an obsession with dive bombers and would insist that aircraft were designed, or redesigned at the last minute, to allow them to dive bomb. There was also great competition between companies and corruption. Indeed, Udet was another to commit suicide as a result of his troubles.

The atomic bomb development under the Nazis also suffered, but in a somewhat different way. As we saw, Hitler's enthusiasm was not great because of its Jewish connection with nuclear research, so, if this project ever saw any real development, it was likely driven by the cartel that surrounded him, their own personal agendas and their interpretation of the Fuhrer's will. Whereas there is some evidence of such a project, it was certainly not from the main physicist, Heisenberg. Instead, there does seem to be evidence that something along the lines of a dirty bomb was considered; that is, a conventional explosive that spreads radioactive material into the environment. However, it is a simple fact that the manpower, finance and technical capability to build an atomic bomb would have diverted all such resources away from conventional weapons like the rocket programme and aviation. Therefore, any real possibility of developing an atomic bomb was soon lost when Hitler gained power in 1933, highlighting one of his first errors, with any significant Jewish scientists working on the splitting of uranium (fission) under the Allies. Indeed, by the time such dismissals were well underway in Germany, physicists were on the point of making major breakthroughs in understanding how uranium atoms split and the consequences that might bring to the war.

Even Speer, as part of his financing duties under Hitler and his dealings with Heisenberg, admitted that too many resources and finance would have needed to be diverted to the atomic bomb project. He also admitted that Hitler's understanding of nuclear physics was obviously strained, saying he was 'unable to grasp the revolutionary nature of nuclear physics'. In fact, out of the 2,200 points raised with Hitler in his conferences, nuclear fission was mentioned only once and then briefly.

There was a clear contrast between the way the Third Reich and the golden years of German science tackled the research, development and production of scientific advancement. During those golden years of prosperity, starting as far back as 1824, the country saw the might of German industry develop alongside academic growth with full co-operation. There were many new universities opened as scientists and students flocked to study and research, resulting in a staggering list of scientific achievements and new products that were exported around the world. These skills were clearly missed by Hitler—essential elements that resulted in no small part in the troubles of the Third Reich. Instead, the Nazis chose the road of segregation, secrecy, competition and corruption within industry and a serious alienation towards academia. Under the Nazis, education and science were drastically reorganized for the worse, partly due to lack of understanding, partly due to prejudices and racism, and partly due to the controlling cartel, which played their parts in irreparable damage. Although there were many occasions when Hitler talked of the golden years and its scientific discoveries, the practices that Germany used to achieve that world status did not seem to be appreciated by Hitler or indeed many in his orbit; however, they were nevertheless essential discoveries that shaped the war machine when it suited.

When considering how Hitler's conventional war machine developed and how it fits with the more exotic pseudo-scientific elements, we find a prime example with Hans Kammler, who was a key member of Himmler's plans. Kammler was a doctor of engineering, as well as being one of the coldest, most ruthless and cruellest characters we will explore. However, before his elevation within the SS, he started his career as an unremarkable civil servant. Starting in the Reich Air Ministry (RLM), amongst his duties he had special responsibility for construction projects such as barracks, administration blocks and aircraft hangars, which proved to be a particular talent. He soon realized by the autumn of 1941 that he was getting nowhere, and his promotion prospects were not particularly good. To escalate up the military ranks, he decided to join the SS, where he first became a brigade leader (Brigadefuhrer) in charge of building projects; this would be the start of his impressive career under the SS.

Kammler first came to Hitler's attention after producing a carefully designed, hand-coloured diagram for the Auschwitz concentration camp. The Fuhrer was impressed, seeing qualities in Kammler that matched his own dictatorial nature; it was obvious Kammler showed perverse capabilities which extended to complete control of a project without relinquishing his grip on the strategic objectives or control over its workforce. Consequently, Hitler delegated more and more power to him as the war drew to a frantic rush for new wonder weapons from 1943 onwards. Amongst his many achievements that struck a chord with Hitler was the re-engineering of the Warsaw Ghetto; after the crushing of the August 1944 uprising, he levelled the contaminated area and saw that all 34 million bricks were used for other more essential building projects. The Fuhrer was suitably impressed. Other duties involved concentration camps, where he increased the daily capacities of the gas chambers and ovens from 10,000 to 60,000. For all his hard work, by the end of the war he had received his reward by rising to the rank of four-star general (Obergruppenfuhrer), at which stage he was effectively only one rank below Himmler.

In many respects, Kammler was more of a dictator than Hitler. In fact, one of Kammler's memorable quotes which shows his true nature was the comment to his staff declaring: 'Pay no attention to the human cost. The work must go ahead, and in the shortest possible time.' As a result, under Kammler and Himmler, the SS created a living hell while power-grabbing just about all scientific projects by the war's end.

Kammler, unsurprisingly, took full advantage of the increasing power bestowed upon him by the Fuhrer. Indeed, while Hitler and his generals huddled together in the

Fuhrerbunker as Berlin was destroyed above them during April 1945, Hitler would rant and rave about the great weapons of mass destruction promised by Kammler, with his claims they would turn the war around to their advantage; like Himmler's promises to the Fuhrer, they fell short of reality or amounted to little at best. Nevertheless, Kammler had an impressive record of pursuing many radical and unconventional ideas for new weapons as he rose in power; he also continued with his building projects, again promising much that did not materialize.

With free range to indulge his dreams during the final years of the war, he drafted a 13-billion-mark programme of construction for the SS, including concentration camps in the newly captured territories from the Soviet Union to Norway. The ambitious plans Kammler had for expanding the camps was encouraged by Oswald Pohl, Himmler's economic authority, who saw this as the engine of growth for the SS's long-term economic plan under Himmler, and freedom from the Third Reich, by using slave labour and charging for the service. Under his plans, Kammler expanded the camps from 4 million to 14 million in just 3 months. However, despite Himmler, Kammler and Pohl's beliefs, Speer did not see the camps as the answer to Germany's manufacturing needs, and constantly thwarted Kammler's efforts. Eventually, as with Himmler and the rocket programme, Speer lost and Kammler won. In his autobiography, Speer admitted his defeat was because, in Kammler, he was battling against a twisted image of himself. The two men came from similar backgrounds—a solid middle-class family, both went to university, both had been discovered as a result of their work in construction, and both had meteoric rises in the fields in which they were trained; it is clear Speer was jealous of Kammler. If there was any significant difference between the two, it was conscience; whereas Speer wrestled with his conscience, Kammler was a cold, ruthless, evil individual without any moral doubts.

It is now clear that Kammler played a significant role in the black side of Nazism. As we will see, details have come to light about this somewhat mysterious member of the Nazi Party. Oddly, one area of his life still has no real smoking gun evidence; that was exactly what role or association he had with Himmler's *Ahnenerbe* and its black magicians or so-called 'knights'. Nevertheless, there are clues that he was as involved as Himmler himself and he was highly likely to be one of Himmler's chosen generals that sat at the Round Table. As we examine the clues, it will be hard to believe he was not part of the inner circle of the *Ahnenerbe*.

As something of a recap, as far as Himmler's *Ahnenerbe* was concerned, all future research of weapons would eventually come under the control of the SS. The SS began as Hitler's bodyguard, but with Himmler's desire to make it a self-sustained economic entity in its own right, it grew and developed during the war, eventually becoming the most powerful entity of the Third Reich after Hitler himself. Its military arm, the Waffen SS, then became the most elite military force in Germany. Over time, Himmler worked his way into many of the research projects and organizations of the Third Reich, eventually taking over just about all scientific projects by the last years of the war. This had direct consequences for both the physicists and engineers researching these projects and Jewish scientists in particular; it also brought into play the horrors of the concentration camps, which were also under the control of the SS and brought in that cheap supply of slave labour, generating a financial income. It was here that the SS economic branch made money by supplying the labour at low cost to many of the industries and research projects both exotic and conventional in nature.

As we have also seen, within this was the secret society element that included the alternative to SS in the form of the followers of the Black Sun, and it appears that this is where many of the pseudo-scientific elements of the SS resided. The Black Sun was where Himmler's Knights of the Round Table and top generals were initiated into the society as its knights. The Black Sun symbolism formed a central doctrine to the pre-Nazi secret society known as the Thule Society, and the Black Sun symbol was adopted as the emblem for von Liebenfels' New Templars. This, together with the swastika itself, in this context, becomes not only a well-known symbol from ancient esoteric traditions, but also a talisman of ceremonial magic on a celestial scale.

Importantly, the methods of de Lubicz found themselves at home in Himmler's *Ahnenerbe*, but they also found a place in Kammler's mindset and his version of the black arts. This was achieved through his own version of the *Ahnenerbe,* generally referred to as the 'Kammler think tank' or *Kammlerstab* (Kammler staff). Like Himmler's *Ahnenerbe*, Kammler's think tank would consider whatever was necessary to achieve its goals; any and all research projects were considered, however weird, out of the box, pseudo-scientific, harebrained, or within the realms of the occult. Furthermore, Kammler's think tank technologies appear to have been developed so that they might be adapted to a variety of uses in the various highly classified weapons developments and black projects. There was considerable overlap of technologies that could be developed and employed across a wide variety of weapons systems and between projects. This served to confuse post-war investigations, whether intentional or not. It was encouraged to follow every available method for the creation of prototypes, 'smart weapons', where German technological and engineering competence was to be exploited to the maximum. This competence was to be pursued in unconventional ways and combinations to create not only new weapons but also a new doctrine of warfare. The idea was that the first generation of such weapons would be extrapolated upon and a second and third generation of technology produced, with long-range goals mapped out. In short, the long-term goal was to create weapons of mass destruction using every known principle of physics and their extrapolations for whatever weapons may be possible. It was even possible for this creative thinking to go against Nazi Party ideology if it produced the goods.

This way of working meant the projects came under the jurisdiction of the SS not only because it was to be kept secret, or hidden, from the German people but also because the SS was best placed to monitor, study, organize and fund the whole process. It seems clear that Kammler's projects and way of thinking was essentially identical to Himmler's *Ahnenerbe* where, if necessary, all normal constraints or orthodox conceptual or moral paradigms were to be laid aside. Given the nature and mutual views of both Himmler and

Kammler, it is likely Kammler was one of Himmler's special generals and a member of his Knights of the Round Table as well as a key member of the *Ahnenerbe*.

Much of Kammler's think tank was based in the key geographical areas now known to be associated with pseudo-scientific research, like Prague, which Hitler feistily defended in the dying weeks of his dictatorship against pleas from his generals to move troops to the north, where they were desperately needed. Hitler's determination to protect Prague at all costs also extended to Norway, with both locations believed to be crucial to winning the war because of the Kammler wonder weapons supposedly being developed in those locations. In the case of Norway, it was believed technologies were evacuated there as the Allies and Red Army swept across occupied Europe, something we will examine later.

A further connection between Kammler and Himmler's *Ahnenerbe* is found with Himmler's belief he had a psychic connection with the famous mediaeval German Holy Roman Emperor Heinrich the Fowler. As a result of this, Himmler had the emperor's remains dug up and reinterred in the cathedral of the little town of Quedlinburg in the Harz Mountains, which was central to Kammler's own empire of underground secret weapon plants and laboratories. Kammler, as we will see, was also responsible for constructing areas like this as part of a grand master plan for last-stand fortresses.

Kammler and Himmler were clearly like-minded. Kammler's think tank with its secret weapons, death camps and consciously organized and orchestrated nature was designed to use massive amounts of slave labour, especially when raising funds for the SS, as well as intellectual and technological capital, on any off-the-books black projects, including the recovery of lost and exotic technology and science, by whatever means and whatever costs it took. At times, it is clearly impossible to distinguish between the Himmler's *Ahnenerbe* and Kammler's think tank; both followed Himmler's *Ahnenerbe* mission statement with the use of the esoteric and occult traditions, including legends and myths often found in ancient texts and traditions, as well as various secret societies associated with them. Furthermore, both appear to have been kept secret from the German people, with Kammler being the more successful in that respect. Kammler also included traditions and legends that are not generally considered to be esoteric or occult in nature in the usual sense. This was due to the belief that all and any possible routes to secret weapons and the winning of the war should be considered. Part of the reasoning behind this was because they remain esoteric or occult as a result of not being well-known to the general public.

There was also the area of buried or partially buried possibilities which formed past or pre-history lost science, hidden in the mists of time. These included old mythologies, legends, texts, and sculptures, talismans and physical monuments that may be associated with them, of various cultures, whether considered canonical or apocryphal by any given community. These cultures, as we have seen with Hitler and Himmler, included Sumerian, Hindu, Mayan, Egyptian, Chinese, Scandinavian-Teutonic, and later Graeco-Roman European cultures.

As with Himmler, it was thought that such texts would yield lost science that was very different from the ideologies, like relativity, condemned as Jewish science, but quite in line with Aryan science, such as vorticular physics, including vorticular spin, polarization, quantum mechanics and their mathematical predictions of the vacuum energy flux or zero-point energy and so-called 'free energy'. These points appear to be particularly associated with ideas of flying discs, or flying saucers, that would be considered as a weapon of mass destruction possibly delivering bombs to places as far away as New York in the United States. As such, there was a lot of similarities between Kammler's think tank and Himmler's *Ahnenerbe*.

Kammler's empire not only consisted of his special unit, where many of the black projects would be based, he also appears to have been a key player in the construction plans of many fortresses that would both research such projects and defend the Third Reich, especially as a last-ditch stand against the Allies. Essentially this came about because the Nazis had two possibilities to follow: the possibility they were going to have to stand and fight, and the possibility they should pursue ever more exotic weaponry to win the war. They chose to pursue both options; therefore, their fortresses would incorporate both options.

When Hitler came to power, one of his earliest decisions was to rebuild the German Air Force; another was to get engineers back to work. As for the new Luftwaffe, that was to be a clean break from the past; it also caused early worries and misunderstanding in Britain when Hitler referred to a new weapon of mass destruction. It took the radar expert and intelligence officer R.V. Jones to work out that this was not some sort of 'death ray' as suspected by the Foreign Office translation, but simply Hitler referring to his plans for the Luftwaffe. For Churchill, the death ray problem was an old worry dating back to the First World War, when ideas to fry the enemy with electromagnetic radiation were seriously suggested. This situation came about partly due to the Croatian physicist Nikola Tesla, who had not only been experimenting with electromagnetic radiation but was actually trying to get military funding in the early 1900s for his version of a death ray. He never did get any financial backing, but what did come out of this was a keen interest by the Nazis in developing a death ray as a wonder weapon, which took many forms as the war progressed. Indeed, many a conspiracy theory has grown up around Nazi research involving such a device. No doubt that was one of the ideas Kammler and his think tank were working on, but considering the secrecy surrounding him, especially during several post-war decades, the facts have become blurred, with all manner of conspiracy theories in place still to this day. That said, it is clear from available records that Kammler was following Hitler's desire to make a clean break from the past and also include pseudo-scientific ideas in general research and development. To achieve this, he was expected to use the finest minds from any branch of the German military.

Tesla's work was certainly a favourite with the Nazis, not only because of possible death rays but also because some of his devices have also been linked to zero-point energy devices researched by Nazis physicists, one of which was free energy; Germany was energy-starved, and as the war progressed, that position intensified. As a result of Tesla, there were also clear links with the Nazi doctrine that supported an ether, and no doubt that would be a source of research for the *Kammlerstab*. Indeed, there are several controversial devices from this part of history that suggest death ray and free energy experiments were a high priority for the *Kammlerstab* and other Nazi physicists. Add to this the 'no limits' and 'overlap' elements of the *Kammlerstab*, and Himmler's *Ahnenerbe*, and it is no surprise these ideas appear time and again within many research projects where appropriate.

In 1978, the British government finally declassified a BIOS report on two curious circuit devices devised by the German naval engineer and inventor Hans Coler (sometimes called Kohler). We have already encountered its cousin in the form of the Karl Schappeller device and submarine research. The report regarding these two circuits (number 1074, item number 31, summer 1946) was titled *The Inventions of Hans Coler Relating to an Alleged New Source of Power*. It considered tests on two strange circuits conducted at the University of Berlin between the two world wars and carried out by Dr W.O. Schumann, discoverer of the Schumann resonance of the Earth. A simple glance explains why these devices attracted such attention, especially by the German Navy: it was said to provide limitless energy and was a quiet-running device, making it suitable for powering submarine propulsion. It consisted of a hexagonal construction of coils and magnets, with two rotating sub-circuits, yet no power input. Coler and Schumann stated they produced, or transduced, a power output from apparently nowhere. Of course, such devices effectively giving something for nothing (power out for no power in) are shunned by conventional physics, but this was simply one of those zero-point energy devices tapping into the zero-point field, or at least that is what the Nazis believed. This was a typical example of overlapping projects.

These devices appear to have the usual air of mystery surrounding them. They are also considered a failure in the hunt for free energy from the quantum background, and the fact the BIOS report is now declassified shows that much, even though in 1926, Schumann decided Coler's device was 'no fault, hoax, or fraud on the part of the inventor'. This story may have more to do with the anti-Semitism and anti-relativity of the 1920s involving the Nazi preference for Planck's quantum physics rather than Einstein's relativity and its dismissal of the ether as unnecessary to physics; there is probably some politics wrapped up with the science, or pseudo-science. Interestingly, the connection with the Schappeller device adds weight to it also being somewhat dubious. Furthermore, there are also conspiracy claims that the devices were captured at the war's end near South America and the Antarctic from fleeing U-boats.

Following the Battle of Britain in 1940, the German air domination over Europe started to decline, setting in motion one of the major reasons for Germany's defeat. Germany's means of industrial, arms and energy production became increasingly vulnerable to attack from Allied bombers. With every possible area of German industry being attacked, including new aircraft production, as well as rockets, tanks, cannons, oil refineries and even the feeble attempts to produce an atomic bomb (which the Allies thought was a major project until December 1944), Germany started to turn to somewhat desperate attempts to produce new wonder weapons. Over the years of 1943 to 1945, in particular, the targeting of sites and massive carpet-bombing raids became ever more accurate as a result of onboard H2S radar developed by British physicists, including astronomers like Bernard

Lovell of Jodrell Bank Radio Astronomy fame. That radar proved extremely beneficial to the Allies and a disaster to the Third Reich.

One plan by the Nazis for just such a situation was a counter-measure of mountain fortresses or *Alpenfestung*—something that brought Kammler back into the story with his construction skills. Originally, these were to be extensively set up in the German-held areas of northern Italy, Austria and Germany, roughly in the area where these countries converged with each other and Switzerland. For example, a fortress in the Harz Mountains of Thuringia was planned with large underground facilities. In total, it would extend from Nordhausen in the north down through Kahla and into the Jonas Valley. A similar complex was planned for the Owl Mountain that separated Poland from Czechoslovakia, which would include *Der Riese* (The Giant). Yet another complex was to be set up in the Black Forest of southern Germany, along with smaller sites of resistance planned for Norway, the Bohemian Forest, and the Bavarian Forest.

These fortresses were to be huge in scale, comprising research, development, production and administration, along with the necessary workers and slave labour from the concentration camps supplied by the SS. They would also have bomb-proof overhangs for aircraft take-off and landing, along with underground hangars where missiles could be fired automatically straight off the production lines. Other weapons would also be manufactured in these fortresses, including research and development of more exotic weapons, such as stealth aircraft and flying discs. To further protect these facilities, they would house soldiers and units from the SS. Further protection would be provided by specially trained mountain troops defending the mountain passes into these fortresses.

History shows these fortresses were never built in quite the grand scale first envisaged; it was one of those extravagant Nazi dreams, along with some of the weapons they planned to develop in them. However, as we will see, elements of this grand plan did materialize as the war progressed and the need for underground facilities became ever more necessary due to the intensive Allied bombing, which escalated from about 1943 onwards, thanks to that H2S radar and other means.

Particular problems faced by the Nazis involving these fortresses were the country's construction capabilities along with the internal infighting, power struggles and corruption within industry and between individuals. There was also a severe raw materials and energy shortage. In short, all this was planned to come together as a solution, but the internal politics and power struggles prevented the completion of many projects or caused such delays that they came just too late in the war.

The Nordhausen in Thuringia is well-known as a site for the production of V-1 and V-2 rockets, while the underground complexes of the Jonas Valley south of Nordhausen were another vast facility which would serve as a centre for government and possibly research for advanced weapons; there were similar complexes in Poland. As for the complex known as *Der Riese*, this appears to have been a site that served as a uranium mine and possible uranium processing plant; however, this never led to the atomic bomb, if conventional history is to be believed. Nevertheless, we will see that the Nazi atomic bomb and its associated nuclear physics research have some interesting stories behind them, suggesting some progress may have been made beyond what is generally accepted, and it is no surprise Kammler's name appears amongst these projects. It was possible other research for secret weapons also occurred at *Der Riese* because many of the ideas overlapped and Kammler was particularly keen that ideas could be swopped around different projects, as we have seen.

Another key underground base was the Wenceslas Mine, which was known to be a further facility for secret weapons research under Kammler, and also carries claims of being a location for nuclear research amongst other projects. It is situated about 50km or so on the other side of Wroclaw (formally Breslau of the German Gau of the Lower Silesia), around 350km from Warsaw. Much of the work resulting in our understanding of this mine's activities under the Nazis is due to Igor Witkowski, who produced a series of books on the subject in Polish. Witkowski spent years sifting through archives relating to the many secrets of the Nazi scientific establishments in and around Breslau (modern-day Wroclaw). Witkowski, a former defence journalist, uncovered a systematic SS-controlled research and development operation in a rat-run of interconnected facilities, most of which were underground in the remote Sudeten Mountains in the south-west of Poland (Lower Silesia as it was then before the handover to Poland after the war).

Interestingly, Witkowski's investigations pointed to a number of nuclear research projects, despite the fact this is considered unlikely because of Heisenberg's work (or lack of it) in that area. It was one site in particular that did not follow the general trend of research, with a series of experiments taking place in a mine close to the Czech frontier beginning in 1944 and continuing into April 1945, and possibly to the end of the war elsewhere. Like many such projects, these 1944 adventures were being raced through against time under the noses of the advancing Allied Forces; in this case, the advancing Red Army. One experiment, the possible nuclear one, was a device called *Die Glocke* (The Bell). We will examine this device later when considering some of the exotic weapons said to have been developed by Nazi physicists and the SS.

Production facilities were also set up to refine synthetic petroleum products from coke to generate electricity and all manner of other forms of fuel for use in aircraft, rockets and flying discs. Such complexes were found throughout Germany, Austria, Czechoslovakia and Poland.

Smaller camouflaged facilities were also planned, and many completed, providing a web where their products were sent to other, often larger, facilities for further work and maybe sent on further still for assembly. However, the overriding dream was to have self-contained facilities where the raw materials entered one end and the weapons were fired out at the other end. To avoid Allied bombing, these camouflaged facilities were often moved around, especially so when they were waiting for underground facilities to become available or to be built. This would become a further strain on power reserves and manpower, but it also produced a problem for Allied bombers because it presented too many moving targets and easily overwhelmed any bombing campaign. Fortunately, there was a weakness in all this, in the form of how they were moved. The sheer scale meant that moving had to be done by railway, and that was a far easier target to bomb; moreover, once the railways were bombed, it prevented further movements until the Germans rebuilt them, putting still more pressure on an already strained construction programme and its energy reserves.

In an attempt to survive, Germany also experimented with radical new types of air defence systems, cannons and anti-aircraft rockets guided by both ground control and infra-red homing devices. In fact, when the war came to an end, some of these infra-red research projects appeared at facilities also researching flying discs and new forms of cannons, including vortex cannons, as well as several other mysterious and unconventional weapons, some of which remain a mystery to this day but are believed to be part of the *Kammlerstab*. It is also clear some of this was connected with the vortex physics so important to the Third Reich's pseudo-scientific research, although not all projects were pseudo-scientific. For example, there were also air turbulence bombs, air explosives, aircraft-trailing long wires that would tangle around propellers, numerous electronic jamming devices, radar-jamming devices (which also seem to be based at flying disc centres), engine- and ignition-stopping devices using electromagnetism (again associated with flying discs), long-range devices based on the microwave and X-ray regions of the electromagnetic spectrum (death rays), magnetically repulsed projectiles, vortex cannons, sun cannons and saucer-shaped interceptor aircraft.

However, serious flying disc research really only appeared close to the end of the war and is probably not as important as modern UFO researchers believe. Nevertheless, it has its origins in around 1941 and was remarkably advanced in many ways, although it was another project that came too late. Some of these discs were somewhat more exotic, with others designed as interceptors, but by the time flying disc technology was seriously considered and developed from 1943 to 1945, the Germans already had jet and rocket interceptors; German skies were relatively full of them. So the disc interceptor versions were not such a high priority then as we give them today, looking back upon it from a UFO perspective. In some ways, the flying discs were just another weapon, but at that stage the SS was in control of just about all science research and new weapons were being considered and promised to Hitler by Himmler and Kammler, so they had their place. That said, there did appear to be projects under development that fit the modern-day flying saucer story as one of those overlapping projects, but it was long drawn out. In fact, one prototype was only ready the day the Nazis surrendered.

By the war's end, so many projects were in the pipeline, the inventory was quite staggering, although that does not mean they would have all come to anything. It was desperate times as Allied carpet bombing was destroying so much of the Nazi war machine, as well as the country's infrastructure generally. As the conflict drew to a close, military planners in Germany considered the idea of concentrating their ground and air defences into specific fortresses for a last stand to buy them time. That time would be used to perfect new *siegerswaffen* or super weapons; many of these SS projects were rushing to a conclusion, and many would never be fully realized.

Considering the power Hitler bestowed on Kammler and the extent of his work, especially in the last 3 years of the war, it is strange how he barely rates a mention in standard works until decades after his death. In fact, much of the mystery surrounding him was only resolved around the early 2000s, although the clues were there from about the mid-1970s in obscure publications and interviews; even enquiries at London's Imperial War Museum would draw a blank. However, one attempt did bear fruit, when Nick Cook, aerospace consultant at *Jane's Defence Weekly*, enquired with them, resulting in one of their researchers tracing a thin volume about Kammler. It had the rather intriguing title *Blunder! How the US Gave Away Nazi Supersecrets to Russia,* penned by Cambridge graduate and foreign correspondent Tom Agoston. The content of this work confirmed many of the claims from former Nazis and was a mine of new information no other researchers had been able to uncover.

Agoston was an air photo interpreter during the war and travelled to the Nuremberg war crimes trials as a result of his war work. There he met honorary SS Standard Leader (Standartenfuhrer) Wilhelm Voss, who was in charge of the Skoda Works, which was used as a cover for Kammler's activities. In the course of many interviews during 1949, Voss was able to explain to Agoston the details of the Skoda Works, Kammler, and the *Kammlerstab,* which was made possible because, while at the trials, Voss was put up at Agoston's home. During the many discussions, Agoston was able to piece together a far fuller picture than previously known as Voss told him everything he knew about Kammler and his special projects office. It turned out that Kammler's office was considered the most advanced high-tech research and development centre within the Third Reich, and was totally independent of the Skoda Works' own research and development while using the Works as a cover. As part of the secrecy, all funding for Kammler was channelled through Voss, who reported progress to Himmler, as did Kammler. Top scientists, chosen for their intelligence rather than their allegiance to the Nazi Party, were also taken from research institutes all over the Third Reich; what was more important was they were experts in their fields, scientists and engineers good at what they did.

One bonus for the many scientists and engineers appeared to be a desire to see their work in print through the technical papers the *Kammlerstab* produced; that was even the case if such papers were secret rather than openly published in top science and engineering journals. That bonus included the fact the papers would be circulated amongst other experts associated with the relevant research areas through the central office and, where necessary, developed into working prototypes and, hopefully, final working versions. This exemplified the secrecy practice of the Nazis, whereby nobody really had the full picture except those high up in the Nazi Party, like Himmler and Kammler; in other words, it was highly compartmentalized. Agoston reported that some of these papers would also serve as a means to recruit other experts, including for the Skoda Works' research.

As part of Himmler's plan, the SS also set up research facilities for politically unreliable scientists. All the usual methods were employed, including the exploration of every possibility; many projects had overlap and, of course, explored possibilities along the pseudo-scientific route. Some of these facilities were set up at Oranienburg, Nordhausen, Mechlenburg, Mathausen and Prague. All used slave labour from SS concentration camps. All this activity was protected by the SS through a triple ring of security around the facilities that consisted of counter-intelligence specialists chosen from the ranks of the SS especially for the task. That triple ring of security had been established by Himmler personally at the Skoda Works at Pilsen and Brno, as well as their administration centre and research at Prague.

What we have here is the region sometimes referred to as the 'Kammler Empire', where visionary projects were pursued in a highly compartmentalized section of the Skoda Works in the Reich Protectorate of Bohemia and Moravia in the vassal Nazi state of Czechoslovakia. This was a giant industrial complex centred on the Czech towns of Pilsen and Brno, and was an SS-run operation. Through the brutal administration of SS Four-Star General (Obergruppenfuhrer) Reinhard Heydrich, the author of the *Final Solution of the Jewish Problem* and protector of Bohemia-Moravia, the SS had come to treat the industry of the entire Czech region as its own private domain. Heydrich was Himmler's second in command but was assassinated by Czech agents in Prague on 27 May 1942—an incident that proved to be a turning point for Kammler. Heydrich and Kammler were cut from the same cloth, and Kammler was now in a prime position to also enter the orbit of Himmler, as well as Hitler. After Heydrich's death, Himmler saw a suitable replacement for Heydrich because of Kammler's cold, ruthless, evil nature and his ability as an energetic executor of his wishes. From that point, the development of the concentration camps was added to Kammler's responsibilities.

Voss described the activities of scientists at the *Kammlerstab* as beyond any technology that had appeared by the end of the war, including research into nuclear physics, particularly nuclear power plants, rockets, aircraft, highly advanced guided weapons and anti-aircraft lasers.

In March 1949, several weeks after he briefed Agoston, Voss was pulled in by the United States Counter Intelligence Corps (CIC) for questioning. He told the CIC agents about the range of research, after which the CIC warned him not to speak about this or the existence and work of the *Kammlerstab* to anybody else. Unfortunately, although he gave his word to the CIC, he had already had his long and detailed meetings with Agoston; he chose not to tell the CIC about those conversations. Shortly after his questioning, he contacted Agoston and asked that he did not mention their meeting or publish the details he had divulged. Although Agoston agreed to this request, causing a further delay in the release of the information to the world, following Voss's death in 1974 Agoston thought it would now be in order to publish his research that included the details he obtained from Voss. Interestingly, in theory, the questioning of Voss by the CIC should be available through the Freedom of Information Act (FOIA), but it appears the powers-that-be deny that any such questioning ever took place and say no files exist; not an unusual response today.

From these details, it is clear that the Kammler think tank was just that: a think tank and not an actual experimental and development institution. However, any work of promise at the *Kammlerstab* did go on to the research and development stage elsewhere, and Kammler was deeply involved in that side of things, travelling between sites regularly with Hitler's full authority. Indeed, by the war's end, Hitler had given him authority to enter any works without hindrance as and when he saw fit.

It comes as no surprise that Himmler's power-grabs included the Skoda Works too. By March 1942, Himmler had formally taken over control of the Skoda Works, bypassing Speer's authority again in the process. In fact, Speer only learned of this arrangement when Hitler told him, explaining it was 'a fait accompli'. Hitler then tasked Himmler with evaluation and duplication of weapons systems captured from the enemy, especially those which appeared to be superior to their own, one of which was Lovell's H2S radar recovered from crashed RAF and American bombers. That back-engineering also came too late for the Nazis. To add to the delay, they were mystified by a broken glass tube in the onboard radar. That turned out to be a simple transmit/receive (T/R) switching device so that the transmitter and receiver could be used as one, reducing the size of the overall equipment. This order from the Fuhrer was completed in record time under the Skoda Works' director, Voss. The speed at which this had been done, Voss told Himmler, was due to the removal of bureaucracy which accompanied projects administered by Speer's Ministry of Armament. This made the Skoda Works beyond oversight and secured the secret location for the Kammler think tank. Furthermore, this appears to explain why Speer knew little about Kammler and his works and why, during interrogations after the war about the think tank's activities, he referred his interrogators to Kammler, who had vanished.

With this move, Himmler had made the *Kammlerstab* so secret and beyond outside control that, to all intents and purposes, it did not technically exist. Moreover, Kammler and Voss now had the remit from Hitler and Himmler to go ahead without any interference from Goering as well as Speer; no wonder details after the war were few and far between. Indeed, the *Kammlerstab* might have remained hidden if it was not for Tom Agoston, because the United States still has Kammler's file classified, and FOIA requests come back with nothing to declare.

Himmler's attempts to take control of all scientific research projects and build his self-sustaining SS included wrestling away control from other areas under Speer's jurisdiction. Although Speer was Hitler's trusted architect and close adviser, scientifically he was essentially lost, like the Fuhrer, having no formal training. However, there is evidence he saw science in a far more conventional way than Hitler, Himmler and Kammler, and was even critical of Hitler's pseudo-scientific approach and amateurish views. This might explain why he was shut out of many projects considered as pseudo-science or even occultist in nature. Speer attempting to understand science resulted in him meeting with Heisenberg to discover the state of the atomic bomb research and its funding. However, he met with the Heisenberg enigma, eventually driving him to put funding into the rocket research leading to the V-1 and V-2 instead. Heisenberg was left with a nuclear reactor project, but even that was half-hearted, and Speer found he came up against the Heisenberg enigma time and again with that too. For example, Speer offered as much funding as it would take to develop the bomb and asked for a list of requirements. What he received was a short list comprising a few metals and a bunker for the research.

However, this only leads us to yet another enigma with the claims the *Kammlerstab* did continue research into a nuclear reactor and may have even developed an atomic bomb just as the war came to an end; it is a controversial theory, with some evidence something was happening. It may have simply been a dirty bomb project; Speer released the Third Reich's store of uranium for ammunition purposes and, with the cartel, it is unclear where some of it may have ended up. Had Hitler known about any possible nuclear research through Kammler, or elsewhere, he must have changed his mind about Jewish science and kept that from the people too, possibly because he was desperate for new super weapons of mass destruction. On the other hand, he may simply have not known, or the project did not exist. There is also the possibility that the atomic bomb believed to have been developed was actually something called the 'fuel-air bomb', which we will look at later.

Eventually, Himmler, with his pseudo-scientific 'training', was able to relieve Speer of many responsibilities at the Ministry of Armament and War Production under the nose of Hitler. This effectively reversed the power Hitler had insisted was Speer's through carefully crafted outmanoeuvring. Himmler also took the opportunity to carry out a similar plan involving the RLM, headed by Goering, as a result of him becoming less powerful after losing the Battle of Britain.

However, it is also clear Kammler's secret work was not the only part of his plan; he was also active in churning out conventional weapons like rockets and aircraft, which fitted with his efforts for all-in-one fortresses and the original idea they would double for his secret projects. This then allowed him the opportunities of follow-on developments and overlapping research where second-generation technology involving secret wonder weapons was pursued. In Agoston's own words: 'In modern high-tech jargon, the operations would probably be referred to as an SS research think tank', or, in other words, it was equivalent to today's black-budget projects carried out within today's military, and as such, was not uniquely Nazi.

Of course, Kammler also found himself involved in the rocket programme through Himmler, especially following a meeting between Hitler and Himmler in August 1943. There had already been a meeting with Hitler about the rocket programme on 11 June 1943, where Hitler raised the priority of the rocket programme above all other armaments production; Walter Dornberger, effectively in charge of the rocket programme, was made a brigadier general the next day. To seal the importance of the programme, Hitler invited Dornberger and Wernher von Braun to visit him at the Wolf's Lair, Hitler's remote headquarters in the forests of East Prussia, on 7 July. At this meeting, Hitler was shown film footage of tests involving the new 'vengeance weapon', which included the footage of the A-4 test in October 1942. However, Hitler expressed one of his tendencies to demand more than was possible while also highlighting again his lack of understanding of science; he demanded that the rocket should carry a 10-ton warhead. However, it had been a task to upgrade the A-3 to the A-4 in order to reach demands of a 1-ton warhead. Hitler also demanded production of 2,000 rockets per month. Dornberger was now in a position of trying to explain to the Fuhrer that these targets were impossible. Dornberger then saw a strange expression in Hitler's eyes, as he feared Hitler would fly into one of his infamous rages. It was at this meeting that Hitler shouted: 'What I want is annihilation, annihilating effect!' Following the meeting, Hitler awarded von Braun a state professorship, signing the necessary paperwork there and then.

The meeting between Hitler, Dornberger and von Braun did help with many of the outstanding problems which greatly improved. However, they did have an immediate problem that needed attention: the lack of labour to meet the demands the programme now experienced, especially with mass production. This shortage of staff was largely due to early decisions to recruit experienced personnel into the armed forces, but the problem could be resolved in several ways. At the meeting, Hitler had also emphasized the secrecy of the rocket programme; as a result, no foreigners should be used as labour. In fact, foreigners had already been used at Peenemunde in 1940 and 1941, when Polish prisoners of war were used as unskilled labour. By the spring of 1941, Peenemunde had around 600 Polish and 100 French workers, with a further 1,000 contract workers from Italy. However, now in 1942, Peenemunde faced full-scale production of the A-4 rocket and the shortage of labour would continue into 1943. Indeed, the need for labour, especially unskilled labour, had become so acute during 1943 that any source was now being considered; so much so that Arthur Rudolph, chief engineer at Peenemunde, was even prepared to accept Russian prisoners of war. This did have its advantages because the number of Russians available had been increasing as a result of the war on the Eastern Front. Furthermore, there were also fewer scientists and engineers being drafted now, and that also eased the problem a little. However, what was really needed was a lot more labour, and to avoid production falling behind schedule, it was a case where Hitler's orders had to be disobeyed.

Another ready source of labour would now come from SS concentration camps. In April 1943, Peenemunde and its two annexes, the Zeppelin plant at Friedrichshafen and the Rax-Werke plant in Austria, still had a serious need for unskilled labour; it was then that the SS offered a solution in the form of slave labour.

It was in August 1943, only 3 months after the first successful test of the A-4/V-2 rocket, when Himmler wrestled away the project from Speer and the Wehrmacht. Himmler was at the Wolf's Lair at the time when Hitler was in the company of his deputy Martin Bormann and the topic of the A-4 manufacture was brought up by Hitler. It seemed that Hitler still had grave concerns about its security and was now making even more impossible demands about rocket production, this time demanding 5,000 rockets put into production immediately with their delivery as soon as possible. This followed the successful test of the rocket where it had landed only 5km off-target at a distance of 265km. This, together with the failings of Goering to win the Battle of Britain, had finally convinced Hitler of the rocket programme's potential. It was here that Himmler saw his chance to gain control of the programme, an important step towards gaining control over all projects and putting them under the jurisdiction of the SS to increase the chances of becoming a self-sustained entity separate from the Third Reich.

Quick to exploit an opportunity, Himmler knew that neither Speer nor the Wehrmacht could deliver under the existing arrangements. Interestingly, Speer's opinion of Himmler was much the same: his promises outstripped his ambitions. What Hitler was demanding was strict security; he wanted those involved in the rocket programme to be Germans, with no foreigners involved. Unfortunately, that was still not possible because there was still not enough German labour, and the programme was still using Poles, Hungarians and Czechs, amongst others. However, Himmler offered him an alternative, and he told the Fuhrer that it was watertight. He would supply the labour from the SS-run concentration camps, which had no way to escape. Moreover, the same source of slave labour could build the Kammler-style underground facilities to protect the programme from the Allied bombing and the same could be done for other projects.

This offer by Himmler to build underground facilities was certainly well timed. Part of his plan revolved around a massive Allied bombing campaign, codenamed Crossbow, that took place on the night of 17/18 August 1943; at 1.00 am, the RAF carried out a raid on Peenemunde using 600 heavy bombers, dropping 1.5 million kg of explosives on the factories. After the raid, the site's residential area of East Peenemunde was destroyed, as was the housing for engineers and the barracks where the slave labourers were housed. Amongst the 700 workers killed out of the 12,000 were 500 foreign workers and Walter Thiel, chief engine designer, along with his family, while in their air raid shelter. The death of Thiel was a particular blow to the programme affecting the missile work for the anti-aircraft *Wasserfall* (Waterfall) and the development of a two-stage rocket that would penetrate even further into mainland Britain. Also extensively damaged were the development works buildings, as well as administration offices. However, the factories where the rockets were assembled escaped largely undamaged. As for rocketeer Wernher von Braun, he survived unharmed, but was said to have been seen rummaging through the debris after the raid looking for lost plans, diagrams and documentation. Following the raid, at first glance, it looked like a devastating attack; in some ways, it was, but in reality, it was less than expected. The Germans left the ruins untouched, hoping the British would think they had done more damage to the site than they had, so they might ease off any future raids.

The effect this raid had on rocket production was to set it back about 2 months, with an estimated loss in production of 740 rockets. Even so, it was clear a more secure underground facility was required; after all, the British were now taking a keen interest in Peenemunde and its activities and had been throughout 1943. That interest included intelligence gathering and photographic evidence, and it was clear that action was needed. All this played out to Himmler's advantage because he was also able to convince Hitler that the RAF raids had been the result of espionage rather than intelligence gathering.

Hitler agreed with Himmler and accepted his offer. However, it did not go all to plan for Himmler. As well as agreeing, Hitler informed him that he would need to co-operate with Speer because he was the minister who had masterminded the revitalization of the German manufacturing economy. That revitalization had achieved month-on-month growth in spite of the Allied bombings since Hitler had appointed him the previous year. As for Speer's opinion, he objected to Himmler's proposal, knowing all too well he would not deliver, but it was not what Hitler wanted to hear.

The next day, Himmler informed Speer that he had assumed control of manufacturing the A-4 instrument, referring to it by that name so as to hide its nature and purpose, and demanded Speer fully co-operate and be his SS subordinate (junior partner). Speer had been outmanoeuvred and had no alternative but to obey.

This was also an important move for Himmler's plan to form his self-sustained SS, putting in place crucial funding through its economic authority, Oswald Pohl, who realized the potential of solving manpower shortages by supplying slave labour to whoever needed it at reasonable rates. In fact, as early as 1942, Himmler had already started a scheme whereby slave labour was provided to private and government industries at an economic rate through the enterprising Economic and Administrative Main Office. This service was also offered to Peenemunde and its annexes. In April 1943, Rudolph visited the Heinkel factory in Oranienburg to see how 4,000 slave labourers consisting of Russians, French, and Poles provided labour as part of the SS deal, all held behind electric fences in cramped conditions. As a result, Rudolph asked the SS for 1,400 slave labourers for Peenemunde while also writing a memorandum to justify the decision on the grounds it would meet Hitler's requirement for greater secrecy. The prisoners arrived 2 weeks later from Buchenwald near Weimar, complete with sixty SS guards. By August 1943, Dornberger was able to order production in all the assembly plants, which now saw an increase of slave labour to 2,500 at Peenemunde, with the other plants getting 1,500 between them. This solved the outstanding labour shortage for now.

Following Himmler's meeting with Hitler after the 17/18 August 1943 RAF Crossbow raid, the site for the new underground factories was quickly chosen by 26 August and consisted of a series of tunnels in the Kohnstein Mountains near Nordhausen in the Harz Mountains, which had been used up to then for the storage of oil and chemical weapons. The new site would be known as Mittelwerke (Central Works). Himmler then told Speer that skilled workers and scientific specialists would be immediately transferred from the camps to begin working on the A-4 instrument, and a young construction expert who had proved his outstanding abilities would take charge of the programme. That expert was Kammler, who was the new head of the SS Building and Works Division, the same division that masterminded and built the camps. Shortly afterwards, Himmler dispatched the first group of concentration camp inmates to build the new underground complex—10,000 Russians, French, and Poles from the Buchenwald camp. Speer was now in his new capacity as a subordinate to the SS, and within a month he and Kammler established the low-profile Mittelwerke GmbH (Central Works Limited) to run the rocket programme.

The slave labour was put to work preparing a tunnel through the length of the mountain. This was the second of two tunnels running parallel with each other between the northern and southern faces of the ridgeline. Tunnel B was the main V-2 production line and stretched to 1.5km in length, just part of 20km of tunnels. Between the two tunnels, fifty galleries were constructed like the rungs of a ladder, each between 100 and 200m long. Many of these galleries were designed as component manufacturing facilities for the rocket assembly line; others were for the manufacture of jet engines, many of which were also assembly lines in their own right. The prisoners would also construct twenty cross tunnels between the two parallel tunnels.

Before the construction of concentration camp Dora nearby, slave workers worked and lived in situ, with over 60,000 prisoners crammed into three tunnels. Those who survived the construction work would go on to man the assembly lines. Initially, they slept on straw, with their surroundings lit by a few carbide lamps. Later, they were allowed to build a four-storey designed set of bunks, touching the roof. Even so, there was not enough capacity for all, but that did not matter, with the prisoners working in shifts to maximize productivity. Ventilation was bad, particularly deep in the mountain beyond Gallery 18, where there was essentially no ventilation, heating or water. Clouds of dust following explosions during construction would add to the misery. There was also the smell of open toilets, consisting of oil drums cut in half with two planks of wood as seats. The evening shift was marginally better, because it was then that the toilets were taken by railroad to be emptied in the open. The result was unbreathable air and high levels of disease, infections and injury, resulting in 6,000 deaths in the first 7 months alone. Some were simply worked to death. Those who became too ill or frail to continue were returned to the concentration camp to be put to death. By the end of the first year, more than 20,000 had lost their lives. This was a typical Kammler design, as was the treatment of slave workers, true to the words to his staff: 'Pay no attention to the human cost. The work must go ahead, and in the shortest possible time.'

Efforts also continued at the Peenemunde site, with the wind tunnels moved to the Bavarian Alps at Kochel. This fragmentation, as well as between other sites scattered around Germany, caused obvious communication problems; even so, it took only 2 months to resume work on the A-4. Following all this work, it was now necessary to bring in even more prisoners for the Mittelwerke site; 4,000 were brought in, mostly Russians, French, and Poles, followed by Jewish prisoners in the summer of 1944, with the figure increasing to 8,000 by November 1944.

By 1943, the occupation of the concentration camps had surged, increasing from 25,000 to half a million and growing. The figures for death camps like Auschwitz, Dachau and Mauthausen were in their millions with diseases, starvation, and gas chambers killing millions by the war's end; conditions were just as bad at places like Mittelwerke. The SS ranks also grew from 250,000 to 800,000 at the same time. The SS provided fighting divisions alongside the Wehrmacht, as well as forming Hitler's bodyguard.

As a result of the work Kammler was putting into designing plants, camps and rocket production, his elevation to the top of the bureaucracy within Hitler's inner cabinet was secured. Mittelwerke would not be the only such project that saw many more deaths of slave labour; indeed, it was intended to be just the beginning of Kammler's grand fortresses plan that never was fulfilled.

As the year of 1943 turned to that key year of 1944, the *Kammlerstab* entered its significant 2-year plan, where many new and often controversial weapons projects took off. As we will see, 1944 appears time and again as the Nazis tried to pull the war back to their advantage amongst the battering from Allied bombers, thanks to the British onboard radar developed to target Nazi industry, research and production facilities. It was also the year of D-Day, as Allied Forces swept across occupied Europe. As for Kammler, like Hitler, he steadfastly refused to believe in anything other than final victory for the Third Reich. This gave added importance to the *Kammlerstab.*

In March 1944, there was the formation of the Luftwaffe's fighter aircraft staff, consisting of senior Luftwaffe and Ministry of Armament officials, intended to increase fighter production in the face of the Allied mass carpet bombing. Kammler's answer was the SS had two primary areas to concentrate on; rapid development and the labour it required from concentration camps. Therefore, as head of the Luftwaffe, Goering tasked Kammler with transferring strategic aircraft facilities underground. Unfortunately, whereas aircraft production improved, the severe shortage of pilots to fly the aircraft as they rolled off the production lines remained a serious problem.

A little over 3 months later, Himmler reported to Hitler that ten aircraft factories comprising underground floor space of tens of thousands of square metres had been successfully completed in only 8 weeks. Of course, the loss of life was, again, staggering. The completion of such a project in such a short time meant that Kammler's reputation was further elevated in the Fuhrer's mind; Kammler was fast heading towards having complete control over these areas in the desperate fight for victory. However, Allied Forces were advancing on many of these facilities faster than research, development and production would have liked. Furthermore, there were also severe delays in rocket production because of a series of date changes, partly due to the Fuhrer's original lack of interest in the project, internal fighting and power-grabs, shortages of raw materials and, of course, Allied carpet bombing.

By 20 July 1944, the plot against Hitler added to Kammler's influence as things entered the final stage. By 6 August, Himmler was in place as head of armaments and the reserve army, adding to his power. At this stage, he was also given responsibility for all aspects of the V-2 operations from research and manufacturing through to deployment as the Nazis raced to finish their wonder weapons and develop super weapons. One such development involved reaching the United States by rocket. Whereas the V-2 was able to reach Britain, it would take the drawing-board rocket known as the A-9/10 to reach the United States. Indeed, as well as adding to Kammler's powers, Hitler himself was heaping more and more onto his own shoulders, which would boil over when trapped in the *Fuhrerbunker* amongst his generals at the war's end.

Despite Kammler's complete control from start to finish, by January 1945 the D-Day troops were now a serious threat to his plans and the Kammler 'Empire'. The Red Army was in Budapest and Warsaw, and the Western Allies were a threat to Germany's Ardennes offensive. At this stage, Kammler had complete control of missiles, both defensive and offensive, with Hitler transferring all air weapons from drawing board to launch over to him; this also included bombers.

Kammler had achieved much of his dream, although the massive fortresses originally planned had only taken a limited form. As a result, Kammler was so powerful only Hitler and his cabinet were more so.

By April 1945, the Red Army was approaching Berlin, Hitler and his generals were trapped in the *Fuhrerbunker* below the party chancellery with Hitler becoming more deranged, while Kammler was outside, effectively the saviour of the Third Reich, now in charge of the whole aerospace programme on behalf of the SS. However, although Hitler had great faith in Kammler, as we will see in the final chapter of our story, Kammler was the realist in all this and had different ideas.

As well as the A-4/V-2 project, there was also the continuation of the pilotless monoplane known as the V-1 revenge weapon (*vergeltungswaffen*), which, unknown to the Nazis, had already been spotted by an eagle-eyed pilot, Lieutenant D.W. Steventon, on a photo reconnaissance flight in his Spitfire on 15 May 1942. Following the usual story of delays, the first V-1s landed on London shortly after D-Day on 13 June 1944. By the month's end, the total number launched was 2,452: a third were destroyed or crashed before reaching England, a third crashed in open country, and the remaining third landed on London and in the vicinity of Southampton. The worse incident happened on 18 June, when a V-1 landed on the chapel of Wellington Barracks in central London, killing 121 people while worshipping, 63 of which were soldiers.

By the autumn, the V-1s were also being fired in large numbers at Antwerp to prevent supplies being sent to invading Allied Forces. In total, about 10,000 V-1s were launched towards Britain; 2,500 landed on London, with 6,000 people killed and 18,000 injured. Things could have been different had it not been for that eagle-eyed pilot, Steventon, flying over the Baltic and spotting something strange on the island of Usedom, and the RAF subsequently bombing Peenemunde in 1943, which saw production of the V-1 put back about 8 months. However, this vital delay came at a cost, with the raid on Peenemunde seeing heavy losses to the RAF, amounting to some 40 bombers amongst a furious defence from German fighters and flak. This delay also helped save lives amongst the Normandy invasion troops, who might otherwise have experienced frightful decimation only a week before the first V-1s started to fall on London.

The V-2 rocket finally went into production in May 1944 at Mittelwerke. Whereas there was limited defence from the V-1s, including some success in shooting them down and even Spitfires attacking them, there was no defence against the supersonic V-2, and by September, they were ready for launch. The first two were launched on 8 September from a site near the Hague in Holland and landed without warning, almost together, at Chiswick in west London, and Parndon Wood, near Epping in east London. At Chiswick, three people were killed and seventeen injured. As planned, they each carried 1 ton of explosives, far short of Hitler's demand for 10 tons. By 27 March 1945, a total of 1,054 V-2 rockets fell, averaging 5 a day, killing 2,700 Londoners, and over 900 were fired at Antwerp during the last quarter of 1944.

As devastating as the V-1 and particularly the V-2 weapons had been, overall, they fell far short of the demands from Hitler and his great promises to the people of Germany. It certainly was not the desired raining down of rockets Hitler spoke of, and certainly did not live up to the words of Hitler when he said: 'What I want is annihilation, annihilating effect!' No doubt this was due to delay after delay provided jointly by Nazi bureaucracy, the cartel's infighting and power-grabbing, constant rearrangements, administrative mismanagement, and Allied bombing raids. Ironically, another contributing factor was the *Kammlerstab*'s desire for pursuing all possibilities, resulting in wasteful duplication and unnecessary overlap. All this meant the true potential was never realized. Indeed, much of this was highlighted during the interrogation of Field Marshal Erhard Milch, Goering's deputy in command of the Luftwaffe, after the war. He said that so much had been tied up in manpower and production of V weapons simply because of the great promises made to the people. An aircraft production chief, Dr Karl Frydag, said during his interrogation that they pursued the V weapons because of propaganda effects, and that it was foolish. As for Speer, he stated the purpose of the weapons was to counter British night attacks with something similar without expensive bombers and losses. However, the main reason was psychological for the benefit of the German people.

As the war drew to a close, Dornberger and von Braun began to speak publicly about the peacetime possibilities of rockets as vehicles for space exploration. In the case of von Braun, his remarks were tinged with regret that the development owed so much to the gods of war. Such sentiments earned him the displeasure of Himmler, such that he was arrested on trumped-up treason charges and interrogated by the SS. The charges were only dropped when Dornberger, now a major general, intervened.

Allied intelligence certainly found a strong element of chaos amongst the infighting higher ranks in many areas but, in general, with rocketry, they found the science and engineering side of things had a high degree of organization and discipline amongst the technological research. As a result, the rush for the scientific spoils of war resulted in many captured advances, although there were also many lost due to attempts by the Nazis to bury plans and technology, destroy blueprints and documents, and even burn and blow up hardware. There was also the problem of scientists, engineers and technicians attempting to escape the advancing Allied Forces. However, much of this had already been considered by the Allies because their objectives surrounding the capture of scientific technology, scientists and engineers had already been planned in Britain and the United States long before D-Day.

In March 1945, before the eventful April when the advancing Red Army forced Hitler and his generals into the *Fuhrerbunker* for the last weeks of the war, Kammler had already moved his headquarters out of Berlin to Munich. He was now working out of the regional Waffen SS and Reich police construction office. With that, he took the authority bestowed upon him by Hitler as the man effectively in charge of all the wonder weapons and super weapons in development, making him the saviour of the Third Reich. As we will see, there was good reason for this move.

Then, on 3 April, 3 weeks after he had received his mission from Hitler to change the course of the war, Kammler delegated Gerhard Degenkolb as industrial plenipotentiary for manufacturing of jet aircraft at Speer's Ministry of Armament and War Production. In particular, he was to assume special responsibility for manufacturing the Messerschmitt 262, Germany's last-ditch hope for superiority in the air. Kammler then met with Hitler and his generals as they prepared to huddle down in the *Fuhrerbunker* in Berlin. Such was the faith in the man following the meeting, on 3 April, Propaganda Minister Joseph Goebbels wrote in his diary about the 'miracle' weapons that could turn the war to the vantage of the Nazis, adding the Fuhrer was left with great faith in Kammler.

Hitler was unaware that Kammler had already moved his headquarters out of Berlin to Munich and that he had other plans, as we will see. Speer also reveals in his autobiography that, given the inevitable failure of these projects, it would be unwise for Kammler to remain in Berlin in easy reach of Hitler. Before leaving Berlin, shortly after his meeting with Hitler, Kammler paid Speer one last visit to say goodbye. Speer said: 'For the first time in our four-year association Kammler did not display his usual dash, he seemed insecure and slippery with his vague, obscure, hints about why I should transfer to Munich with him.' Speer also points out that Kammler's 'Empire', as far as he was aware, was about to be overrun by the US First Army as they approached the giant Mittelwerke underground A-4 construction complex at Nordhausen in central Germany's Harz Mountains. With most of the A-4/V-2 programme and personnel still in place, Kammler was understandably nervous; he needed to get them out. Then, remarkably, Speer says Kammler informed him that 'efforts were being made in the SS to get rid of the Fuhrer.' Speer was also involved in a plot to do the same with a desperate, and ironic, scheme to assassinate Hitler and his generals in their Berlin bunker using poison gas; their own personal gas chamber. So, this assassination news from Kammler was not such a great surprise to Speer, except that the news had come from Kammler's own lips.

Something Speer was unaware of was the fact General Walther Schellenberg, Germany's combined intelligence chief, had already opened secret surrender negotiations on behalf of Himmler with Count Folke Bernadotte, vice chairman of the Swedish Red Cross. Although this offer was passed on to the Allies, it was firmly rejected.

During his last meeting with Speer, Kammler also told him he was planning to contact the Americans and make a deal. In exchange for his safety and freedom, he was prepared to give over everything he was now in charge of: jets, the A-4/V-2 rocket technology and all other important projects, and he was assembling all relevant experts in Upper Bavaria in preparation to hand them over to the US forces. Speer said: 'He offered me the chance to participate in this operation which would be sure to work out in my favour.' Speer turned him down.

Some say that in a late sign of remorse, Speer now saw it his duty to prevent the Fuhrer from carrying out his scorched-earth policy in the face of the advancing Allies. It seemed that, as Hitler was giving orders to destroy factories and instillations, Speer was countermanding them. He found himself fighting with frightened and bewildered plant managers and pointing out that although the war was lost, these plants would be needed to rebuild Germany, yet again, along with its economy.

On 10 April, Dornberger and von Braun, together with their rocket personnel, did evacuate the Nordhausen complex on Kammler's orders. They were informed by Dornberger that if they disobeyed, the SS would shoot them all. The following day, US forces entered and overran the complex. However, plans had already been made for Kammler to meet up with Dornberger and von Braun at the Hotel Lang, near Oberammergau, where evacuated Messerschmitt project teams had already arrived. The meeting took place with von Braun finding a more relaxed Kammler together with his chief of staff, SS Lieutenant Colonel (Obersturmbannfuhrer) Starck. While waiting in the lobby, von Braun overheard Kammler and Starck talk about burning their uniforms, after which they would lie low for a while in the fourteenth-century abbey at Ettal, a few kilometres down the road. At that point, von Braun was ushered into a room by SS guards and met with Kammler and Starck. It was the last time anybody of importance could corroborate seeing Kammler.

On 17 April, as Germany was being destroyed, Kammler dared to send Himmler a message at SS command headquarters in Berlin, denying him the use of a heavy truck that he had requested from the Junkers aircraft factory motor pool. This order was so obsessive in its attention to detail given the inferno burning around Kammler, Speer described it as both 'terrifying and laughable'. The significance is this was the last-ever message anybody received from Kammler, who had disappeared the following day, aware that Germany was on the point of collapse. Speer also said: 'In the course of any enforced collaboration with this man I discovered him to be a cold, ruthless schemer, a fanatic in pursuit of a goal, and as carefully calculating as he was unscrupulous.' The interesting point here is the JU 290 and JU 390 heavy transporter aircraft were often referred to as 'trucks' and were Junkers' designed aircraft, so it has been claimed the 'truck' denied to Himmler was not an army truck, but an aircraft. If true, it may link Kammler to an attempt to evacuate key parts of his Kammler 'Empire', including equipment, documents and personnel, to safe places like Spain, Norway and South America in preparation for his deal with the Allies. We will look at this later with that mysterious device called 'the Bell' and further research by Igor Witkowski into the Wenceslas Mine.

What we will look at next are some of the projects that the *Kammlerstab* and SS in general considered: many of these seem to centre on the last desperate attempts during 1944 and 1945.

Chapter Five

From Phoo Bombs to Flying Discs

As we have seen, the inventory of secret and prototype weapons devised by the Nazis is incredible. However, it comes with a mix of certainty and uncertainty, as well as differing levels of evidence depending on which project we consider; but, collectively, they showed experimentation, with exotic ideas often overlapping with more conventional physics and engineering. Whereas many of these ideas were developed with prototypes and even final versions on occasion, many failed due to their dependence on pseudo-science or even occultism, myth and legends of hidden science. Many were also just pipe-dreams remaining on the drawing board which may, or may not, have come to something. That was a task for the scientists of the Cold War, leading to an active continuation of conspiracy theories surrounding the victors and the spoils of war, a topic for another book. It is also clear many projects, especially the more exotic ones, came too late in the war to be of any use to the Nazis.

For example, in aviation, extensive research into swept-back wing designs for speed and evasion by radar were just coming to the foreground as the Nazis surrendered. One prototype that was just about ready to go into production was the so-called 'Nazi UFO', or Horten 229, a clear prototype of many stealth aircraft designs we are familiar with today. In fact, the third prototype was taken back to the United States. The Americans also clearly picked up on Nazi dreams of atomic-powered aircraft, although less success was found in those designs. The Nazis even had drawing-board dreams of space stations and space shuttles, which again have become reality, although not always with a peaceful nature and more akin to the original Nazi proposals at times. There was also a dream to resurrect a truly ancient idea from astronomy to produce gigantic mirrors in orbit to direct the sun's rays onto the enemy to fry them, a clear variation on death rays using other regions of the electromagnetic spectrum such as X-rays, radio and microwaves. The idea of gigantic mirrors actually originates way back in the history of astronomy as a way to communicate with Martians by burning messages into the deserts of Mars—an early type of crop circles, if we believe today's aliens are communicating with us in that way! The list goes on, but we need to bear in mind all this was a key element of both Himmler's *Ahnenerbe* and Kammler's think tank, where no ideas, however extreme or harebrained, could be ignored.

It was an Italian officer, Luigi Romersa, who claims to have overheard Hitler mentioning such dreams when he said: 'We have invisible aircraft, submarines, colossal tanks and cannons, unbelievably powerful rockets and a bomb with a working that will astonish the whole world. The enemy knows this, and besieges and attempts to destroy us. But we will answer this destruction with a storm and that without unleashing a bacteriological war, for which we are also prepared… All my words are the purest truth. That you will see.' 'Invisible aircraft' clearly refers to stealth projects, which did include radar-absorbing materials, as well as new shapes, like the flying disc. 'Submarines', or U-boats, did also exist, as we have seen, but with mixed results. The 'colossal' machines of war, we can regard as failures, as we have discovered. As for the bomb mentioned, that is open to interpretation. Was it the atomic bomb or something else? We will cover this later. 'Powerful rockets' go without saying—the V-2 and others on the drawing board were clear weapons of mass destruction. However, what are we to make of being prepared for 'bacteriological' warfare?

Many of these and other weapons were considered and were not merely the rants of a madman. However, there was sometimes confusion with such claims from Hitler. One such fear, as we have seen, came from a speech that talked of a terrible weapon that was believed to be a type of death ray. However, when the original speech was revisited, it was found the British Foreign Office had mistranslated it and all Hitler was talking about was the Luftwaffe.

One intriguing piece of evidence for Kammler-type think tank ideas comes from a CIOS report, *German Guided Missile Research G-2 Division SHAEF (Rear), APO413, number XXXII-125*. This ran to more than 150 pages and detailed an additional thrust unit which was to be attached to either the A-4/V-2 or the A-9 to give additional range, along with various other projects. This gave a guided missile a range of 4,630km. It is generally believed this was a drawing-board-only design, although, in the report, that was also said to be an assumption. After the war, von Braun did develop rockets for the Americans with additional attachments to boost rocket performance. There was also a V-3 rocket designed with an incendiary warhead in place of the conventional high explosive. The nature of the warhead was not known, although it might have been a thermite, fuel-air or dirty bomb (we will look at these later). There was also a lengthy part of the report that dealt with guided missile projects under Dr Wagner for the Henschel firm, including the HS-293-B, a rocket-powered glider with a wire guidance system and the HS-294-A rocket-powered glider with torpedoes. A small quantity was built for experimentation between 1941 and 1943.

At the end of the report (from page 139 to the end), there are details about miniaturized television camera guidance systems for a variety of missiles, including the well-known anti-aircraft rocket known as *Wasserfall* (Waterfall). Apparently, many of these failed, but by the end of the war there was a successful test of the television-guided Tonne missile conducted by German physicists for the Allies in Berlin, with the target being the photograph of a little girl's face. The Allied officers were shocked at what they saw. The report also suggests other successes, including radio-controlled surface-to-air missiles, infra-red heat-seeking air-to-air and surface-to-air missiles, wire-guided missiles and torpedoes, and biological and chemical weapons for V-1 and V-2 rockets. Here we have the evidence of bacteriological warfare the Fuhrer said they were prepared to use. Also, the Heinkel and Messerschmitt companies were undertaking modifications in Prague of their He 177 and Me 264 heavy bombers to carry new bomb designs being developed, which might have eventually included an atomic bomb. We have seen Prague was in the heart of the Kammler 'Empire'.

Many of the more exotic ideas originated around 1944 with the height of the Kammler think tank, and a good place to start is with some of those infra-red devices already mentioned. During 1944, section D of the *Deutsche Forschungsanstalt fur Segelflug* (DFS), the German Research Institute for Gliding at Ainring near Salzburg, was working on various apparatuses for infra-red night television using a network of ultra-sensitive thermocouples that would permit distance vision, even through clouds. It is interesting to recall that, at this time, there was surprise that the Allies could see through clouds to bomb cities. This was possible due to onboard miniaturized radar that had been developed by Bernard Lovell and his team. Lovell is best known as the astronomer who established the Jodrell Bank Radio Observatory in Cheshire with its huge 250-foot (75m) dish. During the work, several astronomers and other physicists developed centimetre wavelength radar for bomber and fighter commands to locate and carry out the carpet bombings of Germany during 1943 to 1945. This was known as the H2S radar system.

The Nazis' similar idea to see through clouds using infra-red will bring us to several interesting secret weapons, many of which centred on the main Kammler year of 1944. Certainly, Lovell's H2S radar and its ability to see through clouds was enough to get comments of surprise from the likes of Goering and Goebbels. In the case of Goering, he declared: 'We must frankly admit that in this sphere the British and Americans are far ahead of us. I expected them to be advanced, but frankly I never thought that they would get so far ahead. I did hope that even if we were behind we could at least be in the same race.' Maybe this intense 1944 interest in infra-red research was an attempt to re-join that race?

The British onboard radar may have resulted in a particular phenomenon now famous amongst UFO enthusiasts as 'Foo Fighters'; it certainly highlights many secret Nazi projects developed by them. Without going into huge technical detail, it seems that the experimental radar pumping powerful microwaves into the atmosphere may have produced, as a side effect, these strange glowing balls of light that would sometimes follow the RAF and American bombers; circumstances with atmospheric conditions and pollutants needed to be just right. Regardless, the Foo Fighters existed, and there was great debate as to whether they were natural phenomena of some sort or secret Nazi weapons. Consequently, this one phenomenon resulted in a flood of claims after the war surrounding the possibility that they may be a Nazi weapon. That then led to the claims and discoveries of many other possible exotic devices uncovered and promoted through various individuals.

In August 1944, the highest priority was given to DFS apparatus, a small number of which were built in the plant of the Viennese firm Kepka Werke and equipped with a simplified type of photoelectric 'magic eye' inserted in the centre of a parabolic scanning mirror. The apparatus was also supposed to be mounted in the cone of the Enzian anti-aircraft rocket. However, this was another project that came too late. The advancing Allies forced Field Marshal Albert Kesselring's division to surrender, while the British Eighth Army was moving up from the south to occupy the undefended recesses of the Alpine Redoubt, which was under construction as part of Kammler's fortresses plan.

It is said that this area of Nazi research had produced hundreds of inventions of inestimable value and were found by the Eighth Army's T Unit. Amongst these inventions were infra-red devices that included the minuscule Mucka detector, which was supposed to enable the pilots of the fast night fighter jets 'see' their squadron members by means of infra-red lights mounted in their wing tips and tails. When war ended, these inventions were taken back to the United States, where it is said research continued for some time. However, there is one particular device amongst the claims and folklore that has endured to this day, and that is the so-called *Feuerball* (Fireball), which was said to be amongst the devices returned to the United States.

This *Feuerball* links us to the hot topic of debate within fringe science about the nature of the Foo Fighter phenomenon experienced by both sides. Foo Fighters often seemed to follow a particular squadron, or just one aircraft in particular, sometimes paying attention to just one aircraft engine. So, it is no surprise they were considered a weapon. There are many names for this phenomenon: the Americans called them Foo Fighters; others called them *Feuerballs* or *Kugelblitz* (ball-lightning fighter); while the RAF referred to them as 'The Thing'. Generally, the common name is Foo Fighters, which has developed into a big subject that I can only touch on here.

There are many theories to explain the nature of these sightings; everything from atmospheric plasmas to hidden physics from ancient manuscripts, esoteric phenomena, something 'summoned up' through Nazi occultism, or even aliens taking an interest in our wars. One possibility of particular significance which seems to generate controversy within fringe sciences is the suggested link with the name *Feuerballs* in particular; the suggestion being this was a secret weapon of sorts developed by the Nazis. If this was a secret weapon, it certainly falls into our category of failures. Put simply, the Foo Fighters, by whatever name we choose, had little, if any, effect; they did not attack the aircraft, they did not put them out of action, and they did not particularly spook the crews once they had become accustomed to the harmless apparitions. In fact, they appeared to be exactly what they were, just lights in the sky. However, it is odd these apparitions largely ceased at the war's end, but it is important to note they did not completely cease and that may be the clue. There was also a suggestion they were a psychological device aimed at frightening the aircrew, but again, if that was their purpose, it also failed. A further point to make is the idea Foo Fighters and *Feuerballs* were one and the same is also somewhat flawed; they have a distinctly different feel to one another. It is here that a possible split occurs with the Foo Fighters being a mysterious, maybe, natural phenomenon and the *Feuerballs* being a Nazi weapon.

If we want to consider the Foo Fighters as some kind of weapon, the source usually quoted is Renato Vesco. Much of what Vesco had to say on the matter is contained in his book *Intercept UFO*. Vesco was notoriously reclusive, such that many researchers did not even believe he existed; as a result, some concluded his book was a hoax at best or deliberate military disinformation and misdirection at worse. Any saving grace is down to Nick Cook, aerospace consultant at *Jane's Defence Weekly*, who did track down a group of Italian researchers who had been in contact with Vesco up until his death in November 1999. According to this group, Vesco did not care whether people believed him or not. It is certainly true his book looks like a lot of dodgy claims with some truth included, which is, of course, how disinformation works. However, there are certain elements that can be checked as genuine, but a lot that cannot. Vesco was only twenty-two when the war ended and is said to have been well connected with technical experts within the Italian Air Force at the time he wrote his book. He claims to have pieced together his account of Top-Secret development efforts from sources inside the Italian military and Allied intelligence reports published after the war.

With that in mind, one of his claims was that *Feuerballs* were a weapon to disrupt radar, in particular the H2S system. However, having looked into this myself in considerable depth, and spoken with an astronomy colleague who actually worked on the system, that does not ring true. Nevertheless, it is true that the Germans had various devices they used to confuse radar returns. For example, a whole series of balloons were used to lift all kinds of shapes of various sizes into the air to fool Allied radar by altering the apparent outlines of the land, coastal areas and ports, as well as other areas of importance to British radar identification. One such location that became a favourite for such balloons was the little lakes of Wannsee and Muggelsee, which were basic points of navigational reference.

Another type of balloon sent up by the Germans was their Aphrodite, a type of special black balloon that released sheets of tinfoil during Allied bombing raids in an attempt to confuse the radar returns. These do not account for glowing balls of light, but one version that might was fluorescent balloons of moderate size that were launched by the Nazis in the vicinity of the presumed point of ballistic contact between the raiders and interceptors. These were supposed to fool the escort fighters, causing them to break away from the formation and therefore allow the attacking fighters to speed into the bomber formation. However, given the sighting reports at the time, this does not fit well with Foo Fighters. There have also been claims that some of these lights might have been the white-hot circular exhausts from German jet and rocket interceptors, which also had special fighter tactics, but that does not fit observations either. We are then left with a controllable *Feuerball* weapon as described by Vesco.

Vesco claims there were two types. One was an unpiloted object that was remotely controlled, a flying bomb, in effect, designed to destroy enemy aircraft, while the other was piloted, but only flew once due to the war coming to an end. It was the unpiloted version that was the *Feuerball* (and possibly the Foo Fighters), which had a number of highly advanced technologies and has been described by Vesco as 'a missile'. Vesco also claims *Feuerballs* had an 'older brother' and that was the *Kugelblitz*. Once again, given the many aircrew reports of the way the Foo Fighter lights moved, it is unlikely a missile or a bomb would be a suitable answer, because they did no harm to the aircraft or crew. This repeated return to the fact they were harmless just about dismisses all claims of a weapon of any type. If these devices were a *Kammlerstab* project, they were a failure, but they may have been from another area of Nazi research.

Vesco wrote: 'In the autumn of 1944, in Oberammergau in Bavaria, the OBF – an experimental centre run by the Luftwaffe – had completed a series of researches into electrical apparatus capable of interfering with the operation of an engine up to a maximum distance of about a hundred feet by producing intense electromagnetic fields.' He also reports that there was a parallel effort to produce a 'proximity radio interference' device capable of jamming or spoofing Allied radio and radar systems. These could be combined into a circular, armoured airframe 'powered by a special turbojet engine, also flat and circular and more or less resembling the shell of a tortoise'. The overall shape of the device was considered as disc, or saucer, shape and this would link to other details Vesco gives for Nazi flying discs being developed close to the end of the war, which do appear to have Kammler behind them. Vesco also said: 'Those who claimed to have seen them in daylight describe them as silver discs, or saucers.' Is it possible these were the flying disc interceptors? The device was said to be powered by special flat, circular turbojet engines which Vesco would also claim was the power source of other flying discs being developed (we will look at these later). As a result, there is room for this to be a Kammler overlapping project, one that was considered for other projects and not just its original one.

When in use, the device was steered towards the aircraft's streams by remote ground-based operators, where it would automatically latch onto the slipstreams, 'attracted by their exhaust flames and approached close enough without collision to wreck their radar gear'. Unfortunately, this too does not fit with Foo Fighters, which appeared just about anywhere relative to the aircraft.

Further interesting details were given by Vesco regarding the interruption of radar on Allied aircraft, and in particular the H2S system. He wrote: 'The fiery halo around the perimeter – caused by a rich fuel mixture – and the chemical additives that interrupted the flow of electricity by over ionizing the atmosphere in the vicinity of the plane, generally around the wing-tips or tail surfaces, subjected the H2S radar on the plane to the action of powerful electrostatic fields and electromagnetic impulses (the latter generated by large klystron radio tubes protected with anti-shock and anti-heat armour) since a metal arc carrying an oscillating current of the proper frequency – equal, that is, to the frequency used by the radar station – can cancel the blips (return signals from the target), the Feuerball was almost undetectable by the most powerful American radar of the time, despite its night-time visibility.' It is this reference to Americans that is particularly intriguing. The American aircrews experienced problems in using and interpreting the images on the screen, as did some of the British, which resulted in complaints, especially from the Americans, that the system did not work and was 'unscientific'. Also, many of the case histories which accompany these claims are of aircrew in the various divisions of the United States Army Air Force. However, again this does not fit because the problem was the H2S did not work 'in America' but was resolved when on future bombing missions. At the end of the day, the success of the H2S radar is obvious, and disruption was clearly not a serious issue.

Vesco also goes into details about the origins of the devices. In particular, the *Feuerball* was first constructed at an airfield plant at Wiener Neustadt, south of Vienna, with the help of the *Flugfunk Forschungsanstalt*, the Radio Research Institute, in the village of Oberpfaffenhoffen (also called FFO), an aircraft electronics firm near Munich. It is also claimed Goering inspected progress of the device 'a number of times' in the hope it might also be used to produce 'an offensive weapon capable of revolutionising the whole field of aerial warfare'. It appears that with the advance of the Russians into Austria, the production facilities for the *Feuerball* moved to a number of underground plants in the Black Forest run by the Zeppelin Works, possibly some constructed by Kammler, who did relocate his headquarters to Munich from Berlin.

Following the war, investigation into all kinds of technology and weapons was possible, and it is some of these reports that Vesco used to draw his conclusions, including the British BIOS reporting system and its successor the US/UK CIOS system we encountered earlier. Amongst these reports is one from CIOS about the Wiener Neustadt site and the FFO (report number 156) that tells of the work involved, which included several types of klystron tubes (a source of microwaves) and states a principle purpose of the facility was to develop technology to jam Allied radar. As for any documents from the facility, these appear to have been burned as the Allied Forces approached. However, some documents were said to have been handed over by scientists, but the contents are unknown. Unfortunately, despite these apparent confirmations, Vesco would have known about them anyway, and there is also a lot of elaboration, too, which cannot be confirmed. It is, however, worth bearing in mind some reports are still classified. With these details, we now have a number of elements of the Vesco claims combined. But was it all true? What we can say is similar devices do exist today and might be the spoils of war.

Looking further into official documentation, the nearest that we seem to get to any real supporting evidence for Vesco's claims come from a device called 'Phoo Bombs'. The question is: Are Foo Fighters and Phoo Bombs one and the same? The discovery of Phoo Bombs is thanks to a German researcher, Friedrich Georg, who found an intriguing entry in a microfilm roll giving details of a US Strategic Air Forces in Europe summary entitled *An Evaluation of German Capabilities in 1945*. This was one of those occasions when something was missed by the censors. In that summary report, there is mention of German devices referred to by the American Intelligence as 'Phoo Bombs'. The sources for the information are reports from pilots and testimony of prisoners of war. Phoo Bombs were described as 'radio-controlled, jet-propelled, still-nosed, short-range, high performance ramming weapons for use against bombing formations' and had an estimated speed of 845km/hr. Despite researchers' requests for further details through the Freedom of Information Act (FOIA), denials that anything further was on file was the response. However, a later appeal showed there were, in fact, further documents in existence, but these were simply repeats or re-statements of the original summary document, including one handwritten document which looked as if it was the original text that resulted in the summary. It is an intriguing discovery and may just suggest Vesco was onto something through his contacts given that this is a far more recent discovery.

At the end of the day, these devices may have had some use somewhere, but the *Kammlerstab* and *Ahnenerbe* view that all possibilities and overlap might produce results failed this time, certainly if such devices are to explain Foo Fighters, or The Thing. We only have to look at reports from aircrew involved to see that. For example, one individual who would be in a position to know was RAF Intelligence Officer Michael Bentine, a post-war comedian and member of *The Goons* following his wartime career. Bentine was an officer who briefed and debriefed aircrew and confirms that whereas Foo Fighters were a mystery, they did no harm. Moreover, Bentine had a lifelong interest in the paranormal and all things unexplained, so such a subject would be of particular interest to him. In fact, this was the trend. They were lights following bomber sorties but they did no harm at all; so much for an advanced out-of-the-box weapon.

From a personal point of view, I have lost count of how many UFO sightings I have looked at, including as an astrophysicist and consultant for the newsstand publication *UFO Magazine* (UK) between 1995 and 2004. Many of these showed extremely typical characteristics to the war-time Foo Fighters, yet have occurred in post-war years. These include vehicles on the road followed by the same types of lights, people out walking and being followed by similar objects and even military and commercial aircraft that still see what appear to be Foo Fighters to this day. If all the sightings during the war were weapons, it is difficult to justify post-war sightings as the same. Another significant point is many Foo Fighter–type sightings still get reported, especially around areas employing radar of one type or another, intelligence listening centres like Menwith Hill in Yorkshire, England, and the intense south coast radar still in place where Britain built the Chain Home system in the mid-1930s used to win the Battle of Britain.

It is, therefore, a possibility this phenomenon is a side-effect of radar, maybe a form of atmospheric plasma caused by ionization and other factors that come together for which there is scientific evidence. Certainly, we can create these lights in laboratories where pollutants are suddenly released into cold air and combined with microwaves to produce plasma balls of light. In fact, I have done this myself in the laboratory. The phenomenon is also reported around oily machinery at times, which may link with their interest in aircraft engines. Furthermore, given the experimental and somewhat crude nature of Lovell's H2S radar and battles with power levels, the phenomenon seen by aircrews may have been a side-effect and more prominent during the war years. It is interesting that reports often said the Foo Fighters took a particular interest in aircraft engines, often one in particular; it was here that the onboard radar was wired for power. Foo Fighters may have simply been manmade airborne plasmas.

This radar association continues to this day. In 2017, video footage leaked to the public showed what were called 'Tic Tac UFOs' interacting with pilots and crew from the US

Navy aircraft carrier USS *Nimitz* back in 2004. This is another big subject, but when I looked into the elements of classified details made available to the public, especially the new radar technology being tested, these looked suspiciously like airborne plasmas, particularly those caught on video from the F-18 jets. I could even see details from the magnetic cushion that would form between two interacting plasma balls twisting together.

I now want to return to the Kammler 'Empire' and a further story of a strange device said to be researched in one of the underground facilities under his control. This will then link us with the idea of flying disc technology also explored in his empire and the exotic research into free energy, gravity and anti-gravity.

The underground base in question is the Wenceslas Mine and the strange device is the Bell. As we saw, this mine was known to be a further facility for secret weapons research under Kammler and also carries claims of being a location for nuclear research, amongst other projects. It is situated about 50km or so on the other side of Wroclaw (formally Breslau of the German Gau of the Lower Silesia), around 350 km from Warsaw. Much of the work resulting in our understanding of this mine's activities under the Nazis is due to Igor Witkowski, who produced a series of books on the subject in Polish. Witkowski spent years sifting through archives relating to the many secrets of the Nazi scientific establishments in and around Breslau. Witkowski, a former defence journalist, uncovered a systematic SS-controlled research and development operation in a rat-run of interconnected facilities, most of which were underground in the remote Sudeten Mountains in the south-west of Poland (Lower Silesia as it was then, before the handover to Poland after the war).

The Bell started life in early 1944 at one of Himmler's secret SS-run science facilities near Leubus (now Lubiaz in Poland), north-west of Breslau. However, the Russians were rapidly pushing into Poland in late 1944 and early 1945, so it is claimed the unit was transported to a castle on a hill above the village of Furstenstein (Ksiaz) close to the Lower Silesian coal mining centre of Waldenberg. It is then said to have ended up in the Wenceslas Mine, set up by the SS as part of a neighbouring underground weapons complex codenamed *Riese* (Giant). Operation Giant aimed to convert an entire mountain into a secret weapons complex, but had only been partly completed by the end of the war; it was another of the Kammler fortresses that never saw its potential. Again, much of the tunnelling work was done by slave labour obtained from concentration camps, mainly Gross-Rosen. If time had allowed, it was clear that the Wenceslas Mine was to be connected to the complex via a 10km passage.

The only available outside information about the Bell comes from the secret interrogation of Four-Star General (*Obergruppenfuher*) Jakob Sporrenberg. Opinions surrounding the Bell differ; some say it was a form of nuclear reactor or 'engine' (one of the words used by the Nazis for a nuclear reactor); others say it was actually a version of the atomic bomb; some suggest it was a new form of aviation technique like an anti-gravity device or even a time machine. All we can go on here are the available details from Sporrenberg's interrogation and any scientific clues.

Records show that Sporrenberg was appointed deputy commander of the Waffen-SS VI Corps under SS Four-Star General (Obergruppenfuhrer) Walter Krueger in 1944. Krueger was in charge of several secret SS projects, including some harebrained schemes. Sporrenberg was not a scientist and as such he can only forward limited details about the secret SS science projects he helped to evacuate through Norway in June 1944, one of which was the Bell. This device had two code names: 'Laternentrager (Lantern carrier)' and 'Chronos (Greek for time)'. It is unclear whether these were renames for one project or two separate projects, but both included a device called *Die Glocke*, the Bell, so named because of its shape. It was constructed out of a hard and heavy metal and was filled with a mercury-like substance, although its colour was violet rather than silver. This violet, metallic liquid was codenamed 'Xerum 525' and was stored in a flask, which, in turn was stored in a lead-lined case with walls about 3cm thick. The experiments took place under a thick ceramic cover; the Bell glowed whenever the experiments were underway. Inside the liquid was a pair of cylinders which were spun, rapidly, in opposite directions. Not only Xerum 525 was used; other experiments used thorium and beryllium peroxides, codenamed 'Leichtmetall (Light metal)'. Reports surrounding the Bell told of a 'time dilation' effect akin to Einstein's theory of relativity where time was changed, albeit very, very slightly. This might have sounded fanciful if it were not for the work of German mathematician, and close friend of Einstein, Kurt Godel, who used Einstein's field equations of relativity to show time could be controlled by spinning the universe. Further work along these lines in later years showed the same effect could be achieved (theoretically) with smaller spinning bodies; the best shape was eventually determined as a cylinder.

The Bell experiments took place deep underground in a chamber with a floor space of about 30m^2. The walls were ceramic and covered with a thick rubber blanket or matting. Whenever the Bell was radiating, it required the dismantling and destruction of the material making up the walls after only ten experiments lasting about a minute each. The Bell itself was left in place. While under test, the Bell would emit a pale blue glow, electronics or personnel anywhere within 150m would experience strange effects, and electronics would short out. At the end of each 1-minute experiment, concentration camp prisoners from Gross-Rosen would wash down the walls with what appeared to be brine.

The shorting out of electronics was the less-dramatic side effect. Animals and plant matter left in the region of influence would come off worse of all. Material placed in the region of influence included insects, egg white, blood, milk, meat, snails, frogs, mice and rats. Plants would turn white, with their green chlorophyll decomposed within a few hours. Within about 12 hours, there would be rapid decay setting in; eventually the plants were reduced to a brown liquid akin to axle grease. However, it was strange that there was none of the smell associated with the natural long-term decay of plant matter. Although protective clothing was used, those involved would complain of medical problems including sleeping problems, memory loss, problems with balance, muscle spasms, and a metallic taste in the mouth. There were even reports that about half a dozen scientists were killed from the effects. These side effects are the same associated with radiation poisoning, although some, like metallic taste, are also associated with exposure to certain electromagnetic fields. So, what was this device: a nuclear experiment or an electromagnetic one?

Further modifications took place in January 1945, when effects on objects placed in the region of influence were reduced to about twelve to fifteen per cent. A second set of modifications reduced this further to about two to three per cent. It seemed that the frequent and numerous 1-minute experiments were an attempt to fine-tune whatever the Bell was designed to do. But what was it designed to do? Clearly, the tuning out of such a dramatic set of side effects meant those were not the purpose of the Bell, even though they appear to provide a dramatic weapon to use on the advancing Allies.

It is at this point that the Italian scientist Enrico Fermi enters the story. Fermi was associated with nuclear physics and worked on the atomic and hydrogen bombs at Los Alamos. However, Fermi's interest in atomic matters began before the war. While based in Rome during the 1930s, he systematically researched the properties of neutrons. Fermi was only 22 years old when Hitler came to power, but he had already made a name for himself by developing a statistical method for analyzing sub-atomic particles. In his Rome laboratory, Fermi used his equipment to generate neutrons. This consisted of a source of radioactivity, radon and a vial. The vial contained beryllium. Was there a connection with the beryllium peroxide in the Bell? Could the replacement of the rubber tiles and radiation sickness effects be due to neutrons striking the surroundings of the Bell? Neutrons striking various materials can transmute them into different elements and split atoms, causing further radioactive effects; after all, that is the basis of the atomic bomb. Indeed, it was this work on the transmuting property that secured Fermi a top-level position on the Manhattan Project at Los Alamos. So, was the Bell simply a nuclear device associated with the Nazi research into an atomic bomb, or something even more exotic?

During his Rome experiments, Fermi subjected each element of the periodic table to neutrons, transmuting them into radioactive isotopes. He performed many of his experiments in the goldfish pond outside his laboratory and discovered that radioactivity of a metal bombarded with neutrons increased 100-fold when the neutrons had been slowed by water or paraffin. Had the Nazis been doing the same thing by using the mercury-like liquid in the Bell? Fermi also discovered that when he bombarded the heaviest element, uranium, he produced a variety of new radioactive elements which he called 'artificial transuranic elements'. What he had actually done was to split the uranium atom, a key starting point when producing the atomic bomb.

At the same time as Fermi's experiments in Rome, Leo Szilard (later to become a colleague of Fermi at Los Alamos) had been working on the idea of sustaining a chain reaction using neutrons. He even tried to convince sceptical scientists in Britain about his ideas of a chain reaction and the release of large quantities of energy producing a 'human-devised explosion unprecedented in history'. What he meant was the atomic bomb. The British physicists were having none of it and refused to listen. In the end, Szilard filed for a patent on the idea which was granted in Britain on 12 March 1934. Eventually, with the help of his close friend Einstein, his ideas were taken seriously in the United States after the two wrote directly to the president; their fears that the Nazis might already be building an atomic bomb were taken seriously enough to result in the setting up of the Manhattan Project.

Of all the interesting snippets of information associated with the Bell, one of the most intriguing must be the involvement of Professor Walter Gerlach, another German nuclear physicist. After the war, Gerlach always stuck by his belief that he was never developing the atomic bomb for Nazi Germany and that, furthermore, neither were any of the other scientists. He claims that he was working on an 'engine'. However, was Gerlach aware of what was possible with such technology? While detained by the British after the war at Farm Hall (a former MI6 safe house), he fell into a deep depression and was reluctant to talk about the matter, even to his fellow scientific detainees. Worried by his mood, the MI6 officers asked his fellow scientists to keep an eye on him, especially after they broke the news of the Japanese bombings using atomic bombs in August 1945. The news caused further distress for Gerlach. It is also interesting that after the war, when he returned to Germany, he made the decision not to return to his scientific work but instead became rector of his old Berlin University. It begs the questions: What were Gerlach and his team really up to? What could have been its ultimate conclusion? Maybe it is significant that Dr Ernst Grawitz, head of the euphemistically named SS Medical Service, was interested in the results of the Bell and its effects on living matter. Grawitz was the boss of Josef Mengele, the infamous doctor of Auschwitz. Whereas this medical application might be an added bonus to Nazi atrocities, the original purpose of the Bell was not an early form of atomic bomb, if Gerlach is to be believed. If it was not nuclear, could it have been electromagnetic?

One thing is clear: there is certainly suggestion that the metallic liquid was radioactive because it was contained in a lead-lined box. The destruction of materials like the walls and other objects in its region of influence also suggests radioactivity, as do the medical effects reported by workers, including a half-dozen deaths. But there are other interesting clues. Sporrenberg picked up on key words and phrases which, being no scientist, made no sense to him. One of these was 'vortex compression'. This term could be applied to the subject of plasma physics, resulting in a whole new meaning. Plasmas are electrified gases where the negative electrons and positive nuclei of atoms are split apart by pumping energy into gas. Within the plasma, electrical filaments tend to attract and twist up into larger filaments, a form of twisting compression or, maybe, 'vortex compression', also known as 'the pinch effect'. This is like lengths of string twisting up into larger rope-like structures. Another phrase was 'magnetic fields separation'. This, again, fits well with plasma physics, having magnetic and electric fields. The fact that some of the side effects might have come from electromagnetic radiation is further suggestion this could have been a plasma physics experiment. Further interesting details include the glowing effect whenever the Bell was working and the spinning cylinders. Were the cylinders an attempt to get those electromagnetic filaments to twist up in some way? More intriguing is the fact SS officials took an interest in the goings-on of Hannes Alfven and his associates during their occupation of Norway; they were experts in plasma physics. After the war, these experiments left behind strange concrete structures and evidence of colossal power cables feeding them from powerful generators; the production of plasma would require high levels of energy. It is by no means conclusive, but intriguing, nonetheless. Of course, we also have to ask: Was there a connection between plasma physics, Alfven's work in Norway and the eventual evacuation of key experiments like this to Norway at the end of the war by Kammler?

Intriguingly, the new type of nuclear-fusion reactors being developed today rather than the fission reactors involving uranium depend on Alfven's plasma physics discoveries. So, are we back to nuclear reactors? It seems unlikely, because fusion reactors are far too advanced for the time unless it really was a highly speculative, out-of-the-box project. Although all this allows for both sides of the argument, if the Bell really existed I would consider it to be electromagnetic in nature rather than nuclear, because it just fits far better.

Another popular possibility that has been suggested for the Bell is an anti-gravity device. In particular, this idea links with the development of disc-shaped aircraft, or flying discs, especially the so-called 'field propulsion discs' that were said to use free energy from the zero-point field as a power source. It is particularly intriguing that Gerlach has links to gravity research and this, it is said, links to anti-gravity devices and disc technology. It is also said this explains why a nuclear physicist became involved with such devices. The evidence is found in missing details and anomalies in Gerlach's curriculum vitae. Again, it is a case of looking for what is missing rather than what is present in documentation and reports.

During the 1920s and 1930s, Gerlach was interested in spin polarization and spin resonance, as well as magnetic fields, all of which were to do with gravity research. Moreover, one of Gerlach's students published a paper in 1931 entitled *About Gravitation, Vortices and Waves in Rotating Media*. There was also that desire by the Nazis to use quantum mechanics to circumnavigate the Jewish gravity theories of Einstein, which plays a part here. Furthermore, when looking at the nuclear or electromagnetic suggestions for the Bell, a long-standing colleague of Gerlach (also at Farm Hall) was Heisenberg, who, in turn, was a close friend and colleague of Einstein and the quantum mechanics/gravity connection. Here, the quantum background foam of Heisenberg's Uncertainty Principle (HUP) was to provide free energy and non-Jewish anti-gravity. The connections are present and very intriguing. However, does it all fit together? What we now seem to have are three possibilities for the Bell; a nuclear, plasma or gravity experiment.

Different conspiracies exist for all three possibilities. The Nazis put a lot of faith in the ether theory, which led them to anti-gravity, vortex physics, spin and free energy, but Einstein had shown through relativity theory that the ether was unnecessary. All this fiddling and tinkering with experiments in mines also occurred with gravity and anti-gravity devices elsewhere, as we will see, and there is a lot more documented evidence when we meet the likes of Viktor Schauberger. Given the early stage in unification of quantum ideas and relativity, such theories were more believable back then than they are today, although they have not been totally dismissed.

The story of the Bell might sound fanciful if it were not for the testimonies and connections we have seen above and the fact certain modern-day discoveries suggest spinning cylinders in liquid helium can produce artificial black holes, a rich area of relativistic ideas and time travel, as well as parallel universes and the multiverse, but that is one for another book and is unlikely to be what the Nazis were really doing. Furthermore, it is unlikely the strange Xerum 525 liquid in the flask was liquid helium.

Let us now look at that Kammler evacuation programme. Amongst his investigations, Igor Witkowski found details of the special unit of the Soviet secret intelligence service known as the NKVD, the forerunner to the KGB. Attached to the unit were two Polish officers, General Jakub Prawin, head of the Polish military mission to Berlin, and Colonel Wladyslaw Szymanski, a senior member of his staff. During a debriefing of a former high-ranking official from the *Reichssicherheitshauptamt* (Reich Council Security Office or RSHA), they learned of General Plan 1945, an enigmatic evacuation plan. Their investigation subject, Rudolf Schuster, had worked for the RSHA, one of four security organizations run by the SS-controlled *Sicherheitsdienst* (Security Service) until his deployment on 4 June 1944 to the Special Evacuation Kommando Unit, which was unknown to the NKVD despite their pride in knowing everything. Schuster's responsibility was for transportation arrangements.

Schuster had been kept from the bigger picture regarding this plan, in accordance with SS practices. However, much of the kommando's activities centred on Lower Silesia and clues come from Jakob Sporrenberg. On 28 June 1944, he commanded a section of the kommandos attached to the Gauleiter of Lower Silesia, Karl Hanke. Gauleiters were the party's representatives in the gaus, or regions, answerable directly to Martin Bormann, the party chief. Sporrenberg was eventually handed to the Polish because he acted as a general for the SS in Poland where the SS ran many of their death camps.

It is claimed that Martin Bormann, Hitler's deputy, was behind General Plan 1945. However, if this was some type of secret plan to secure his safety after the war by doing a deal unknown to the Fuhrer, along the lines of others like Himmler and Kammler, it did not go to plan. Bormann did not benefit from it because he is said to have left the *Fuhrerbunker* on 1 May 1945 and was killed, although his body was never found.

It appears the British were unaware of Sporrenberg's other activities, otherwise they may have held onto him. He was a senior SS police general of high status and in a position to give Himmler absolute power throughout Germany in the war's closing years. He also carried the same rank as Ernst Kaltenbrunner, the brutal Austrian who succeeded Heydrich as head of the Reich Security Office, which was the Third Reich's central agency for internal counter-espionage and repression. For Sporrenberg to be assigned the command of the Special Evacuation Kommando Unit attached to Hanke's gau of Lower Silesia shows how important Bormann's evacuation plan was considered to be.

Sporrenberg was sent for trial and sentenced to death in 1952, but shortly before this, he testified in secret before the Polish courts about his role at Lower Silesia. This included evacuation of secret technology, documents and workers under Gauleiter Hanke and how he was tasked with operating the northern evacuation route to Norway. As we saw, it was here that the SS took an interest in top plasma physicists like Hannes Alfven. In fact, the SS once paid a visit to one of Alfven's scientists who managed to escape through a window to seek safety in Alfven's laboratory. It is therefore claimed the Bell was transported to Norway as part of the technology and further suggests it was a plasma experiment, not nuclear. Here we see why Norway, as well as Prague, were so important to Hitler in his final days.

All southern route evacuations were under the command of Lieutenant Colonel (Obersturmbannfuhrer) Otto Neumann, commander of the kommando detachment in Breslau. These shipments were destined for Spain and South America. Neumann was never caught but was thought to have escaped to Rhodesia, where he was supposedly sighted after the war. In total it is said that 12,000 tons of high-tech equipment, documents and blueprints were evacuated to Spain using any Luftwaffe aircraft available.

The Germans maintained a special detachment of heavy transporter aircraft believed to be JU 290s and a single JU 390 based at Opeln (Opole today) about 100km from the mines. According to witnesses, these aircraft were heavily camouflaged; some also had blue and yellow identification marks painted on them as if they were hiding as Swedish aircraft. It is believed they were a unit of the KG 200, the Luftwaffe special operations wing, because they were known to frequently fly under the flags of enemy or neutral countries. This allowed the evacuation kommando to transport thousands of tons of equipment, documentation and even personnel. Intriguingly, as we have seen, these aircraft were often called 'trucks', which appears to support the claim that Kammler refused Himmler a 'truck' from the Junkers transport pool mentioned above.

Following his death sentence, Sporrenberg was smuggled to Russia and further interrogated by the NKVD, who then disposed of him. Schuster died mysteriously in 1947, while Szymanski and Prawin also met untimely deaths, Szymanski in an air crash and Prawn by drowning.

Whatever the Bell was and where it ended up is still a mystery, as indeed are the other items evacuated. Nevertheless, it appears Kammler had quite an empire and there were many secrets about which we may never learn. However, one area that does appear to have much to say about these secret projects is the flying disc technology, to which we now turn. In particular, it illustrates nicely how many of these Kammler-style projects progressed at times.

We start by returning to Vesco's investigations, which reveal interesting possibilities about the Nazis and experiments involving disc-shaped aircraft and weapons of several types. However, a word of warning is important here because, when we look at this area of his research, we find a familiar level of uncertainty to begin with, but later we find a considerable amount that suggests this type of research was being done and associated with the SS and Kammler. In particular, there is a lot of documentary proof from one engineer called Viktor Schauberger, and again, it is Nick Cook who discovered much of worth from Schauberger's archives.

Certainly, the idea of a disc or saucer-shaped aircraft leads to many controversial avenues of fringe science, for example, the post-war sightings of flying saucers throughout the world and in particular the United States that has led to claims of extraterrestrial visitations. However, with this subject we also find a more conventional terrestrial element to explore because of that surprising amount of scientific evidence to support such an aircraft was being developed by the Nazis. Maybe also of significance is that we have already met this idea in a slightly different form with the so-called 'tortoise shell device' proposed to explain Foo Fighters and claims from Renato Vesco in his book *Intercept UFO*. It is, therefore, not surprising that Vesco also has much to say about flying discs generally.

The idea of an aircraft shaped as a disc can be traced back to the year before Hitler came to power. In 1932, Henry Coanda came up with what is now termed 'the Coanda effect'. What he realized is a disc-shaped aircraft could be used in such a way that its entire airframe would essentially act like the wings of a conventional aircraft. As such, it was considered along the same lines as the Horten 229 and similar aircraft being developed in 1944 and 1945. If shaped just right and with a powerful fan placed at the centre of the disc, air would be drawn above and over the airframe, then down below the craft, giving it lift. This is essentially the same way the wings of a conventional aircraft work; in doing so, the air pressure would be lowered above the craft and increased below it, giving lift, or what is known as the Bernoulli principle. As a result, the disc would rise into the air, and by careful manipulation of its shape and aerodynamics, possibly by using other fans, vanes or jet engines it could act like the wings of a conventional aircraft to control its flight. Essentially, as we will see, many of the disc designs have this idea as a basic principle of operation one way or another.

Much of the more exotic aviation designs, including discs, occurred as the war drew to an end and Nazi physicists were becoming desperate for new wonder weapons; all the more so as by then, Hitler and Himmler's esoteric, even occultist, views had got out of control. What essentially started as some isolated ideas in 'garden shed'–type workshops of the early 1940s had become much more by the last couple of years of the war; once again much of this was coming together around 1943 to 1945. The subject of flying discs falls broadly into two areas: projects that are factually better known and understood that deal with conventional propulsion methods, such as fans, vanes and jet engines; and lesser known projects that tackle the problems through exotic propulsion systems and free-energy ideas, sometimes called 'field propulsion discs'. The latter is less well-documented, but depends on the exotic ideas of quantum mechanics, anti-gravity, the Heisenberg Uncertainty Principle, and zero-point energy. As such, it did away with conventional fuels to power the discs.

Although these flying saucer designs are controversial, it is somewhat ironic that many ridiculed in the subject as 'UFO nutcases' have actually unearthed documents, personal accounts and general evidence to support the subject. Amongst these documents are intelligence reports from the time, as well as personal files and diaries from those involved that escaped destruction as the chaos of war came to an end and Allied Forces descended on the factories and institutions involved. As a result, it seems clear that between three and seven, maybe eight, different disc designs were considered, with some built and tested, although some debate remains as to the exact number because of variations on the same designs and overlap as they developed. Again, this was typical of the Kammler 'Empire'.

To start with, and to set the scene nicely, we will first look at one of the key characters, Major (Sturmbannfuhrer) Rudolf Lusar, who served as the commanding officer of a German Army technical unit. In 1956, he spoke out about the secret weapons of Nazi Germany in a book titled *German Secret Weapons of World War Two*. The book is detailed and became a bestseller in the United States and Britain. However, it has the theme of clear bitterness about it because of the way the technical achievements of a 'small industrious and honest nation which lost the war' have been handled, in his words. The book shows how Germany was ahead in some key areas like jet engines, rockets, missile guidance seekers, aircraft and airborne weapons systems, infra-red and thermal-imaging systems, proximity fuses, technologies for bringing down enemy aircraft with sound waves, air vortices, intensely focused beams of light, and jets of compressed air, much of which we have touched on already. Many of these technologies were in their infancy in the 1950s, yet he pointed out that Germany had been working on them a decade and a half earlier, which is true enough in some respects. However, one area of the book was somewhat more sensational and at the time got Washington worried; that area was the wonder weapon of flying disc technology.

In support of some of these ideas, in 1958 the United States Air Force commissioned a special study group within their intelligence division headed by Austrian-born technical consultant Dr Stefan Possony. It was Possony's job to give appraisal to Lusar's book. The exercise was classified as Secret and only came to light at the end of the 1990s, when it was uncovered by aerospace consultant Nick Cook of *Jane's Defence Weekly*.

In Lusar's book, there is a section devoted to flying discs, in particular the post-war flying saucers of UFO fame which Lusar claimed were developed by Nazi physicists. The first projects were called 'flying discs' and originated in 1941, which may suggest it was in development before the Horten 229. Lusar also mentions key experts who worked on the projects, including Rudolf Schriever, Richard Miethe, Giuseppe Belluzzo, and Otto Habermohl. In his book, there are detailed descriptions of the craft, with two principal centres of development mentioned: one in the vicinity of the lower Silesian city of Breslau in what is now Poland and headed by Miethe; the other at Prague in Czechoslovakia. The claims of Lusar's book were basic, but they did allow further investigations guiding the way to a fuller picture about his claims. Some of that investigation was quite remarkable, as we will see.

The best-known flying disc project is usually referred to as the 'Schriever-Habermohl project', or sometimes just the 'Schriever project' because of the uncertainty about exactly how much input came from Habermohl. It is also a bit of a mystery as to who was actually in charge; it is said that neither Schriever nor Habermohl actually headed the project. What we do know is Rudolf Schriever was a Nazi engineer as well as a test pilot; rather less is known about Habermohl, except that he, too, was an engineer. Flight Captain (Flugkapitan) Rudolf Schriever was one of four flying disc engineers who in 1950 spoke out about his work to the West German media. His ideas stemmed from work he undertook for the Heinkel Aircraft Company at Marienehe, near Rostock, on the Baltic coast. This location suggested to some that this, and similar, projects also fell under the control of Peenemunde and the rocket scientists. Indeed, there is some evidence to suggest it may have, and as a result, an alternative name for at least some of these aircraft was 'Peenemunde discs'. We also know that Schriever started out as a test pilot in the Luftwaffe and later developed advanced ideas for aircraft that could take off and land vertically: the idea being this would get around the Allied bombing of airfield runways. After he was drafted to Heinkel's design section, he came to the attention of Professor Ernst Heinkel in early 1940. Heinkel then encouraged Schriever to develop a small prototype of his idea.

It may be significant that key to these types of flying discs was the jet engine, which Heinkel had been funding since 1936 while Frank Whittle had developed and patented his version in Britain. This would also be a key form of propulsion in further disc developments after the war, the Canadian Avro Car being an example. However, those post-war projects also carry a lot of uncertainty and, for those who have investigated the subject, a definite amount of military disinformation, too. What we can therefore say is the development of the jet engine spanned 3 years and fits with claims of early disc development from 1941 onwards.

In the spring of 1941, Schriever's blueprints were used to develop a model to prove the concept worked. This he did in a garage away from prying eyes, again something which fits with Heinkel's way of development. The location of the garage is unknown, but was probably amongst the huge complex at Marienehe, a 3km^2 complex of Mecklenbury State Park. However, somewhat confusingly, this device was codenamed V1, although here the 'V' stood for *versuchs* or 'experimental version 1' and does not appear to have associations with the Peenemunde V-1, or doodlebug, except for claims a common engine was used. More informally, it was referred to as the 'Flying Top'. At this stage, it was just a model, measuring about 1m in diameter and powered by an electric motor or a two-stroke engine.

It appears that, by June 1942, the 'Flying Top' was proving to be promising enough to get Top-Secret funding from the Air Ministry to provide a full-scale version complete with a cockpit for one pilot. This version, again somewhat confusingly, was codenamed the V2, although again it had an informal name of the *Flugkreise*, or 'Flight Wheel'. Development began in early 1943 at Marienehe with a version measuring 8m in diameter and powered by one, maybe two, Heinkel-Hirth jet engines. It is said that, being a test pilot, Schriever himself flew his creation on its first test flight. Accounts also suggest it was an overengineered device and proved difficult to control or even get off the ground, so it was scrapped. That said, it seems to have shown enough promise to develop further into what would become the V3. At this point, the project moved to Prague in Czechoslovakia, home of flying disc technology.

Following the move, the project appears to have been centred on Prag-Gbell (Prague-Kbely) Airport, which was one of the Luftwaffe's airfields. Indeed, it appears that by now this was a Luftwaffe project which received technical assistance from the nearby Skoda Works, the Skoda division at Letov and possibly elsewhere. It therefore was almost certainly connected with the *Kammlerstab*. According to one key outspoken player in the disc programme, Joseph Andreas Epp, the Junkers firm at Oscheben and Bembury were also involved, as were the Wilhelm Gustloff firm at Weimar and the Kieler Leichtbau at Neubrandenbury. This move to Prague was also partly due to the Allied bombing campaign, which was now penetrating deep into the Reich. However, there was also another advantage to the move: it could be centred on a restricted area outside Prague belonging to Munich-based Bayerische Motorenwerke engine company (BMW), where real cutting-edge research on gas turbines was being perfected. In particular, there was also a connection with BMW's Bramo (Brandenburgische Motorenwerke) division located at Spandau in Berlin, which they bought from Siemens in 1939.

It is estimated that, by the middle of the war, the BMW-Bramo works had 5,000 full-time employees working on the gas-turbine research. This research was ultimately responsible for the BMW 003 jet engine, which was the best of its time. The engine went on to power the Me 262, the world's first operational jet fighter, as well as the Ar 234, which was the Luftwaffe's advanced jet-propelled reconnaissance bomber; both were well ahead of their time. Another engine design that could have been employed in this disc research was the Junkers Jumo 004, which was a substitute for the BMW 003. Rocket engines may also have been employed, such as the Walter HWK 109, which powered the Me 163 rocket interceptors. One witness, Epp, reported the Jumo 211/b was used because of shortages of other engines, possibly supporting this view. Furthermore, as rocket-powered aircraft are involved in this story and given Goering's Luftwaffe alliance with rocket engineers and rocket aircraft, it is possible Peenemunde may well have been involved too. It is also the case that early discs were being considered as interceptors, leading to early versions such as the tortoise-shell devices proposed as an answer to Foo Fighters. Another engineer associated with the disc physics, Hermann Klaas, reports that the Argus pulse jet (Schmidt-duct) based on Peenemunde's V-1 was also considered. However, just about all these engines were difficult to obtain at about the time because of their need on higher priority fighters, shortages of materials and manpower, and Allied bombing of factories, as we have seen. This may explain why serious disc technology did not advance significantly until later in the war, when Kammler needed the new super weapons he promised Hitler.

Not so much is known about the other name associated with this flying disc project: Habermohl. His job at Prague seems to have been to integrate the disc with a new power plant known as the 'radical-flow gas turbine', or RFGT. This RFGT was certainly recognizable technology by today's standards, even if it was somewhat extraordinary. Basically, it was a jet engine, but unlike regular jet power plants with a compressor, combustion chamber and turbine mounted one behind the other in a big tube, the RFGT formed part of the aircraft itself. The construction was a whirling turbo-machinery rotating around the aircraft's centrally mounted cockpit, which meant there was only one shape this aircraft could take on—a disc.

Epp reports much of his knowledge of this research in his book *The Reality of the Flying Discs* (*Die Realitaet der Flugscheiben*) with that knowledge coming from claims he served as an engineer and consultant to the Schriever-Habermohl project, as well as a separate, parallel, project known as the 'Miethe-Belluzzo project'. Epp states that some fifteen prototypes were built in all, the final version of which is the disc described by engineer Major Rudolf Lusar in his book. Interestingly, Lusar worked in the German patent office, so he was able to see the technical designs for the Schriever-Habermohl project. He describes it as a central cockpit surrounded by rotating adjustable wing-vanes forming a circle. The wing-vanes were held together by a band at the outer edge of the wheel-like device. The pitch of the vanes were adjustable, so that during take-off, more lift was generated by increasing their angle from a more horizontal setting; in level flight, the angle would be adjusted to a smaller angle, similar to the way helicopter rotors operate. The wing-vanes were set in rotation by small rockets which were placed around the rim, somewhat as a Catherine wheel, or pinwheel, arrangement. Once the rotational speed was sufficient, lift off was achieved. When the disc reached the required height, the horizontal jets and rockets were ignited, and the small rockets shut off. From this point, the wing-vanes would be allowed to rotate freely as the disc moved forwards, as in an autogyrocopter. It also seemed that the wing-vanes' speed, and hence their lifting value, could be increased by directing the adjustable horizontal jets slightly upwards to engage the vanes, thereby spinning them faster at the discretion of the pilot. Rapid horizontal flight seems to have been achieved with the jets or rocket engines.

By the autumn of 1944, the V3 version is said to have been completed. However, there was now a change of plan, or 'administrative change' as it was described; the V3 was abandoned in favour of another prototype called the V7. The jump in number is unclear but the sudden change of plan just as a prototype was complete certainly is consistent with Nazi aircraft production. There was also the suggestion this had happened because, although it started out as a Luftwaffe project under the control of Ernst Udet, it eventually fell under the control of Albert Speer's Ministry of Armament. After that, it is said to have been controlled by the engineer Georg Klein and finally, like so many scientific research projects, it ended up under the control of Himmler's SS in 1944, specifically under the jurisdiction of Kammler. The SS, and particularly Kammler, would also take control of other disc project at the same time, and the familiar changes would also take place with them, too. This was almost certainly against a backdrop of panic and chaos to win the war during its final year or so. The new plan was to build the V7 with a propulsion system involving the experimental RFGT from BMW-Bramo, which allowed for a much bigger disc of 18 to 20m in diameter and a crew of two or three pilots. It is possible the increase in size was to allow it to go into action sooner and carry bombs. Placing some figures on the Habermohl RFGT, it would have to generate 2,250 to 3,350 Newtons of thrust to have made this design feasible.

The end result is unclear, but according to Klein, he saw this device actually fly on 14 February 1945, although Schriever himself speaking after the war never claimed the device flew or even worked. However, another witness does support Klein's claim, saying he saw it in flight in earlier August or September 1943 at the Prague facility, but given the time scale, this was probably the V3 disc not the V7. The witness in question was in flight training at Prag-Gbell when he saw a short test flight of a disc, describing it as 4 to 5m in diameter and as tall as a man, with an outer border of .3 to .5m, aluminium in colour and standing on four thin legs. Interestingly, it flew only 275m at an altitude of only 1m off the ground. This would fit with post-war flying discs like the Avro Car, which never really flew long distances before crashing into something due to instability, or far off the ground. Klein's account of his V7 sighting was far more impressive. He claims it climbed to 12,400m in 3 minutes, reaching a speed close to the speed of sound (about 1,200km/hr); a claim backed up by Epp, who says it achieved Mach 1. However, there is some confusion here because Epp might be describing an earlier test flight in August 1944, where he took two fuzzy pictures of a disc in flight, pictures that have been doing the rounds in UFO books ever since. Epp goes on to say the following night the sound barrier was broken in manned flight, but the pilot became concerned with the vibrations he encountered. As for the official flight of 14 February 1945, Epp claims it obtained a test speed of 2,200km/hr, close to Lusar's claim of a top speed of 2,000km/hr, in line with claims from others.

As remarkable as all this may sound, there are some doubts over such high speeds. For one thing, the disc shape of such an aircraft with its large frontal area makes claims of a Mach 1 speed appear impossible; the atmospheric resistance would slow the disc to a point below the figures quoted. Then, there is a problem with the available power plants achieving such speeds in the first place. Therefore, some researchers have suggested there may be confusion with other projects, like Project 8-346, which was not a disc but a swept-back wing design; given the time scale, this would fit with projects like the swept-back winged Horten 229, also known as the 'Nazi UFO'. Further support for this comes from Allied intelligence reports that suggest the Germans designed the 8-346 to fly in the region of 2,000 km/hr. That said, one intriguing point is it was designed to use the Walter HWK 109 rocket engine, which was one of the engines claimed to be involved with the Schriever-Habermohl project. This may be significant, if only to show the practice of overlapping within Kammler's projects. Of course, given all these claims as well as confirmable details, and taking into account the obvious free rein designers had, and the funding thrown at them, there could be a good mix of fact, myth and pseudo-science in all these possibilities. Discrepancies like these persist to this day.

Schriever claimed he continued to work on his project until 15 April 1945, when Prague was threatened by the advancing Red Army. It is also claimed the technicians at the plant ran amuck as the Russians approached, looting the facility and pushing the prototypes at Prag-Gbell onto the tarmac to blow up the evidence under orders from the SS. Habermohl then disappeared and is assumed to have gone over to the Russians. This may have been true if Lusar's claim is correct when he says many experts were captured by the Russians and sent to Siberia where work on the discs was 'successfully continued'.

As a result of the advancing Red Army, Schriever decided to pack the plans for his disc into the boot of his car and, with his family in tow, drove to southern Germany. He then travelled north to his parents' home in Bremerhaven-Lehe after hostilities came to an end. It was here that he set up a new workshop which was later raided on 4 August 1948, with the plans and models stolen. After the raid, Schriever says he was then approached by 'foreign powers' enquiring about his work with the Nazis. He refused their 'offers' and went to work on menial tasks like driving a truck for the US Army. He died shortly afterwards in 1953. This approach may be true; as we will see later with disc engineer Viktor Schauberger, he too was approached by foreign powers, in his case the United States, and asked to continue his work, except here there is actual documented evidence of the fact in the Schauberger archives.

The Schriever story continued, however, even to the extent that his death was said to be faked so that he could take up work with the United States beyond just driving a truck. It is claimed he did post-war research on the flying discs, which led to the famous flying saucers and UFO reports in the country from 1947 onwards. It is at this point the story gets controversial beyond many people's taste and opens up a whole new can of worms, leading us into the domain of modern ufology (UFOs since 1947), a topic beyond this book, but one that can be followed elsewhere.

Epp always insisted it was he who originally came up with the type and design used in the Schriever-Habermohl project. In his book, he explains that the imbalance in the ring of wing-vanes that plagued the prototypes, especially in the early stages, was due to a deviation from his original design. That deviation amounted to a lengthening of the wing-vanes; he explains that when they were returned to his original specifications, the disc was able to take off. It appears the unofficial test flight of August 1944 had the lengthened wing-vanes. Indeed, Schriever's change in the length of the wing-vanes caused long-term problems; he was still trying to correct the instability of the disc as the Russians overran Prague. Habermohl, who also continued his work with the corrected wing-vane length, had two or three successful flights, whereas Schriever probably had none. Remember, Schriever never did claim his design flew. We will see later how this wing-vane length played out in claims of post-war developments.

There is also the claim that the Schriever-Habermohl project was actually two projects: the Schriever project and a parallel Habermohl project, giving support to discrepancies in accounts. Of course, it is possible that the two merged, but if we look at the account of Georg Klein, he states there were 'three constructions' all finished at Prague by the end of 1944, but destroyed as the Russians approached in 1945. Klein acknowledges that one of these discs was the Miethe-Belluzzo disc and that Peenemunde and its nearby facility at Stettin retained and developed the third Miethe-Belluzzo design as an unmanned vehicle. In short, he claims the third disc was designed by Dr Richard Miethe, sometimes referred to as Dr Heinrich Richard Miethe, with the other two discs being the Schriever disc and the Habermohl disc. We will look at the Miethe disc later, as our second main disc project.

There seems to be good reason to believe the words of Epp and Klein that both Schriever and Habermohl each produced their own designs, and that Miethe worked on a somewhat different approach with a fourth main engineer in this area of research, Professor Giuseppe Belluzzo. Epp claims that Habermohl's design was the one that flew in August 1944 and again on 14 February 1945, which was the disc witnessed in flight by Epp and Klein. Epp also claims Miethe was a 'known V-weapon designer' and this is why the project became connected with Peenemunde, where disc projects were set up, probably by Dornberger himself. It seems that Miethe and Belluzzo worked at the Dresden and Breslau plants, but had brief associations with Schriever and Habermohl at Prague, according to Epp. Furthermore, Epp claims he sent his design and model of his version of a flying disc (the Schriever-Habermohl design with the original length of blade dimensions) to Ernst Udet of the Luftwaffe. Udet is said to have passed this to Peenemunde for development.

In conclusion, the most likely answer is Epp's claim that it was his design which formed the basis for this project is correct. This version was given to Udet and forwarded to Dornberger at Peenemunde. Dornberger then had it tested and recommended the project go ahead, a detail confirmed to Epp by Dornberger after the war. A facility was then set up in Prague to explore further developments, where both Schriever and Habermohl were assigned to work on it. In the beginning, it was Goering and his Luftwaffe who took charge. Later, it transferred to the control of Speer and his ministry, maybe when Hitler put Speer in charge after falling out with Fritz Todt and his subsequent death in a mysterious plane crash in February 1942. At this stage, Klein took charge of the disc projects. Finally, in 1944, the SS took complete control, along with other disc projects, at which point it fell under the jurisdiction of Kammler. Of course, this may be wrong, but based on the claims from all those concerned, that seems to be the likely scenario.

Politically, this control-grab by the SS in 1944 is said to have come about because Himmler decided to replace Speer's appointee, Klein, with Kammler, making him overseer of combined disc research projects. However, there appeared to be something strange because Kammler kept Klein as his employee. A better way to interpret this is Kammler, Himmler's employee, replaced Speer, while Klein continued doing the job he had done up to then. Nonetheless, the final result was that Himmler's SS had now taken absolute control of the disc projects from that point until the end of the war, as they had for other scientific endeavours.

This brings us onto the next major disc design: the Miethe-Belluzzo project. Although this is regarded as a flying disc, it is more likely to have been yet another variation of the flying wing research from more conventional aviation projects. It is said to have begun in 1942 under the authority of Dr Richard Miethe; however, like many of these unconventional off-springs in research, Miethe is yet another participant that we know little about. Indeed, just about nothing is known about him before the war, although afterwards it is rumoured he worked on the Anglo-American flying disc projects coming out of Avro Aircraft Limited of Canada. Certainly, much more is known about this company and their research into flying disc aircraft; there is no doubt the research existed and Avro did produce working full-scale aircraft of that nature, but those who have studied this see much military disinformation, smoke and mirrors. However, just how this is connected with Nazi research is the point at which it becomes even more blurred and uncertain. Those who claim Miethe did go over to the Avro projects have only word of mouth from Klein, Epp, Lusar and Michael Barton, amongst many other sources, so whereas there appears to be considerable argument amongst these and other flying disc researchers, hard proof is lacking again. Nevertheless, the claims are interesting in themselves.

The other scientist working with Miethe has a better proven history. He was Professor Giuseppe Belluzzo, senator and minister of the national economy under Mussolini. In some paperwork, his name is given as 'Bellonzo', for example, in Vesco's book *Intercept UFO*, but Vesco was probably talking about Professor Giuseppe Belluzzo, because he fits the engineering specifications outlined in the book. Belluzzo also has a proven record of turbine research, having written several books on the subject, including *Calculations and Installations of Modern Turbine Hydraulics* in 1922 and *Steam Turbines* in 1926. In fact, Belluzzo was considered to be something of an authority in these areas; we also know he was considered a senior scientist within Nazi disc research and regarded as invaluable. After the war, Belluzzo retired to Italy, where he had a quiet life. He died on 22 May 1952.

Like many of the other disc researchers during the 1950s, shortly before his death, Belluzzo started talking about the work he had conducted with the Nazis. In 1950, he told of how he had developed the idea of a disc-shaped 'flying bomb' which he worked on during the war. He then passed this over to the Nazis for further development into prototypes. There are two particular articles which are often quoted as containing such claims: one is in the popular 1950s Los Angeles paper *The Mirror* dated 24 March 1950; the second is in Belluzzo's obituary in the *New York Times* dated 22 May 1952. Belluzzo also stated he was convinced that these prototypes were the basis of the so-called 'flying saucers' that made headlines in the United States during the latter half of the 1940s and beyond. However, that claim was made by just about all the designers at about the same time. He further claimed they were then under development in the Soviet Union. However, these claims, like similar claims by Schriever and others, remain unverifiable, although intriguing, given flying saucer history. One further intriguing point is there was only a few days between Schriever talking to the media for the first time and Belluzzo doing the same; this resulted in some researchers claiming both had the same idea to cash in on the topic because many such former Nazi figures were struggling to make ends meet.

Although it is claimed that we are really dealing with three main disc projects with different aspects, the Miethe-Belluzzo was quite different. This version was a disc-shaped design whose outer part did not rotate. To add confusion, the Miethe-Belluzzo disc also had three designs. Details of the first design came from Klein's article in the Swiss newspaper *Tages-Anzeiger fuer Stadt und Kanton Zuerich* on 16 October 1954 (the same design is reproduced by Epp in his book). This was a disc that was not intended for vertical take-off and landing, but designed for an angular take-off, as with a conventional aircraft. There were twelve jet engines mounted 'outboard' which powered the craft, and a cockpit mounted to the rear with a periscope to monitor direction that was visually impaired by the design. At the centre of the craft was an internally mounted gyroscope to provide stability. The overall size was 42m in diameter.

However, there has been some challenge to the feasibility of such a design, especially from aeronautical writer Hans Justus Meier. It appears that the configuration of the jet turbines is incorrect. Furthermore, there appears to be confusion with a central bloated body if this was an outboard jet turbine design. What did this central part serve? It seems more likely there was one engine at the centre with twelve jet nozzles. For this to be so, Klein may just be retelling stories from others and never saw the disc himself. He certainly does not claim to have personally witnessed it.

The second design originates with another article in 1975 from the May/June publication *Luftfahrt International* titled *Deutsche Flugkreisel Gab's Die?* In this version, there is a cockpit above and below the centre of the craft, with four jet engines lying behind the cockpit as power plants. Unfortunately, there are really no significant details to be found in the article; the text, instead, deals with the Schriever-Habermohl project, adding more confusion. Of course, much speculation has been put forwards elsewhere about this design, but no proof has appeared beyond these brief details, and no link with the Miethe-Belluzzo project has been found. This might, however, explain confusion about whether there were two or three designs to the Miethe-Belluzzo craft.

The third design comes from yet another article. This one was written by Jan Holberg on 20 August 1966 in *Das Neue Zeitalter*. With this design, the disc is capable of vertical take-off and is based on details which come from connections between Michael X. Barton, Carl F. Mayer and Hermann Klaas. It is Klaas who provides internal details. At first sight, this design shows signs it is a push-pull propeller system driven from a single engine, but it is not. It also appears the twelve jet nozzles are not supported in any way as depicted in the article, which seems to be due to the drawing being incomplete. When the completed parts are depicted, we have a radical turbojet engine of special type.

Design one differs from design three inasmuch as design three is controlled by selectively shutting various jets through the use of a surrounding ring. This is achieved from a centrally located cabin and a symmetrical arrangement of the twelve adjustable jet nozzles. All this is what allows for a vertical take-off, as well as the ability to make turns. As for the incompleteness of such designs it has been proposed by a German researcher, Klaus-Peter Rothkugel, that an engine design does exist which links designs one and three, and possibly design two, while also supplying the missing pieces required to make the depicted engine air worthy. This appears to resolve these and other issues. It is also significant that this engine would have been available to the Nazis following their occupation of France, seeing as it was invented by a French engineer, Rene Leduc. It is further intriguing that if such a disc equipped with this engine was viewed from the outside, no rotating parts would be visible; the rotating part would be completely enclosed within the outer metal skin with an air space all around the spinning engine. This was a radical-flow jet engine and is said to have powered all of the Miethe-Belluzzo designs. Moreover, it is also the prime candidate for a post-war design by John Frost called the 'Flying Manta', which actually flew on 7 July 1947. There are even photographs of its test flight at that time by William A. Rhodes as it flew over Phoenix, Arizona, in the United States.

Exactly when, or if, there were any test flights of the Miethe-Belluzzo designs in Nazi Germany is unclear. Nevertheless, it is the post-war details from Epp that come to the rescue as the main claim for such events, although Klein does back up claims to some extent. Epp claims models were under test by 1943, which is also claimed by Klein; indeed, both Epp and Klein claim they were tested from Stettin, north Germany, close to Peenemunde, at a location where the Oder River meets the Baltic. It is also claimed a disc crashed in Spitsbergen, which are the islands to the north of Norway. Pinning down a date for these test flights is also problematic. There have been claims that the Miethe-Belluzzo disc flew in December 1944, with this date possibly arising because of Klein's claim 'three constructions' were completed by the end of 1944. Another date, 17 April 1944, comes from an article dealing with the work of Miethe in the Italian newspaper *Tempo* dated 6 September 1952. Interestingly, this article contains a photograph of the Miethe-Belluzzo disc in flight. It is a bit fuzzy, but is claimed to be a type-one design, or maybe a type three.

Yet another intriguing event during 1944 involves claims that all such patents were taken away by the Allies as the war ended; indeed, literally truckloads of paperwork were removed. Again, details come courtesy of the book written by Lusar who, as we have seen, was an engineer working in the German patent office at the time. After the war, these patents were reproduced from memory by Lusar and appear extremely detailed. Amongst them are also details of the Schriever-Habermohl disc, as well as the Miethe-Belluzzo discs.

A final bit of intriguing information comes from a book not about flying discs, as such, but about the atomic bomb project. In the 1958 book by Robert Jungk, *Brighter Than a Thousand Suns: A Personal History of the Atomic Bomb,* there is an interesting footnote: 'The only exception to the lack of interest shown by authority was constituted by the Air Ministry. The Air Force research workers were in a peculiar position. This produced interesting new types of aircraft such as the Delta (triangular) and "flying discs". The first of these "flying discs," as they were later called – circular in shape, with a diameter of some 45 yards – were built by the specialists Schriever, Habermohl and Miethe. They were first airborne on February 14, 1945, over Prague and reached in three minutes a height of nearly eight miles. They had a flying speed of 1,250 mph which was doubled in subsequent tests. It is believed that after the war Habermohl fell into the hands of the Russians. Miethe developed at a later date similar "flying saucers" at A. V. Roe and Company for the United States.' Of course, this book was written in 1958, after the disc scientists and engineers went public with their own books and articles in 1950 to 1952.

However, it is interesting that such a footnote should appear in a book essentially about the atomic bomb. The connection might be the suggestion that Nazis physicists were also working on atomic powered flying discs; we will touch on this again later.

Another key point to make here is 1952 was a big year in UFO history, as was 1947, with high numbers of flying saucer reports and sightings—even sightings over the White House. The Soviet Union also had its fair share of sightings at the same time. The debate over whether the technology lived on in these two superpowers and developed as a Cold War weapon, or whether many Nazis strapped for cash eased their positions by writing books and articles about a far lesser achievement, will rage for some time yet. However, it is interesting that many of these wartime claims appeared during those years when flying saucers and UFO sightings were big news worldwide.

At the end of the day, hard evidence for much of the claims about Nazi flying discs are few and far between. Individual claims are not so significant, but collectively they do carry some weight. Certainly, it seems research existed on the drawing board and maybe models were made, like the 'Flying Top', for example. Certainly, aviation engineers and designers were given a field day when it came to new ideas, designs and technology development, all backed by huge sums of money as well as corruption. This was all the more so in the panic years of 1944 and 1945, when it looked like Germany was losing the war and new wonder weapons were demanded by the Fuhrer. But how far did it really go? We may get a clue later when we look at an extremely well-documented individual: Viktor Schauberger. But first, we need to look at an area of aviation physics that may give a clue and support to how and why all this flying disc research occurred in the first place.

Almost 10 years after the Second World War, a German engineer by the name of Heinrich Fleissner filed a patent application for a flying disc with the United States Patent Office (number 2,939,648). This act had a curious story associated with it inasmuch as the patent application was made on 28 March 1955, but was not granted until over 5 years later, on 7 June 1960. The reason for the delay is still unclear; sometimes such a delay can happen, but given the detailed history of flying saucer sightings in the United States throughout the 1940s to 1960s, some have claimed the authorities held back the application as part of the post-war military research, in particular with Project Y2/Silverbug. What we can say with certainty is the United States military was trying to recruit ex-Nazi saucer scientists during this period. However, to fully understand the Fleissner disc, we need to return to Nazi research and, in particular, to look at the problem area of atmospheric drag on aircraft and something called the 'boundary layer effect', which was key to flying disc development back then.

The boundary layer is that small layer of air only a few molecules thick that sticks to a lift surface, such as a wing, with the slowest moving sheet closest to the wing. As the aircraft moves faster, the layer increases the drag on the lift surface and therefore weakens the aircraft's efficiency; this, in turn, means the aircraft requires more energy to move. At high speeds, these slower moving layers collide with oncoming air molecules, which, in turn, cause areas of turbulence, translating into atmospheric drag. As the speed further increases, and depending on the configuration of the wing itself, this turbulence can become even greater, and builds up behind the wing as a result of the thickening of the boundary layer, which leads to the increasing of the aerodynamic resistance. As a solution, it appears necessary to move the point of transition as far to the rear of the aircraft as possible in order to minimize the expenditure of energy required to propel it through the air. If there is an elimination of the boundary layer, this allows the aircraft to fly faster and expend less energy when flying at any given speed. Prior to the war, British, American and German researchers concentrated on finding a solution to this problem. Various methods were tried, one of which was microporous sinterized metal the Germans called *Luftschwamm* (air sponge) as both a lift surface and an intake vent for jet turbines. The goal was simply to suction off the boundary layer from the lift surface, thereby dramatically decreasing drag and increasing efficiency and performance at high speed.

As part of the German response to the problem, they decided on the innovation of swept-back wings on an aircraft because it was discovered that air passing over such wings at an angle reduced boundary layer formation, meaning turbulence was less likely to develop. It is considered likely that the swept-back wings of the Me-163 rocket interceptor may have been the result of this research. Furthermore, an advanced model of the Me-262 jet fighter incorporated fully swept-back wings. Then, of course, there was the Horten 229, appearing at the end of the war. That said, reduction was one thing, but the ideal goal for the designers was to eliminate the boundary layer problem completely, and that is where matters became particularly interesting.

In an attempt to do this, they proposed the idea of suction wings. This goal started in the early 1940s: aviation designers cut slots into experimental aircraft, then auxiliary engines were employed to suck in the boundary layer through the wings and redirect the air into the fuselage and out of the aircraft's rear. However, although this might appear straightforward, it actually proved to be far more complicated than first thought. The problem was that the eddy currents of the turbulence caused the boundary layer to move across the wing from front to back as the air speed increased; a slot in one position on the wing worked at one speed, but not at another. An obvious answer was a series of slots covering the whole wing, but this proved impractical for a number of reasons. Another problem was the requirement for multiple engines, with the first providing power for flight and a second mounted in the fuselage to draw in air from the slotted wings.

Later it was found that the boundary layer could be eliminated by sucking it in or by blowing it off using a strong flow of air to disrupt it, and so full-scale suction-wing aircraft were built to test this solution. Examples of such aircraft were the Junkers *Absaugeflugzeug* (suction-aircraft) AF-1 and the Fieseler *Absaugestorch* (suction-stork) AF-2. In his book *Intercept UFO,* Vesco states that the flying disc experiments were the off-shoots of designs to suction the boundary layer from the lift surface of aircraft; in other words, the disc-shaped aircraft actually began as experiments to transform the entire lift surface into an intake vent for a jet turbine. The early discs were simply standard suction aircraft of an unusual, experimental shape that were designed to suction the boundary layer from the lift surfaces of aircraft.

Vesco also claims that, because of this research, the Germans gradually reached some intriguing conclusions. One was that transformation of ordinary aircraft was not a practical solution because the suction principle was deprived of its best attributes, and there were difficulties with construction, which did not compensate for the limited advantages. At the time, the engineers were also planning a special turbine-powered project, so the conclusion was to combine the two mechanisms into a single whole whereby the air was fed into the turbine taken from the wing instead of by the means of the usual forward-ram air intakes. Therefore, it was better to combine different projects so that the result was a new aircraft—a disc- or saucer-shaped craft, the entire surface of which was both the turbine intake as well as the lift surface, with fuselage and air intake as one and the same. There is also a suggestion this was achieved close to the end of the war, because such ideas had also occurred to the British. Details are found in a post-war report, *A.R.C. No. 9672: Notes on German Theoretical Work on Porous Suction*, showing the Germans had good success in combining microporous 'sinterized' air-permeable lift surfaces and turbine intakes. These notes were compiled by a special team of investigators through the examination of German research on porous materials and compared with similar British work done during the war.

In parallel with this German research, there were ideas being carried out into circular-wing designs beginning in the 1930s, and generally credited to Professor Ludwig Prandtl. This effectively meant the wing tip would curve back into the fuselage, making a circular wing. Experimental research into this type of aircraft has a long history dating back many years before the outbreak of the Second World War. However, in the case of Nazi research, such ideas began with two scientists who wrote scientific papers on the subject: Wilhelm Kinner in 1936, and M. Hansen in 1938, while working at the Aerodynamic Research Facility at Gottingen. Further such research was later carried out in 1941 at the Messerschmitt aircraft company in Augsburg by Dr Alexander Lippisch, who was also a pioneer of the delta-wing aircraft, holding unconventional theories about the design. However, his work would be proved correct when the Horten brothers used his ideas to build the Horten 229. During that time, Lippisch was working with Dr F. Ringlib on the *Drehfluegel* (rotating wing) when he was visited by Dr Giuseppe Belluzzo. It was also said that the *Drehfluegel* was another aircraft that was tested at Peenemunde as one of the so-called 'Peenemunde discs'. Whether the Peenemunde link is justified is still debated; what we can say is a large body of scientific literature exists to support these circular-wing experimentations. It also appears that one of Lippisch's designs, the J1253, was actually tested in the wind tunnel at Gottingen.

The ultimate goal of the aircraft designers was to combine the suction idea with the circular-wing design, housing the mechanism in the wing and eliminating the fuselage, essentially producing a disc-shaped aircraft and hopefully eliminating unwanted drag. It is important to realize this circular-wing design, although somewhat disc shaped, was not the same as the Schriever-Habermohl or Miethe-Belluzzo discs; it seems to be a more conventional project in aviation design rather than the more unconventional spinning-type flying discs. Nevertheless, it puts into context how these different projects may have worked together with obvious connections and varied approaches. Certainly, there is overlap between all these projects and key names, but exactly how they fit together is still not fully understood to this day. A further point to bear in mind is that the suction technique will enter our story of flying disc developments again when we look at the work of Viktor Schauberger and that wealth of documented research that appears to have escaped the wartime censors.

Having introduced the idea of suction aircraft, we can now look in detail at the work of Heinrich Fleissner. In the May 1980 issue of *Neue Presse,* an article appeared by Fleissner that also makes claims that flying disc research was carried out at Peenemunde, this time with his own design, that he later patented in 1955. Fleissner was a German fluidics engineer, designer and advisor to what he referred to as a '*Flugscheibe* project'; the word *Flugscheibe* being a German folk-word for 'flying disc'. Fleissner's flying disc was based on his area of expertise, fluidics, which included ways of investigating boundary layer flows. As a result, Fleissner's design, he claims, would be capable of speeds up to 3,000km/hr within the Earth's atmosphere, but he goes further by claiming it could reach 10,000km/hr outside the atmosphere, in space. Of course, this does suggest a link with Wernher von Braun working at Peenemunde and his preference for rockets being used as a means of space travel rather than weapons, but again, there is little evidence to support a connection.

What evidence we do have for a Fleissner disc is obviously found in his 1955 patent, so we do have some design details with which to work, regardless of whether it was a Peenemunde project or not. To begin with, the engine employed in the disc rotated around the central cabin on the outside of the disc itself, so this was essentially another rotating disc or flying saucer similar to those we have already seen. Again, the engine was set in motion by starter rockets in the same way as the Schriever-Habermohl disc, and might be where a link to Peenemunde originates. However, what makes this design both different from the Schriever-Habermohl disc and interesting is it really amounted to a form of ram-jet engine. This design also had the feature of slots which ran around the periphery of the disc into which air was gathered up in a suction boundary layer-type solution. The slots continued obliquely right through the disc, aiming the jet thrust slightly downwards and backwards from the rotational direction. Within the slots, there were fuel injectors and a timed ignition, which insured a power curve in accordance with the speed and direction of the disc, much like an automobile's fuel injection is timed to match the firing of the spark plugs. In order to steer the craft, the direction of the airflow was adjusted using internal channels which contained a rudder and flaps running alongside the central cabin. The cabin could be held stationary or turned in the direction of flight using a system of electromagnets and servo-motors coupled with a gyroscope. There are also various design features found with the Fleissner disc that are associated with Prandtl and Lippisch. The slot air intakes near the edge of the disc would suck in the boundary layer before it could form; then, below, jets would blow off the boundary layer at a similar point. Because the disc is in a state of spin, it would move any further development of a boundary layer at an angle, nullifying it in the same way as a conventional high-speed jet aircraft with severely swept-back wings. A further claim is this arrangement may even prevent the disc from generating a sonic boom. Interestingly, the lack of a sonic boom is often reported by witnesses of flying saucers and other UFOs.

It was also claimed that, apart from acting as a ram-jet, the Fleissner disc could be powered by a number of different fuels—liquid gas and even powders of solid fuels—to overcome shortages being experienced by the Nazi regime at the time. In particular, the disc could use finely powdered coal dust, or foam coal (*schwammkohle*), in a suspension of liquid air. It is also known that during the war, the Germans used hypergolic fuels—fuels which ignited simply on contact with one another—possibilities were C-Stoff and T-Stoff, which were designations for use in the Me-163 rocket interceptor and in rockets. Fleissner also mentioned in his 1980 article that liquid hydrogen and liquid oxygen could be used in a similar way as rocket fuel. This gave a further Peenemunde association, as well as suggesting that with the right fuel and expertise, the disc could function as a rocket. In its basic form, the Fleissner disc could therefore operate as a ram-jet on jet fuel; at a higher functioning level, it could operate outside the Earth's atmosphere on liquid hydrogen and liquid oxygen. With the correct development, it could function as both.

If such claims are true, it would make sense to have this project connected with developments in rocketry at Peenemunde and its associated plants. However, there is little proof the disc was built or even considered outside claims in books and articles by those working on weapons development in Nazi Germany, and it would seem unlikely a disc shape would be suitable as a rocket or missile. However, Vesco did use the word 'missiles' when he spoke of the disc weapons that he claimed were Foo Fighters. Nevertheless, Fleissner claims his disc did fly at Peenemunde and a nearby test facility at Stettin, but there is no smoking gun evidence. If any proof is alluded to, it is in the form of three photographs. These photographs appeared in a Dutch article about German discs and are also attached to a letter from Prague sent to Epp. The photographs show a small disc with features similar to those proposed by Fleissner where the air intake is located at the periphery of the saucer and seen in the ring just inside the disc's edge. The directional control is also clearly visible in the rudder mounting on the top of the cockpit or central cabin. However, the control is external and not as sophisticated as that shown in Fleissner's patent, but they are similar.

There is also so-called 'confirmation' that this was a Peenemunde disc, with a somewhat sensational report in a Stockholm evening newspaper, *Aftonblodet*, dated 10 October 1952. The paper reports that a flying saucer, or 'space ship', was developed by the Germans at Peenemunde under von Braun and his rocket team, with a test model flown in April 1944. The model was only 6m in diameter, but the full-scale version would have measured 42m and was said to fly at an altitude of 300km. This all sounds extremely fanciful and, again, there appears to be no real proof to support it. It is interesting that the size given is the same as the Miethe-Belluzzo disc, but this proves nothing of substance. It is also interesting to note that the altitude quoted is higher than the first Earth-orbiting satellites later developed by the Americans. It is further claimed in the article that the Americans hold design plans and so do the Russians.

However, the claims go further by suggesting the problem with the design is the fuel consumption needed to achieve the altitude, with the solution being an atomic engine. It is here that Heisenberg and his reactor enter the story with even less supporting evidence, especially as Heisenberg clearly did not come anywhere close to producing a reactor that worked, let alone an atomic engine. As a result, the failing in Nazi atomic physics means such ideas as atomic discs are just about universally dismissed by researchers. However, it is also worth bearing in mind the claims that the Fleissner disc was capable of getting into space without an atomic engine.

One historian, Thomas Powers, has looked into the atomic research area in his 1993 book *Heisenberg's War: The Secret History of the German Bomb*. The book concentrates on the historical sequence of the German atomic programme and the people involved, as well as their relationships with each other. It also follows the various organizations employed in such research, one of which was a group called *Heereswaffenamt* (HMA), or Army Ordnance Office. The director of this department was Dr Erich Schumann, a scientific advisor to Field Marshal Wilhelm Keitel. Schumann had the interesting position of being both a professor of military physics at the University of Berlin and holding a commission in the army, which allowed him to mingle and jump between both worlds with ease. Although he was a professor of military physics, he was more of an administrator than a research scientist; the research side was said to have been left to Dr Kurt Diebner, one of the Farm Hall detainees and one who was a full member of the Nazi Party. As a physicist, Diebner had been associated with the HMA since 1934, and it is claimed he headed his own atomic research project. It seems that any such project followed the view that atomic weapons were unnecessary to win the war, so the thinking was to de-emphasize to energy production through a reactor or engine. It is said that this became more important as the war dragged on and energy supplies from foreign powers, like coal and oil, dried up.

The controversial claim of this story is that whereas Heisenberg's efforts came to just about nothing of significance, Diebner's research resulted in a full-scale reactor and maybe an atomic bomb, in proposal at least. Furthermore, he repeatedly pressured Schumann about the possibility of bringing his proposal to a practical conclusion. Schumann is said to have finally given in and put the proposal to top Nazi officials in early 1942. Not surprisingly, the eventual result was to stress energy production rather than a bomb, a conclusion not much different from that of Heisenberg. However, where things differed somewhat is with Diebner's optimism that nuclear reactors could power submarines, something now commonplace. Unfortunately, the completion date for this was given as 1945, so it is open to debate as to whether an atomic disc existed before the end of the war, if at all, and evidence does not seem to support Diebner being a more successful version of Heisenberg. As such, this may only have boiled down to a drawing-board proposal, like so many others.

Powers also mentions two further characters, industrial physicist Carl Ramsauer and Ludwig Prandtl; the latter we have already met during the discussion of circular-wing aircraft. Ramsauer, on the other hand, was the head of the German Physical Society and a leading researcher for the electrical company *Allgemeine Elektrizitaetsgesellschaft*. Interestingly, a particular characteristic of Ramsauer was his desire to get rid of 'ethnic physics' and concentrate on using science to win the war. Prandtl was also of the same opinion, insisting that the Nazis let scientists do science without worrying about the ethnic background or politics; he also had practical experience of fission power. Prandtl's connection in all this is he was both an aeronautical engineer and supporter of nuclear power. Moreover, attention is drawn to why there was such urgency for Ramsauer and Prandtl to intervene in areas outside their usual expertise. One possibility is Ramsauer's ability to put technology into large-scale production, while Prandtl's interest was circular-winged and disc-shaped aircraft and atomic power. One conclusion to all this is the combining of all areas—circular-winged suction aircraft, flying discs and overcoming limited fuel capacity by using atomic engines—was the ultimate goal. The particulars of these characters make for an interesting story, but what of any hard evidence?

As we have seen, from time-to-time certain documents come to light that are more official and may shed some light on an otherwise uncertain subject. One such document is the BIOS report, number 142, written in 1946 and titled *Information Obtained from Targets of Opportunity in the Sonthofen Area*. The report includes details of the chemical physicist Josef Ernst and claims about a high-speed fighter, designated P-1073, being developed by Messerschmitt. Details are given of three different engines. The first was a BMW 003 engine using petrol as a fuel; the second was an engine using crude oil; and the third was an atomic engine. The atomic engine is described as 60cm long and 20cm in diameter. Ernst said it could produce about 2,000 horsepower and had a speed of 2,000km/hr with a ceiling of 18,000m. It was made at Camp Mecklenburg, with apparently only one model ever being manufactured, which was reported as destroyed, along with Camp Mecklenburg, by the SS shortly after Allied Forces arrived. Although it was believed this level of atomic efficiency was never achieved by the Nazis, British intelligence thought it was worthy of inclusion.

There is also a report obtained under the FOIA on a particular German scientist working at Wright Field (later known as the Wright-Patterson United States Air Force Base). This is a report from December 1946 titled *Effect of Power-Plant Weight on Economy of Flight (Project Number NFE-64)*. The German scientist concerned is Dr Neugebauer, who was brought back to the United States under Operation Paperclip. He is described in the report as the foremost German authority on this subject, an expert on internal-combustion engines and a specialist in diesel compound aircraft engines. During his time in Germany, he held leading positions at Junkers in Dessau and Munich from 1924 to 1943 and was director of the engineering department of the Institute for Aeronautical Research at Munich from 1943 to 1945. In the United States, he was employed in the propulsion section of the analysis division, intelligence (T-2), AMC, Wright Field, Dayton, Ohio, according to the report.

It appears strange that Neugebauer was an expert in diesel-powered aircraft, but that does not appear to be the reason he was brought to the United States. For one thing, at that time diesel-powered engines were much heavier than piston engines. As a result, it has been claimed the interest in him was due to his knowledge of the effects of heavy engines on aircraft, which was part of his expertise. The fact that the words 'atomic' or 'rocket' are not included in the report has led some to suggest it is implied because of the need for heavy radiation shielding on atomic aircraft.

Even before the FOIA request, it was known that Junkers in Dessu had associations with disc projects designated *Schildkroete* (Tortoise/Turtle), which some believe might have been connected with the idea that Foo Fighters were a tortoise shell–shaped weapon or, as Vesco claims, a 'proximity radio interference' device capable of jamming or spoofing Allied radio and radar systems, which also resembled the shell of a tortoise. However, the word *Schildkroete* appears relevant because one interpretation of the word's translation involves 'shield', in the way a tortoise shell is a shield. Claims that such atomic shielding would add significantly to an overall weight increase leads to Neugebauer's involvement. In fact, even allowing for weight reductions as a result of no conventional fuel and its associated components, the shielding would increase the weight of an aircraft. An interesting part of the report to consider is its introduction: 'Power-plant weight is a factor which affects flight performance; the greater the weight, the greater is that portion of the airplane and the drag which is affected by the power-plant. In contrast to the effect of fuel consumption, the effect of power-plant weight cannot be easily determined. For example, it cannot be easily determined whether a certain reduction of fuel consumption is still advantageous if it involves an increase in power-plant weight. This report aims to facilitate insight into these and similar questions.' Because of this report, some believe that Neugebauer was needed to deal with the weight problems of radiation shielding on atomic aircraft.

This brings me to the American nuclear physicist Stanton Friedman and my conversations with him over the years. Friedman worked on many government projects in the United States after the war involving aircraft using atomic power and was involved specifically with radiation shielding and its weight problems. He never made any secret of the fact, although he did not go into great detail. However, he did say that the United States successfully developed an atomic engine after the war, but it was never put into use. Furthermore, he was also a world-famous lecturer and supporter of flying saucers, often giving lectures along the lines of 'Flying Saucers Are Real'. That said, he claimed their origin was down to aliens visiting the Earth, which is taken by some as military disinformation. There have also been several rumours about Friedman's work; some say he was involved with the CIA, while others claim he was involved with a secret rocket team employed at McDonnell-Douglas. So, did the United States further develop Nazi ideas of atomic discs by combining the Nazi drawing-board dreams with their atomic bomb achievements to develop an atomic engine for aircraft, or maybe an atomic flying saucer?

Let us now summarize these many claims. The Schriever-Habermohl disc employed a whirling set of vane-blades and one or more rocket or jet engines in a spinning top affair. It may also have been capable of supersonic flight. The Miethe-Belluzzo disc differed inasmuch as it employed an internal spinning turbojet, first invented by Rene Leduc. Depending on the exact configuration, its thrust could be vented in any direction to steer the craft. Again, it may have been capable of supersonic flight. What we can say in support of this design is it was picked up by John Frost as part of his Flying Manta project after the war, and it has been claimed this, with other designs, may have been responsible for the spate of flying saucer sightings throughout the United States during the 1940s and 1950s. This same design was also referred to as a 'Flying Shoe' and may have been further developed by A.V. Roe Limited in Canada. It is suggested that the third design of the Miethe-Belluzzo disc, often alluded to by designers in various books and articles, was kept under special control at Peenemunde as the best of the three, often referred to as the 'Peenemunde Disc', and probably based on Fleissner's work helped by other key names we have encountered. This craft could use a variety of fuels and engine designs. As a result, it could function as a turbine–ram-jet within the atmosphere or convert to a rocket engine for high altitude. It is said that its speed and altitude limits would be much greater than either the Schriever-Habermohl or the other Miethe-Belluzzo designs and less complex than the advanced radical-jet engine designs developed in Canada as part of Project Y2/Silverbug. Therefore, claims the Fleissner patent of 1955 was delayed until 1960 because of Project Y2/Silverbug may be true. There is also the A.V. Roe developments and subsequent Avro Car design, which may account for the abandonment of the A.V. Roe work. It is then claimed this was followed by the release to the public of the Avro Car design, which was immediately discredited by its own engineers as part of a cover story. Work then continued on a Fleissner-style alternative; we will look at this in the next part of the flying disc story when we examine the work of Viktor Schauberger and the post-war part of his story. As for atomic discs, there seems to be much speculation, but at the end of the day, it is unlikely this was anything but a Nazi pipe-dream further considered by the United States, the results of which are unclear.

Until now, we have considered physicists and engineers, together with their work, who were qualified in their fields and often held impressive academic posts. However, there is one major name in the area of flying discs who had no scientific qualifications or academic posts to his name, yet was one of the biggest names in the subject: Viktor Schauberger. At first sight, it may be thought that Schauberger's lack of any formal scientific training would have gone against him, but that position needs to be put into context. Certainly, within the academic world, that was often the case; all the more so today when scientists want to distance themselves from such taboo subjects. However, in reality he was actually a skilled engineer in his own right, and even before the Nazis made available the necessary expertise to help with his research, his son was certainly a qualified physicist, mathematician and engineer.

What makes Schauberger different is there is an impressive archive of documentation to back up his claims and work, including a wealth of documented details like letters, diaries, blueprints and general records of his work under the Nazis, particularly under the SS. It is also significant that this achievement survives to this day and, in doing so, puts into context not only his own work but also that of others. Furthermore, the Schauberger devices went beyond just a flying disc—they incorporated other areas like water purification and energy production, including the controversial free energy ideas and its link to the Nazi belief in an ether of some sort. His work also included suggestions of atomic physics, which worried the Allies. Whether we choose to believe Schauberger's work is correct or not, the fact remains it is well-documented compared to other projects and shows how the Nazis were thinking and working as the war came to an end. It also highlights the rush to develop new wonder weapons as defeat became a real possibility.

When I first read of the Schauberger diaries and his relentless efforts to design, develop and put his devices into production, rushing between sites with a team of physicists and engineers while dodging enemy attacks, it showed a chilling parallel with the efforts of Bernard Lovell and his team to develop the various types of onboard radar systems. This was all the more so given the dates of both: 1943 to 1945. What we had was a British effort, a race against time, to target industrial sites and research establishments like those used by Schauberger perfecting new 'V- weapons' for use against the Allies, while the likes of Schauberger were in a desperate race of their own to develop their devices and dodge the Allied bombings. To top it, like Lovell, Schauberger was keeping detailed diaries and notes for future reference. So, what does the wealth of this paperwork show? There have been many researchers who have used the archives, but much of the credit for recent details, especially in bringing the story into a wider public domain, must go to Nick Cook of *Jane's Defence Weekly,* who travelled to the Schauberger's family home on the outskirts of Bad Ischl, Austria, to gather details.

However, let us start at the beginning. Basic details about Schauberger have always served to diminish his standing in any serious scientific study of Nazi physics. His early life was as a forester and naturalist who had focused on water effects found occurring in streams, rivers and lakes, particularly observing the flows, eddies and vortices. As a result of this, he formulated his own ideas about its movements and energetic properties. In physics, it is important to remember that both water and air are fluids obeying the laws of fluid mechanics, so in that respect, the flow of air in and around the discs we have looked at so far is analogous to the flow of water for Schauberger. As a result of this, many of his observations and subsequent work applied equally to both air and water flows. What caused immediate problems, however, and still does to this day, is many of his ideas appear contrary to accepted views and are still not fully understood due to the taboo nature of the subject. His ideas and lack of formal education therefore combined to brand him as something of a charlatan within physics, a situation not helped by the fact there are many strange terms used by Schauberger in his work which also go against any credibility. One such term he often used was 'implosion', which many simply cannot understand in the context of his work. This was essentially his new form of propulsion; implosion was at the heart of a radical new turbine and by all accounts he had, like Schriever, built a working model. Indeed, the results of the test had been highly impressive, with one test seeing the craft rise rapidly towards the ceiling trailing a 'glow of ionisation' in its wake. Unfortunately, by the time he became known to the post-war community, much of the stories about him had developed sufficiently to totally discredit him.

Schauberger is now long dead, but in 1991, Nick Cook was able to talk with his son, Walter, about his father's work and travel to the family archives to see the documentation to back up claims. Cook's contact with the family confirmed that Schauberger was not one of the professors of physics or an engineer in the same way as other characters in our story. It was also true that he had developed his ideas about energy and propulsion from observing nature, and his only professional training was as a forester. However, it was possible to confirm Schauberger was a skilled engineer in his own right and his son, Walter, was qualified as a physicist, mathematician and engineer. Walter completed his studies at the technical college in Dresden, after which he took his father's work into a respectable domain of scientific research. Sadly, by the time Cook was able to get to the Schauberger archives, Walter had also passed away and contact had passed to the grandson, Joery.

The institute holding Schauberger's achieve is a large, impressive house with a tower rising from one of its wings. Also obvious are 6-foot (2m)-tall letters painted on a wall which stand for 'Pythagoras-Kepler System', and here, again, we find an element that further discredits him within mainstream physics. What Walter did was to merge his father's ideas with Pythagorean concepts of harmonics. Furthermore, he had included ideas from the laws of planetary motion developed by the astronomer Johannes Kepler. Walter also believed that the cross-section through a Pythagorean hyperbola of the elliptical planetary orbits plotted by Kepler showed an egg-shape in a similar form that was found in nature: in fact, nature's highest expression of energy and strength. Although there was now some element of science to this work, it was still a little bit 'New Age' and was not going to go far enough to convince many establishment physicists, but that fitted well with Nazi doctrine. Moreover, the archives would reveal a better understanding to all this and also the baffling word 'implosion' that many physicists today still find a problem.

Schauberger's ideas centred on 'comprehend and copy Nature', and the key to this is the understanding of vortices, the whirlpools in nature visible everywhere from the horns of a kudu's antlers to shells, tornadoes and even the structure of the DNA double-helix molecule. These natural vortices are, in effect, an extremely efficient conduit for the transmission of energy according to Schauberger. This was the key to understanding that mysterious term, 'implosion'. When a three-dimensional spiralling energy pattern is channelled inwards rather than outwards, it becomes endowed with higher order properties; that is what Schauberger called 'implosion'. This process also explains another problem with the Schauberger story involving his term 'atomic', which is yet another word he used to call this process; we will see why later. In fact, Schauberger was famous for using several different terms for the same thing, as his archive clearly shows.

The use of the word 'atomic' also led to further confusion, because Allied intelligence believed it was associated with atomic energy, atomic bombs and atomic engines, especially when applied to atomic flying discs. It therefore came to the attention of intelligence officers looking into the work of the likes of Heisenberg and the possible building of the atomic bomb. In reality, it is a most unfortunate use of the word because Schauberger was not involved in any atomic, or nuclear, work in the way Los Alamos, Heisenberg or others would understand it; quite the contrary. Schauberger was interested in natural forms of energy, not artificial manmade ones like a nuclear chain reaction leading to a bomb. So, the problem here was essentially Schauberger's habit of using somewhat unconventional terminology, often using two or more different words to mean the same thing. This picking, mixing and swopping of terms led to much confusion at the time, although when understood, there is a kind of logic to his thinking, as we will see.

When the implosion process was used in his machinery, it generated phenomenal levels of force and, with this, he coined yet another unfortunate term for it, 'biotechnology', which incorrectly suggested to some a biological connection rather than referring to nature and the biosphere. This new term had come about because Schauberger believed mankind's regulation of the movement of water using devices like dams and irrigation systems had obstructed the complex vortices and flow patterns water naturally adopts. This, he believed, causes degeneration and decay in the ecosystem, and in this unnatural state, water becomes a pollutant, not a life-force. Certainly, this is an interesting view given today's environmental problems. This pollutant element was a driving force for Schauberger as he developed his ideas and promoted them through writing books; in fact, it was these books that came to the attention of Berlin and some very high-ranking Nazis, including Hitler.

Soon after Hitler came to power, Schauberger was summoned to the German capital in 1934 to meet the Fuhrer. Also present at the meeting was quantum physicist Max Planck. The purpose of the meeting was for Schauberger to explain his ideas on nature, water, and the relationship to soil, vegetation and a viable society in harmony with itself. This was clearly connected with Hitler's idea of a radically hygienic body of clean living and the vision of the 'body politic' expelling unwanted pathogens. Hitler listened to what Schauberger had to say and then turned to Planck for his opinion. However, Planck's response was somewhat testy, responding with: 'Science has nothing to do with Nature.' After giving his opinion, he withdrew from the meeting. Hitler then talked to Schauberger about incorporating his ideas into Nazi doctrine, but he, too, was equally blunt, telling Hitler that his belief it could be part of the country's 4-year economic plan was impossible. He informed the Fuhrer that such a short-term plan would undermine and ultimately destroy Germany's biological foundations, adding that it would result in the 1,000-year Reich lasting only 10 years, if lucky. Nevertheless, Hitler decided to seek advice from others in his familiar way, but nothing came of the plan. Later, things did change when Himmler got involved, possibly because of his love of the unconventional and pseudo-science; in some ways, Schauberger's ideas did fit. In particular, they fitted well with views of vortex physics, the ether, a perfect Aryan race and various pseudo-scientific areas of interest, including numerology, the workings of the universe and even occultism. So, let us look closer at Schauberger's ideas and how his devices worked.

In a nutshell, the devices Schauberger developed were impellers, the opposite to propellers, incorporating a vortex effect where air at the top enters the device and flows right through the centre, somewhat different from the Coanda effect that had air flowing over the surface of the saucer. To understand the idea and the key shape of the vortex involved, we can consider everyday examples by looking at tornadoes and hurricanes, where such vortices are found, although his devices also worked with water. There are two directions of vortex movement key to the devices: centripetal, or an inward-moving vortex, and centrifugal, or an outward-moving vortex. The centripetal spiralling air (or water) takes up less space and is cooled by the motion, according to Schauberger, who called this centripetal movement 'implosion'. This implosion is always accompanied by explosion as the air (or water) expands against an outward, centrifugal spiral. So, the process is first centripetal, then centrifugal. The form taken by this vortex, according to Schauberger, is really dictated by another of his terms, 'function', which is the energy flow, and the spiral vortex is the shape the energy flow takes in its movement. With energy flowing in at the top of the vortex, it adopts the characteristic double-spiral manner with the air (or water) molecules first imploding; in other words, they are made denser and therefore yield heat. As they progress in this manner, the air (or water) molecules are squeezed together tighter and tighter as they move down the vortex until the sub-atomic particles themselves become 'unglued', according to Schauberger, and then transform into new and unrecognized forms of energy. This is where his term 'atomic' appears. As the vortex decreases in diameter, the implosion and speed increases until they reach the point in the vortex where centripetal forces stop and centrifugal forces take over and the air (or water) becomes less dense. With this process, energy is radiated out from the centre of the vortex. The best way to visualize the vortex is as a figure 8, where the energy radiates outwards at the narrow mid-point between the two loops of the '8'. The somewhat-controversial end of this process and its radiating energy is to produce levitation, and it is here we get the connection with flying discs. Schauberger referred to this energy as 'diamagnetic energy'. We will expand on this later, as it is somewhat controversial in particle physics, but key to the misunderstandings within Allied intelligence when investigating Nazi atomic research.

Schauberger's early experiments resulted in him producing designs for flumes to transport logs. He also used his impeller to draw water through a tube and found that the output he was getting from his egg-shaped implosion machines was nine times greater than could be achieved with conventional pressure turbines. From there, he built water purification machines using the same vortex process. This then led to the production of electric generators, heaters and coolers using air as a fuel. However, this research came with some controversial claims from Schauberger. For example, he claimed vortex machines could auto-rotate, achieving speeds between 10,000 and 20,000 revolutions per minute. These speeds may appear impressive, but what was more controversial was the claim of auto-rotations; in other words, once started with a starter motor, the device would continue without further power input. In conventional physics, this sounded like an impossible perpetual motion machine, and essentially was dismissed as nonsense. However, to the Nazis with their belief in an ether, free energy from the background quantum foam (zero-point energy) and the Heisenberg Uncertainty Principle, it all sounded exciting. Besides, as we have seen, there were several other apparent perpetual motion devices that interested the Nazi physicists.

A key element to Schauberger's devices was the replacement of water with air in his early models. That led him to further developments, including a new type of aircraft engine that sucked rather than pushed its way through the atmosphere, and as war broke out in 1939, a device that could be used either as an energy generator or a power plant for aircraft and submarines. This idea for powering submarines was yet another to add to the list, like the Schappeller device we saw earlier.

The following year, Schauberger lodged an application with the Reich Patent Office for his invention. He described the essential characteristics of his device as a 'multi-stage centrifuge with concentrically juxtaposed pressure chambers'. Interestingly, he then wrote to his cousin to say he had invented an aircraft that made no noise. With a patent application for a new turbine engine, and the SS eventually taking control of scientific research and patents, it was inevitable that he would again come to the attention of high-ranking Nazis as he had done in 1934.

As war started, Schauberger concentrated on developments of several different versions of his machine. For example, there was the 'repulsator' and the 'repulsine' for water purification and distillation, an 'implosive motor' for generation of electricity, the 'trout turbine' for propelling submarines and flying discs—all of which demonstrated the interchange of water and air in his devices. All of these devices work on essentially the same principles and, as was common with Schauberger, he would often interchange the names of these devices and their applications when it suited him, seeing them as fundamentally the same device.

The development of these devices was helped along by Schauberger's son, Walter, who helped his father with the physics, mathematics and engineering; indeed, it was Walter's faith in the Pythagoras and Kepler connections that led to the egg-shaped design of the machine with the pipe work also following a mathematical or geometrically based design. For example, the bend of the spiral pipe was calculated using the golden section or ratio from mathematics. These mathematical rules shaping the various parts were key to air (or water) flow within the device, which even today is not fully appreciated, or so it is claimed. Another important element to these designs, repeatedly pointed out by Schauberger, is that they incorporated diamagnetic materials in their construction. To understand this, we must look at some accepted physics.

To begin with, diamagnetic materials are repelled by a magnetic field. This is caused when an applied magnetic field creates an induced magnetic field in the material in the opposite direction, causing a repulsive force. To put it another way, diamagnetism of a substance or body tends to become magnetized in a direction 180 degrees to the applied magnetic field. In contrast, a paramagnetic and ferromagnetic material is attracted by a magnetic field. Diamagnetism is a quantum mechanical effect that occurs in all materials; when it is the only contribution to the magnetism, the material is called 'diamagnetic'. As a result, all of Schauberger's devices were constructed of diamagnetic materials, with him considering copper the best. This meant that the surfaces of his devices that came into contact with air (or water) were made of copper.

We can now bring together these features and summarize the device from a flying disc perspective. The disc version looked somewhat different, inasmuch as it did not have the dome-shaped intake on the top; effectively, this gave it the appearance of a standard flattened flying saucer, compared to the version with a dome on top of a saucer. Other versions did have the domed appearance, which is another familiar flying saucer shape. The key element to this device relied on a turbine plate taking on a waviform construction fitted onto a similar moulded base plate. The form of the gap between these plates was a pattern of spirals, or whorl shapes, like a corkscrew and similar to a kudu's antlers. With air drawn in through the intake, the turbine rapidly rotates and propels the air into the rim of the rotating mass by centrifugal force. The rapid cooling of the air is caused by the waviform gap between the plates. This action also increases its density and is accompanied by a massive reduction in volume, which, in turn, generates a tremendous vacuum. The result of this is the device sucks more air into the intakes, which makes the process self-sustaining. By attaching the device to a gear shaft, it is also possible to generate electricity; alternatively, if left alone, it can be made to take off as a flying saucer. Schauberger believed the ability to make his device fly was due to the creation of the vacuum in the region immediately above the plates, somewhat similar to the Coanda effect. As for the primary energy source, he believed that came from a reaction between molecules in a new excited state caused by the body of the device itself and involving that figure 8 visualization we saw earlier. That was the so-called 'atomic' nature of his device.

The history surrounding the development and construction of this device follows a familiar pattern. After Germany annexed Austria in 1938, Schauberger became involved in research at the Nuremberg Laboratories of Professor Kotschau, where he was also assisted by his newly qualified son, Walter. The two worked with a Dr Winter on developing his electrical energy ideas from water flow with some success. However, no practical results appear to have come of this association at the time, despite claims of obtaining 50,000 volts output.

In 1940, Schauberger wrote that, at his own expense, he had commissioned a company in Berlin, called Kaempfer, to build a repulsator. At the time, the company was unclear about the exact purpose of this device; after great difficulty producing it to the extremely precise specifications demanded by Schauberger, it became apparent to them the nature of its function. By February 1941, he had changed contractors to the Kertl Company in Vienna. Here, Schauberger wrote that the device had a two-fold purpose: the first was to investigate free energy production, and the second was to test his theories on levitation flight. While the device was being constructed at the Kertl Company, an assistant of Schauberger decided to make an unauthorized test without Schauberger's knowledge or presence. The result was an unexpected powerful levitation of the device, which shot up to the roof of the hangar, smashing into it. The force of the impact was so great, it caused serious damage to both the hangar's roof and the device itself. A company official was far from amused, giving a frosty reception to one of Schauberger's representatives when he later visited the company to check on progress.

Further details in the Schauberger records show correspondence, highlighting March 1941 as the time when things really started to happen. Work was now taking place at the Kertl Company to repair the device (and presumably the roof) when the SS arrived. It is not surprising they had been made aware of events at the company, and it was at this point that they took an interest in Schauberger and his inventions. However, it was not only the SS who had an interest in matters; the archived correspondence also shows Professor Ernst Heinkel was interested too. This interest also occurred in the spring of 1941, when Schriever's blueprints were being used to develop a model of his disc as proof of concept in a 'garage' at Heinkel's works. Furthermore, this year of 1941 is also mentioned in Major Rudolf Lusar's 1956 book, *German Secret Weapons of World War Two*, as the year flying disc technology started, while also mentioning key experts who worked on the projects including Schriever, Miethe, Belluzzo and Habermohl.

Interestingly, Heinkel was already aware of Schauberger's devices before the accident at the Kertl factory because he had illegally obtained a copy of Schauberger's patent application form lodged at the Reich Patent Office in 1940. Without Schauberger's knowledge, Heinkel had already begun work to incorporate the ideas into at least one of his aircraft designs. According to some who have examined the Schauberger archives, they believe this is likely to be the He 280 fighter, which made its maiden flight on 30 March 1941, but not all agree and independent confirmation has not been possible. Whereas it is known the He 280 ran into problems involving its problematic HeS 8 turbojets, it is thought more likely the true aircraft in question was Schriever's flying disc, or 'Flying Top'; the time scale fits better, for one thing. Another interesting point is Heinkel used his influence to convince the Reich Patent Office to grant a patent to Schauberger only for his water purification and distillation versions of the device, not the aircraft or flying disc version. This they did, leaving Heinkel free to fraudulently use the aircraft version. Schauberger was not happy and refused the offer. As a result, the Reich Patent Office rejected his whole application.

It was not long before the SS returned, this time in May 1941, where, in the presence of Schauberger and his patent lawyer, they informed him that they were not going to restrict his work but encourage it; the condition was that it would now have to be done in secret. From this point, things really started to move for Schauberger, bringing in a period of frantic research and covert activity. It is therefore not surprising that the archives get less detailed at this point. Nevertheless, there are some intriguing details available. A few weeks after this second meeting with the Gestapo (in typical Schauberger style he interchanges

'Gestapo', 'secret police' and 'SS personnel' in his records) he wrote to his son, Walter, to tell him he was now working in Gablonz (present day Jablonec) in Czechoslovakia, stating: 'What I am doing is secret.' This location was on the Czechoslovakia border with Germany and Poland, and just happened to be right in the heart of Kammler's high technology regime, or Kammler 'Empire'. A follow-up letter to Walter told of how he now had an agreement with a factory in the Sudeten region where unspecified research was taking place. A further intriguing point is Gablonz is between Prague and Breslau, which again gives possible support to other less-proven stories of flying disc research in this area. It was in the second letter that Schauberger also confirms he is aware that Heinkel had stolen his ideas, and that he had had this reported to him by the secret police.

The problems Heinkel had reportedly been experiencing at this time seem to have some truth, because in July 1941, Schauberger confirms he was approached by a middle man in the hope that he might be able to solve the problems Heinkel was having. The main problem is said to have centred on the stolen patent details and appeared to be down to Heinkel's engineers making an error when they copied them. This is where the belief originated that the He 280 was involved when Heinkel was trying to replace conventional engines with Schauberger's. However, the trouble with this idea is Schauberger's engine was a centripetal compressor, which made no sense when considering the air flow of the HeS 8 turbojet; it was diametrically opposed. Moreover, there would be problems with the aerodynamics of the He 280 because of the suction nature on which Schauberger's engine worked. It is possible this was one of the typical SS-style covers because again, in hindsight, suspicion falls on the 'Flying Top' being the real project, which makes far more sense, especially as it had been given Top Secret classification. In the end, the He 280 project was scrapped because the Air Ministry wanted the BMW 003 or Jumo 004 engine fitted, both of which were impossible to fit anyway.

Schauberger was now involved in research at several sites according to correspondence with his son. By late 1941, he was at a 'weapons factory' in Neudek (now Nejdek), 120km south-west of Gablonz. Then, in December, he was back at Gablonz, where he was to take delivery of a starter motor. From there, he travelled frequently by train from Reichenberg (today Liberec in the Czech Republic) to Gablonz to check on work. In early 1942, Schauberger was then at the Messerschmitt works at Augsburg, Bavaria, to do further work on his device. It is unclear whether this was the same version as elsewhere but, remember, they were essentially the same, just used for different purposes. Given the importance of the flying disc version over water purification it is likely to be the flying disc version.

We know from the archives that by 1942 onwards the shortage of raw materials generally in the Third Reich and the sub-standard quality of available salvaged materials was also causing problems with Schauberger's demanding quality and precision requirements. For example, there were failures and disasters when welding failed; repairs were often needed, delaying progress. The outcome of this brought to an end the Kertl device due to lack of suitable quality and quantity of materials, and the Messerschmitt project ended in failure too because of sub-standard materials. Not deterred, there was some attempt to salvage something from these failures; there was a Fuhrer directive ordering the Ernst Kubiznak company in Vienna to repair the device, but this amounted to nothing.

Whereas it is reasonable to assume the Heinkel company, and similar, continued to take advantage of the significant funding thrown at them and freedom to experiment, for Schauberger, problems continued and activity dwindled. Eventually, activity ground to a halt, with a year of stagnation resulting in Schauberger receiving a summons to a Waffen-SS draft panel in April 1944. There are stories that he was then drafted into the army due to his project's inactivity but this appears unlikely; for one thing, his age, at 59, was against him. According to the archives, it seems more likely that he got a kick-start to his work from the SS, now desperate for last-minute V-weapons to turn around a lost war, especially as there appears to be many claims of activity during 1944 to develop flying discs and new wonder weapons, generally. Even Hitler had convinced himself, if not his generals, that there were secret weapons about to come online to turn the war around to his favour.

Only 2 months after this mysterious draft panel story, in June 1944, the SS was now over a year into their efforts for complete control of scientific research, and that included Schauberger's project. To put this into context, D-Day had begun and the Allies were advancing. Further evidence for this draft panel story being faked, or a cover, comes from Himmler's intervention. Schauberger tells how he was ordered by the SS to attend the Mauthausen concentration camp. On arrival, he was told Himmler himself had approved his project and he was, under his orders, to hand-pick any engineers, technicians or labourers suitably qualified to make a new team for his projects. This apparently was under threat of execution should he refuse. This episode is also confirmed by the records in the Schauberger archives. In short, the SS had decided he was to stop 'tinkering around' and get on with serious development; the ultimate plan was to take his various versions from prototype to full-scale weapons. From here, Schauberger set up his office in the SS technical engineering school in the Rosenhugel district of Vienna with twenty-five inmates. This naturally meant an environment of oppression and strict SS control, but at least things could progress after a year of stagnation. Initial work was to draw up design plans ready for the production process, which were approved by August 1944 and then passed on to the factories from the technical school. Once again, Schauberger found himself rushing between sites to monitor and advise.

By October, according to his diaries, Schauberger had started cutting metals and mill components for the devices, here referred to as 'the Repulsine'. However, bear in mind that was one of many interchangeable words he would use. By now, the advance of the Allied Forces pushed ever further into occupied territories and the pressure was mounting amongst the Nazis. To add to the race against time to put new weapons into mass production there was also ever-increasing bombing raids on factories and industry; this was as a result of Lovell's team developing ever-better H2S radar. This eventually took its toll on Schauberger and his team. Nevertheless, on 6 October, Schauberger had drawings ready so that his air intake could be put into production: it was a rounded cone-shaped attachment for the top of the Repulsine which he called the *Schaufelentwurf.* Given the nature of the device, this probably best translates as 'blade design' or 'shovel design', given that it fed air into the Repulsine. When attached to the device, it made it look like the stereotypical flying saucer shape with a dome that would become familiar in many 1950s B movies, comics and sighting reports from the general public from about 1947 onwards. In that respect, it was somewhat different in appearance to the other familiar flying saucer shape of a flattened disc.

On 11 October, production halted when the first of a series of bombing raids hit Vienna from American 'Flying Fortresses' on daylight missions against local industry; by now American aircraft like the Flying Fortresses had been fitted with the H2S radar sets. These bombing raids now included the nearby Hermann Goering Works, a giant heavy-engineering complex. On 14 October, there is an entry in Schauberger's diary, saying: 'I wish I could work longer, but I have to stop at four in the afternoon. There is a shortage of materials and tools. I had to construct parts today from an old tank.' To add to the delays, Schauberger experienced a further 10 days loss of work when, on 23 October, he was required to develop a more efficient carburettor for Opel Blitz army trucks. By 4 November, he was back working on his devices, this time a water-based version. On 26 November, he was then working on his Repulsine again; it seems a starter motor had finally arrived and needed fitting. Work continued on the Repulsine, with Schauberger and his team even working on Christmas Day and into the New Year.

All during this time, the work continued under the onslaught of air raids and power cuts, but by 28 February 1945, to escape the bombings, the team moved to a small village called Leonstein in upper Austria. This move now dictated who would eventually take control of the project once the war came to an end: the move placed the operation in the future United States zone of occupation; if it had remained, it would have been in the Soviet zone. However, these spoils of war were open season for all sides and even zones were not always respected. It is also worth bearing in mind the Soviets would be the ones to advance into another flying disc region of Prague. This no doubt gives rise to the post-war back-and-forth claims of whether the United States or Soviet Union got the spoils of war associated with flying disc technology. In reality, it was probably both with each side getting a piece of the jigsaw in the same way as they did with rocketry and aviation generally.

The long road to develop his Repulsine had now reached the point where a final assembly was made on 8 April 1945; a month later, on 6 May, it was finally ready to test. The day of reckoning arrived, but to Schauberger's surprise, he arrived to find no SS officials present, as they had fled that night. Work stopped on 8 May and the war ended the next day at one minute past midnight with the surrender of German forces. The position had now changed to presumably, a working device and the United States rather than the SS in charge. It was only a matter of days before the United States Intelligence Corps found Schauberger and made contact. It transpired they were already well-briefed about his work. In Schauberger's own words: 'It was as if somebody had guided them.'

Schauberger still had an apartment at Vienna which shortly afterwards was entered by the Russians, who removed anything of importance or value, then blew it up. It is unclear how well informed they were about Schauberger's work or what was taken. Fortunately, his archives, including correspondence with factories, etc., as well as his diaries, were all safe and still are to this day at the family home in Bad Ischl, Austria. It would also appear any 'clean up' by the United States fell short.

After the war, Schauberger was held under house arrest by the technical intelligence of the United States; it seemed that their main interest was with his 'atomic' work, which had intrigued them the most. As a result of this, Schauberger faced a detailed debriefing until March 1946. No doubt this was due to the nuclear physics intelligence team, Alsos, and their agent, Boris Pash, who must have heard of Schauberger's 'atomic' research, setting in motion an intelligence-gathering operation. Certainly, Schauberger was rushing between key locations and contractors. However, what Alsos found was a different, but nonetheless, important research project that was not part of Heisenberg's nuclear work or the atomic bomb after all.

The reality of the word 'atomic' actually came from Schauberger's belief that the atoms had been 'unglued' by his device producing new forms of energy, so it is understandable how this got confused with nuclear fission and a chain reaction. However, even after being debriefed, Schauberger was warned by the intelligence agencies not to talk about this part of his work, or continue it, after the war.

To explain this confusion, we need to understand that the atom consists of a nucleus made up of protons and neutrons, with the electrons occupying the outer region of the atoms; these are usually regarded as orbiting the nucleus, although from a quantum mechanical probability viewpoint, this is not strictly the true picture, but we need not worry about that here. Within his device, Schauberger believed the nucleus was altered by the diamagnetic material (copper) separating the nucleus into its separate protons and neutrons, effectively stripping the protons from the atomic structure; this would also strip the electrons from the atoms too. The positively charged protons and negatively charged electrons then combine (unlike charges attract) and annihilate, yielding energy between the two loops of the figure 8 analogy above; hence Schauberger's terminology of 'atomic'. During this process, the particles would then reverse their spin and alter their rotation. This is somewhat unconventional, to say the least, and will not be easy for particle physics to accept because it is essentially a nuclear reaction and unlikely to occur in such a device. However, that was not fully understood at the time and may explain why Schauberger was told to keep quiet anyway in case there was some form of nuclear process taking place. There was also a problem with the interpretation of spin, because that is a misleading term even in conventional physics.

Yet another controversial view was with the left-over neutrons that do not appear to be part of this process. Although neutral in charge, they were believed to be magnetic in this device; again, this goes against accepted views. Schauberger believed these neutrons were then expelled from the disc centrifugally along with any unaltered air (or water) and together with water vapour. The 'magnetic' neutrons were also thought to (maybe) increase the diamagnetic properties of the copper causing a push away between the ground and the cloud of surrounding 'magnetic' neutrons. In other words, the disc would fly by repelling away from a magnetically charged atmosphere which it had itself created. Incidentally, this is still one of the propulsion mechanisms claimed to be at work even to this day amongst ufologists. Obviously, given the role neutrons play in the uranium chain reaction, this may also explain why Schauberger was told to keep quiet about the atomic nature of his devices at the time; remember, the subject was in its early days.

Interestingly, although the separation of the protons and neutrons in the nucleus would essentially be a nuclear reaction requiring something much more than the Repulsine to achieve, it is possible to separate the nucleus (consisting of the protons together with the neutrons) and the electrons. That would not produce separate neutrons; they would remain with the protons as a positively charged nucleus, but this would produce plasma with the separation of the nucleus and electrons into a charged gas of positive nuclei (protons and neutrons still combined) and the negative electrons. Plasma effects, including surrounding glowing clouds, are often reported with flying saucers and UFO sightings and, as we saw when Schauberger's device took off and hit the factory ceiling, it was accompanied by a glow. But was that the true answer? Was this a plasma effect? Recall the possibility the Bell may have also been a plasma device.

Although documentation showed something was clearly happening, the rush of the war's end meant all these ideas came together at once and would require some working out. Maybe that was done in the leisurely times of post-war research and went further in a way not unlike Lovell's rush with radar and a more leisurely assessment and further development in peace time.

From that point, a whole new can of worms was opened—one that would lead to suggestions of flying saucer development back at places like Wright-Patterson Air Force Base in the United States, leading to strange sightings of flying discs with domes on the top not a million kilometres away from the appearance of the Repulsine. From there, we had the start of the modern post-war flying saucer era that began in June 1947 with Kenneth Arnold's sighting, although their shapes appear much closer to the Horten 229 that also returned to the United States. The term 'flying saucer' for that sighting did not really tally with Arnold's description and was coined by journalists. Whatever view individuals may take about the flying saucer subject, it is worth remembering that one of the most common shapes described was remarkably similar to Schauberger's Repulsine and he did have a flattened disc version without a dome. This was long before the general public had ever heard of him and his devices.

Eighteen months after Schauberger was warned not to speak about, or work on, his 'atomic' research, an interesting incident happened. General Nathan Twining, head of the United States Army Air Force's Air Materiel Command (AMC) admitted to a subordinate in a classified memo that it was possible 'within the present US knowledge - provided extensive detailed development is undertaken - to construct a piloted aircraft with the operating characteristics of a UFO; a craft that seemingly defied the laws of physics.' Post-war military intelligence with UFOs would centre on the AMC at Wright-Patterson, leading to decades of sightings investigations from Project Sign to Project Grudge and then Project Blue Book, yet another big subject for another book.

Schauberger's story does not pick up again until 1957. Now aged 72, he was in bad health with emphysema and heart disease. What happened next, according to his archives, is a brief mention of an approach from two aircraft companies, one American and one Canadian. They offered him facilities and 3.5 million dollars for the rights to acquire his propulsion device. Neither company name is mentioned by Schauberger in his records; however, the time scale matches that of John Frost's secret group and the design of a Mach 3 flying saucer for the United States Air Force known as Project Y2/Silverbug. In the case of the Canadian company, this most probably was the Avro Company, because they were the only Canadian company known to be involved in such work at the time. This assumption is further supported by declassified documents that show, at a Canadian/UK government instillation in Canada, John Frost had met with an engineer who worked at Prague during 1944 and 1945 on Nazi flying disc projects. If this person was not Schauberger, it is likely to have led to his work. The other company is believed to be the Martin Aircraft Company because of similar work being carried out and their announcements of a new era in clean, free energy and how one day it would take us to the stars. But the identity of the two companies is only educated guesswork by researchers.

Whoever these two companies were neither would meet Schauberger's demands which were that it should be used for the 'common good', or 'commercial aviation purposes', and it should be transparent and announced to the public. Consequently, Schauberger rejected both offers. The other intriguing connection with the Martin Aircraft Company is that it set up the Research Institute for Advanced Studies (RIAS) which was 'to observe phenomena of Nature and to encourage, promote, and support investigations in search of underlying knowledge of these phenomena, to discover fundamental laws and to evolve new technical concepts for improvement and welfare of mankind'. Clearly there are a lot of common desires between this company and Schauberger and it is surprising they could not come to an agreement. A possible answer is military secrecy was behind the offers which leads us to the next part of the story.

Shortly after this episode, Schauberger was visited by Karl Gerchsheimer, a German-American acting on behalf of a United States financier and multi-millionaire, Robert Donner. Donner heard of Schauberger's devices and was particularly interested in the 'free energy' version—the part where the device was set in motion with a starter motor and became self-sustaining so that a gear mechanism could be attached and generate electricity. Donner certainly had a colourful past; he was involved in counter-espionage, ending up as an intelligence agent (possibly with the CIA). Post-war, from 1945 to 1950, he was the United States civilian property administrator-in-chief in charge of all logistics, transport and accommodation for the army of occupation in the United States zone. He then set up a metal fabrication business in the United States and eventually worked for NASA.

When Gerchsheimer approached Schauberger in Austria, he told him there was millions of dollars just waiting for him to continue his work, and there was an engineering works at his disposal in Sherman, Texas, ready to go with his say so. Eventually, despite his severe health problems, Schauberger agreed to accept the offer and headed for the United States with his son, who would oversee the project after Schauberger returned to Austria.

However, suspicion that this offer may involve the intelligence agencies became a real worry when the two arrived in Texas. It was then that Donner and Gerchsheimer secured physicists from the National Atomic Research Laboratories at Brookhaven, Long Island, to help. Yet more suspicion appeared when Schauberger and his son were separated to write up their reports on implosion technology, which were then forwarded to Brookhaven. Weeks dragged into months with no progress, it must have seemed all too familiar to Schauberger. Then his health deteriorated further and to ensure he could return to Austria for his final days, he was presented with a contract he did not understand because it was in English. He signed it so that he could get back home. Later, he found out he had signed away everything to the Americans. Five days after returning to Austria, on 25 September 1958, Viktor Schauberger died. Some claim this was a late American 'clean up' that had failed to take place after the war; however, if that is true, it failed again because the archive still exists.

Although Schauberger thought the levitation of his disc may be due to it pushing against a magnetically charged atmosphere caused by its cloud of surrounding 'magnetic' neutrons, there was another suggestion—anti-gravity. Interestingly, anti-gravity was big news in 1956 just before Schauberger was approached by Gerchsheimer, with several news items in aviation publications and even articles. However, things changed suddenly; it all went quiet very quickly. This leads to an interesting question: Was the approach by the two aerospace companies and Donner/Gerchsheimer due to that interest in anti-gravity? Certainly within this subject the ideas of free energy and anti-gravity are strongly linked to this day, even within government departments. Whereas there may have been private interest, according to Gerchsheimer, there was no government involvement. However, he was the go-between of a known figure from the intelligence world.

The free energy and anti-gravity elements of flying discs brings into play a part of the subject that is just about universally dismissed by aviation experts as nonsense, citing no real evidence— 'field propulsion discs'. This particular part of disc technology does not deal with standard propulsion engines for power like jet turbines, but instead uses the so-called 'free energy' said to be obtainable from the zero-point field that permeates the whole universe. However, physicists today do not really see it that way and many believe the quantum effect cancels out over the expanse of the whole universe leaving, maybe, just enough to boil a kettle of water. However, having said that, this area of physics does have problems at the moment, leading to what is termed a 'cosmological crisis', leaving room for many claims and counter-claims. Outside conventional physics, opinions vary depending on which side you support, but a typical claim is that just one cubic centimetre (.06 cu. in.) of space has enough energy to boil away the Earth's oceans.

Certainly, what is generally unappreciated is the fact that in certain quarters, there is solid scientific support for this idea. Moreover, that support has come from some big names in the aviation industry as well as NASA. This serious research is what first came to the public notice in 1956 and has continued behind the scenes ever since.

However, back in the days of Hitler, the gravity and anti-gravity mix was clearly different. As we saw, one of the beliefs of Schauberger was the spin of particles played a part in his 'atomic' process and it is here that controversy involving Walter Gerlach enters the equation. Particle spins and resonance effects were areas of Gerlach's work; in fact, he was a Nobel laureate, winning the prize for his work on magnetic spin polarization. He also published post-war papers on the subject. Added to this is the claim his interests in this area of particle physics, together with nuclear physics and gravity, leads to the idea nuclear physics and gravity are linked. Whereas this may have been a Nazis belief it is not generally the case today.

However, Gerlach's exact work involving gravity under the Nazis is strangely unclear; we know he worked in the area, but after the war his curriculum vitae seems to have had parts of that element removed. We do know that another Nazi physicist, Dr Ott Christoph Hilgenberg, did use Gerlach's work to take research one step further. Hilgenberg was a student of Gerlach, going on to work in mainstream physics; however, he also had a taste for the unconventional concepts of the subject. In 1931, he published a paper titled *Gravitation, Tromben, und Wellen in bewegten Medien* (*Gravitation, Beats and Waves in Moving Media*). Essentially, this involved the ether. However, it must be appreciated that Hilgenberg was thinking of an ether that was not static in the relativistic way but a dynamic ether which was also a view the Nazis held. The paper had its problems inasmuch as it was mysterious in nature, even secretive, and quite difficult to understand in the extreme. However, in common with relativity, it treated gravity as a complex geometry, but in Hilgenberg's version, mass was a geometric result of the interiors of rotating bodies, bringing us back to vorticular physics. Hilgenberg suggested a massive rotating astronomical body, such as the Earth, expanded and contracted over time in huge wave-like patterns with his interest inspired by Alfred Wegener's continental drift. He then went on to write his work *Von Wachsenden Erdball* (*The Expanding Globe*) showing how all continental shelves would fit neatly together if the Earth's diameter was about half the size of today. This also had an appeal to the Nazis because one alternative to the relativistic nature in Mercury's orbit was a sun that expands and contracts in an oscillating fashion, a view still held today by anti-relativists. While working at the Technische Hochschule in Berlin between 1934 to 1938, from where he qualified in electro-mechanical engineering, he wrote a thesis titled *Uber Stromungsversuche mit Senken und Quellen, die das Wesen der Schwerkraft grundlegend erklaren* (*Flow Experiments with Sinks and Sources, that Explain the Fundamental Nature of Gravity*). This was rejected by the faculty because it went against Einstein's theory of relativity by using the luminiferous ether.

This paper was followed up by another extraordinary piece of theoretical physics in 1938 titiled *Quantenzahlen, Wirbelring-Atommodelle und Heliumsechserring-*

Aufbauprinzip des Periodensystems der Chemischen Elemente (*A Quantum Number, Vortex Atom Model and Hexagonal-Ring Construction Principle of the Periodic System of the Chemical Elements*). What this paper amounted to was a system of modelling complete atoms according to vorticular rotational principles of the ether. This was a return to Ionian ideas; the idea of reality being formed out of vortices first suggested by Anaxagoras 2,500 years ago, highlighting the faith the Nazis had in ancient knowledge. In modern times it was raised by the Soviet Physicist Lev Landau in the 1940s.

The end result of these two papers was to create a mathematical and theoretical development that predicted a number of effects completely at variance with relativity. In doing so, relativity could be rejected and quantum physics could replace it. The new 'vorticular quantum mechanics' was taken a step further by Carl Friedrich Krafft, who proposed atoms as a geometric, or topological, construct of the ether that acted as 'ether pumps' and in doing so took in, and gave off, energy based on the rotations of various rings of dynamic ether around them. He then went further still by developing the notion by assuming various combinations of vorticular, rotating geometrics were the basis for the known sub-atomic particles. Krafft was left to self-publish his work and as a result by the war's end it was promptly lost to physics; many say maybe for the better. Nevertheless, it can be seen how Schauberger's work fitted in with these ideas as well as anti-gravity. Of course, we must bear in mind that many of these ideas may appear to make sense at the time when the science was new, but with hindsight and almost a further century of discovery, the position today is different. That said, in a strange way this does conjure up thoughts of modern-day string theory with one dimensional vibrating strings rather than the vortex idea. String theory, however, hopes to unite general relativity with quantum mechanics to develop a theory of quantum gravity.

It is open to debate as to how far these many non-Jewish alternatives went during the war with flying disc technology, rotation, atomic and nuclear physics, and the boundary layer problems. There is certainly no shortage of conspiracy theories. Another certainty is Nazi physicists were encouraged by the SS ideology to investigate relationships such as these under Himmler's *Ahnenerbe* and Kammler's think tank.

When considering the physics of the Third Reich the real question is: Where does it fall in the spectrum of genuine research to complete pseudo-science? Certainly there was an element of conventional physics involved, with the pseudo-science believing in 'hidden physics', but from the angle of ancient manuscripts, myths, legend and even occultism and the black arts. Many of their ideas revolved around vorticular physics and free energy, which is why Schauberger's work was important. Such ideas also included the Vril society and how Nazis originated from middle, Vril energy (free energy) and life force energy amongst other ideas. It may also explain why Himmler stepped in to save Schauberger's work under threat of execution. As such, Nazi and modern research does obviously split significantly into a preference for pseudo-scientific and one of only conventional physics respectively.

Chapter Six

Hitler's Ashes

Hitler is as mythical in death as he was in life especially with the circumstances of that death. This has resulted in many conspiracy theories and myths, many as controversial as the science he followed and the beliefs he held. In the end, his support by even the faithful was severely strained; he was even betrayed by Himmler and Kammler, both of whom seem to be more focused on doing a deal with the Allies to save their skins than victory for Germany.

Kammler's peace deal is less certain, but Himmler had secretly started peace talks with the Allies through the Swedish government. The one-time designated Deputy Fuhrer and Party Chief, Rudolf Hess, was in a British prison and his designated replacement Reich Marshal of the Greater German Reich (Reichsmarschall) Goering was now claiming leadership in the chaos of a collapsing Reich to the denouncement by Hitler of treason.

In Berlin, far below the ground, in the dying weeks of the war and the Third Reich Hitler and his generals found themselves in the bizarre, even surreal, world of the *Fuhrerbunker* where he and his generals huddles together as Allied and Soviet bombs reduced the once beautiful city above to piles of rubble. Hitler, with his left arm shaking uncontrollably, and a grey, pallid complexion ranted as he squinted over the maps before him. His health was shattered, his doctors having drugged him up so as to keep the ever-diminishing Fuhrer going throughout the war. He now sits in conference.

His generals, desperate for more forces to be sent to the north, find Hitler more interested, even obsessed, with defending Prague to the south, believing it is crucial to winning the war. He also maintains thousands of troops in Norway, which he considers another essential location; a country that had long since ceased to be of any strategic or operational value to the Third Reich. Paradoxes like these have led to many myths and theories after the Fuhrer's death, which was only weeks away; given what we have seen, this actually makes sense in the deluded mind of the Fuhrer. Considered as just the ranting of a madman, we now see why he thought these locations so important; Prague was a key location in the Kammler 'Empire', and Norway was the destination of the northern evacuation of secret weapons developed by the *Kammlerstab*. At this stage, Hitler was still convinced that the likes of Kammler would save the day.

There were other oddities at these *Fuhrerbunker* conferences. Delusional insanity or not, on more than one occasion his generals were told that Germany would soon be in the possession of weapons that would snatch victory from the jaws of defeat at 'five minutes to midnight'; all that the Wehrmacht had to do was hold out a little longer and hold Prague and Lower Silesia (in other words, the Kammler 'Empire').

Hitler was not alone in this belief, because on 3 April 1945, only weeks before the Fuhrer's suicide, he held a meeting in the *Fuhrerbunker* with Kammler. We know the outcome of this meeting because Hitler's Propaganda Minister, Josef Goebbels, wrote an account of it in his diary for 3 April. He wrote: 'The Fuhrer has had prolonged discussions with Obergruppenfuhrer Kammler who now carries responsibility for reform of the Luftwaffe.' He also writes about the 'miracle' weapons to turn the war to the vantage of the Nazis, saying: 'Kammler is doing excellently and great hopes are placed on him'. It was clear the Fuhrer was left with great faith in him. At the end of the war, Goebbels also boasted in a speech that he has seen 'weapons so frightening it would make your heart stand still'.

Hitler also found confidence for a victory within the pseudo-science of astrology. As Germany faced defeat, he regularly consulted a file of astrological reports and favourable predictions based on his personal horoscope. This file was regularly updated and supplied by Goebbels. Hitler's positive interpretation of such things was given a boost when he heard the news that on 12 April President Roosevelt had died. With great enthusiasm he said: 'Here we have the great miracle that I always foretold.' He added: 'Who is right now? The war is not lost. Read it! Roosevelt is dead.'

A further point we need to bear in mind is Hitler's heavy dependency on medication, some of it considered highly addictive and illegal today, and how this affected him by the end of the war. Hitler was becoming ever more dependent on these, as well as being deprived by Allied bombers as they destroyed the factories that manufactured them, along with those that produced his military hardware; in effect, Hitler was 'going cold turkey' at the time. How far this was a factor is open to debate, but it does not account for the earlier years.

Hitler committing suicide on 30 April 1945 is itself not without its own occult significance, being the date marking the eve of a witches' Sabbath, the *Walpurgisnacht*. Moreover, in mediaeval Cathar doctrine, which was well-studied by the *Ahnenerbe*, suicide was a permissible act if done in concert with a soulmate. It is, therefore, no surprise Hitler chose to commit suicide on that particular day with his newly married soulmate of many years, Eva Braun.

Before committing suicide, Hitler relinquished power to an unlikely candidate, Grand Admiral Karl Doenitz, who, for a brief period of a little over one week, became Nazi Germany's second dictator. Doenitz would then order his armed forces to surrender. It is said the choice was because Doenitz was in a good position to arrange the escape of fleeing Nazis to South America, amongst other places, using the new XXI class U-boats just entering service. This starts yet another long-lasting conspiracy theory with many claims and counter-claims.

Linking to the evacuation plan of Kammler that we have already seen, at about the time Kammler's think tank was gaining more power from the Fuhrer, Doenitz alluded to something similar on more than one occasion. He alluded to the German Navy's role in exotic secret weapons research and construction of secret bases for the Reich homeland. For example, in 1943 he is reported to have said: 'The German submarine fleet is proud of having built for the Fuhrer, in another part of the world, a Shangri-La on land, an impregnable fortress.' This is considered by many as a somewhat strange statement from someone with cold calculation in military strategy and tactics and not known for his mythical statements.

Then again, in 1944, at the height of activity within the *Kammlerstab,* he provided further details: 'The German Navy will have to accomplish a great task in the future. The German Navy knows all hiding places in the oceans and therefore it will be very easy to bring the Fuhrer to a safe place should the necessity arise and in which he will have the opportunity to work out his final plan.' It looked like plans were in place to evacuate Hitler as well as Kammler's secret projects.

There were then rumours at Nuremberg that suggested these safe places included the polar regions. Here he boasted of 'an invulnerable fortress, a paradise-like Oasis in the middle of eternal ice'. This may well point to the belief of the Aryan race originating from ice and the glacial cosmology theory of Hitler and the SS, including their expeditions, one of which was the Antarctic Scientific Expedition. In 1938, the Germans undertook an expedition to Antarctica, specially fitting out a seaplane carrier for the purpose, the Schwabenland, at a cost of millions of Reichsmarks. This was under the personal direction and mentorship of Goering. The inspiration for the expedition may have had hidden occult motivations for the occult *Thulegesellschaft*, or Thule Society, which subscribed to a Nordic Atlantis hidden beneath the polar ice, from which sprang the Germanic race (according to legend). There was also a small team of biologists and other scientists onboard to carry out experiments. This would certainly place the expedition, like others, within the brief of the SS *Ahnenerbe.*

Whether any return to the Antarctic at the end of the war was connected with the evacuation, or fleeing, of Nazis, with or without Hitler, is still unclear; nevertheless, this is a big theory that persists to this day regarding where the Nazis may have eventually gone after the war. Another location is South America.

This connection to the Antarctic is also a big part of UFO theory and is linked to the idea that flying saucers were developed under Kammler and may have ended up at the polar regions, especially Antarctica. Indeed, I recall it being a popular topic when I was a consultant at *UFO Magazine* (UK), and there was even suggestion the Nazis had moved a nuclear power station there as part of their evacuation plans to melt a region of ice to produce that 'paradise-like Oasis in the middle of eternal ice' that Doenitz spoke about. Another less-exotic variation is that the expedition of 1938 allegedly found ice-free ponds, heated geothermally, in which grew various unknown species of algae. This, too, led to conspiracy theories suggesting deep under the ice there was a world of virus and bacteria as well as other life forms—even aliens have been mentioned! It also links with ideas of flying saucers originating from the polar regions and even from inside a

Himmler-style hollow Earth. Whereas a hollow Earth is highly unlikely, they did discover the southern tip of the fault line that runs from New Zealand through Queen Maud Land and up to the Atlantic Ocean: the famous Atlantic trench. Queen Maud Land was claimed by Denmark, but the Nazis decided it was ideal for them and claimed it for themselves; they had concluded that features of the fault line might indicate rocky caverns on the continent heated geothermally, and that was the perfect place to hide a base in the world's most isolated wilderness.

What we can say is there was certainly U-boat activity in the Antarctic months after the war. For example, U-boat U-530 surrendered at Mar del Plata, Argentina, on 10 July 1945, followed by U-977 at the same location on 17 August, while U-465 was scuttled off the coast of Patagonia the same month. Another U-boat of unknown number surrendered to the Argentine Navy on 10 June.

The surrendering of these U-boats so long after the defeat of Germany caused the Allies concern. As a result, they dispatched agents to interrogate Captain Schaeffer of U-977 and Captain Wermoutt of U-530. The captains stated they had made the 3-to-4-month journey specifically to surrender to the Argentines, which would make sense because that country was sympathetic to the Nazis and considered a safe haven. Schaeffer was the last to surrender and was taken to the United States for a month, then onwards to Britain for more questioning. Interestingly, both captains said no politically important persons were deposited in South America. After the interrogations, both captains were released, but in the case of Schaeffer, he found he could not live in occupied Germany; it was intolerable. He therefore relocated back to South America, where he decided to write a book about the incident and explain his voyage and actions; however, nobody believed him.

The whole South America and Antarctic episode is surrounded in mystery; over the decades, speculation has produced myth upon myth with claims and counter-claims as a continuation of the myths held by the Third Reich while in power. The possible interest in Antarctica in the past only adds to speculation. One claim, or myth, is that Hitler did not commit suicide but travelled to South America to ponder his 'final plan', as Doenitz claimed, but given his health, that seems highly unlikely.

During the closing stages of the war back in Germany, the advancing Allied Forces were heading for Nazi technology as the spoils of war. Sir Roy Fedden, a British specialist, was sent to Germany to investigate Nazi secret weapons research after the war; he had no doubts, certain that the weapons research had deadly potential. In his assessment in London 1945, he said: 'The Nazis' V-weapons matured too late.' He went on to say: 'In these respects the Nazis were not entirely lying. In the course of two recent visits to Germany, as leader of the technical mission of the Ministry of Aircraft Production, I have seen enough of their designs and production plans to realize that if they had managed to prolong the war some months longer, we would have been confronted with a set of entirely new and deadly developments in air warfare.' This is certainly a result of cartel infighting, bureaucracy and delay piled upon delay.

However, whereas this is taken to refer to standard weapons of warfare, a possible starting point for the examination of more exotic weaponry is often said to be March and April 1945, as a race occurred across southern Bavaria, with General George S. Patton's Third Army making a beeline for the huge Skoda Works at Pilsen. Although the Works had been destroyed by Allied bombing, for this race to start, Patton must have thought there was something of worth that survived.

As we saw, this was a region of the Harz Mountains in Thuringia, known by Germans as the Dreiecks (Three Corners), an area encompassing the old mediaeval towns and villages of Arnstadt, Jonastal, Wechmar, Ohrdruf and Prague, a major part the Kammler 'Empire' that Hitler was obsessed with protecting and might have been part of his last stand. This sets the scene for more developing mystical, even occult, stories amongst some post-war researchers.

Of course, as we have seen, what had been constructed only amounted to part of that grand plan for a last stand, or their Alpine fortresses, sometimes referred to as the Alpine National Redoubt, one of which was the Harz Mountains. However, what was the rush? Officially, it is said that the Third Army was attempting to cut-off the escape route of Nazis fleeing the carnage of Berlin, but others suggest it may have had something to do with Kammler's evacuation of technology, and that would have been of interest to the Allies, along with other developments like rocketry. It is certainly true that aerial reconnaissance and other intelligence would have told them such fortresses were never as grand as planned and what was present was no National Redoubt at all, but that same intelligence may have spotted something more. What throws a spanner into the works and elevates this rush to a conspiracy theory is the sudden death of General Patton.

Some suggest that Patton was eliminated because of his remarks about turning the Germans 'right back around' to let them lead an Allied invasion of Russia. Others say it was because he knew about the Allies' knowledge of the Soviet's execution of British, American and French prisoners of war and threatened to go public; he was known for his outspoken ways and outbursts. However, that said, this incident leads post-war theories and myths down the route of whether the Nazis had developed the atomic bomb and Patton was racing to get to it before the Russians.

We have seen the ideas behind the Bell and similar devices, but if Kammler had evacuated these, what was left?

On 6 May 1945, 5 days after the announcement of Hitler's death, trucks of the US 16th Armored Division passed through the landscape that was neither German nor Czech. Despite it being almost the end of the war, a hardcore of Waffen SS was defending in and around Prague. There were also ragged columns of Wehrmacht troops heading westwards to the comparative safety of the US zone of occupation. The rumour was that Patton wanted to reach Prague ahead of the Russians, which resulted in a confrontation with the SS. As troops pushed onto the heartland of Czechoslovakia, they met with blue and white Czech flags; it was like the liberation of Paris all over again. By 1800 hours, they were delayed by the crowds lining the streets; it was chaotic. Then, an hour after the US troops had arrived, German snipers opened fire and the crowds ran for safety.

The 16th Armored Division soon found General Georg von Majewski, German army commander for Pilsen, and 35 of his staff in the Wehrmacht's town HQ. Majewski surrendered his troops, pulled a pistol from his desk, and shot himself through the head in front of his wife. By this time, a second unit of the 16th Armored Division, 'Casper', had taken the airport, while a third, 'Able', had the Skoda Works secured. The Works were 80 per cent damaged as a result of the air raids several weeks earlier.

SS Standard Leader (Standartenfuhrer) Wilhelm Voss was hiding at a hunting lodge on the Skoda estate of Prague when he heard of the troops' arrival. That night, he headed back with a truck full of documents and blueprints to surrender to the US troops because he did not want the Russians to get hold of them. By this stage, Voss had been sacked by Goering because he refused to back nominees proposed by Goering for the board of the Skoda Works. Voss bluffed his way back into the Works, where he made contact with the officer in charge of the US troops. Although offering to hand over all the documentation, which included details of the *Kammlerstab,* the officer told Voss everything was to be handed to the Russians. That duly happened and any secrets were lost to the Americans. This is the story behind Agoston's book title *Blunder! How the US Gave Away Nazi Supersecrets to Russia.*

It seems that Kammler never got to the Skoda Works, but then, maybe that was not his plan. It is, however, strange that this mad dash came to nothing if the documentation was handed to the Russians anyway. According to Voss, it appears the officer in charge had told him a US ordnance team had arrived earlier that week. It also appears that they may have entered with 'Able' and already taken anything of value. The story is unclear, and no official documentation can be found outside that supplied by Voss. However, there is some indication that those looking for nuclear weapons had gained entry to the Works and obtained records and documentation, including details of an SS cell's work with Junkers at Dessau on nuclear propulsion for aircraft. Were those the details Patton was after? Voss had confirmed such research was a top priority of the Skoda Works and under the control of Kammler. It is, therefore, suggested that Patton's dash was for the nuclear details and that is something Hitler was keen to protect with SS troops as he sat in his *Fuhrerbunker* at the end of the war. Furthermore, that research was alongside laser and guided weapons, something now a reality in both the United States and Russia.

We do know that a British-led BIOS team entered the Skoda Works on 12 May and got the runaround from the new Czech managers, who only wanted to deal with the Russians. There is also a US/UK administered CIOS report (Trip no. 243), the successor to the BIOS, which included details of the United States entering the complex on 16 May. Nothing of importance was found except for some new project details in ammunition research and advanced designs for guns and munitions.

On 10 May, the United States tested their atomic bomb; a bomb that one senator, James F. Byrnes, had earlier complained was way behind schedule. Is it possible, as some suggest, the final finishing touches were courtesy of Kammler's research? Of course, this is all uncertain and goes against the conventional history, but there is more to tell from those who believe it to be true.

For those who know about the development of the atomic bomb and Germany's efforts, it is well established that they got nowhere. Albert Speer, in his autobiography, says it was 'scuttled by the autumn of 1942', with funding going to the rocket scientists instead. The tons of uranium were then released for ammunition. The conspiracy suggests that given the considerable chaos, corruption and power-grabbing throughout the Third Reich, some of the uranium did find its way into a secret SS-run atomic bomb project. It is intriguing that, according to post-war theories, a pilot by the name of Hans Zinsser actually saw an atomic bomb detonation in Germany.

On a night in October 1944, Zinsser, a pilot and rocket expert, was flying his Heinkel 111 twin-engine bomber in twilight over northern Germany. He was close to the Baltic coast in the province of Mecklenburg while avoiding Allied fighters; German airspace was now wide open to the Allies and all but undisputed. What he saw that night and reported to the Allied intelligence would remain secret until his affidavit was declassified and released just before the start of the millennium. That affidavit is contained in a military intelligence report dated 19 August 1945, (roll number A1007) filmed in 1973 at Maxwell Air Force Base, Alabama. His account is found on the last page of the report.

The report refers to Zinsser as a Flak rocket expert, describing his sighting as being at the beginning of October 1944. Zinsser was flying from Ludwigslust (south of Lubeck) about 12 to 15km from an atomic test station when he noticed a strong and bright illumination of the whole atmosphere lasting about 2 seconds. There was also a clearly visible pressure wave escaping the approaching and following cloud caused by the explosion, with a diameter of about 1km as it became visible to him. The colour of the cloud changed frequently and was dotted after a short while of darkness with all sorts of light spots, which contrasted with a normal explosion; it also had a pale blue light.

After about 10 seconds, the sharp outline of the exploding cloud disappeared as the cloud took on a lighter colour against the sky's colour, which was a grey overcast. By now, the still-visible pressure wave had a diameter of at least 9,000m and remained visible for 15 seconds. The colour of the exploding cloud was an almost blue-violet shade; during this manifestation, reddish-coloured rims were seen changing to dirty shades in rapid succession. The explosion was lightly felt at the aircraft as a pushing and pulling sensation.

After an hour, Zinsser started off again with his He 111 from an A/D (assumed to mean aerodrome) at Ludwigslust and flew in an easterly direction. Shortly after take-off, he passed through the almost complete overcast between 3,000–4,000m in altitude, where he could see a cloud looking like a mushroom with turbulent billowing sections about7,000m in altitude. It just stood over the location where the explosion had taken place earlier.

During this experience, Zinsser also reported strong electrical disturbances and the impossibility to maintain radio contact because of lightning. He also reported that because of P-38s operating in the area of Wittenberg-Mersburg, he had to turn north, where he was able to observe the base of the cloud where the explosion had occurred, showing its full extent. However, it did not seem clear to him why these experiments had taken place in what was a populated area clearly still controlled by the Germans.

This is a strange report because it appears to suggest, against all historical fact, that the Nazis had an atomic bomb and were even able to test it successfully some 8 months before the Americans tested their atomic bomb. This is supported in the report, where it says: 'When Germany was at this stage of the game, the war broke out in Europe. At first investigations on this disintegrating of U235 were somewhat neglected because a practical application seemed too far off. Later, however, this reason continued, especially in methods of separating isotopes. Needless to say the centre of gravity of Germany's war effort at that time lay in other tasks.' In the next section of the report, it goes on to say: 'Nevertheless, the atomic bomb was expected to be ready towards the end of 1944, if it had not been for the effective air attacks on laboratories engaged in their uranium research, especially on the one in Ryukon, Norway, where heavy water was produced. It is mainly for this reason that Germany did not succeed in using the atomic bomb in the war.'

This is interesting wording, suggesting it was known that the Nazis were working on a bomb, and it is no surprise that those who believe that to be true cite this report as evidence. It is also interesting that Norway is mentioned here because, as we saw, there was an evacuation plan by Kammler to get Nazi research to that country, and there were some intriguing suggestions this included possible atomic or nuclear devices like the Bell. Was that the real reason for Patton's mad dash? Some say it is. However, the full story of this is still unclear and those joining such dots may, or may not, be onto something. Nevertheless, whatever we make of Zinsser's affidavit, it has become a boost for those who believe the Nazis had perfected the atomic bomb, albeit just too late to win the war. It is also unclear whether this was one of Kammler's last-minute wonder weapons Hitler was sure would win him the war.

It is, of course, possible Hitler was unaware of this particular weapon, having given over the entire research of wonder weapons to Kammler by that stage. That said, we must take into account Hitler's view that the chain reaction that governs the bomb is 'the spawn of Jewish pseudo-science' and would turn the Earth into a glowing star. Here, he would be going against his seething anti-Semitism. So, in those desperate last days, is it possible Jewish science was seriously considered after all? If so, it was continued after Speer gave up on Heisenberg's bomb due to his lack of interest. But where might that have been done? Only, it seems, under Kammler. If true, that might have been Kammler's way of doing a deal with the Allies, who had not yet perfected their atomic bomb. It might also explain Patton's mad dash and the US senator's comments.

There may be an alternative answer to the Zinsser sighting. The atomic bomb is clearly the ultimate weapon of mass destruction, but at the lower end of the scale, there is a type of bomb that the Nazis had that was considered a lower cousin of the bombs of mass destruction; it was known as the fuel-air bomb. As such, it is the only known conventional explosive device with enough power to produce the blast and heat effects of a small tactical nuclear weapon. Today's tactical nuke would therefore be the Second World War's strategic weapon. Therefore, even if the Nazi physicists did not develop the atomic bomb, they certainly had the ability to develop the fuel-air bomb. This is evident from declassified documentation which shows the Nazis developed it long before we might like to believe. It is unclear whether this was one of Kammler's devices, but the chances are it might well have been; it was just the sort of project that fitted his think tank.

The evidence is again found in a BIOS report *Information Obtained from Targets of Opportunity in the Sonthofen Area* (BIOS target numbers C28/8-211, C25/549, C6/137, C30/338, C4/268, C22/2182 and C21/601). Initial experiments were carried out using ordinary powdered coal, which were unsuccessful, but extremely good results were obtained from a mixture of 60 per cent finely powdered dry brown coal and 40 per cent liquid air. The technical expertise came from Dr Zippelmeier (note that his name has several spellings, including Zippermayr). The first trial was carried out at the Doeberitz grounds near Berlin, using a charge of about 8kg of powder in a thin tin-plate container. The liquid air was poured onto the powder and the two mixed together using a long wooden stirrer. The result was significant; in an area of radius about 500 to 600m, trees were all completely destroyed. After this, the explosion started to rise and only the tops of the trees were affected, although the intensive explosion covered an area of 2km in radius. Zippelmeier then had the idea for a better effect if the powder was spread out in the form of a cloud before the explosion. Trials were made with a paper container impregnated with some waxy substance. A metal cylinder was attached to the lower end of this container and hit the ground first, dispensing the powder. After a short time interval of a quarter of a second, a small charge in the metal cylinder exploded and ignited the dark funnel-shaped dust or liquid air cloud. The bombs had to be filled immediately prior to the departure of the aircraft. Bombs with charges of 25 and 50kg of powder were dropped on the Starbergersee, with photographs taken of the explosion. Standard Leader (Standartenfuhrer) Klumm kept one of the photographs to show Rudolf Brandt (Himmler's personal advisor). The intensive explosion covered an area of 4 to 4.5km in radius and the explosion was still felt at a radius of 12.5km. When the bomb was dropped on an airfield, considerable destruction was caused 12km away, with all the trees on a hillside 5 to 6km away flattened. Within a radius of 12.5km, only the tops of the trees were destroyed.

As the Allied Forces penetrated deeper and deeper into Nazi Germany, teams of experts including scientists and intelligence officers scoured the Fatherland for secret research projects, wonder weapons and patents, including anything to do with atomic and nuclear research. To begin with, they were uncertain as to the level of development of the atomic bomb, or whether it had even been seriously considered. The British were fairly certain it had not as a result of their intelligence gathering, but the Americans were unsure and did not really come to the same conclusion as the British until December 1944, if conventional history is to be believed. This conclusion was partly due to searches of research instillations and partly due to the capture, or surrender, of key scientists and engineers, some of which carried high ranks. However, as we saw, Kammler and much of his personnel and projects are said to have not been amongst this sweep through occupied Europe and the intelligence officers remained quiet about Kammler until recent evidence appeared. The main evidence for the opposite appears to be Patton's mad dash towards Pilsen and the Skoda Works and Prague. That remains something of a mystery for now.

However, much of the more conventional weapons and research captured, like von Braun's rocketry, was highly advanced but recognizable. Even so, amongst this was certainly some notably unconventional science pursued by Himmler's SS, which clearly came from a different culture and mindset altogether. It was, therefore, essential that the scientists and engineers responsible for these advances were acquired. Of course, there was a mixture of individuals involved; some were clearly faithful to the Nazi cause, but many were simply scientists, technicians and engineers just doing their jobs. This would be a problem when justice was administered after the war, and that tricky problem fell to Operation Paperclip for a solution.

For now, the race for Nazi technology and scientists resulted in considerable competition from all sides, each with its own goals and agenda. This meant trespass into each other's zones of interest at best and at worse threats, kidnap, blackmail and general gangster-style behaviour; the Americans did not want to lose any post-war advantages to the Russians and the Russians did not want to allow the same losses to the Americans. Whereas Britain and the United States were less aggressive towards each other, there was still an air of distrust and a race for the spoils of war. However, one example of British-American co-operation involved the British helping the American team led by Colonel Holger Toftoy, chief of the US ordnance rocket branch, to ship the V-1 and V-2 rockets and their spares, together with tons of documents and blueprints, back to the United States. They also shipped the entire supersonic wind tunnel from Bavaria which would later be essential for von Braun when developing the space rockets for the United States, including the Saturn V, which took men to the moon. Much of this was initially transported to the Air Document Research Center at Wright Field. The Russians, too, grabbed whatever they could, including rocket research.

Indeed, there is no doubt the Soviet Union's behaviour was worse than the Allied teams, and much is still secret to this day. It is unclear exactly how many scientists and technicians ended up in the Soviet Union; estimates range from 5,000 to 100,000, but an often quoted figure is 6,000. Those that did end up in the Soviet Union were pressured and lied to, many forced from their beds on the night of 21/22 October 1946, following many others who had been pressured to join the Soviets between May and August 1945. These specialists also included nuclear scientists, some taken to the MI6 safe house, Farm Hall, in Britain, and some taken elsewhere. Most rocket scientists went over to the United States, many surrendering willingly. In fact, just about all areas of armament were liberated. Then, of course, there were many who had fled to Britain and the United States before the war as part of Hitler's dismissals.

One such name who did not return with the Allies but chose instead to go over to the Russians was Helmut Grottrup, a key member at Peenemunde. It is said he made his decision because his colleagues had accused him of betraying the location of Nazi rocket documents. Grottrup therefore became Russian's answer to von Braun, being made head of the Soviet rocket programme initially set up near Mittelwerke; he eventually transferred to Moscow. Many of his colleagues who had been forced at gunpoint to join him were eventually imprisoned; however, Grottrup himself lived in relative comfort.

Other technologies grabbed included submarines, conventional and exotic-shaped aircraft, propulsion systems and various unconventional weapons, some of which remain a mystery or classified to this day. It is said one of the top classifications included the flying saucers or discs which many UFO enthusiasts believe evolved into the sudden flying saucer and UFO sightings of the late 1940s and 1950s in the United States. As we saw, Wright Field, where much of the rocket and aviation devices ended up, would become the centre for investigating UFO sightings. These sightings included many strange lights in the skies around vital instillations in places like New Mexico, including the spate of mysterious green fireballs from 1947 until the 1950s. Furthermore, some of the rocketry transported back to the United States was also located near New Mexico close to several claimed flying saucer crashes in and around the 1940s, an area already rich in the history of rocketry. This included the infamous July 1947 Roswell flying saucer crash.

These fireballs became a real worry, resulting in arguments throughout military intelligence as to whether they were natural phenomena or the Soviets testing missiles over the United States. Moreover, many of these bases were doing nuclear research. The UFO investigations essentially ran from 1946 to 1969 through projects Sign, Grudge and Blue Book. For decades, it was claimed the matter was over with the closure of Project Blue Book in December 1969, but we now know it continues to this day under different projects. It is one of the longest-running legacies left by the Nazis.

The American troops also seized the Mittelwerke fabrication plant, taking parts for nearly 100 rockets as well as the wind tunnels at Peenemunde, all shipped in pieces to White Oak, Maryland, along with 13 years of records found hidden in a mine shaft by von Braun. The Soviets also had some luck themselves when they discovered two completed V-2 rockets in Poland complete with service manuals, which were shipped back to the Soviet Union. Even Britain profited from the rocket technology, and if things had been different, may have become a bigger player in the space race.

No doubt von Braun must have known all too well the horrors of his research involving slave labour, but, sadly, the Americans showed no conscience when colluding with him and his team; besides, there would be ways around this problem under Operation Paperclip. This grand programme to liberate technology and scientists was authorized as early as July 1945, barely 2 months after the war's end in Europe, and was originally codenamed Operation Overcast. The US Joint Chiefs of Staff gave the operation the remit to 'exploit.... chosen rare minds whose continuing intellectual productivity' America wanted to use in the continuing war against the Japanese and the gathering Cold War against the Soviet Union. The Joint Chiefs of Staff directed that this top-secret project should see 350 specialists, mainly from Germany and Austria, brought immediately to the United States, including von Braun and Dornberger. By March 1946. amongst the gathering stand-off against the Russians, the Pentagon's Joint Intelligence Objectives Agency decided to recruit even more former Nazi scientists. However, there was a problem with this plan. US immigration laws forbade entry into the country of any former Nazi Party officials as bona fide immigrants, so President Harry Truman was forced to authorize a more extensive effort than Operation Overcast. That move produced a change to Operation Paperclip, which formally replaced Operation Overcast as a means of circumnavigating or 'bending' the rules to place matters on a formal legal footing.

In particular, von Braun and his team were technically guilty of war crimes involving slave labour from concentration camps like Mittelbau-Dora who were worked to death producing the V-2 rockets. Such was the importance for the United States to develop these rockets into intercontinental ballistic missiles (ICBMs), and later, space rockets, the team had to be protected from war crimes investigators. However, whereas the world was clear about these crimes, in a similar fashion to the nuclear physicists being detained at Farm Hall in Britain, the rocketeers convinced themselves they carried no blame for their actions, including von Braun. Instead, to them, the blame for the atrocities of concentration camp detainees lay squarely with the SS and not the Peenemunde scientists and engineers themselves. This, of course, suited America and its new Operation Paperclip rules. In the case of von Braun, there was an added bonus to support such a view; as we saw close to the end of the war, he had been arrested and interrogated by the SS, so he was actually considered a victim, not a villain.

Operation Paperclip was officially cancelled in September 1947; however, it is claimed that it continued and simply changed its name and funding, becoming a 'denial programme' which was said to be so ultra-secret and deep-black, not even President Truman was aware of its existence. From there, it is claimed it continued to recruit scientists into the mid-1950s. It is estimated that Operation Paperclip recruited thousands of former Nazi scientists, engineers and technicians over the years, many of whom had extremely undesirable backgrounds; all were permitted entry to the United States and employed on cutting-edge defence and aerospace projects, including NASA's Apollo missions to land men on the moon before the Russians.

As for those who chose to go over to the Soviet Union, or were forced or tricked to do so, they had a far more brutal reception, as did their families. Indeed, it is still a matter of debate within astronomy as to exactly how much they contributed to the Soviet space programme; the Soviets already had a rich history in rocketry, like the Germans, and that industry was already well-established with their own experts in place.

In fact, it is true Soviet engineers had already been secretly working on rocket development for more than a decade following the work of Friedrich Tsander, a Lithuanian who had corresponded with rocket pioneer Konstantin Tsiolkovsky, working on rocketry from the early part of the century. Tsander died in 1933, the year Hitler came to power; his leadership in rocketry passed to Sergei Korolyov, a test pilot who had turned into a designer. Following this change of leadership, Soviet rockets developed to such an extent they were reaching altitudes of around 10km—nearly four times as high as those of American rocketeer Robert Goddard's best attempts. However, by the late 1930s, progress ground to a halt as Korolyov, together with hundreds of other engineers, was banished to the Siberian gulag as part of Joseph Stalin's political purges; they would not be released until 1946. During the post-war years, Korolyov would then oversee the production of hundreds of V-2s. At the same time, the Soviet Union would see itself in a furious arms race with its former ally, the United States, and, as a result, began to develop a much larger missile known as the *Pobyeda* (Victory), which was designed to deliver a heavy warhead over a range of 1,450km. In 1949, the *Pobyeda* went into secret production; the same year, they tested their first atomic bomb.

It is said the Nazi scientists and engineers who ended up in the Soviet Union really only contributed to the development of anti-aircraft missiles. The exact details may never be known for sure because the Soviet records are heavily classified to this day; more so than the United States', where von Braun's work is better known, although still classified in some areas.

One of the best testimonies supporting this limited role in Soviet rocketry comes from Werner Albring, who was a leading German aerodynamics expert for the Third Reich. Albring was one of those to go over to the Russians with promises that his family could join him and that they could remain in Germany. These were lies, as they were for many others. According to Albring, scientists and engineers had to work under enforced conditions in wooden huts in a forest surrounded by barbed wire and would be fined if late for work. Working conditions were considered extremely primitive. There were also restrictions on relaxation and socializing, with no collaboration or contact with Russian scientists working in the same research fields. Albring, Grottrup and their teams were regularly assessed and evaluated by the Russians in what was described as 'confrontational sessions'. They were never allowed to see how their work added to the Soviet research, if indeed it ever did. Albring became convinced that the work he and others did contributed little, if anything, to the Soviet space programme, and the plan was really to prevent them from going over to the West.

Meanwhile, by mid-August 1945, back in the United States, some 300 railroad freight cars of V-2 components captured in the European theatre of operations had trundled westwards across the wilderness from the Gulf of Mexico to the Organ Mountains, deep inside the dry, desert hinterland. Such was the operation, every railroad siding from El Paso, Texas, to Belen, New Mexico, consisting of some 338km, was full of cars. Their ultimate destination was the White Sands Proving Ground 193km to the west of Roswell, not far from Goddard's test site at Mescalero Ranch, the US centre for rocket research under Goddard. However, Goddard would not play a role in the post-war research; he died in August 1945. In tow with this spectacular sight was a collection of forty captured German scientists, led by von Braun.

By September, von Braun and his scientists had been joined by more members of the Nazi rocket establishment, all initially resuming their work at Fort Bliss near El Paso, Texas. Eventually, a total of around 120 engineers had been hand-picked by von Braun to accompany him to the United States. The race to be the first in space between the already advanced Soviets and the Americans had begun, as had the race to develop these rockets into ICBMs for a possible future world war.

There were many other spoils of war that did not involve weapons per se, including mind control practices carried out by the Nazis which found their way into US government research, such as MK-Ultra. Evidence of this has appeared in declassified documents, as well as duplicated copies of documents found in files which the powers-that-be were unaware of following the destruction of the originals. For example, the CIA continued mind control experimentation which was clearly Nazi in origin under the MK-Ultra umbrella, consisting of many individual projects over many decades. There were even projects in remote viewing on a far grander scale than those of the Nazis and their paranormal or psychic experiments. That was another favourite with the post-war military, producing psychic spies in both the United States and the Soviet Union. Indeed, it is said that the Soviets were far more advanced in such skills than the West. These spies would effectively sit at their base, yet be able to view remote locations such as enemy installations, meetings and the like. Other results from medical experimentation on death camp detainees found their way to the Allies, along with such research and practices.

We may never know the exact extent of Nazi-style medical research undertaken in the United States and elsewhere, however extreme that might have been, but that which is known about showed a similar trend, including experimentation on prisoners, the mentally ill and even the general public.

For those who were not protected by Operation Paperclip, there were the Nuremberg trials. After the war, the wrestling away of power from Speer to Himmler, and indirectly to Kammler, and its effects are found in a comment from Speer during his interrogation. When the Reichminister of Armaments was confronted by prosecutors enquiring about these black projects, including chemical and biological weapons tests near Auschwitz, he suggested they take up the matter with Kammler. There was also an element of bewilderment which also extended to others. This bewilderment might come from the ultra-secret nature of what Hitler, Himmler and Kammler were doing; as we have seen, many of the black arts and practices were being kept even from the German people.

Unfortunately, asking Kammler was impossible because he had disappeared after the war, leading to the conspiracy that he had already done a deal with the Allies to secure his safety and start a new life. Whether this is true or not, it is certainly the case no real hunt for Kammler had been undertaken; in theory, the horrors he was responsible for should have placed him high on the list of SS officers sought by the Allies for war crimes. So, did he do a deal with the Allies? We may never know for sure; there is no real evidence to support this theory. Nevertheless, there are some interesting details surrounding Kammler's behaviour as the war drew to an end, some of which come from Speer's autobiography.

Whereas Himmler vainly believed he could enter into armistice negotiations with the Allies and emerge with a leadership role in the reconstituted Germany, Kammler, on the other hand, was more of a realist. Kammler knew all too well he was in a difficult position in more ways than one. He was heavily involved in the construction of the concentration camps; then, there was the cold and clinical way he had attempted to boost the efficiency of the gas chambers and ovens; and the part he played in levelling the Warsaw Ghetto. He also had an obvious record in the use of slave labour and the horrors that involved. Oddly, unlike Himmler, Kammler did have something to bargain with: something tangible. As we saw, by early April 1945, Hitler and Himmler had placed every secret weapons programme of any real value under his control, especially those that had no equal in the three powers of the Allies bearing down on Germany from both the east and west. Given his record in construction and development of many projects, he would have been in a position to do a deal and the clues were there from the beginning of that month.

The Kammler think tank and the *Ahnenerbe* gave a peculiar blend of reasoning, logic, conventional science and pseudo-science with the metaphysical and speculation, but it seemed the *Kammlerstab* went further than the *Ahnenerbe* by putting technological ideas into practice. It was a paradigm that was readily and easily adaptable to the German turn of mind, developed before the war, and continued until the fall of the Third Reich, as Hitler huddled in his Berlin bunker, still holding onto his beliefs and hopes that Kammler would save the day. However, Kammler seemed to have different plans; maybe because, like Himmler, his promises to the Fuhrer were too ambitious and would come to nothing in time.

So, what do we know about those plans and the fate of Kammler? It is no surprise that this is also surrounded by mystery and confusion amongst the chaos of the war's end. If we assume he died, there are four stories about how he met that fate, three dated 9 May 1945. The first tells of how he committed suicide in a forest between Prague and Pilsen 2 days after Germany's unconditional surrender. The next is that he died in a hail of bullets as he emerged from a cellar of a bombed-out building to confront Czech partisans. The third story is he shot himself in a wood near Karlsbad (Karlovy Vary in today's Czech Republic). There is also a fourth story that comes from two documents held by the Austrian Red Cross. One posted him as missing, with a second updating the situation, saying he was dead. The first post was apparently made by a relative, last placing him at Ebensee in Steiermark, Austria. The second was based on the testimonies of unnamed comrades, with no burial place given.

Kammler certainly knew Ebensee well; under his orders and supervision in 1942, he worked on a giant underground complex for the international A-9/A-10 rockets planned for use on New York. This was codenamed Zement and based near Lake Traunsee, a location considered the epicentre of Kammler's 'Empire'. On the eve of surrender, this was the place where many gathered for protection, with heavy German troops guarding the complex and Nazi Party members looking for some place to lie low.

Gauleiter Siegfried Ueberreither, the Nazi's chief administrator at Steiermark, had left his office for the complex, but later materialized in the Argentine. Was it possible, like so many others, that South America was the final destination for Kammler and his comrades? The posting that he was dead was maybe just a cover to buy him time.

Wherever Kammler ended up, dead or alive, Prague was a common theme in many of these stories surrounding his fate. In fact, according to Tom Agoston, one witness to these events was said to be an official with the Prague regional office of the Buildings and Works Division of the SS Economic Main Office, who claims Kammler arrived at Prague in early May 1945. Furthermore, his arrival was unexpected, with no advanced notice being made; nobody knew why he had suddenly turned up, especially as the Red Army was fast approaching.

A further possibility is Kammler may have beaten the Allies to the Skoda Works and removed the *Kammlerstab* records to make his deal. He was well-known for taking any documents with him during his war-time activities to cover his tracks, which is possibly why little was known about him at the war's end. Even when Voss turned up with records to hand over to the Allies rather than the Russians, he was not only told the records would be given to the Russians but that the Allies showed no real interest in Kammler or his whereabouts. Had the deal been done? On the other hand, maybe Voss had beaten Kammler to the only records, and Kammler made his escape in fear of prosecution for war crimes.

At the end of the day, there may have been a clean-up job, even a deal and maybe some form of protection under Operation Paperclip, or it may just be uncertainty as a result of the chaos of the time. Indeed, there are so many uncertainties, we may never know the true story. What we do know is Kammler appears to have just disappeared.

As evil as Kammler and others were, there is a mystery surrounding the Nuremberg war crimes trials that remains to be addressed.

We know that many top Nazis, including Hitler, had interests in the occult and the black arts. Indeed, occultism clearly ran deep throughout the Nazi regime, yet it is particularly significant that this element of the Nazis did not come to life in the war crimes tribunals after the war. The answer to why that situation came about can be found in the autobiographies of Michael Bentine, who was an RAF Intelligence Officer during the war. Bentine was also famous for being a comedian and founding member of the Goons, but in these paranormal autobiographies, he goes into great detail about his war years. During the Second World War, Bentine trained as an intelligence officer at a special MI9 (escape and evasion) course under Captain (later Colonel) Airey Neave, after which he was posted to Bomber Command's Number One Group. He was also heavily involved in paranormal research from a young boy as a result of his father's interests and penned several books on the subject. In his paranormal autobiographies, *The Door Marked Summer* and *Doors of the Mind,* he talks in detail about the Nazis and their occult beliefs, and in the latter book, he mentions that many years after the war he asked Colonel Airey Neave 'why none of the evidence relating to the perverted ritual practices of the Nazi hierarchy, such as their blood sacrifices to the ancient gods and the dark initiation ceremonies of the SS, was even mentioned in the court records at Nuremberg?' Neave was a leading member of the Allied legal teams which prosecuted the Nazi war criminals, and he replied: 'It's really quite simple. If we had, as the prosecuting team, brought such hard evidence of these practices to the court, the defence would undoubtedly have used it as proof of their clients' insanity. The war criminals would have been acquitted on the grounds of diminished responsibility.'

Bentine also speaks of his meetings with Air Vice-Marshal Sir Hugh Dowding in his book *Doors of the Mind.* Dowding also researched the paranormal, which included his time during the preparation of his airmen for the ordeal ahead. In his final years, Bentine interviewed him about his views on Hitler. Dowding confirmed that 'Hitler was a black magician and used dark forces.' He also accepted Bentine's views that the principles of destructive ritual magic form the basis for the techniques of modern power propaganda and disinformation.

This comment from Dowding has always made me think along the lines of the sceptics and debunkers of modern times who go to great lengths to dismiss such paranormal beliefs as nonsense in whatever form they may appear. Is it possible that this so-called 'uniquely Nazi practice' and Dowding's view about it being the basis for the techniques of modern power propaganda and disinformation is the real reason behind such dismissals? All I can say is: Look at the world and make up your own mind.

Appendix

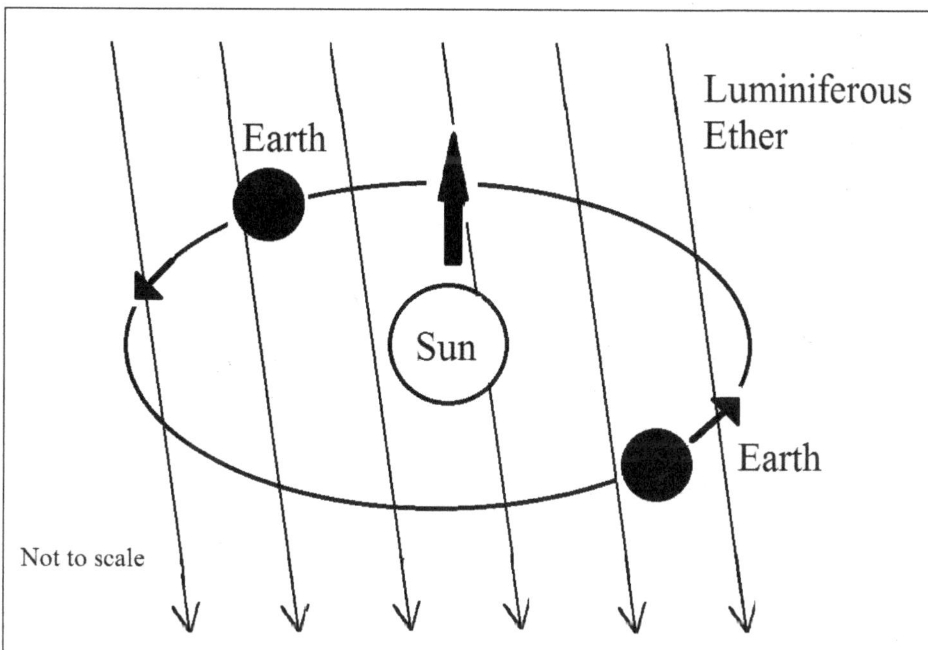

The luminiferous ether in relation to the motion of the Earth. This idea would become a long running battle. The Nazis had great faith in an ether that Einstein's Jewish relativity theory showed is unnecessary for science.

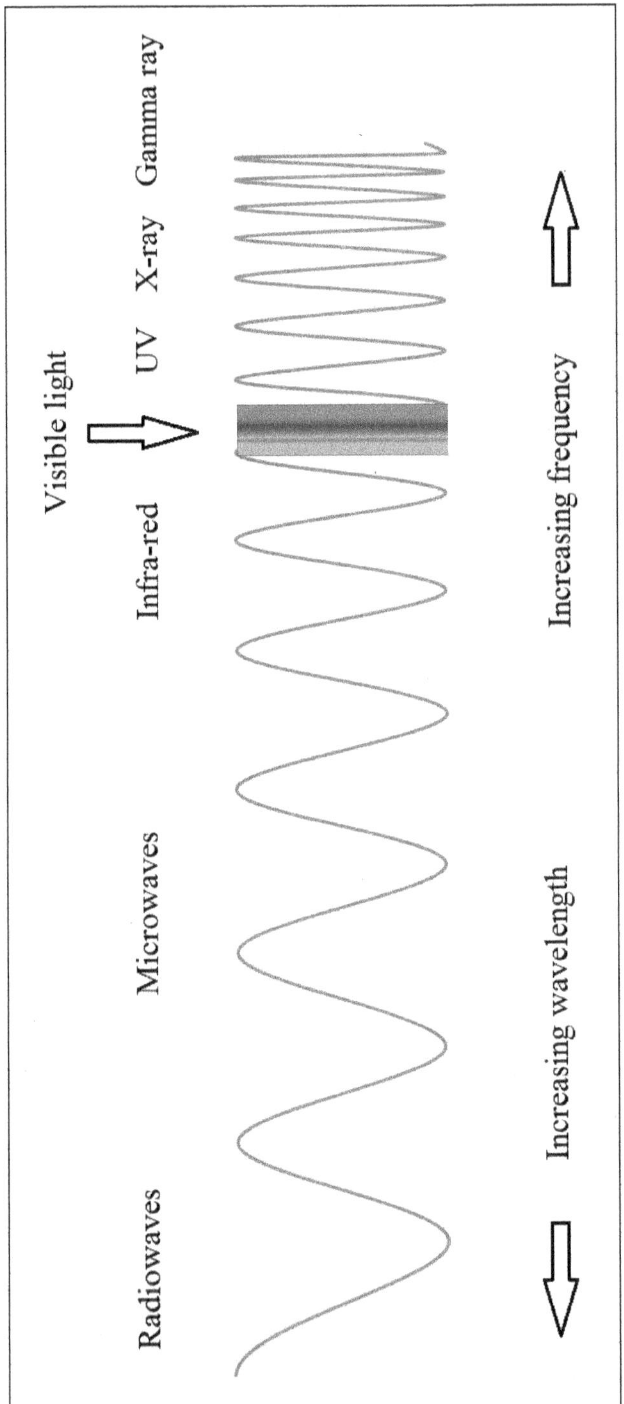

The electromagnetic spectrum showing wavelengths and frequencies from Radiowaves to Gamma rays.

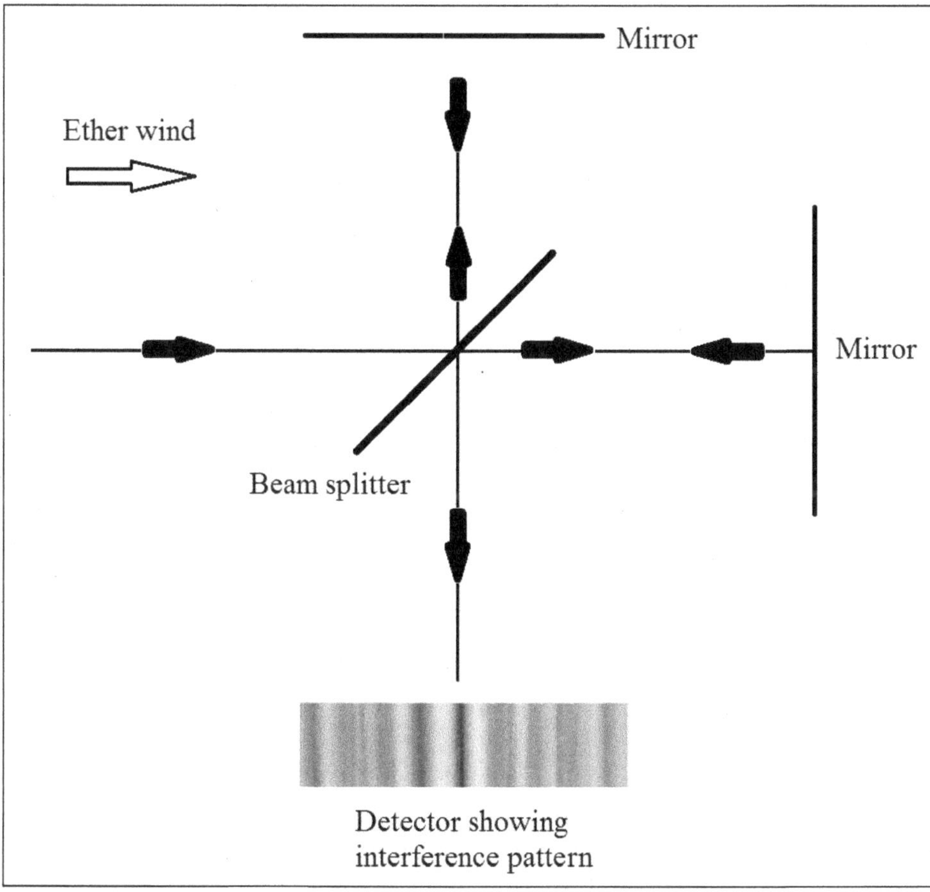

Above: Michelson Morley Interferometer Experiment designed to detect the luminiferous ether. If the ether existed the recombining of the two split light beams should show an interference pattern.

Right: Graph of the Ultraviolet Catastrophe showing deviation at the UV frequencies.

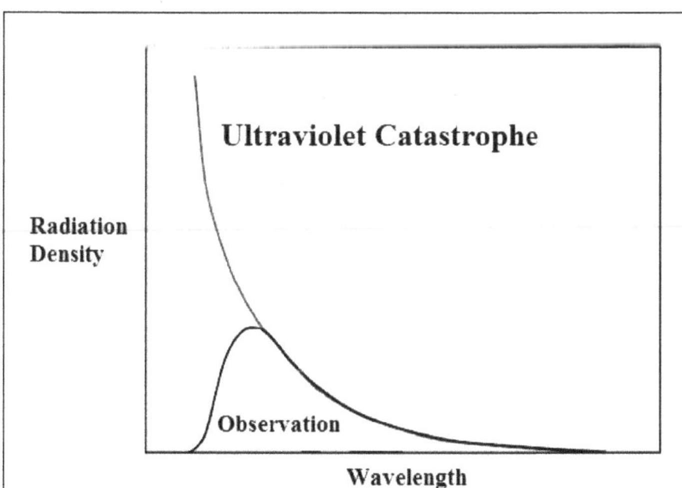

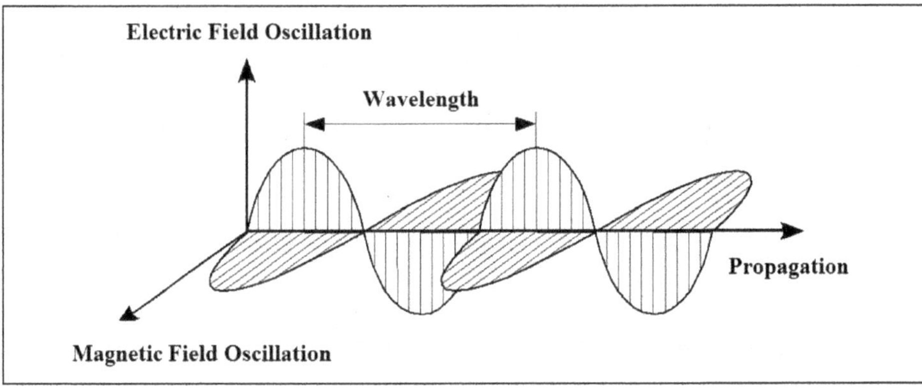

Propagation of electromagnetic radiation without the need for the ether. Due to the nature of the electric and magnetic fields the waves are self-propagating.

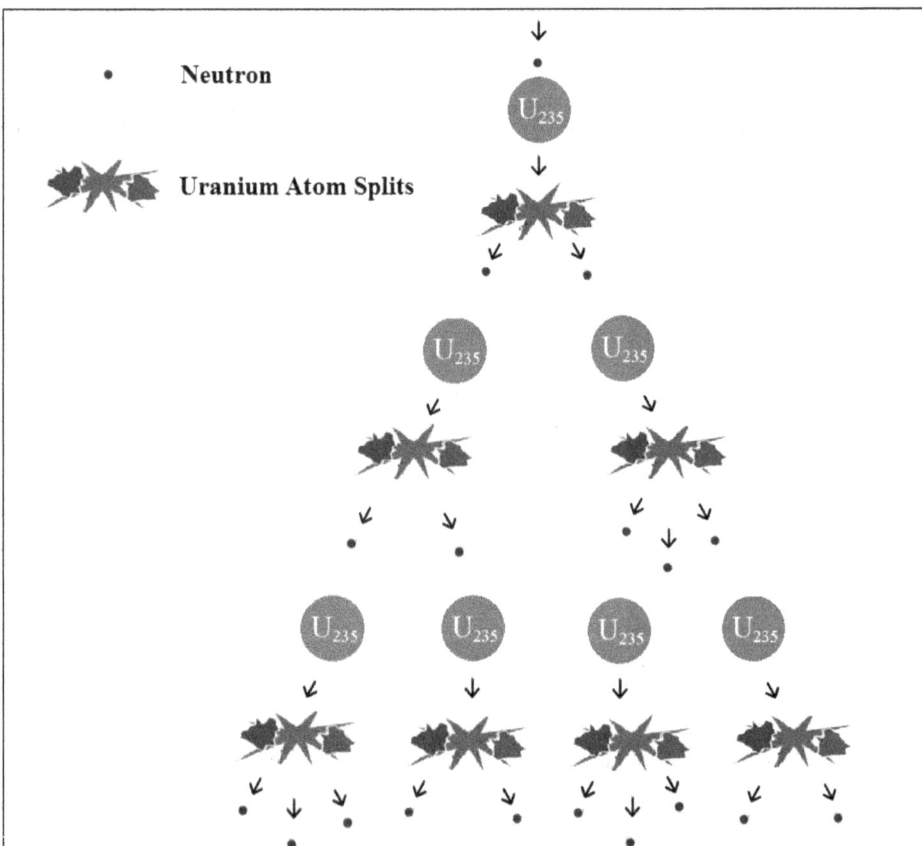

Uranium 235 chain reaction. A neutron fired at the uranium nucleus slits it releasing two to three further neutrons, which in turn each do the same. This rapid multiplication causes a runaway chain reaction.

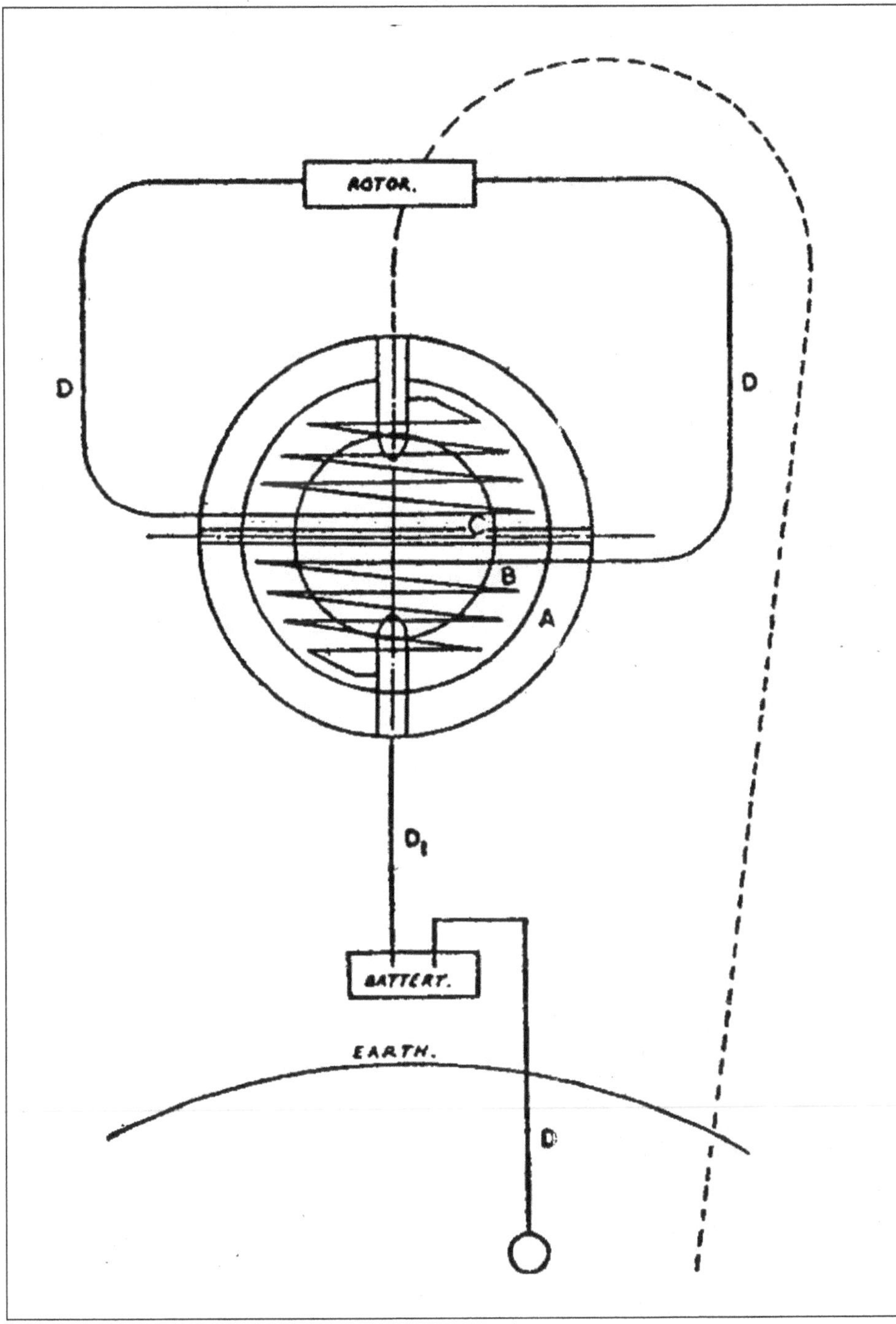

Schappeller Coil or Device. It was said to be a source of free energy from apparently nowhere. It was also said to have anti-gravity qualities.

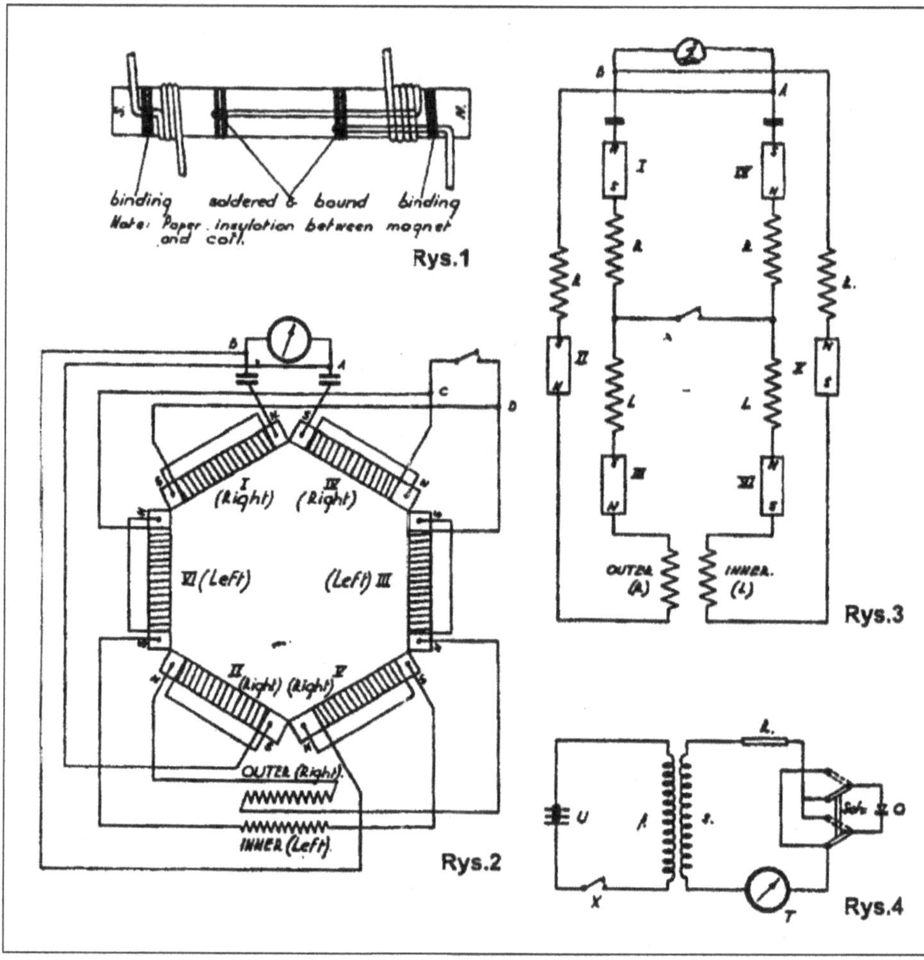

Above: Coler Converter. Another example of a Nazi free energy device. It was patented by Hans Coler in 1937.

Left: The Black Sun Emblem.

Foo Fighters during World War Two (at night). These were strange glows that followed aircraft on both sides. The RAF called them The Thing.

Foo Fighter seen over the Pacific in 1943 (during daylight). It was sometimes the case that daytime Foo Fighters were seen as silver spheres.

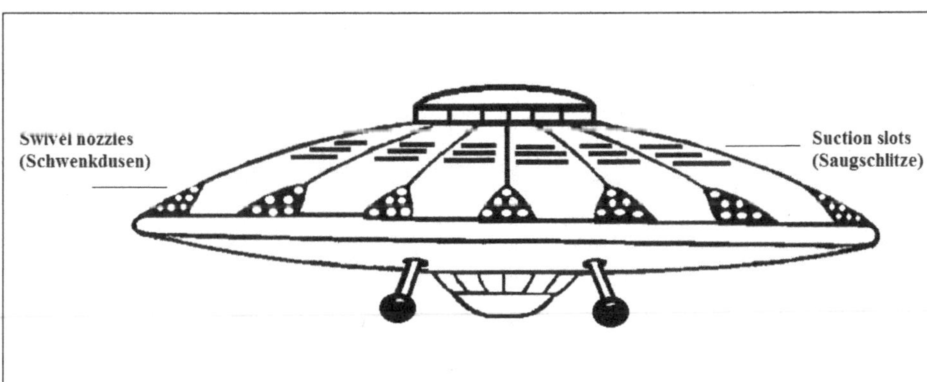

Schriever-Miethe-Belluzzo Disc. This was said to be a typical Nazi flying disc after years of development.

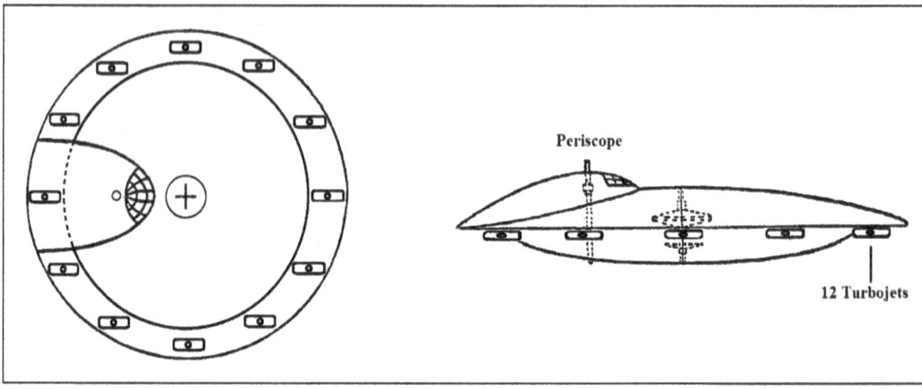

Miethe-Belluzzo design one.

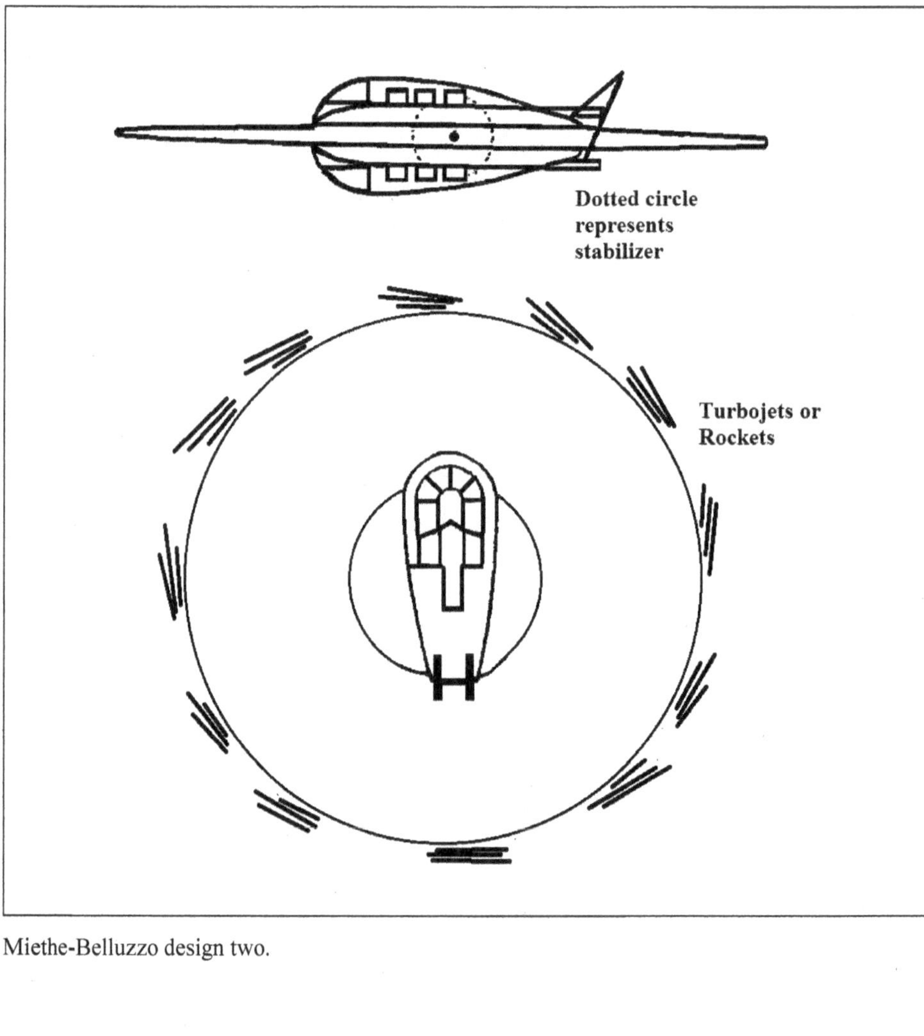

Miethe-Belluzzo design two.

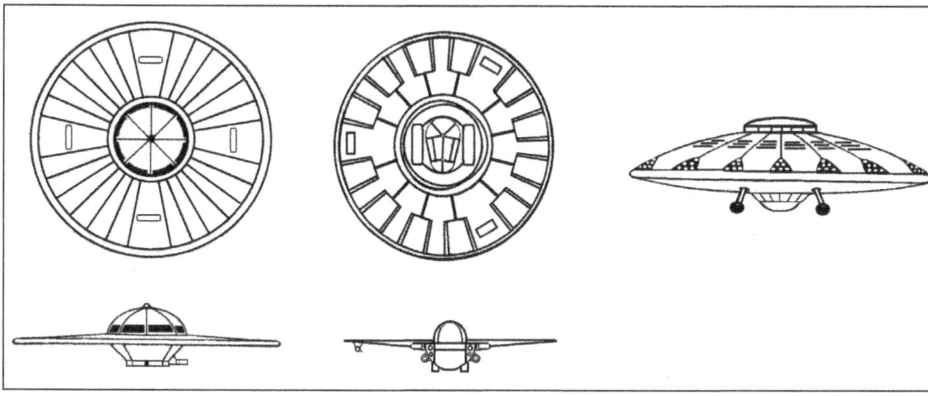

Comparison between the Schriever disc (left), the Habermohl disc (centre) and the Miethe-Belluzzo disc design three (right). Many of the Nazi designs followed a familiar style with differences in the way they worked.

Schauberger with one version of his device. He had several devices all for different tasks but essentially the same basic design.

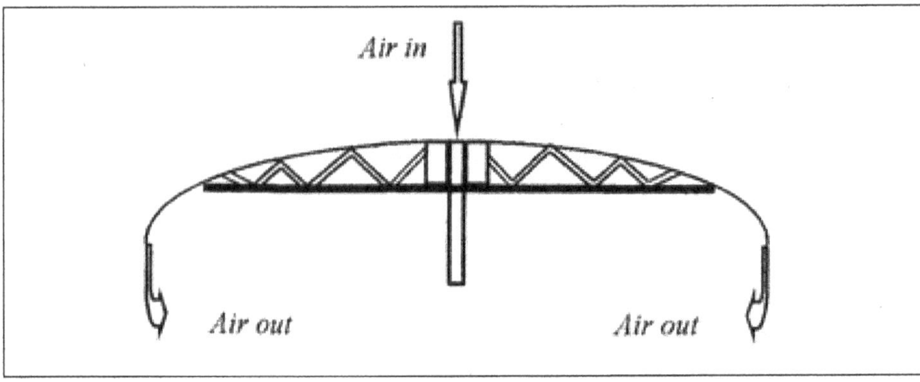

The Schauberger disc showing its plates and air flow. This was based on his main design but worked differently from the Coanda Effect inasmuch as its air flow was internal rather than external flowing over the disc.

Schauberger devices. This is the Repulsine with and without its cone shaped intake. Both had a familiar flying saucer appearance.

Index